Millionaire Babies
or Bankrupt Brats?

Love and Logic Solutions to Teaching Kids About Money

Donated by
Chester Investors
December 2008

Millionaire Babies
or Bankrupt Brats?

Love and Logic Solutions to Teaching Kids About Money

Jim Fay & Kristan Leatherman

Love and Logic® PRESS Inc.

Love and Logic Press, Inc.
2207 Jackson Street, Golden, CO 80401-2300
www.loveandlogic.com
800-338-4065

Library of Congress Cataloging-in-Publication Data

Fay, Jim.
   Millionaire babies or bankrupt brats? : love and logic solutions to teaching kids about money / Jim Fay, Kristan Leatherman. -- 1st American pbk. ed.
   p. cm.
ISBN 978-1-930429-95-6 (pbk.)
1. Children--Finance, Personal. 2. Teenagers--Finance, Personal. 3. Child rearing--Economic aspects. I. Leatherman, Kristan. II. Title.
   HG179.F375 2008
   332.0240083--dc22
   2008021066

Project Coordinator: Kelly Borden
Editing by Jason Cook, Denver, CO
Cover and interior design by Michael Snell, Shade of the Cottonwood, Topeka, KS
Illustration by Steve Ferchaud, Paradise, CA
Indexing by Dianne Nelson, Shadow Canyon Graphics, Golden, CO

Dedicated to raising children
who have all that it takes
to make their dreams come true

Contents at a Glance

Table of Contents

Introduction

Life is challenging. Life is an even more challenging without knowing how to manage money wisely. The negative effects of money mismanagement can have a lifelong impact—overspending, mounting debt, collection calls, poor credit scores, repossession, and eventually bankruptcy. It's like financial triage every day. And that's not all. Friendships, marriages, and family ties can break down over the devastation of debt.

These problems are frequently the profile of a person who has not learned the difference between needs and wants, or how to delay gratification—at a cost more painful than the initial pleasure of the purchase. While we wish it were different, few of us are granted financial immunity.

While we wish it were different, few of us are granted financial immunity.

Why Every Parent and Grandparent Needs a Copy of This Book

Money problems are pesky, nagging annoyances that don't go away unless resolved. Constant money problems can feel like monkeys climbing on our backs, stealing our peace of mind. But what if we knew how to get those little "money monkeys" off our backs?

> Monkey see?
> Monkey do?
> Monkey hears ... monkeys?

One monkey that parents face is the "monkey see" monkey. It is our children's constant hounding (complete with the hound dog look), begging, and manipulating to get us to buy them this or that.

**Millionaire Babies will teach you how to set limits
with your children without losing their love.**

A second monkey is the "monkey do" monkey. What difference could we make if we knew how to show our children the mistakes others have made, especially costly financial blunders?

**Millionaire Babies will show you how to do what's best
for children without feeling guilty.**

Still another monkey is the "monkey hears" monkey. Sad stories abound of parents taking care of their adult children financially long after they should be self-supporting.

**Millionaire Babies will show you how to do what's right in the
short term to prevent financial problems in the long term.**

This book will help you learn how to get life's little "money monkeys"—now and in the future—off your back.

How This Book Was Born

Regardless of your children's age—from toddler to teen to young adult—the answers to these and hundreds of other questions are found in these pages.

The authors of Love and Logic have conducted countless seminars for parents. Invariably, questions and issues about kids and money surface. Questions like:

"Should I give my kids an allowance? How much?"

"Should I pay them to do chores?"

"How can I say 'no' to buying something for my child and not lose my mind?"

"How can I get my kids to earn their own money—or save it?"

"How do I handle overindulgent grandparents?"

"How do I deal with an irresponsible young adult who should be self-supporting?"

If you've picked up this book, you too are probably seeking solutions.

Regardless of your children's age—from toddler to teen to young adult—the answers to these and hundreds of other questions are found in these pages.

While there are other books about kids and discipline, and other books about kids and money, *Millionaire Babies* is really two books in one. It combines teaching *both* personal responsibility and financial responsibility, because the two are inextricably intertwined.

Millionaire Babies is a straightforward, practical collection of effective tools and strategies for raising personal and fiscally responsible kids. Love and Logic is used to teach personal responsibility, and everyday opportunities are used to teach personal money management skills.

No parent or grandparent wants to see their children or grandchildren struggle financially. If you are interested in raising personal and financially responsible kids, you've picked up the right book.

It's the Principle That Counts

This book is not just a book with new and great ideas. It is a book based on time-tested principles. Principles are guidelines that can be adapted to fit the uniqueness of each circumstance. *Millionaire Babies* uses Love and Logic principles to teach personal responsibility, and key financial principles to teach fiscal responsibility. Once you understand how to apply the basic principles, you can use them over and over again, unlike short-term prescriptions and one-time only fixes that eventually lose their effectiveness.

You won't find timelines to tell you what your children *should* know by now; only what they need to know to prepare them for their future. You can begin using the principles at any time, with any age. The principles work when you work the principles. Your values and some common sense are the only things you need to add to make these principles work for you and your family.

How This Book Is Organized

Millionaire Babies is divided into two parts. Part One, "Teaching Personal Responsibility," forms the foundation for teaching kids how to become accountable. It gives you an overview of Love and Logic and covers the essential building blocks of allowance, chores, needs versus wants, and delayed gratification.

Part Two, "Teaching Financial Responsibility," moves from making character count to making money count. It covers spending, saving, borrowing, earning, investing, and sharing money.

Quick Pick Topics

Millionaire Babies is designed with busy readers in mind, readers who may only have time to read in short spurts. Each chapter is a collection of short articles, woven together by stories and examples. Each article, listed in the table of contents, is indicated by enlarged lettering and underlined for easy identification. For example:

Eight Ways to Say "No" to "Buy-Buy"

Sidebars, indicated in italics in the table of contents, are supplementary topics that may be of special interest to you and are found in shaded boxes like this:

> ## *"It's not fair!"*
>
> It's Saturday morning. Taylor, Tyler, and Tommy have just finished the weekly drawing for their family contributions. Eight-year-old Tyler starts complaining immediately: "It's not fair! Taylor always gets to do the easy stuff. I never get to pick anything I want to do." Taylor, the eldest, chimes in with, "Yeah, but Tyler only has to do eight contributions and I have twelve!"

The road to mastery is always under construction. Take your time. Learn a little bit at a time, and practice it until you are in the habit. Then move on to another new skill or concept.

For a "quick pick" read, you have several options:

- Scan the table of contents and browse randomly for titles that interest you.
- Use the one-paragraph introduction at the beginning of each chapter for a "quick synopsis."
- Open the book to any page and use the subject headings at the top to figure out exactly where you are. The top left heading gives you the chapter topic, and the top right heading gives you an idea about the specific content (for example, p. 246 has "Saving" in the top left corner and p. 247 has "Compound Interest" in the top right corner).

The road to mastery is always under construction. Take your time. Learn a little bit at a time, and practice it until you are in the habit. Then move on to another new skill or concept. Like all learning, each step builds on the next—for you and for your children.

Icons

Icons are invitations to interact in some special way with the information. Using them will help you navigate and personalize the information to fit your own needs.

Cross-Reference

Signals to reference another place in the book. It may be a recommendation to review a related topic, or it may refer you to complementary or more extensive information such as charts, worksheets, and sidebars.

Love and Logic Heart Logo

Signals a description of a Love and Logic technique, or a special application of a Love and Logic skill or strategy.

Exercise

Signals an opportunity to exercise—at least with paper and pencil or a computer/calculator. *Millionaire Babies* contains numerous financial exercises and games to help make money lessons fun and more concrete.

Note

Signal a special message or common mistake that might render a suggestion ineffective, but than can be avoided by heeding the information.

Bottom Line

Signals a simple summary statement that reinforces the current topic.

A Note About Financial Resources

An abundance of financial information are available online, in libraries, and from professional financial sources. It is in your best interest to choose your own financial resources, as changes in the financial industry happen so frequently that specific referrals and references become dated quickly.

In *Millionaire Babies* we give you a set of financial principles instead—and invite you to supplement them with the most accurate and current resources you can find to fit your unique financial needs.

Turn Cents into Sense

Are you, or is someone you know, in the position to influence the life of a child?

- Are you searching for a way to teach a child personal and financial responsibility?
- Do you want to help a child avoid repeating the same mistakes you made?
- Do you feel that it's important to educate the next generation?
- Have you tried other methods, but are still looking for something more effective?

Millionaire Babies is for anyone who answers "Yes!" to the above, anyone— whether parent, grandparent, godparent, aunt, uncle, friend, educator, or financial professional—who wants to teach kids about the relationship between life and money, and money and life. You will find *Millionaire Babies* a handy reference for yourself and a valuable resource to share with others who are searching for answers to these essential topics.

Our influence can have a profound and lifelong impact when we teach our children how to manage money responsibly. We can increase the chances that our children will be able to fulfill their potential, support their dreams, and give back to society.

Raising responsible kids takes time, patience, and lots of practice. There are no grades and no tests in this book, just many generous chances to practice and learn personal and fiscal fitness, every day, with your children.

Open to any page—anywhere in this book—to begin your move toward a more prosperous and abundant future for your children, and yourself, today.

You can do it! Your kids can do it!

Teaching Personal Responsibility

Six Ways to Build a Foundation of Accountability

Introduction

Responsibility, in simplest terms, means the "ability to respond":

> To pick up after yourself.
> To thank someone for their gift.
> To pay for something you broke.

That's the purpose behind Part One of *Millionaire Babies*—to learn how to teach personal responsibility. The chapters in Part One are based on a three-key combination:

- The teacher.
- The instrument.
- The opportunity to practice.

Key #1: Adults are the teachers.

Chapter 1 looks at how parents can use everyday opportunities as lessons. Chapter 2 gives an overview of Love and Logic's principles and strategies, which provide the methods for teaching responsibility. The teacher, the method, and the lessons form a fundamental part of the foundation.

Key #2: Money is the instrument.

Chapters 3 and 4 address the issues of allowance and money, respectively. Kids will need practice if we are to teach them how to manage money wisely. Just as we can't expect our children to learn how to play the piano without practicing on a piano, we can't expect them to learn how to use money if they don't have any money with which to practice.

Key #3: Chores provide the opportunity to practice becoming responsible.

Chapter 5 addresses the significance of chores—the vehicle by which parents can teach character, family values, and self-discipline. Chapter 6 addresses the importance of needs versus wants, and delayed gratification, as building blocks for teaching fiscal responsibility.

A Foundation That's Key

Foundations, of the financial kind, conjure up words like *endowment, long-term investment, legacy,* and *self-supporting.* Teaching your children how to be responsible endows them with a lifetime legacy. A legacy that will enable them to grow into young adults who think and say, "I am responsible." A legacy that will create financially self-supporting, happy, contributing members of society.

From Baby Shoes
to Nursing Home Blues

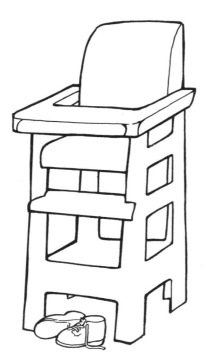

This chapter presents two perspectives on teaching our children about money. The first perspective, the story of Jack, shows how everyday opportunities are the key to teaching our children how to manage their lives and their money wisely. The second perspective shows why missing these opportunities will be costly, in more ways than one.

From Baby Shoes ...

A baby is born. He or she is beautiful—an incomparable bundle of joy! The feeling of love is forever redefined as you hold your newborn in your arms.

You know without a doubt that you are looking into the eyes of someone who is very, very special. Someone who has great potential ... who will be smart, talented, and creative ... basically a chip off the ole' block, right?

You have dreams for your child's future. Dreams that your child will grow up to be a happy, confident, and contributing member of society. You picture in your mind the fun of being a part of your child's first moments—the first word, the first step, the first birthday party, the first holiday—then kindergarten and elementary school, followed by graduations, weddings, baptisms, and of course, grandchildren.

Life comes full circle. Just as you have dreams for your children, your children will grow up to have dreams of their own.

Let's begin with the story of how one child moves through the normal ages and stages of growing up. Let's see what kinds of opportunities exist to teach our kids about responsibility. It's a brief story, in five short chapters, but it may surprise you. Parental discretion is advised.

The Story of Jack

The baby is named Jack. His proud parents bring him home to his new, carefully prepared baby room. They want to be the best Mommy and Daddy their son could ever have.

Jack's days as an infant zoom by quickly. Mom and Dad use every opportunity they can to help him grow up healthy and happy. Before they know it, he starts to walk and talk. It seems like only yesterday they celebrated his one-year birthday.

Chapter One

Jack is a toddler now. He naturally begins to test Mom and Dad. Things are starting to shift a little as he asserts his desire to be independent and develop a mind of his own. He can be a tyrant and an angel many times in a single day.

One day, just after Dad and Jack have lunch together, Dad remembers he needs to go to the grocery store on his way home.

Everything is going smoothly until Dad gets to the cereal aisle. Jack wants to snack on the cereal Dad has just put in the cart. Of course, Dad knows that Jack isn't really hungry, since they just finished lunch.

So at first Dad tells him "no" and explains why: "Things do not belong to us until we pay for them." But Jack throws such a fit—kicking, yelling, and screaming—that Dad is totally embarrassed. After trying to calm him down, Dad finally can't take it anymore and gives in. He opens the cereal box, hands it to Jack, and lets him munch just for the peace of mind.

Dad tells himself: "The cashier will be okay with this … she looks like she has kids too. She knows we're not stealing; he's too little to understand. He'll learn to wait when he gets older."

Notice how this is an opportunity to give Jack an early lesson in delayed gratification.

"But … I waaannnt it."

Some may argue that not letting a toddler eat cereal when he is being fussy at the grocery store is a little over the top. But notice that Dad could have still taught the lesson of "waiting for what we want"—delayed gratification—by paying for the cereal in the express line and then letting Jack munch on it while continuing with his shopping.

Chapter Two

Jack is school-age. Mom needs to pick out a birthday present for Jack's best friend. Before they leave the house, Mom tells Jack that they are going to the toy store only to buy a present for the birthday party next weekend. He agrees to this "concession" with a reluctant nod.

Mom and Jack pick out the gift together and head for the cashier. Jack asks her if he can go "over there," pointing to a nearby aisle, while Mom waits in line. He wants to look at the most recent addition to a popular series of collectibles. (Mom has bought him every item in this series since the prized inaugural piece.)

It's time to leave. As Mom calls him over, she knows exactly what's coming as Jack walks toward her, toy in hand. "Will you buy this for me … ?" he asks, followed by lots of "because" reasons.

Mom looks into his pleading eyes as she reminds him that they agreed only to buy a birthday present: "Why are you asking me to buy you one more thing when you knew that … ?"

Jack continues to plead, cajole, and manipulate Mom by promising to pay her back when they get home. With the time ticking by, Mom finally caves and buys him the next piece to his prized collection.

Mom notices she is feeling annoyed as they head toward the car. She spent more time *and* money than she wanted to. She knows she should not be doing this, but tells herself, "Oh well … he's still a kid. And he offered to pay me back. Jack gets lots of pleasure from playing with his toys. He'll have plenty of time to work and pay for things he wants later in life. Besides, it's easier to give in than listen to his constant begging."

Notice how this is an opportunity to give Jack an early lesson in the difference between needs and wants,

plus a lesson in delayed gratification.

Chapter Three

Jack is a tweenager. Mom takes him on a back-to-school shopping trip for clothes. He has outgrown, stained, or torn almost everything he wore this summer.

On their way into the mall, Mom tells Jack that her spending limit is $200. Jack argues that it's "not enough." Mom explains that her plan is to help him buy a variety of interchangeable tops and bottoms to give him at least a week's worth of outfits for school.

Mom sees that Jack has another plan as they begin shopping. He wants to buy the coolest and trendiest "designer" clothes (and thus the most expensive) on the market. He gripes that $200 is "nothing" and that he should get "at least twice that amount," because that's what all his friends get from their parents.

Mom is getting more and more exhausted as they move through the store. They can't agree on any clothing they both like. Everything Mom likes, Jack shoots down as "ugly" or "uncool." Everything Jack likes is out of Mom's budget. Things are getting very unpleasant, so Mom tells him that she will only spend $50 more, and "That's it!"

Still feeling like it's not enough, Jack grumbles and complains, but gives in to some of Mom's "stupid" choices in the interest of "getting this over with."

Still feeling like it's not enough, Jack grumbles and complains, but gives in to some of Mom's "stupid" choices in the interest of "getting this over with."

Mom silently thinks to herself: "Ingrate! Where did he learn to be so ungrateful? Here I am giving him a generous clothing allowance and it's still not enough! Wait until he has to start working and earning his own money. Then maybe he'll appreciate me more."

Notice how this is an opportunity to give Jack an early lesson in gratitude versus entitlement,

plus a lesson in the difference between needs and wants,
plus a lesson in delayed gratification.

Chapter Four

Jack, now a teenager, wants a car when he gets his driver's license this summer. He has been surfing the Internet lately to check out all the latest models. His first choice is a brand new BMW, but if not that, at least a four-wheel-drive pickup truck, which he reminds his parents "are really hot right now."

Based on his extensive research, he says to Dad one night: "Would you like to know what kind of car I want you to buy for me?" Dad knew a question like this was coming someday, but isn't sure how to answer it. Part of him wants to buy Jack a car, but another part thinks: "Don't do it."

Dad and Mom go back and forth in their minds about whether they should pay for all of it, some of it, or none of it. They decide it would be good for Jack to get a job so he can earn some money for his own car. When his parents share their decision, Jack complains bitterly that he'll never have enough time to save "that much money," let alone earn it.

"Get real … with homework, afterschool sports, and time with friends? Why can't you just buy it for me?" he asks persuasively. "Besides, it will take me forever, because I'll only make a pittance. Plus, everyone else …" The argument gets more heated and ends (as it usually does) with the tagline: "You don't understand. You just don't want me to drive."

Mom and Dad feel terrible, but they stick to their guns—he's got to learn sometime.

Jack Goes to Work

To their surprise, Jack gets a weekend job! He tells his parents that he can't wait to get his own car, so he won't have to rely on them to take him to school and work. Mom and Dad say to themselves, "Yes! This is working!"

Jack loves the new freedom and independence that come with having some money of his own. Even though Jack talks about saving some of his earnings, his parents notice him spending it frivolously on junk food, excessive CDs, movies, and other luxuries when he's out and about with his friends.

Jack is arguing with Mom and Dad almost every day now that they should buy him a car. They get tired of the hassles. They start to think: "Maybe it's just easier to buy the car. Plus, Jack will be safer driving than riding with those irresponsible friends of his."

They figure: "Well at least he's a good kid. If we get him a car, maybe he'll settle down, quit his complaining, and spend some of that time raising his grades. And maybe if we tell him what a sacrifice (or privilege) this is, he'll see the light."

Notice how this is an opportunity to give Jack a lesson in personal money management skills (earning, saving, and spending wisely),

> *plus* a lesson in gratitude versus entitlement,
> *plus* a lesson in the difference between needs and wants,
> *plus* a lesson in delayed gratification.

(But, he has developed and refined some great manipulation skills that he can use on his parents later.)

Chapter Five

Jack, now a young adult, moves out. He gets an apartment with some of his high school buddies in order to share living costs. He is delighted because he's finally out from under his "clueless" parents and their "constant harassment."

In the first few weeks of apartment living, things go okay. After a while, however, Jack's roommates start to notice that he is sloppy and inconsiderate. So they cover for Jack, just "to cut him some slack." They aren't sure if he even notices that they pick up after him, since they never get as much as a word of thanks.

His roommates also notice that Jack eats up their groceries without replacing them, forgets to empty the trash, and abandons his dirty plates in the kitchen sink. One roommate decides to put Jack's dirty dishes on his bed—thinking he might get the hint, but Jack ends up putting them on the floor, which attracts ants.

When Jack is out with friends and short on cash, his friends loan him the money. What are friends for, after all? But Jack never seems to pay his friends back—not even a goodwill gesture of "sodas for the house" or some other favor. It seems like Jack always has enough for his own entertainment and snacks, but when it comes to splitting the washing machine repair bill, he's flat broke.

It doesn't take long for his roommates to realize that Jack isn't holding up his end of the new living arrangement, in terms of housework or money.

Home Sweet Home?

Getting some heat from his roommates, Jack begins to drop by his parents' house for a few more meals (and to drop off his laundry bag). He doesn't say too much when his folks ask him how it's going, but Mom can tell things aren't going very well at all with his newfound "freedom."

A few weeks later, Jack asks Mom if he can move back home.

Mom thinks: "What am I going to do? I can't say no." His parents eventually learn that Jack's roommates kicked him out for not "pulling his own weight."

Just when Jack's parents thought their official job as parents was over, they're now pondering privately if his problems have anything to do with not requiring him to help out at home. They didn't make Jack do many chores around the house because he was always busy playing with friends, doing his homework, and participating in extracurricular activities—all of which were important, of course.

Besides, Mom and Dad learned long ago that it was often just easier to do the housework themselves. They figured Jack wasn't capable when he was little, and when he got older it wasn't worth the hassle of trying to get him to cooperate.

Notice how this is an opportunity to give Jack a lesson that life will always have its chores,

> *plus* a lesson in personal money management skills
>   (earning, saving, and spending wisely)
> *plus* a lesson in gratitude versus entitlement,
> *plus* a lesson in the difference between needs and wants,
> *plus* a lesson in delayed gratification.

Chapter Six and Beyond

How do you think chapter six might turn out for Jack? What about chapter seven, eight, and so on? We know that Jack isn't your kid, but we bet you know someone like him. As we look back on his life so far, we see those intrinsic opportunities to teach life's lessons. The names, faces, and details of each story are different. Yet the patterns created by the problems of personal and fiscal irresponsibility are the same.

Not My Kid

You may be thinking: let kids be kids … they have a lifetime to learn. True, but at whose expense? Yours? Your son's or daughter's? Your own parents'? Why wait until our children are *forced* to learn about personal responsibility and money the hard way? Why miss those opportunities when the lessons are easier to learn on a daily basis, and when the price tags for mistakes are so much more affordable?

Jack's story illustrates both the good news and the bad news. The good news is that you don't have to be a perfect parent to raise a great kid.

> And, these lessons do not need to be taught in any special order.
> And, opportunities to teach them are found in everyday interactions.

The good news is that you don't have to be a perfect parent to raise a great kid.

The bad news is that if we miss those teaching opportunities, the unlearned lessons accumulate into a combination of bad habits and bad attitudes with undesirable consequences for both parent and child.

Jack's story demonstrates the compound effects of many underutilized opportunities. What we *haven't* taught our children about personal and fiscal responsibility sneaks up on us until—quite literally—the results end up staring us in the face. Is that our intention when we bring home *our* beautiful baby? Absolutely not. But perhaps it is easier to see how and why Jack ends up back home when we take a satellite view or look at it from a long-range perspective.

And what's your guess about Jack's behavior once he returns home? Will he be a delightful, contributing member of the family, happily returning home to help out where needed and appreciating what's provided for him? Or will he continue to experience money problems? We all know the answer.

What's the moral of this story? *You want the buck to start with you but not end with you.* The purpose of this book is to help turn around these kinds of problems before it's too late. Jack's story *can* have a different ending when we teach ourselves how. We'll look at how we can change Jack's story at the end of this chapter.

Reasons to Make Money Matter

While the value of the dollar may change, the value of learning to manage a dollar wisely will always be necessary.

Jack's story illustrates the importance of using everyday opportunities to teach *personal* responsibility. Let's look at several reasons why it is essential to teach *financial* responsibility.

Here are three reasons to teach your children why money matters in life.

Reason #1: Life is hard ... without enough money.

Few of us can go for more than a day without some kind of money transaction or exchange. Whether we earn, spend, save, share, borrow, or invest, money is a ubiquitous part of life. And guess who's often at our sides? Our kids.

Parents are in the land of many, many golden opportunities, as Jack's story illustrates. Each lesson can build upon the next, providing your child with lots of fiscal practice as he or she matures. While the value of the dollar may change, the value of learning to manage a dollar wisely will always be necessary. Wise parents look for the day-to-day opportunities to teach their children the values and skills associated with life's fiscal transactions.

Bottom Line: When there is a lack of understanding about how money works, life gets harder.

Reason #2: The school of hard knocks is expensive.

Here's a question for you: What school teaches our children how to manage money if the neighborhood school is not teaching them? (For a look at the role of school in our children's financial education, see "Who's Filling the Fiscal Education Gap?" on p. 15.) We learn at the school-at-home if we're lucky. We default to the school of hard knocks if we're not so lucky.

Let's take Joe, for example, a married nineteen-year-old private in the Army. Joe hasn't yet learned the basics of managing his money. On a meager salary, he bought an overpriced vintage 1970s muscle car. He discovered *after* his purchase that he couldn't afford the extra insurance, the extra gasoline, the costly repairs, or the traffic tickets (his red car was a magnet for cops).

Joe's understanding of how money works is so faulty that he borrowed money using his gas-efficient and already-paid-off Jetta as collateral to buy the vintage car. If he defaults on the loan, he'll not only lose his Barracuda, but will also risk repossession of his main source of transportation to work!

Without transportation, he'll have to depend on his buddies and curtail some of his social freedoms. Joe is missing the important link between cause and effect, and between valuing money and good judgment. Because he wasn't taught earlier in his life, Joe must learn the hard way.

Financial literacy doesn't come naturally, it is learned. Understanding how money works is a concrete discipline that requires a concrete understanding of basic economics. Few of us, including Joe, become financially literate using only our impulses and intuition. We need to be taught the meaning and the value *behind* the exchange of money.

An examination of recent statistics supports the fact that many adults in the United States are not financially literate. Consumer debt is at an all-time high, Americans routinely spend more money than they earn, and they aren't saving for retirement. And even though the red flags are waving wildly, we fail to notice that the United States is headed for bankruptcy as a country if the elected leaders in our local, state, and federal governments do not change their collective financial course.

What comes around goes around. Our children may well become the financial stewards of our future (and for sure, the stewards of our country's future.)

Financial literacy doesn't come naturally, it is learned.

Bottom Line: When it comes to learning money management skills, there is only one school with automatic enrollment and expensive tuition—the school of hard knocks.

Reason #3: An ounce of prevention is worth a pound of cure.

Unless children grow up with parents who share their money stories, they rarely hear about the real life relationship between family, money, and life.

Family values are often passed along from one generation to another through storytelling. Financial lessons—the good, the bad, and the ugly—are no exception. Unless children grow up with parents who share their money stories, they rarely hear about the real life relationship between family, money, and life. There can be unintentional consequences to keeping money a secret from our children.

Parents do talk to their children about money, but not often enough about the specifics, or the consequences of different choices. Kids need to hear that Aunt Susie used powdered milk in order to make real milk last for a week, or that Uncle Fred's kids wore hand-me-downs because he and his wife didn't have enough money to buy each child new clothes.

Everyone has financial stories to tell—stories of success and failure. Share your family's stories, as they can provide compelling and memorable lessons about the virtues of saving early and the dangers of spending too much.

Ever heard the wise saying "You cannot teach what you do not know"? I (Kristan) had a friend who, when she first got married, spent much more than she and her husband earned. She, her husband, and their two children ended up living with her parents, struggling for six years before she was able to live with her own family in a new home of their own, free of debt.

She learned how to live beyond her means from her parents, who learned the same values from their own parents. How might her life have been different had she been taught how to manage money better? How might her parents' lives in their golden years have been different had they learned how to manage their own money better?

There are numerous statistics to support the argument that many of us are learning about money management the hard way. We need experience, knowledge, and role modeling in the ways of successful money management to avoid becoming statistics ourselves. The school of hard knocks is a tough, unforgiving school, and should be reason enough to make sharing and learning from our mistakes a priority for us and our children.

 Bottom Line: Our children are destined to repeat our fiscal mistakes unless we show them a different, more effective way to manage their money wisely.

Who's Filling the Fiscal Education Gap?

How many of you remember completing worksheets about money in elementary school? You would match the names of the coins to corresponding pictures, learn the dollar and cents symbols, and fill in blanks with corresponding numerical equivalents.

This type of learning helped us understand that five pennies equal a nickel, that two nickels equal a dime, and so forth. We learned how to add and subtract money using decimals and place value. Later, we learned how money could be understood in fractions, and perhaps how to calculate percentages related to compounding interest.

These lessons would also include word problems. For example:

1. You go into the ice cream store with $5.00. How much change would you receive if you bought an ice cream sundae that costs $3.45?
2. Using the same example above, how much more money would you need if you wanted to buy your friend a sundae too?

Such knowledge incorporated into school math curricula is a good beginning. But it's not enough to develop personal money management skills.

Knowledge Is Wisdom

Understanding the value of *numbers* in operations with dollar and cents symbols is not the same as understanding the value of *money*. Such lessons are merely exercises with money *on* paper (abstract) versus experiences with money *in* paper (concrete coins and dollars).

In the first word problem above, for example, I (Kristan) might figure out as a kid that I would receive $1.55 in change. Good start, but not enough to develop the deeper, more profound *economic* understanding, related to the second word problem: that if I also want to treat my friend to a sundae, how will I *get* the additional $1.90 I need?

In order to figure that out, I need to learn the money management concepts of earning and saving. (Of course, as a child, I could ask my parents for the additional money, but we all know that kids are already expert at this!)

While these types of exercises in school appear to indicate understanding when answered correctly, they lack the real life challenge that turns knowledge into wisdom through experience.

While these types of exercises in school appear to indicate understanding when answered correctly, they lack the real life challenge that turns knowledge into wisdom through experience.

Research shows that schools in the majority of U.S. states do not offer personal finance education courses prior to graduation from high school. While schools in some states require an economics course before graduation, understanding economics is not the same as learning personal financial skills. Kids are learning the concrete mechanics of numbers without understanding the cause and effect of earning, spending, and saving money. In many schools today, students gain only an *abstract* understanding about how money works.

Bottom Line: Teaching your kids personal money management skills is essential, especially if these skills are not being taught at school. Wise parents fill the financial education gap at home.

Back to Jack

Let's revisit the story of Jack. Let's turn back the hands of time and pretend that Jack's parents prepared him for his future by teaching him how to be personally and financially responsible. What can Jack's parents do differently to raise Jack to become a responsible and happily self-supporting adult?

When Jack was a young child, his parents began by giving him an allowance. They gave him lots of opportunities to spend his allowance within limits by saying "no" to *their* money but "yes" to learning how to use *his own* money. Living with limits taught Jack the difference between his needs and wants, which in turn taught him how to prioritize wants, delay gratification, and earn his own money. This led him to understand and appreciate the value of saving money for his bigger wants. Finally, Jack learned the meaning of family and work by doing household chores at an early age. Contributing to the quality of his life, while enriching the lives of others, gave him important experiences in character development, personal accountability, and gratitude.

When it comes time for Jack to leave home, get his first real job, and receive his first paycheck, how will Jack be better prepared?

First, Jack understands what to do with his first paycheck besides spend it all in one weekend. He understands how to budget, and the importance of paying his bills on time, because he had kid-sized opportunities to practice how to live within his means. He already knows that a portion of his paycheck goes to deductions for taxes, disability, and retirement, because Jack's parents taught him how to divide his allowance among competing needs and wants. Jack also knows that he needs to save a portion of his paycheck for emergencies and more expensive purchases, and to invest in his dreams for the future.

Jack's future looks bright because he has learned some of life's most valuable and necessary lessons. And, not by accident, the future for Jack's parents, in their retirement years, looks bright too. Why? Because Jack may someday become his parents' caregiver, financially and otherwise. While it was very challenging at times, Jack's parents knew it was far better to teach him personal responsibility and financial literacy now than have to deal with irresponsibility and financial lunacy later.

From Baby Shoes to Nursing Home Blues: Summary

One day at time, just like Jack, opportunity by opportunity, your children have the chance to become financially successful and happy because you taught them. You can be proud that you gave your children the skills to be able to support and pursue their dreams, because they have the personal financial wherewithal to make it happen. The effect boomerangs in many positive ways when we teach our children well.

The following list summarizes why teaching our kids about money is important:

1. Life is hard … without enough money.
2. The school of hard knocks is expensive.
3. An ounce of prevention is worth a pound of cure.
4. Our kids may be the ones who pick our nursing home
   (more about this in Chapter 13).

Any *one* of these reasons stands alone as an excellent reason. All four together make for a compelling argument too important to ignore.

Most kids today know that money buys them things they want. However, most kids are not connecting the dots between what money can buy and how to manage it without depending upon their parents. *Millionaire Babies* will show you how to be your children's best teacher.

Money does not need to be a problem if we take the time to understand and teach the value and meaning it brings to the quality of our life. It is vital to their future, and yours. Just by reading this book, you are already making the commitment and gaining an understanding of the importance of getting started.

The next chapter introduces the Love and Logic philosophy, a way to set limits with our children without losing their love.

CHAPTER 2

Love and Logic

From Introduction to Application

This chapter presents an overview of the principles of Love and Logic, and introduces many of the tools and strategies used throughout this book to teach responsibility. We use a common scenario—and a typical kid, Emily, who needs to clean her typically messy bedroom—to explore four types of parenting styles. Each style offers its own special way of illustrating what happens when we pay our children to do their chores.

An Overview of Love and Logic

You may already know about parenting using Love and Logic. If you're familiar with Love and Logic's principles and strategies, this overview will serve as a refresher. If not, this overview will serve as an important primer to understanding the philosophy and principles that serve as the foundation for this book.

What Does "Love and Logic" Mean?

The words *love* and *logic* can mean many things to many people. What do they mean when referring to the principles of Love and Logic?

The word *love* in Love and Logic reminds us of the love that is required to allow kids the latitude to make little mistakes—the little mistakes that teach life's lessons while the price tags associated with those mistakes are small. A bruised knee can teach an important lesson without doing permanent damage. Bruised emotions and disappointments can do the same. Watching kids experience these important lessons can be difficult for parents. It is a wise parent who knows that bruised limbs and bruised emotions are short-term. Being protected from these experiences causes damage that lasts a lifetime.

The word *logic* in Love and Logic is about what happens inside the child's mind when the parents love him or her enough to allow the consequences of mistakes and poor decisions to do the teaching. When parents allow the consequences to do the teaching, the child starts to develop an internal voice that says, "I wonder how my next decision is going to affect me." That is real logic. Lecturing, threatening, and reminding can never do this. All these do is cause the child to think, "When I make mistakes, it makes my parents angry. I better make sure they don't find out next time."

Love allows kids the latitude to learn from their mistakes. *Logic* allows kids the latitude to learn from the consequence of those mistakes.

The Four C's of Love and Logic

These descriptions of what *love* and *logic* mean are supported by the use of four guiding principles or goals of Love and Logic:

1. Maintain the self-respect and dignity of both the adult and the child, which builds a positive self-concept.
2. Share control whenever possible.
3. Share thinking and decision-making opportunities through choices.
4. Use empathy before delivering consequences.

An easy way to remember these principles is to think of them as the Four C's: Self-Concept, Control, Choices, and Consequences. Each C connects to the next C, and as such, can succeed or fail with each step in the process.

In adult-child relationships, the use of these principles can repeat itself many times in a single day. It begins with everyday interactions as simple as asking your child to put their shoes on or asking them about how their day went at school. Ever wonder, for example, how a simple order such as "Hurry up!" can escalate into World War III with your child in a matter of minutes?

When this happens, chances are that we have forgotten to begin with the first principle—maintaining dignity. Then, before we know it, we are nagging our kids out of frustration in ways that do not enhance anyone's self-concept, including our own.

Interactions between you and your child move through each of the C's, for better or for worse, in a fairly predictable pattern that repeats itself daily. The Four C's of Love and Logic's—self-concept, control, choices, and consequences—provide a set of guiding principles for parents to use in their day-to-day their interactions with their children. (For a more complete grounding in the Love and Logic approach to raising responsible kids, read the book *Parenting with Love and Logic*.)

The Love and Logic Process
Using these principles is a process. It begins by learning how to

> share healthy control …
>> by giving children appropriate choices …
>>> using empathy first, to learn through consequences,
>>> or encouragement …
>>>> to develop a positive self-concept built on
>>>> increasing capability and confidence …

all enveloped in an atmosphere of respect and dignity for each other.

This process is illustrated in the chart on the next page, which shows how Love and Logic can be viewed as a circular process—one that allows adults to be both loving and logical at the same time.

Love and Logic: The Essential C's
Control, Choices, Consequences, and Capability

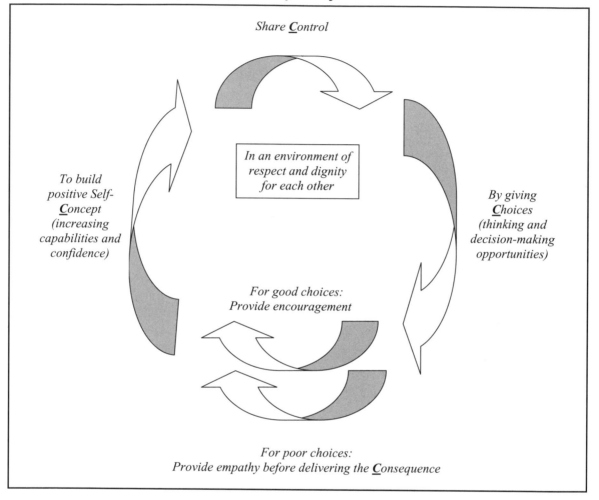

Share Control

In an environment of respect and dignity for each other

To build positive Self-Concept (increasing capabilities and confidence)

By giving Choices (thinking and decision-making opportunities)

For good choices: Provide encouragement

For poor choices: Provide empathy before delivering the Consequence

When we give children the latitude to make choices by sharing control, they will make either good choices or poor ones. And they will experience either positive or negative consequences, respectively. Notice, logically, that our response is different depending upon which way the child chooses. We respond with encouragement when the child makes a good choice, and we respond with empathy if he or she makes a poor choice. Consequences always follow choices, either way.

Surely if love—in the traditional sense—were enough to raise our kids, few of us would have any trouble. We naturally love our children. Yet how many of us secretly vow to stop yelling at our kids and in a matter of minutes find that we have already broken our promise? Or how many of us promise ourselves to follow through and then, in a weak moment, give in to our children's whims? Yet when we learn how to deliver empathy before the consequence, or encouragement, as the case may be, we build our children's positive self-concept.

It's the combination of using the four principles, *plus* love, *plus* logic (as defined at the beginning of this chapter), that will increase the odds of raising responsible and respectful kids. Learning how to share control, give choices, and deliver empathic consequences to develop your children's positive self-concept will—literally and figuratively—keep you on the winning track in your daily "rounds."

The Rules of Love and Logic

One of the beauties of Love and Logic is its profound simplicity. There are only two rules, which in combination with the four principles make it a very effective method:

> Rule #1: Adults set limits without anger, lectures, threats, or repeated warnings. When we describe what we will do or allow, that's setting a limit. When we tell a child what he or she should or shouldn't do, that's a potential flight-or-fight situation.
>
> Rule #2: When children cause problems, for us or anyone else, adults hand the problem back to the child in loving ways. We hand the problem back by replacing anger and lectures with a strong dose of empathy, followed by a logical consequence or by requiring the child to solve the problem he or she has created.

Love, Logic, and Money

While the concepts of Love and Logic can be adapted to many situations, the purpose of this book is to apply them to teaching kids fiscal responsibility. Toward that end, you will recognize the use of Love and Logic's four principles and two rules as we learn how to teach our kids about the value and meaning of money.

For example, Love and Logic suggests separating allowance from chores. Love and Logic recommends *giving* your kids an allowance instead. Why? So that we give them some practice with Control over the use of their own money, allow them to make spending or savings Choices, and learn from the Consequences of those choices in order to build a positive Self-Concept about their financial capabilities. (For a closer look at Love and Logic's view of allowance, see "The True Purpose of Allowance" on p. 25.)

Learning how to share control, give choices, and deliver empathic consequences to develop your children's positive self-concept will—literally and figuratively—keep you on the winning track in your daily "rounds."

You may notice in specific examples that we recommend the use of lots of empathy when the child makes poor use of his or her money, thereby allowing the negative experience, rather than our negative reaction to his or her choice, to be the consequence. Conversely, Love and Logic recommends using encouragement when the child makes a wise financial choice, so that the positive experience (i.e., a positive consequence) can be the teacher.

Regardless of whether a child makes a poor or a wise choice, Love and Logic allows him or her to make mistakes when the price tags are small, and affordable. Love and Logic helps kids to learn how to solve their own problems by providing opportunities without reminders, lectures, or warnings. (For a sample list of affordable mistakes from a financial perspective, see "Affordable vs. Unaffordable Mistakes" below.)

And yes, in case you're wondering, Love and Logic parents don't bail kids out when they overspend. Kids must be allowed to experience the consequences of their actions if we truly want them to learn basic money management skills and if we truly want them to be fiscally responsible.

When children discover that they can solve the problems they create, or live through an uncomfortable or disappointing situation, they start to build their own healthy self-concept, which results in increased self-confidence, resiliency, and the discovery of their many capabilities.

Bottom Line: Love and Logic gives parents the methods and tools to raise responsible kids, financially and otherwise, in effective ways that are both loving and logical.

Affordable vs. Unaffordable Mistakes

One parent brags, "We follow all our lessons about money to the penny with our child. Craig knows to *not* spend any of his money without our presence and prior approval."

Another retorts, "What a great day! Carey forgot her lunch money today and had to beg off her friends. That's the second time this week! With all these mistakes and consequences, she'll have a Ph.D. in life by the time she graduates!"

Which child will be better prepared for a financial life that's full of wise decisions? Our bet is on Carey.

The authors of Love and Logic understand that the road to wisdom is paved with mistakes and their consequences. The list on the next page establishes patterns of affordable versus unaffordable mistakes around money. Which pattern do you want to establish with your child?

- Not having enough money to buy a toy car.
- Not having enough money to buy a real car.

- Not receiving full pay for an incomplete job at home.
- Not receiving a full paycheck for an incomplete job at work.

- Defaulting on a family loan and having his or her bike repossessed.
- Defaulting on a bank loan and having his or her car repossessed.

- Saving money early and often.
- Saving money late and sporadically.

- Making financial restitution for unpaid bills to Mom and Dad.
- Making financial restitution to a credit card company or collection agency.

We can turn our children's mistakes into powerful learning opportunities simply by letting them experience the consequences of their mistakes. What are some of the affordable mistakes your kids need to make, today, to avoid serious financial difficulties in the future?

The True Purpose of Allowance

The authors of Love and Logic suggest separating allowance from chores. What, no strings attached? You mean my kids do not have to do work to earn allowance? That's right. The authors of Love and Logic recommend that allowance should be given to kids with no strings attached ... because an *allow*ance, in the truest sense of the word, *allows*.

Allowance *allows* your kids the opportunity to experiment with money. It also:

- *Allows* your kids to make mistakes and learn from them.
- *Allows* your kids to make their own earning, saving, borrowing, and spending decisions.
- *Allows* your kids the opportunity to make better choices, or not, and experience the financial consequences.

The best kind of allowance simply *allows* for free market opportunities to practice and learn.

Perhaps you are thinking, "But what about chores? I can't just give my kids money without having them do something to earn it." We will discuss what you *pay* your kids to do in Chapter 10, on earnings. What we pay kids to do gives them opportunities to *earn* money, whereas an allowance gives kids opportunities to spend, share, or save money. Earning and spending money, as we all know, are two different processes! (For an interesting look at the pitfalls of paying children to do their chores, see "Three Reasons Why Allowance Tied to Chores Is Ineffective" on the next page.)

Bottom Line: Love and Logic uses allowance purposefully, truly giving children the opportunity to practice, to make mistakes, and to fix them financially without the burdensome attachment to doing their chores.

When Allowance Doesn't Allow

Allowance should not be considered a salary and it is not an entitlement. Kids need to know that there may be a time when allowance does not fit into the family budget due to other, more pressing expenditures.

Once your children are old enough to understand how money works, this is a good time to discuss when an allowance increase (related to cost of living and birthdays, for example) might not be given, such as during a period of financial hardship.

Financial life is susceptible to highs and lows just as much as other parts of life. I (Jim) have experienced times in my life when there was not even a dime left at the end of each week to share with my kids. My wife and I felt guilty about this, given that their friends received allowances.

If we could do it over again, we would have been more open with our kids about our financial situation, sharing information about our family budget and how it worked. I'm sure we would still have felt bad about the situation, but we would not have felt guilty. Allowances are great when parents can afford them, but giving an allowance should not feel like an obligation, nor should denying an allowance feel like an earth-shattering event.

Take a moment to explain to your kids that you are happy to give them their allowance as long as you are able to afford it. This reinforces the way adult life works—we give when we have the money and when times are good, and we exercise caution and restraint when our circumstances change and we need to budget.

(For more information about how to present allowance as part of the bigger financial picture, see "The Family Budget" on p. 199.)

Three Reasons Why Allowance Tied to Chores Is Ineffective

Still not sure about giving allowance as "practice money" to your kids? Let's take a look at this issue through the eyes of three different parenting styles to learn about the pitfalls of paying our kids to do chores.

In the first home, we have the drill sergeant–type parents—parents who believe that "when you live under my roof, you'll do as I say." These parents give their kids an allowance for doing chores because they believe kids "should have to earn it." Things appear simple in the drill sergeant's house: no chores, no allowance.

In the next home, we have parents who are like helicopters—they rescue, hover, and overprotect their kids. They believe that giving allowance to kids is a good idea some of the time, but find it necessary to remind or warn their children in advance of subsequent consequences. These parents might give their kids an allowance but then bail them out when they get into a financial pinch.

For example, a helicopter parent might protect a child from disappointment by giving him or her extra money, above and beyond what the child has in hand, to purchase something wanted. Or this parent might rescue the child from paying for repairing a neighbor's window broken by an errant baseball. In the helicopter home, the use of allowance tends to waver and fluctuate with the wind.

In the third home we have the jellyfish parents—parents who believe that anything goes. The noncommittal "whatever" works for them. Allowance is a wishy-washy kind of thing: sometimes money is given for doing chores and sometimes it isn't. Sometimes allowance is forgotten altogether.

Jellyfish parents tend to give their children most of what they want, either to avoid a conflict or to be their friend. They don't like to set any rules or deal with any discipline. They believe that kids should be able to figure it out on their own, or that they will be able to make their own rules and choices around money when they grow up, without any adverse effects.

Let's Go Visiting!

To illustrate the differences in parenting styles, let's go behind the scenes. Here's the scenario: All good parents know that a kid needs to keep a clean bedroom, right? It's Saturday, and before Emily can go out to play she needs to clean her room.

Behind Door #1: The Drill Sergeant Style

In the drill sergeant home, there are few "if, and, or but's." On this particular Saturday morning, Emily, eight years old, *will* clean her room. "Now!" *Before* she can go out. "You know the rules!" Mom says.

But Emily has other plans. She glares back at Mom and says, "I don't want to clean my room." Probably Mom's commands would be effective in a military dormitory, but not on this Saturday morning. Mom says, "Oh yes you will, young lady! You get into your room right now, and don't you even think about coming out until it's clean!"

Does Mom have a control battle on her hands? You bet. Is this how she wants to spend her morning? Bet not. No fun for either one of them. And you can be sure Emily has much more time on her hands than Mom, who has a long list of things to do today.

So, what does Mom do? She threatens, warns, and lectures Emily about the pitfalls of not cleaning her room. Not only will Emily not be able to go out to play today, but she will also not get any allowance this week until she cleans her room.

As the argument escalates, Mom heaps one threat on top of another in the hope of motivating Emily to get started. Because Mom is sure all good kids need to keep a clean room, she is going to win this one if it takes her all weekend.

"It's not fair. Lilly's mom doesn't make her clean her room. Her mom cleans it for her."

Emily stands firm: "It's not fair. Lilly's mom doesn't make her clean her room. Her mom cleans it for her." Emily's mom explains—again—why a clean room is important and why what she has asked Emily to do is fair. Emily, angry at Mom's unwavering stand, resorts to: "You're mean. I want a new mom."

In total frustration, Mom feels her only option is to teach Emily a lesson for being disrespectful and disobedient. She drags Emily back into her room, spanks her, and leaves, closing the door behind her.

Mom feels fine about this … for the first fifteen minutes … and then the guilt begins. She tells herself: "I know I should have handled that better, but she just won't listen. She knows she is supposed to keep her room neat. I offered her an allowance, so what more can I do? Maybe I should go in there to see how she is doing. When she complains that it's not fair, I can tell her one more time that she cannot go to the Kite Festival, and that she won't get her allowance until she cleans up her room."

Mom opens the door slowly. Emily is playing on her bed. It appears that nothing in the room has changed. Mom says softly, "Emily, you know you need to clean your room on Saturdays. Why are you acting this way? You know better than this …"

What happens? You guessed it. The argument starts all over again, and the cycle continues, leaving both Mom and Emily feeling frustrated and defeated.

Notice the problem when allowance is tied to a child doing their chores. What happens to our ability to control this outcome? When the child does not clean their room, the parents are still left with the problem—a child who still needs to clean their room.

Apparently in the drill sergeant home, the "no chore, no allowance" rule is not enough to motivate Emily to clean her room.

Behind Door #2: The Helicopter Style

The second home is different. Emily is the same child, and the parent still wants her to clean her room for an allowance, but the approach changes. In this home the parent is of the helicopter variety, and tells Emily she will get her weekly allowance *if* she does all her chores, one of which is cleaning her room. Here's how the dialogue might play out:

Mom: "Emily, today is Saturday. It's time to clean your room … and remember … you'll get your allowance if you do."

Emily: "But I don't want to clean my room."

Mom: (trying to persuade her daughter to cooperate) "But Emily, if you get your allowance, you can spend it when we go to the fair today. Remember? We're going to the Kite Festival with the Smiths. You love hanging out with Lilly, don't you?"

Emily: "But I don't want to clean my rooommm …"

Mom: "I know, honey, but it's messy."

Emily: (moaning and starting to whine)

Mom: "Here, let's go and see what we have to do."

Emily: "You do iiittt."

Mom: (feeling pressed for time, dragging Emily like dead weight across the floor toward the bedroom) "I'll help this time, but *only* because we have to meet the Smiths by eleven o'clock. I can see we won't get it clean unless I help you."

Emily: (moaning, getting up slowly, and walking reluctantly with Mom toward the bedroom)

Guess who will be doing most of the work in this house? You're right! Mom is going to pick up the slack as well as the room. Mom's way of handling the problem is to basically do it by herself. What might that teach Emily? Whining wins.

The Pitfalls of *We*

Notice how Mom inadvertently used the word *we*. Be careful when using this word. To a child, the word *we* translates into the child thinking: "Far out, Mom's gonna do this for me, so I can get by with the least amount of work!"

Using *we* is fine if you mean "you and me"—literally. Otherwise, parents heed: we means "me"!

In the helicopter home, the parent usually gives in to the child's resistance. Mom just couldn't bear to let Emily join Lilly and the rest of the Smith family at the Kite Festival without any spending money. Simply by insisting that she didn't want to do it, Emily was able to manipulate Mom into cleaning her room—and ended up getting her allowance anyway!

As in this scenario, helicopter parents tend to avoid control battles by giving lots of reminders and warnings and then, when that doesn't work, by not following through and enforcing consequences. Guilt is often a technique of choice with the helicopter parent: "You'd think, after all the things I do for you, that you could just cooperate once in a while."

Behind Door #3: The Jellyfish Style

In the third home, the jellyfish parent has it easy. Mom makes few limits, or none at all, so control battles rarely break out. Whereas the helicopter parent gives in, the jellyfish parent gives up. Mom still wants the same thing from Emily—a clean room, with the promise of an allowance. She gets different results, but they are equally unsatisfactory:

Mom: "Emily, today is Saturday. It's time to clean your room … and remember … you'll get your allowance if you do."

Emily: "I don't want to clean my room."

Mom: "Emily, your room is a mess. You really need to pick up after yourself. I can't even see the floor."

Emily: "But I said … I don't want to clean my room … duh."

Mom: "If you clean your room, I'll give you some allowance that you can spend at the Kite Festival today."

Emily: "I'll clean it tomorrow."

Mom: "You know, there are some kids in the world who don't even have half of what you have, and they manage to take better care of their possessions."

Emily: "Yeah? Where? What are their names, Mom?"

Mom: (feeling frustrated) "Well if you want to live like a pig … wait until you grow up and live with others … you'll learn then."

Emily: "I can keep my room any way I like."

Mom: "This is my house too, you know."

Emily: "Whatever. Can I have twenty dollars?"

Mom: (hesitating, sighing) "Well … okay … I guess it's better you're busy doing something instead of nothing."

Here the jellyfish mom tried to teach a lesson in gratitude to motivate Emily. When that didn't work, she figured it would be best to just avoid a conflict. So she convinced herself that her daughter would learn good housekeeping skills in the future.

Once again, the problem of a clean room falls back into the lap of the parent. This laissez-faire mom is allowing the world to raise her daughter—no doubt a harsher, less kind version. Imagine the kind of roommates Emily will attract when she has few or no housekeeping skills? How does the saying go: "Birds of a feather flock together"?

* * *

What's wrong with all three of these scenarios? The problem of a clean room has not been resolved. The promise of an allowance didn't seem to change the outcome, nor did lectures, warnings, reminders, or punishment.

What's In Store Behind Doors 1–3?

Basically, when allowance is tied to chores, it raises the odds that in the struggle for control, we become either a tyrant or a wimp.

The drill sergeant parent is destined for a control battle—it's not a matter of *if*, it's simply a matter of *when*. What if your child doesn't want to do what you asked, *now*? What if your child doesn't want to earn any money today? Or what if your child does the chore halfway? Does he or she get paid for only half? These are all formulas for additional control battles.

What do you think might happen when allowance is freely given as practice money and not tied to chores? Control battles are greatly reduced. As one mom so succinctly put it: "In our home, I give choices, but chores are required. That way my kids can't opt out of them if they don't want the money."

The jellyfish parent and the helicopter parent are not exempt from control battles either. Their inconsistent and pandering methods waste time and are equally ineffective. What will happen to the value of our word over time if we say one thing and do another? What kind of respect and trust will our children develop toward authority figures? What will happen when we are too permissive, not requiring any effort on the part of our kids?

With any of these approaches, we are slowly training our kids to become future anarchists. No doubt, as parents, none of us want any of those outcomes.

Notice how all three approaches forgot the importance of Love and Logic's basic principles—the first C, of sharing control, and the second C, of giving choices. And all three approaches forgot the importance of maintaining the dignity of both the adult and the child.

 (For more information about the relationship between Love and Logic's principles and the different parenting styles, see "Where Are *You*? Four Parenting Styles" on p. 36.)

"Not *my* kid!"

Even in the face of these commonsense reasons, one mom still thought, "*My* kid will never be like that!" Until the day she heard the reason that changed her mind forever: roommates will not pay her son to clean his personal space when he leaves home. Bingo! She could immediately see the dangers of setting the payment precedent.

The authors of Love and Logic suggest that we should not tie allowance to chores for two reasons. First, we cannot control whether or not our kids will be motivated by money on the day we ask them to do their chores. That was one of the fundamental problems we found when visiting the drill sergeant, helicopter, and jellyfish households.

Second, paying kids to do their chores robs them of fulfilling their basic need to be a valued, needed member of their family. We must remember that when this need is not fulfilled, all kinds of problems start to emerge as kids get older. (We will cover the connection between chores, character development, and cooperation more fully in Chapter 5, on contributions.)

Now let's take a look inside the home of Love and Logic's consultant-style approach to see why giving allowance to children without any attachment to chores is a more effective idea.

Behind Door #4: The Consultant Style

Same child, Emily, who still needs to do the same thing—clean her room. But this time, Mom will use the consultant approach:

Mom: "Emily, would you like to clean your room this week, or pay me to do it?"

Emily: "I don't know. Maybe Jennifer will do it."

Mom: "If you're the one who does it, would you like to use the mini-vac or the large vacuum cleaner?"

Emily: "I don't want to clean my room. I think I'll ask Jennifer to do it."

Mom: "Okay. Would you like to have it clean by two o'clock on Saturday, or by four o'clock?

Emily: "By four o'clock."

Mom: "Great. Thank you."

Jennifer, Emily's younger sister, declines to clean her room, despite the wages Emily offered, a whole one-dollar bill. Emily ends up doing it herself, by the appointed time. Sound like a dream?

Not when you understand that Emily has been raised on a steady diet of Love and Logic principles—shared control, and a share in the decision-making process through choices. (We'll learn what happens to Emily and her allowance in a Love and Logic consultant home when she isn't so cooperative, as the chapter continues.)

One of Mom's secrets to success with Emily was her use of choices. Bedrooms are notorious battlefields for control. In Chapter 5, you'll discover that kids don't have to clean *their* bedroom as long as they are contributing to cleaning *something* in the house. By giving choices effectively, parents can avoid painting themselves into a corner—a bedroom corner or otherwise.

(To learn more about how to use choices effectively, see "Love and Logic Guidelines for Giving Effective Choices" on p. 35.)

The Consultant Difference

Let's examine what makes the consultant parent more effective in this particular scenario:

1. Love and Logic parents remember the importance of sharing control. Emily's mom shared control by offering choices in three different areas:
   a. Who cleans her room.
   b. What vacuum she uses.
   c. When she would like to do the job—by two o'clock or by four o'clock.
2. Mom did not remind, warn, or lecture Emily prior to the deadline. The price tag of Emily making a mistake in this case is not life-or-death. It will not hurt her to discover, possibly to her shock, that things don't go well when she makes bad decisions.

Basically, Mom's effectiveness can be attributed to the use of the first two C's— shared control and giving lots of little choices. Note that the continual use of the first two principles can sometimes avoid the need for the third C—an unfavorable consequence for the child. (For a look at how the consultant parent handles Emily on a day when she doesn't clean her room, see "Money Back Guarantee Options" on p. 41.)

By the way, what positive "consequence" did Emily experience as a result of getting her room cleaned by the deadline? She improved the quality of her *inner life* through a sense of achievement that comes with effort, and she improved the quality of her *outer life* through a more organized, tidy room. Plus, she got some encouraging words and a hug from Mom.

In the consultant home, the fourth C—positive self-concept and confidence—comes into play because Emily gets the job done without being nagged, threatened, yelled at, or punished. And who else's self-concept gets a positive boost? Ours!

Taking the Consultant's View of Parenting

In general, consultant parents are always there to give advice and let the child make the decision, with the idea that they will let the child make as many mistakes as possible when the price tags are affordable. The message that consultant parents send says:

You'd best do your own thinking, because the quality of your life has a lot to do with the decisions you make.

In the pages that follow, you will find many examples about how consultant parents take very good care of themselves:

- They never tell a kid what to do.
- They get better results by saying what *they* are going to do.
- They offer choices and alternatives instead of orders.
- When confronted with a problem that their child created but is unwilling to fix, consultant parents use meaningful words and few actions. They wrap consequences in a loving blanket of empathy.

Love and Logic Guidelines for Giving Effective Choices

What is one of best ways to bring more harmony into your home *today*? Choices. By giving kids choices, we give them opportunities to think and make decisions, and to share the highly coveted need to feel in control.

Give your kids choices, choices, and more choices—with one caveat: give them choices only about things that affect your children's lives directly.

The authors of Love and Logic use the analogy of a savings account at a local bank to teach about control theory. Wise parents build up a "bank account" of choices in their child's mind *before* misbehavior or defiance. When the "bank account" is laden with choices on the deposit side (delivered when things are going smoothly), then a withdrawal (a time when no choice is offered) gets a bit easier.

Choices around how much money to earn, spend, share, save, or borrow are used throughout the examples and stories in this book. In fact, sharing control through choices can be one of the most effective techniques for avoiding power struggles with kids over all kinds of issues, not just money.

Here are a few generic guidelines to keep in mind as you give your children choices:

- Only give choices that fit your value system.
- Give 99% of your choices when things are going well.
- Give choices *before* the child becomes resistant, not *after*.
- For each choice, gives two options, each of which you like.
- Use care not to disguise threats as choices. To keep the threat out, begin with phrases such as:

  "Feel free to _____ or _____."

  "You are welcome to _____ or _____."

  "What would be best for you: _____ or _____?"

  "Would you rather _____ or _____?"

Caution! It's very easy to turn choices into threats. For example: "You can either clean you room or lose your right to watch television." This is like the boss giving an employee the choice: "Would you rather do your report today or get fired?"

Here are three choices about cleaning a room that avoid threats:

"Would you rather clean your room, or mop the kitchen floor so *I'll* have time to clean your room?

"Would you rather clean your room on Saturday or Sunday by four o'clock?

"Would you rather clean your room, or hire someone else to do it?

- Don't be afraid to make a withdrawal. You can say: "I usually give choices, but not this time. It's my turn. Thanks for understanding."
- If your child doesn't choose within about five seconds, there is always an implied third choice: *you* will choose.

Next time an issue arises around money with your children, ask yourself: "How can I offer them a choice?" Then expect things to go more smoothly.

Where Are You? Four Parenting Styles

Love and Logic is about teaching the importance of setting loving limits. When your kids make excuses about cleaning their room or helping out in other ways, Love and Logic has the tools and strategies to help. (For a look at why parents should not buy into their kids' typical excuses, see "Three Traps to Avoid with Kids' Excuses" on p. 38.)

The chart on the next page illustrates the four parenting styles according to the Four C's of Love and Logic. Use this chart to examine what happens during the challenging times with your children. It can help you understand what step or steps you can take to improve your parenting. Then you can literally chart a new course of action.

For example, if you lean toward the drill sergeant style, you'll notice in the chart a need to share more control by giving choices. If you tend toward the helicopter style, then sticking to choices and allowing your children to experience the results of those choices, without reminders or warnings, should help.

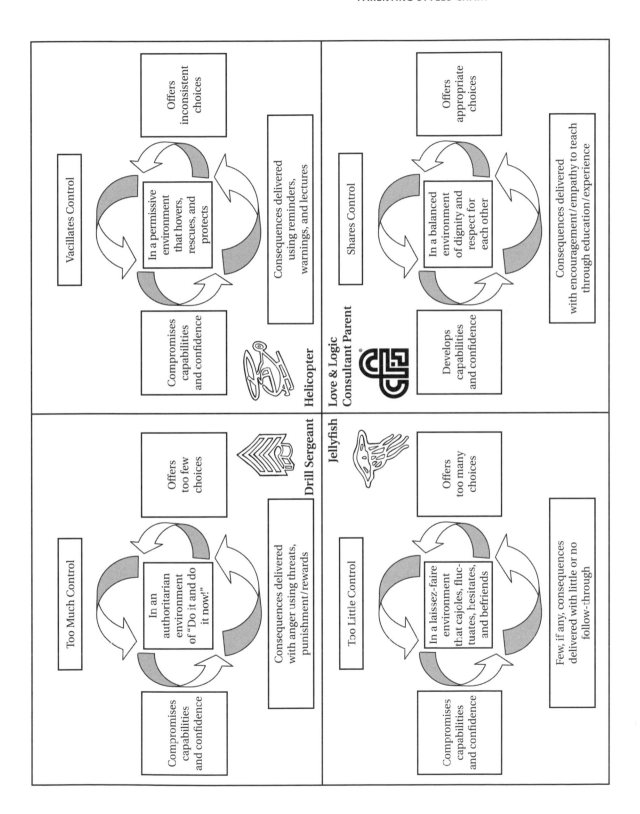

Helicopter

Drill Sergeant

Love & Logic Consultant Parent

Jellyfish

Vacillates Control

Offers inconsistent choices

In a permissive environment that hovers, rescues, and protects

Consequences delivered using reminders, warnings, and lectures

Compromises capabilities and confidence

Shares Control

Offers appropriate choices

In a balanced environment of dignity and respect for each other

Consequences delivered with encouragement/empathy to teach through education/experience

Develops capabilities and confidence

Too Much Control

Offers too few choices

In an authoritarian environment of "Do it and do it now!"

Consequences delivered with anger using threats, punishment/rewards

Compromises capabilities and confidence

Too Little Control

Offers too many choices

In a laissez-faire environment that cajoles, fluctuates, hesitates, and befriends

Few, if any, consequences delivered with little or no follow-through

Compromises capabilities and confidence

Three Traps to Avoid with Kids' Excuses

Children often challenge us when it comes to helping out. All across the country, parents have the same reasons for granting their children immunity from chores.

It's easy to lull ourselves into thinking that doing chores are not really that important, or not worth the battle. In Chapter 5, we'll show how kids who make contributions meet their basic human need to feel important, significant, and needed. That reason alone is worth its weight in gold. But there are some other excellent reasons to resist granting immunity from chores.

Below are three of the most common traps that confuse many parents about involving their children in doing household tasks. The typical responses to such traps may be accurate in the short term, and might help you get through the day. But wise parents remember that they will be far more effective at preparing their kids to live in a home—other than their childhood home—if they think about the long-term benefits of raising responsible, contributing kids.

Challenge #1: When kids say, "I can't."

There are lots of reason why your children might say, "I can't" when asked to help out. Sometimes it's legitimate, and sometimes not.

What do we sometimes hear ourselves say when our children tell us they can't do something? "Here, I'll do it!" or "Here, honey … do it this way!" as we take over without involving them in the process. Then we wonder why our kids do not take the initiative to do something on their own later in life. Ask any parent if they wistfully long for the days when their children used to say, "Me do it, Daddy, me do it!"

Unknowingly, we tend to be our children's ever-ready battery when it comes to doing it for them. While this is the perfect choice when it comes to helpless infants, we often forget to wean ourselves from doing everything for them *when they could be learning how to do it themselves.*

When the "I can't" rolls off the lips of your children, it could be legitimate. Maybe they really can't do all or part of the task. Clearly, more training is in order if that is the case. But what if you know that *they can* do it? What if you have actually seen them complete the task before without the kind of frustration that stems from not knowing how?

An "I can't" may not be legitimate. Sometimes it is used to emotionally hook us as parents. We need to be careful not to buy into our children's manipulative efforts to get us to do the task for them. A good response at times like this is, "Aren't you glad I don't believe that?"

Sometimes the "I can't" mantra is a cover-up for "I won't."

Bottom Line: The time and patience you invest now to teach your kids to be contributing members return bonus dividends later. When your kids say, "I can't," show them they really can.

Challenge #2: When kids say, "I won't."

Parents may think: "Well … I don't know how to get them to cooperate … and it's probably faster, easier (and usually better) if I just do it myself. Sometimes a swift swat to the rump helps too."

Many kids, by creating a hassle, train their parents to not even ask for help around the house. Many of us end up doing it ourselves, because it simply gets us through another day more peacefully.

One dad complained, "My son makes more of a mess than if I had just done it myself!" This is a common reaction for most of us, who just want the task crossed off our "To Do" list. Unfortunately, this is a shortsighted view. We unintentionally tend to cross opportunities for building character and life skills off the list at the same time. How? Easier and faster *now* means harder and more difficult *later*.

Here's a sneak preview of what can happen when we buy into the "faster … easier … better" idea when our kids say, "I won't." It's not as far-fetched as it sounds:

The four-year-old who makes a big mess (therefore we do it for him) …
becomes the fourteen-year-old who argues (therefore we do it for him) …
becomes the twenty-four-year-old who still lives at home
(because we do it for him) …
becomes the married forty-four-year-old who never helps out
(because his spouse does it for him) …
until no one lives happily ever after.

It probably is faster and easier to do it yourself, for a time or two. But if you add up all the times you do things *for* your children, the short-term gain becomes a long-term drain. The time you save by doing it yourself becomes time wasted for a more independent, happier future when you and they are older.

Getting our children to do their chores can feel like pushing a boulder uphill!

Nonetheless, we need to create as many positive training experiences as possible, so that kids will not only learn how to contribute to the family, but also learn that helping others feels good and is fun too!

Bottom Line: It may be tempting to just "do it yourself" when your kids say, "I won't." But important opportunities for building character and life skills toward independence will be missed.

Challenge #3: When kids say, "I'm busy."

You may be thinking, "But it's my kid's job to go to school and play sports … plus they need time with their friends." Yes, yes, and yes. School, extracurricular activities, and time with friends are important—but family needs still come first. The issue is not who is the busiest; the issue is one of setting priorities.

"Too busy," your kid says? Is this just a kid problem? Look at what you, as an adult and parent, have learned to juggle. Why not prepare your kids for adult life by teaching them how to prioritize their social, entertainment, recreational, educational, and job pursuits just like you do?

"Too busy," your kid says? Fast-forward to their first job in life. Are they going to be able to tell their first employer that they're "too busy" to show up for work, or "too busy" hanging out to complete a team task? Learning how to manage time and set priorities is a life skill, no matter what the age or setting.

What else do you think happens when we allow our kids to get away with not doing their chores because they're "too busy" or they have "homework" or they "need to see friends" or whatever?

It teaches an attitude of *me, me, me* entitlement and cripples empowerment, motivation, and achievement in school. "Me first" kids do not learn that life takes effort and compromise for the good of the whole family. "Me first" kids also don't learn the important life skills of time management, scheduling, and advance planning.

Bottom Line: Parents who are too busy to teach their children how to make contributions raise kids who are too busy to put anyone else but *me, me, me* first.

What's School Got to Do with Chores?

The words *housework* and *homework* both share the root word *work*, translated loosely to mean "effort." A minor difference between housework and homework is that the first deals with the process of living and the other deals more with the process of learning … although *homework* still implies "effort at home," whether it involves the house or not.

What's housework got to do with homework? Some parents think their kids are too busy with their homework to do any housework. But we miss giving our kids an important learning opportunity when we let them off the housework hook. Why?

Because the character traits instilled by making family contributions are universal to success in all walks of life. There is simply no substitute for perseverance, determination, and effort, and the resulting satisfaction of being a needed member of the family. The best experiences for developing character come in the face of a challenge.

Parents who do not require their children to contribute to life at home create kids who do not want to contribute to life at school. Don't expect your child's teacher to be able to motivate him or her to pick up their pencil at school if they're not required to lift a finger at home. As one teacher said: "No wonder some kids have a tough time with motivation and achievement in school, when they have different expectations at home."

> *P*arents who do not require their children to contribute to life at home create kids who do not want to contribute to life at school.

Bottom Line: Wise parents do their kids a favor by *requiring* contributions at home, so they'll have more of what it takes to fulfill the requirements at school.

Money Back Guarantee Options

Many of you might be thinking: "Choices won't work with my kid. My son still won't clean his room." If so, let's continue with the story of Emily to illustrate how a Love and Logic parent uses their skills on a day when she isn't responding to Mom's choices.

It's a month later. Same scene. Only this time, it's four o'clock and her room still hasn't been cleaned. Emily hasn't bothered to hire someone else, beyond her one-dollar effort to con her younger sister, nor has she cleaned it herself. What would the Love and Logic consultant parent do now?

It's time to use a heavy dose of empathy before delivering a consequence. Why? Because the purpose of any consequence is to hand the problem back to the child so he or she can resolve it, and learn from it. A heavy dose of empathy hands the problem back not only kindly, but also firmly and without anger. We want to create a consequence that makes it the child's problem that his or her room is not clean, not your problem. (For more information about the Love and Logic approach of using empathy prior to giving a consequence, see "The Core of Love and Logic: Empathy" on p. 44.)

Mom has several ways to hand the problem back to her daughter.

Money Back Guarantee Option A: Bill 'em

Once the deadline has passed, Mom can tell Emily, "No problem. I'll take care of it." Then she cleans Emily's room herself, and encloses a bill for her services in Emily's allowance envelope. Should Emily notice that Mom is cleaning her room, Mom can calmly say, "No problem. I'm taking care of it." (Some parents may want to avoid a potential control battle by cleaning their child's room when he or she is not around to notice.)

Option A allows Mom's non-emotional billing for her work to do the teaching. The fact that the bill will be a surprise increases the chances that the consequence will be more effective.

It's allowance day. Here's how the scenario plays out:

Mom:	"Emily, it's Friday. Here's your allowance."
Emily:	"Great!" (counting it out)
Mom:	"Is that right? Eight dollars?"
Emily:	"Yeah. Thanks!"
Mom:	(sighing) "Ohhh, and here's my bill."
Emily:	(opening the bill) "Seven dollars?! For cleaning my room? That's not fair!"
Mom:	"I know."
Emily:	(whining) "If I pay you, then I only get one dollar for allowance this weeeeeek."
Mom:	"I know."
Emily:	(giving Mom a wide-eyed, dumbfounded look) "But you didn't tell me you were going to charge me seven dollars."
Mom:	"I know."
Emily:	(begrudgingly handing back the money) "Here."
Mom:	"Thank you."

What just happened? Notice that Mom said nothing about Emily "learning a lesson." She didn't threaten or warn Emily, nor did she use the "I told you so" lecture. She used empathy instead, by repeating "I know" in a calm, soft voice. This way, Emily was guided to see herself, not her Mom, as the source of the problem.

As for the consequence? Mom set up the situation so that Emily was surprised. She handed the problem back to her in the form of a cleaning bill. Love and Logic teaches that empathy should precede the consequence.

Seven dollars, you ask? That's right—adult wages for adult work; children's wages for children's work. (Use the prevailing minimum hourly wage as your guide.) It's important for your children to understand that when adults do adult work, we charge adult wages.

But I Do Enough Housework Already ...

You may be thinking that you don't want to clean your kid's room. That's their job! Remember how the whole dialogue started? Mom asked her daughter, "Emily, would you like to clean your room this week, or pay me to do it?" She offered her a choice of two things, one side of which involved Mom doing the cleaning.

Can Mom choose to *not* offer her cleaning services? Of course. Ever have the experience of offering a choice of two things and your child invariably picks the one you don't like? This puts us in a negative predicament, because we have lost control of the outcome.

One of Love and Logic's guidelines for offering effective choices is to only offer choices that are acceptable to you. In that way, no matter what the child decides, it will be a choice you can live with. In other words, if you do not want to clean your child's room, then don't give your child the choice.

You could say instead, "Do you want to clean your room by Saturday at two o'clock, or do you want me to *hire* someone to do it?" Then, if the room hasn't been cleaned by the deadline, hire a professional cleaning service and dock your child's allowance for the cost (as in the example provided in "Money Back Guarantee Option B" on p. 48).

Pinch Without Being a Grinch

There is a tendency in such a billing situation to make an automatic deduction by giving the child the remainder of their allowance and explaining why. Cancel that impulse. We want the child to "feel the money crunch" so that the lesson is learned from the inside out. The clincher is when you hand the bill to the child and the child has to physically hand back part of his or her allowance—the part that he or she *thought* was going to be given for "free."

It's not until that moment that a child learns the *real* cost of not cleaning their room. No need to be a grinch to help your children feel the pinch. Simply use your favorite empathic statement and let the consequence of the financial loss do the teaching.

What do you think might happen the next time Mom asks Emily to clean her room? Once she understands that Mom will follow through by collecting what is owed, *and* once she values what her money can do for her, chances are Emily will be more motivated to follow through on her commitment next time.

Is Mom teaching Emily how the real world works? Yes. Do we, as adults, have to come up with the money when bills are due, or face the consequences? You bet. Emily is lucky. She's learning this lifetime lesson at the young age of eight, for the small sum of $7.

You may be thinking, "… but how do I bill my kids?" Billing your children for chores left undone can be as simple as a sticky note, or as elaborate as a formal notice. Sound over-the-top? Not really, because wise parents who use Love and Logic understand that real world lessons are best taught in real world style. (For more information about how to set up an allowance system that includes bills for your services, see "Kid-Sized Bills" on p. 78.)

Finally, what if Emily turns into a serial whiner about this? Or wants to argue with you? In that case, see "What to Do When Your Kids Argue: How to Use Love and Logic One-Liners" on p. 46.

The Core of Love and Logic: Empathy

Many of the strategies used in the stories and examples throughout this book employ empathy, or an expression of sadness for the child's situation, to soak up the emotions of a difficult or challenging moment. Empathy is the keystone in the Love and Logic philosophy, and a big part of the *love* in "Love and Logic."

For many parents, empathy is the antithesis of our typical reaction when our children misbehave. Thus it probably won't feel like a natural response at first when parents practice its use.

From our early life, we become hard-wired to think: "When a kid does something wrong, I should get angry." That's because we ourselves were programmed as children by the adults around us. Through the influences of early modeling, this reaction becomes automatic. (Just recall the last time you reacted to something your child did with the very same words your mother or father used with you … and yet you promised yourself you would never do or say those things when you had children.)

This can change with awareness and practice. Parents can learn to deprogram their typical reaction of anger or frustration and reprogram themselves to respond with empathy.

Parents who are successful with this core skill keep it simple by using just one empathic statement that fits their personality, temperament, and culture, and using it every time they are about to deliver a consequence. Some examples:

"This is so sad."
"Oh no. That's too bad."
"Dang. That's awful."
"What a bummer."
"That's never good."
"This stinks."
"Oh sweetie …"
"Uhmmm."
"Uh oh … oh man …"

The expression of empathy has to be genuine to be effective. A sarcastic, condescending, or angry tone of voice, or disapproving body language, will undermine empathy's effectiveness in a heartbeat. The way we say our empathic statement (our tone, inflection, body language) is far more important that *what* we say.

Some parents practice making sounds like "Hmmm" or "Ohhh" while keeping their lips closed if they aren't sure they can muster a genuine or empathic tone using words. Other parents use a "sing song" style or whisper their empathic statement to hide any hint of sarcasm.

Regardless of your style, an authentic delivery can make the difference between a child learning responsibility or learning resentment. Parents who benefit the most from being empathic are those who have personalized their statement, memorized it, and practiced it so often that it's the first thing off the tip of their tongue when their child misbehaves or when they don't know what to do.

"I'm sorry" Is Not Empathy

Some parents, when first practicing this skill, respond with "I'm sorry." For example: "I'm sorry. Because you haven't cleaned your room, I can't take you to the mall."

"I'm sorry" is an expression of sympathy, not empathy. While the difference may be subtle, the focus moves toward how *you feel*, and away from the child's *poor choice or misbehavior.*

The expression of empathy has to be genuine to be effective.

Top Five Benefits of Using Empathy

Many parents have discovered that empathy seems almost magical as a method to use while disciplining their kids … without losing their love and respect.

Here are the top five benefits of learning how to use using empathy effectively:

- Empathy makes the child's decision the "bad guy" while keeping the adult the "good guy."
- As a result, the child has a harder time blaming the adult for the problem.
- This forces the child to look inside and to learn from the consequence.
- The child tends to go into the thinking mode instead of the fighting mode.
- This reduces the likelihood of the child becoming revengeful or resentful, or withdrawing from the adult.

What to Do When Your Kids Argue: How to Use Love and Logic One-Liners

Money, unfortunately, is the topic of many an argument in relationships, among family members, spouses, and with our children. Regardless of whether the topic is money or not, kids are able to engage their parents in all kinds of arguments. For example:

"You don't love me anymore! If you did you would buy it for me …"

"That's not fair! Jason's parents would pay him."

"Dad never does that."

We've all been hooked by our kids like this, at one time or another. What is the best way to keep our cool when things get hot?

Here are some Love and Logic one-liners that will help parents neutralize the moment without getting hooked. You'll recognize the use of these statements in the stories and dialogues throughout the book:

"Probably so. And what did I say?" (The question "And what did I say?" is a good way to establish the fact that you have set a limit and that you intend to stick with it. Parents who use this way of enforcing limits find that it's very effective, and that they can fall back on it most of the time.)

"I know."

"Nice try."

"I bet it feels that way."

"What do you think you're going to do?"

"I don't know. What do you think?"

"I'll love you wherever you live."

"I love you too much to argue."

"Thanks for sharing that."

"That's an option."

"I bet that could be true."

"I'm not sure how to respond to that. I'll have to get back to you on it."

"I'll let you know later what will work for me."

Let's take a look at how to use these one-liners.

Step 1: Go brain dead!

That means you don't engage in the content of the argument, or think about what the child is saying. You may be tempted to reason with your child if you think too much. It's likely that an argumentative child will try to trap you with your own words when you try to reason with him or her. When children play our words back to us, the color of our face may change, our voice may get louder, and the veins in our forehead may budge. This does nothing but embolden an arguing child.

Step 2: Softly repeat a single Love and Logic one-liner.

Pick one of the statements above and repeat it softly. The parents who are the most effective at using these statements find they don't need to be creative. They pick one that fits the situation and their personality and just repeat the same line ... over and over again. Some parents successfully end the matter by following their one-liner with: "And what did I say?" as they walk away to continue their day.

Remember, these statements tend to backfire if used sarcastically. They are never intended to be flippant remarks or to discount the feelings of a child. The problem will only become worse if a parent uses these responses to try to get the better of their child.

When we argue with our children, or allow them to manipulate us, we reinforce those behaviors as acceptable ways for kids to get what they want. Your ability to understand this and your genuine desire not to argue or get hooked by whatever your children say is the key to your success.

Money Back Guarantee Option B: Let a Pro Bill 'em

But let's say Mom doesn't want to clean Emily's room. She feels like she already does more than her fair share of the household work. If that's the case, here's how to hand the problem back to the child in a different way:

Mom: "Emily, would you like to clean your room by four o'clock Saturday, or hire someone else to do it?"

Emily: (shrugging her shoulders) "I don't know … naaa.

Mom: "Oh, this is so sad. This is a problem. I'm not sure what I'm going to do about it. I need to think about it. I'll get back to you … but in the meantime … don't worry."

Emily: (mumbling) "Yeah right, whatever."

In this scenario, Emily does not clean her room. When Mom says "I need to think about it," Emily mumbles "Yeah right, whatever" and thinks she's gotten away with it. Little does she know that the consequence is on its way.

Guess what? Four o'clock Saturday comes and goes. Emily hasn't cleaned her room. Mom remembers not to warn or remind. Mom will just say to Emily, "No problem. I'll take care of it," if Emily inquires, and nothing more. This gives Mom time to calm down and think about the best way to hand the problem back to Emily.

Mom uses a Love and Logic delayed consequence: "Oh, this is so sad. This is a problem. I'm not sure what I'm going to do about it. I need to think about it. I'll get back to you … but in the meantime … don't worry." (For information about a consequence to use whenever you need time to think, see "It Pays to Delay: The Delayed Consequence" on p. 52.)

This gives Mom time to make a plan. She decides to hire a cleaning service, because she doesn't want to do it herself. With Mom's continuing use of "No problem. I'll take care of it," it won't be long before Emily begins paying serious attention those words.

The Monday Blues

It's Monday. Emily comes through the door after school:

Emily: "Hey, Mom … Hi! Can you take me to the mall?"

Mom: (with empathy) "Oh, no … this is so sad. My energy was drained trying to figure out what to do with your room. I'm too tired. I'm going to rest on the couch and just pretend I took you to the mall."

Emily: "What do you mean 'too tired'? You only have to drive me there. You can drop me off. It will only take a few minutes."

Emily does not understand yet that Mom's talk of an "energy drain" is about having had to hire, supervise, and pay a professional cleaner while Emily was at school. That discovery comes later.

Emily: "Come on, Mom … it will only take a few minutes …"
Mom: (with empathy) "Probably so. And what did I say?"
Emily: "But Lilly's mom would do it for her."
Mom: "Probably so. And what did I say?"

Emily is beginning to notice that her manipulation isn't working, so now she tries the "good manners" route, complete with pleading eyes that melt Mom's heart. But Mom stands firm because she's been practicing for this moment:

Emily: "Pleeezzz, Mom, pretty pleeezzz …"
Mom: "I really need some rest. There are some energy replacement options on the refrigerator. If you want to do some things for me to restore my energy, please feel free to choose anything from that list. Maybe after you get a few of those done, I will have some energy to take you to the mall."

Emily just stares at Mom. She wants to say something, but decides not to, and instead of heading for the kitchen to review the energy replacement list, she races off to her bedroom.

One Problem for the Price of Two

The energy drain technique works when you can engineer a situation that holds the child accountable. Love and Logic parents know that engineering just a few of these situations causes a dramatic change in a kid's behavior. In the above example, the problem shifts from Mom wanting Emily to clean her room (Mom's problem) to Emily wanting Mom take her to the mall (Emily's problem).

This transfer of responsibility becomes the consequence that teaches the child that his or her poor choice is causing them to have even more problems down the road: the parent's energy drain. (For more information about the energy drain technique, see "Earning Energy Back" on p. 53.)

The true-to-life lesson here is that when we don't solve one problem, it often creates more problems.

Emily's first problem is that she has to replace Mom's energy in order to be driven to the mall. Her second problem is that she needs to pay Mom back for the cleaning service hired on her behalf. The first problem—a ride to the mall—is handled once Emily makes some sort of concerted effort to replace Mom's energy. Mom will be too "drained" to do most anything else until she sees Emily making some effort to restore her energy.

Now for the second of Emily's problems—repaying the money Mom spent on getting her room cleaned. What about the minimum two-hour fee the cleaning service charged? How will Mom recoup the money? All part of what Love and Logic calls a strategic training session. Wise parents figure out their strategies and "plug the holes" before they ever begin a training session in cooperation.

So Mom takes a moment to think through her options before talking to Emily again.

Mom's Options

Emily can repay Mom in several ways:

- *Earning:* She can bid on and earn money from the standard list of jobs on the refrigerator, or complete odd jobs in the neighborhood equal to the amount of the bill (more about earnings in Chapter 10).
- *Borrowing:* Mom can hold collateral—in the form of toys or possessions equal to the amount of the bill—until the bill is paid. Items are sequestered until the child earns the money back doing jobs or doing *your* contributions as payment (more about borrowing in Chapter 9).
- *Spending:* The cleaning service bill can be paid back via allowance, or with forfeited possessions of equal value that are not returned to the child (more about saving in Chapter 8).

"So, Emily ..."

Let's continue this story to see how we might present these options to a child. What might happen once Emily discovers that Mom's way of solving the problem was to hire someone else to do it? Here comes Emily, emerging from her bedroom:

Emily: "Mom, there is a *bill* in my room from Merry Maids for cleaning services!"

Mom:	"Yes, I know."
Emily:	"Why is this in my room?! Did *they* come clean my room?"
Mom:	"Yes. So, how do you plan to pay me back?"
Emily:	(after a long pause, looking back and forth between Mom and the bill) "This isn't fair! I don't know how I'm going to pay you back. I didn't hire them—*you* did. *You* should pay them!"
Mom:	"Yes, I bet it feels that way. I took care of it. Now you have a clean room. So what's your plan?"
Emily:	"I don't know."
Mom:	"That's a bummer not to know."
Emily:	"That's a ton of money! I don't have that kind of money. That's just not fair."
Mom:	"I know. Would you like to know what some other kids have tried?"
Emily:	(reluctantly, since Mom isn't budging) "Yeah … I guess."

"Okay, okay, I'll *dooo* it …"

Parents can proceed here by using Love and Logic's five steps to guiding kids to own and solve their problems. Mom offers Emily some options to consider. In the end, Emily decides on a combination of using her allowance and doing some extra jobs. (For a more complete description of the five steps to guiding children to own and solve their problems, see "Accountability 101" on p. 55.)

Notice how easily Mom was able to drive the lesson home, without anger or frustration. She refrained from the more typical parent reactions in favor of using one-liners repetitively and a consequence that hands the problem back by saying, "No problem. I'll take care of it."

Mom knows that when empathy precedes the consequence, the child's poor choice becomes the bad guy, not her. In either case, whether she hired herself or hired someone else, the room got clean. Emily discovered, to her dismay, that she lost her choice in the matter when she didn't deal with the problem herself.

What do you think is going to happen the next time Mom asks the very same question: "Do you want to clean your room, or do you want me to hire someone else to do it?" Chances are Emily will have a different thought process. And you never know … her sister Jennifer might even get a pay raise if she wants the job—without even asking!

You may be asking, "My kid won't clean their room no matter who does it or how much I charge. What do I do then?" You'll need to up the ante on the consequence a little bit more in order to hand the problem back. (For a series of strategic training steps to help kids who are having trouble remembering the importance of cooperation, see "Eight Steps to Motivate the Unmotivated" on p. 148. These expanded training steps will help any child remember the same principle—that they'd better solve their own problems before they make a problem for their parents.)

It Pays to Delay: The Delayed Consequence

Ever find it challenging to come up with an appropriate consequence in the heat of the moment? Or get stumped after the umpteenth time of telling your child to do something?

In these kinds of situations, Love and Logic uses a delayed consequence. This strategy can be used in many different ways, but wise parents make it the strategy of choice *whenever they don't know what to do.*

One of the biggest benefits to parents who use this strategy is that it gives them time to think and calm down. And it gives the child time to think and worry about what the consequence is going to be.

Ever feel the pressure of thinking you need to come up with an immediate consequence? There are several problems with immediate consequences such as "You're grounded for a week!" or "Go to your room *now!*":

- We tend to react while we *and* the child are too upset to think.
- We don't have time to put together a reasonable plan and a support team to help us carry it out. (As a result, we often end up making threats we can't back up, or setting limits we can't enforce.)
- We tend to forget to respond with empathy because we are too busy trying to deal with the moment. This leaves the child in the fighting mode.

Next time your child does the unexpected or you just don't know what to do, delay the consequence. Here's an example of what to say:

This is so sad (or whatever your empathic statement is). *This is a problem. I'm not sure what I'm going to do about it. I need to think about it. I'll get back to you … but in the meantime … don't worry.*

When we follow the words "I'm going to do something about it" with a meaningful consequence, then "I'm going to do something about it" become a consequence too—an anticipatory consequence.

Perhaps you know the value of anticipation if you're from the generation whose own parents would say, "Just wait until your father gets home!" Love and Logic's delayed consequence is different, however, because it uses empathy—not anger, threats, warnings, or lectures—in order to keep the child in thinking mode.

As soon as a child hears "No problem. I'll take care of it," he or she will learn that things turn out better when they choose to solve the problem on their own. Why? Because they learn that it's much sadder for them when they leave it up to their parents to solve the problem for them.

Parents solve the problem in a way that usually causes the child to be inconvenienced or uncomfortable. In the example of Emily, she learned that when she didn't get her room cleaned by Saturday at four o'clock, her mom took care of the problem—in this case to the tune of much more effort than she bargained for.

Bottom Line: While it pays for parents to delay a consequence, children soon learn that it doesn't pay for them to delay.

Earning Energy Back: The Energy Drain Technique

Many parents can identify with feeling that their energy has been drained by their children's misbehavior. The logic behind the energy drain idea suggests that those who contribute to draining your energy are the ones who need to replenish it!

From such a perspective, "energy replacement options" become consequences for your children. Energy replacement options are basically anything that is on *your* contribution or *your* job list, or anything that might help *you* relax and rest.

The energy drain consequence is a great choice for those times when kids leave you speechless. Next time you find yourself stumped for a consequence, try this:

Step 1: Say with empathy, *Oh, no. When you* _____ (describe the behavior briefly), *it really drains my energy. We'll talk about this later.* Alternatively, the script can go something like this: *Oh, this is so sad. That behavior* (choice, etc., briefly describe if necessary) *drains my energy. You can replace some of my energy by doing something on this list. Let me know what you decide.*

Step 2: Give yourself some time to calm down and think.

Step 3: Ask your child how they plan to replace the energy they drained. Kids can replace energy by staying home while you rest, hiring themselves a babysitter, cooking dinner, and so forth.

Step 4: Give them a deadline for "energy replacement," and enforce it if they forget or refuse. Some parents find it necessary to delay a privilege until the work is done, or supervise a "withdrawal" at allowance time if their energy isn't replaced by the deadline. (For an example, see "Money Back Guarantee Option A: Bill 'em" on p. 42.)

Paying the Piper

One mom used the energy drain technique one night when the babysitter called her and her husband to come home because "the kids were out of control":

Oh, this is so sad. When your father and I have to come home early because you guys are behaving so poorly, it really drains my energy. Tomorrow, when you get a chance, you can replace some of my energy by doing some of the things on this list. Let me know what you decide. In the meantime, try not to worry about it.

This turned out to be a double consequence. First, her children had to do jobs to re-energize Mom … before they could get her to do anything else for them. Second, the children had to do jobs for free that they might have otherwise been paid to do. (They also had to reimburse Mom for the babysitter's fees.)

The energy drain strategy has an added bonus: it teaches the value of work and appreciation for the ones who provide it. That's because the source of "energy replacements" should always be the things that adults *do for* kids. Kids get a firsthand experience with the energy or effort it takes to carry and put away the groceries, or clean the kitchen, when they are the ones who are doing it.

Another dad, once he had trained his child with anticipatory consequences, used the energy drain as a preventative measure. All he needed to say to his son, using his oh-so-tired voice, was: "Oh man … I feel an energy drain coming on."

His son has been heard to say, "No, not the list!" and then begin doing what he was asked to do.

When your child creates a problem, you can use the energy drain technique—a type of consequence that holds kids accountable for their poor choices by "recharging" their parent's energy. Next time your child leaves you speechless, experiment: take a rest from doing things for your children while your children get busy doing things for you!

Accountability 101: How to Guide Kids to Own and Solve Their Problems

Love and Logic uses a five-step approach to guide kids to own and solve their problems. It's designed to help children with problems during those times when the parent has no control over the situation. This strategy teaches kids to be their own problem-solvers and is effective for teaching "cause and effect" thinking. (For specific examples of the use of this strategy, see "Crossing the Double Line" on p. 166, "Five Kid-Sized Reasons to Save Money" on p. 250, and "Care to Share?" on p. 406.)

Five Steps for Guiding Kids to Own and Solve Their Problems

Step 1: Use empathy.

"How sad."

"What a bummer."

Step 2: Send the "power message."

"What do *you* think you're going to do?"

Step 3: After asking permission first, offer choices.

"Would you like to know what some other kids have tried?" If they agree, proceed. If they don't agree, the consequence—of not solving the problem—is built into saying, "Well, let me know if you change your mind."

If they agree, offer a variety of choices that range from bad to good. Begin each suggestion with "Some kids try …" and "Other kids try …"

Start out with a poor choice. This approach has benefits for two reasons: first, it reminds the child that he or she is in control of solving their own problem, and second, it gives them a chance to reject your first idea. (Plus, all of the other ideas look better by comparison!)

Each time a choice is offered, go to step 4, requiring the child to state in his or her own words the consequence of his or her choice *in advance*. This means that you will be alternating between step 3 (giving an idea) and step 4 (asking him or her how it would work) about three to five times.

Step 4: Have the child state the consequences in their own words.
"How will that work for you?"

Step 5: Give permission for the child to solve the problem on their own, without asking them what they are going to do.
"You have figured things out before. I hope it works out."

Remember: This is the child's problem. It is important to let the child either solve or not solve the problem. Have no fear. If the child is fortunate enough to make a poor choice, he or she may benefit from a double learning lesson. That's because if the child solves the problem poorly, or not at all, there are still consequences: first, not solving the problem is a consequence, because the problem does not get resolved, and second, selecting a choice that does not work for the child is a consequence. Notice how both outcomes offer learning opportunities.

 It is important to use this strategy only when the child has a problem, or as a way to hand the problem back to the child. In the example of Emily, it was not a problem for her that she didn't want to clean her room. But it soon *became* Emily's problem when she resisted.

The Five Most Common Mistakes Parents Make When First Using This Strategy

- Not being genuinely empathic in step 1.
  Being flippant or sarcastic will backfire. Whisper, use a singsong tone of voice, or use one word that allows you to keep your lips closed to express yourself authentically (e.g., "Hmmm," "Ohhh," "Mmmm").
- Forgetting to ask permission to give suggestions.
  Drop the subject if your child says "no" to "Would you like to know what other kids have tried?" Chances are, any idea you mention will fall on deaf ears. "No" means they're not interested in solving the problem yet, or that the problem is not big enough yet to motivate them to want to solve it. Let the consequence of still having the problem continue to do the teaching.
- Forgetting to begin suggestions using the key phrases: "Some kids …" and "Other kids …"

Referring to what friends and peers do tends to open the eyes and ears of your children, because the suggestions sound like kid-sized solutions even if they're your thoughts.

• Passing judgment on the child's answers in step 4: "How will that work for you?"

The authors of Love and Logic want your children to make as many affordable mistakes as possible. Give them the precious opportunity to figure things out on their own.

• Asking the child which suggestion they're going to try.

Resist the temptation to pressure the child into making a decision; simply express confidence in their ability to solve the problem, and let them know that you're there to offer support.

Short on ideas? Most adults have difficulty launching into a list of possible solu-tions that other kids have tried. Don't rush into this part. It's often best to say, "I need a little time to remember what other kids have tried in these situations. Give me a day or so and I'll get back to you." This gives you a chance to consult with others for ideas. This alone could result in the child solving the problem on his or her own.

CHAPTER 3

Allowance

Training Wheels to Financial Freedom

In this chapter you'll discover what giving kids an allowance can teach them about personal accountability. You'll find answers to questions about how much allowance, when to start, how often, and how allowance can pay you back in "teaching responsibility" dividends.

Allowance Vows

Parents are milling around the refreshment table during a break from their PTA meeting, laughing and chatting with one another. The conversation turns to allowance:

Mom #1: "I don't give my kids any allowance at all."

Mom #2: "You don't? Gosh … I've been giving my kids an allowance since they were five years old."

Mom #3: "Really? Well … My kids have to do their chores before they get any money from me!"

Allowance is a regular and often controversial topic when the subject of money and kids bubbles up in conversations. Many parents think that kids should earn their allowance. Others think not. Let's examine allowance from two different perspectives—first, how giving an allowance benefits kids, and second, how giving an allowance benefits parents.

Cameron's First $10

Seven-year-old Cameron looked so surprised the first time his mother experimented with an allowance. After the cashier gave him change from his first $10 bill, Mom could tell he had no comprehension of why the clerk handed him money in return. He looked up at Mom wide-eyed, as if to say, "Do I get to keep this?"

Mom wished she had a camera. A picture of that incredulous look on Cameron's face would have been worth a thousand words. A picture of a child who had no comprehension of what had just happened. And, it was instant validation that she was on the right track.

Guess what Cameron did with the change? He must have reasoned that if some spending is good, more is better. On the way out of the toy store, he spent his last few coins on one of those gumball-type machines that issue trinkets for 50¢ each. She wisely told herself over and over again to keep her mouth shut. She knew it was not a wise purchase, but *he* was the one who needed to pay the price in order to learn this lesson.

Cameron was so pleased with himself as they left the store. He chatted away as he played with the trinket. Of course, it broke on the way home, thank goodness. Why thank goodness? The lesson—buying cheap doesn't reap—only cost him 50¢. What a bargain! What if Mom had told him, "Don't buy that, it will break before you get home?" Mom would have robbed him of the opportunity to figure that out all by himself. What if he hasn't learned this lesson by the time he buys his first computer or his first car?

A Hands-On Experience

Money is just as fundamental and purposeful as anything else we can give our children in order for them to learn. For Cameron, at this point in time, money was just an everyday object to him without any real meaning.

How else will kids learn about money unless they are given opportunities to use it or lose it? If we give pencils to children so they can learn how to write, and books so they can learn how to read, then why not give children money so they can learn how to save and spend? How can a child learn to ride a bike without access to a bike? By giving them money in the form of an allowance, our kids get to experiment and practice with the basic concepts of saving and spending.

Allowance is often our kids' first real hands-on experience with learning about the value of money. That is, *if* we give our kids an allowance. I (Kristan) was rarely given any practice "money" as a kid growing up. All that I knew about money was that it bought me things I wanted, and that if I could manipulate my father or mother into giving me what I wanted, I was happy—until the next time I wanted something. That experience was a great foundation for learning how to manipulate others, but not great for learning personal money management skills.

Hands-on experience with money, early and often, offers essential practice if the goal is to prepare our children for their future. Let them make as many mistakes as possible when the stakes are small. By giving kids allowance when the price tags are affordable, both literally and figuratively, they have opportunities to both fail and succeed at making money choices.

Too bad Cameron's mom didn't have a camera that day. Cameron could be the poster child for the true purpose behind giving kids an allowance. It provides hands-on experience to practice with their own money—with no strings attached.

If we give pencils to children so they can learn how to write, and books so they can learn how to read, then why not give children money so they can learn how to save and spend?

Bottom Line: Wise parents realize that the only way kids will truly understand the value of money is through hands-on experience.

How Much Allowance?

One Sunday morning, Julie had asked her five-year-old daughter at least ten times to pick up her toys. Her daughter kept playing and playing as Mom was scurrying around to get ready for church.

Finally at her wit's end, after numerous pleadings, Mom said, "Tina, if you don't pick up your toys *now*, there's going to be hell to pay!" Immediately and very innocently, her daughter responded: "Mommy, how much does hell cost … one or two weeks' allowance?"

Good question.

Wise parents keep it simple when it comes to the question of how much allowance to give their children. They use a formula that's easy to remember, simple to use, and developmentally appropriate.

Two Approaches

There are two basic approaches to determining the amount of allowance. The first is the "flexible" approach, whereby parents involve the children in deciding what amount works. This might be a good choice if you already have an allowance system but it isn't working very well, or if you have older or more experienced children.

The second is the "flat rate" approach, whereby the parents decide the amount. This approach is a good choice if you are just beginning an allowance system, or if you have young or inexperienced children.

The approach you adopt depends on the age of your children, your family's financial resources and values, and common sense.

The Flexible Approach to Allowance

To involve your children in deciding about allowance, sit down and discuss with them the reason for, and possible uses of, allowance: how they plan to spend, share, and save it, and for what purpose.

Important money decisions should never be made in haste. Don't agree on anything initially until both you and your children have had adequate time to discuss it. Once you've introduced the subject, invite your children to think about it and come back later with a proposal about how much they would like and how they plan to use it (some parents even ask for this proposal in writing).

Before accepting any proposal, written or otherwise, give *yourself* some thinking time to make a reasonable counter offer. Many kids quite naturally name a higher amount than their parents are willing to give. Other kids might underestimate what will be needed based on inexperience with how they plan to use it.

Regardless of what amount is finally agreed to, be sure to give your children enough money to experiment and practice with, otherwise you'll undermine the point of giving them an allowance in the first place.

Regardless of what amount is finally agreed to, be sure to give your children enough money to experiment and practice with, otherwise you'll undermine the point of giving them an allowance in the first place.

Once an initial amount has been agreed to, announce to your kids that allowance can go up or down according to changes in how it is used, inflation, a change in the family's finances, or increased expenses the children assume over time.

By using the "flexible" approach at a young age, kids will already have had numerous experiences with budgeting, saving, and spending by the time they become tweens and teens.

Each year, as allowance increases, the children assume more risk and responsibility, using clothing, lunches, school supplies, and gas budgets as practice. This approach allows parents to gradually build on their children's changing needs and offers the opportunity to match monetary increases with fiscal responsibility.

By the way, parents who request a proposal the first time around are often the same parents who request proposals to justify allowance increases in the future. Good practice for the real world? You bet!

The Flat Rate Approach to Allowance

The flat rate approach to allowance is exactly that, a fixed amount. Many parents who are interested in this approach give $1 for each year of age. A $1 (more or less) "cost of living" increase can be given every year on a child's birthday. The $1 increase per year tends to reduce sibling squabbles, because the "birthday" becomes the boss that determines a raise.

Some parents decide to use the same formula, but cut the amount in half if $1 per year of age seems like too much money, especially for young children. For example, a four-year-old child would get $2; a seven-year-old child would get $3.50.

Some families factor in other variables besides what they can afford. For example, you may want to consider where you live and how much others kids of the same age, with similar needs, are receiving. Giving kids allowance is not an exact science, so follow whatever amount feels fiscally right to you.

If the dollar or half-dollar amount is not enough, double or triple the formula. The important thing is that an impartial formula is used and that enough money is given to allow your children to learn how to use it—that is, to save it, spend it, or share it.

Allowance Chart

The chart on the next page suggests amounts of allowance to give to your children using $1 per year of age as a guideline. It also offers some progressive suggestions about what children can do with their allowance money.

Allowance Chart (based on $1 per year of age)

Ages 3 or 4	25¢ (10 pennies, 1 nickel, 1 dime)	Provide a piggy bank to play with, and careful supervision; child's first experience naming coins.
Ages 5–6	$5–6 (add quarters, half dollars, and dollar bills)	Piggy bank shifts from toy to storage and use; child's first experience with "savings" and spending.
Ages 7–14	$7–14 (add $5, $10, and $20 bills)	Open an official custodial savings account at a bank, plus a wallet or purse for carrying their money safely.
Ages 15–18	$15–18 (more as necessary for pre-approved expenses)	Open custodial checking and debit accounts as privileges (credit card at legal age).

When Should I Start?

Naturally, money is an abstract concept in the early years. A young child, for example, will think that a nickel is worth more than a dime simply based on its size. Or that the same $10 bill they deposit into a savings account at the local bank will be the same $10 bill they receive at withdrawal time.

Very young children can be given money to play with—*under vigilant supervision*—to develop a more concrete familiarity with the different types of coins and bills, and their shapes and names. Chances are that very young children will use the piggy bank as a toy. At this age, they will simply enjoy the novelty of playing with money until they tire or become interested in something else.

Allowance readiness varies among children.

Not to worry. Money takes on a new meaning beyond round metal coins and green rectangular paper as soon as your child understands that money buys things they want. That's a good time to begin a real allowance system.

Allowance readiness varies among children. Here's the story about what one father did to prepare his son for the concept of an allowance.

Freddie's Gone Crackers

Four-year-old Freddie was about to learn about the value of allowance in a backhanded way. Freddie loved graham crackers. In fact he lived for graham crackers. It was all his parents could do to keep him out of the cupboard.

So one day his dad took him to the store and said, "Freddie, you are now old enough to get your own box of graham crackers. You may have one box each week. But you need to know that when they are gone, there will be no more until next week when we go to the store."

"So, Freddie," Dad continued, "you might want to think about how you're going to eat them. Some kids eat all of them on the first day and cry the rest of the week for more. They have to wait until the next time their parents take them to the store. Other kids find a way to divide them up. They eat a few each day so that the box lasts for the whole week. I'll be interested to see how you take care of your crackers, Freddie. Good luck."

The realization that he had a whole box of crackers all to himself was too much for Freddie to believe. He ended up eating the entire box on the first day. And, as fate would have it, he got sick to his stomach and threw up.

Dad was good to his word. No matter how much Freddie begged and cried for more crackers, he had to wait until the next week.

Throughout the next grocery shopping trip, Freddie was asking questions like, "How many days are there before I get my next box, after the one I get today?"

Dad helped him make seven piles of graham crackers when they got home. Freddie was very careful to make sure each pile was the same height. After this, he ate one pile each day. Dad was also amazed to see that Freddie always knew exactly how many crackers were in each pile and was quick to notice if anyone else had eaten any of his treasures.

Later, when Freddie was six years old, his parents started his allowance. His dad had taught him lessons in spending and saving with a simple box of crackers. It was easy for Freddie to associate coins with crackers.

From Crackers to Coins to Currency

Naturally, as kids grow, you can expand from graham crackers to coins to paper money by giving allowance amounts in $1, $5, and $10 dollar bills. By the time you introduce paper bills, children should be able to understand equivalencies; for example, twenty-five pennies equal a quarter, four quarters equal a dollar, five $1 bills equal a $5 bill, and so forth.

This is an important time to give your kids a way to store their money, because it helps to teach them that money is something of value. A piggy bank for younger children is a toy, but it's also their first experience with savings. Isn't storing something a form of saving something for later use?

Throughout the next grocery shopping trip, Freddie was asking questions like, "How many days are there before I get my next box, after the one I get today?"

As your kids grow older, teach them that money should be put in a safe place such a purse or wallet. Once your kids have received enough money to constitute the minimum amount required to open a savings account, introduce the idea of using a bank to store money (more about savings in Chapter 8).

Finally, teaching your kids about the value of money is more than teaching them about nickels and dimes. We are also teaching them about the meaning of money. Lessons in both the meaning of money (its significance) and the value of money (its worth) can begin as early as three or four years old.

Now that you have an idea about how much allowance to give your kids, the next question is how often.

How Often to Give Allowance

Parents have lots of choices about how often they give an allowance. Wise parents keep it simple. Many parents choose weekly, biweekly, or monthly allowances depending on *their* payday.

Lengthen the time period as your children become more fiscally responsible—for example, a weekly schedule while in grade school, a biweekly schedule in middle school, and a monthly schedule in high school. It is generally recommended to save the monthly system for more experienced kids, after they have demonstrated basic budgeting skills on a weekly or biweekly basis first.

Let's look at eight-year-old Nikki and twelve-year-old Bryan. Using $1 per year of age as a guideline, Nikki would receive $8 and Bryan would receive $12 in each allowance period. Depending on your financial resources, you can figure payday in many different ways using these amounts. For example, you could give Nikki and Bryan, respectively:

- $8 and $12 each week
- $4 and $6 every other week
- $8 and $12 each month
- $2 and $3 each week

Regardless of what you decide, the important thing is to come up with a simple system that works for your family and your own unique financial situation. The best allowance system is one that's best for you.

"You forgot ... *again*?!"

> "Dad," said Alana as her father walked into the kitchen, "you forgot my
> allowance, *again*!"

Wondering how you'll remember to give your kids their allowance? Some parents remember by picking the same time on the same day every week or month. For example, allowance is given out every other Friday at dinnertime, or weekly on Saturday mornings. Other parents use their own payday as a reminder. As one parent stated, "It's easy to remember: When I get my money, my kids get their money."

Some parents wonder about whether they'll be consistent about giving an allowance. Wise parents *give their children the responsibility* for making sure they receive their allowance. (Of course, if it is money due to a child for a completed job, it is ultimately the parent's responsibility to see to it that the child receives that money.)

One mom shared that she asks her children to date a series of envelopes in advance, so that they take responsibility for remembering and receiving their allowance. No envelope, no allowance.

No need to worry too much about forgetting. Kids who have learned the value of their allowance will remind you. In fact, you'll know you're making progress in teaching your kids about the value of money as soon as your kids don't let you forget their allowance. How sweet, for a change, to make it *your children's responsibility to remind you!*

You'll know you're making progress in teaching your kids about the value of money as soon as your kids don't let you forget their allowance.

Allowance: A Hand-to-Hand Experience

Once you've decided how much and how often, you're ready to begin giving your children an allowance. This works best when it's a tangible, hand-to-hand experience. The younger or more inexperienced the child, the more important it is to make the feel of money and its transfer concrete—cash on the table. The best results happen when parents can physically hand their children coins and paper bills.

Some parents find that a prepaid money card in an amount equal to their allowance works well with children who have had lots of prior experience using cash. Some kid-friendly banks offer renewable money cards for specified amounts. Parents can buy as many cards as they need, in advance of allowance time, as a convenience.

Other financial institutions issue ATM access cards that are linked to revolving joint accounts. Parents transfer, or give the bank permission to automatically transfer, a set (prepaid) allowance amount on a regular basis into a custodial "checking" account.

Whichever way is chosen, wise parents start with the method that is the easiest to implement and track. Whether it's cash or some type of money card, keep it simple by using a method that has built-in overspending controls. Both cash and prepaid cards share the best kind of common ground we can give our kids—a limit, meaning: when the money is spent, it's gone. (For more detailed information about the right money tools to use for allowance, see "Paper or Plastic?" on p. 88.)

Let Allowance Make a Statement

Many parents simply use an envelope, labeled with their child's name, to distribute allowance. Put the cash or prepaid money card inside, along with a simple "allowance" statement.

An allowance statement is your child's first "income statement," and is an essential step in learning how to budget. Some parents simply record the allowance amount on the statement and hand it to their child. Other parents ask their child to count the money and record the allowance on the statement as an introduction to basic bookkeeping (and practical math skills too).

The statement can include other sources of income for the week. This could be money received as birthday gifts from grandparents or the tooth fairy, money the child earned for jobs around the house or neighborhood, or even money found in-between the cushions on the couch! Even though the "other income" space on the statement may remain blank for quite some time, that's fine. This space "holds the place" for your child to expand their understanding of "income."

The "other income" space also encourages children to understand that they can gain some independence and control over the size of their income. Naturally, there are other income sources they can be responsible for creating in addition to what their parents provide. The statement can be expanded to include a variety of other types of income as they grow older. A sample income statement that accompanies an allowance might look like the following:

Income Statement

Date: _____

Name: _____

Allowance amount: _____

Other income: _____

Total income: _____

Your Child's First Expense Sheet

Expenses naturally follow income. Include on the expense statement (see example below) any spending allocations designated for specific purposes, such as buying lunches, birthday gifts for friends, or clothing. For example, a $15 weekly allowance might include the understanding that your child pay for his or her school lunches. Special spending allocations are pre-designated, sometimes negotiated expenditures that are the child's responsibility. (For more information about how to set up specific spending categories, see "Categorical Spending" on p. 197.)

Expense Statement

Snacks: _____

Lunch: _____

Clothing: _____

Gas: _____

Other: _____
[may include bills and a loan repayment plan]

Total weekly expenses: _____

Income minus expenses: _____

Grand total: _____

Use the "grand total" on the allowance statement to illustrate that income minus expenses is the real deal when it comes to discretionary spending.

At this step, some parents invite their children to record their expenses on the statement. Filling out the statement on their own, even with zeros, helps to solidify the numbers. This assists the child in developing a better understanding of where the money goes. Use the "grand total" on the allowance statement to illustrate that income minus expenses is the real deal when it comes to discretionary spending.

Other parents ask questions to foster their children's understanding. For example, "How much will you have left over from the $15 after you've paid for your school lunches this week?" or "If you spend all of your money on the pink T-shirt you want, what will you do for lunch?"

Some kids will need both approaches—asking questions and "doing their own math." The point is to form a solid foundation for making choices. This also helps children understand the consequence *in advance* of being, or not being, fiscally responsible.

Love and Logic parents, however, remember that the final spending decisions are up to the child. The girl who buys the T-shirt she wants, but then feels hungry at school, will quickly learn a lesson about the virtues of saving, much sooner than a parental lecture will impart.

Putting It All Together: Income Minus Expenses

Based on your agreements and discussions with your children, help them combine the two concepts—income and expenses—into one bottom line: "So here's your allowance, honey, along with an allowance statement that we'll go over together."

Income and Expense Statement

Date: _____

Name: _____

Allowance amount: _____

Other income: _____

Total income: _____

Expenses: [lunch, clothing, gas, bills, loans, etc.] _____

Total weekly expenses: _____

Income minus expenses: _____

Grand total: _____

Drum Roll .... And Now for the Envelope

On the outside of the envelope, you can write something like, "Here's your allowance, just because we love you. Spend it wisely and make it last."

[child's name]:

Here's your allowance, just because we love you.
Spend it wisely and make it last.

Love,
Mom & Dad

Some parents use an envelope that is recyclable, so the child can bring it back each time for replenishing. Other parents help their kids find the kind of container they want to keep the allowance in, such as a wallet, purse, or billfold.

In either case, kids need to figure out a way to carry their money safely. Safe-keeping is an important lesson, because they'll need to bring *their own* money to the store, to school, and everywhere else. Their money is now in their hands—the perfect place for learning how to use it, or as the case may be, lose it.

"But I lost iiittt!"

Losing an allowance is a wonderful opportunity for exploring different ways of preventing loss or theft. The consequence of losing money is usually immediate and very effective if the child is not rescued.

If this happens to your child, you can simply offer your empathy and let the natural consequence do the teaching. A parent might offer the following empathic consolation for lost money: "That's a real drag, honey, but maybe when we come back another time, you'll remember to keep it in a safer place." Or, a parent can ask simple questions that begin with "What" or "How" to help the child realize their mistake. This way they can learn about what they can do differently the next time to prevent the loss from happening again.

Remember, your tone of voice is more important than your actual words in such situations.

Going Once ... Going Twice ... Gone!

Kids will need to understand that once the allowance is gone, it's gone. No more money until the next regularly scheduled allotment. Do not replace the money if your child loses it or spends all of it before the next allotment. Shortcuts, such as bailouts and "Johnny on the spot" loans, result in shortchanging kids from the opportunity to learn from their mistakes.

And if they spend it all, guess what? Love and Logic uses a heavy dose of empathy followed by the consequence. The consequence is ... no more allowance until next time. Lectures, warnings, reminders, and threats are no longer necessary, because it's *the child's* unfortunate decision to spend it all, *not yours*. Their choice becomes the "bad guy," not you!

**If your child has a money meltdown, wise parents remember:
Rescue now, repent later.**

Some parents are probably thinking: "It's not that simple. Give them an allowance and that's it? I bet lots of other issues will arise after giving my kids money. What if my kids want to buy things I don't want them to have? Or what if my kids spend their money foolishly? Shouldn't I lay down some rules?"

Introducing an Allowance: Rules or No Rules?

We've discussed a process for giving children money that's simple, straightforward, and apparently risk-free. Yet restrictions, limits, and qualifications immediately spring to every parent's mind when the subject of money and children occupy the same space. Because, for whatever reason—whether it's a power trip, a control issue, or simple concern—most parents want to know how "their" money is being spent.

What's the best way to handle this issue? Should there be rules, or not? And if so, what are they?

Naturally, parents need to consider whether or not allowance comes with limits about its use. Some parents simply give their children an allowance, hold their breath, and see what happens. Other parents give their children allowance with some definite strings attached.

One mom, happy to give an allowance but stumbling over the next step about its use, said to her child: "You can spend your allowance on anything you want as long as you ask first." This ended up driving Mom nuts. "Mom, can I have *this*?" "Mom can I have *that*?"

Another father told his kid he could spend his money on just about anything … anything but candy. But this created problems every time they went to the store, because, as Dad learned, "candy" was subject to interpretation and resulted in lots of arguments.

Let's look at several ways to introduce allowance limits to our children. When it comes to learning how to use money wisely, some kids will need to learn the hard way through real life experience. Other kids will learn the easy way, through a little education and encouragement. And for some, learning happens using a combination of both.

Allowance Limits: Plus or Minus

Love and Logic offers two basic approaches to allowance: "money plus" and "money minus." Their difference lies in the degree to which you offer guidelines about how the money is used. Choose the approach that fits for you and your child, and that fits with your financial resources and family values (more about family values, age appropriateness, and spending issues in Chapter 7).

The "money plus" approach gives allowance with several qualifications. Parents who choose this approach routinely divide their children's allowance into saving, sharing, and spending categories.

The "money minus" approach gives allowance without limitations, qualifications, or suggestions. With this approach, parents allow the children to experiment with the allowance any way they choose, "as long as it doesn't cause a problem."

In the chart below, notice how the option to save/share money is present with both approaches, but the "minus" approach comes with the freedom not to make those choices. Notice also how the words *plus* and *minus* have the user's benefit built right into the name.

Allowance Approaches

Approach	Teaching Method	Guideline
Money Plus	Education and encouragement	"Use it to spend, plus save and share some."
Money Minus	Real life experience	"Use it any way you like as long as it doesn't cause a problem. Saving and sharing are optional."

One parent adopted this idea for her teenagers by substituting the word *income* for the word *money*. Her kids could choose between an "income plus" or an "income minus" allowance account. Sounds even more beneficial.

Let's take a look at each approach in more detail.

The "Money Minus" Approach

*W*hen we give an allowance with fewer strings attached, kids tend to learn faster than when we attach a lot of rules about how it should be used.

To experiment with the "money minus" (no-strings-attached) approach, give your kids allowance without any reference to what they should do with it other than, "Feel free to spend your money any way you like, as long as it doesn't cause a problem." Many parents find that this approach works best with older kids—we all know those kinds of kids: the kids who know it all already.

With the "money minus" approach, as long as children aren't engaged in any kind of illegal activity, or using their money in a way that will hurt or harm themselves or others, they can spend, save, share, or waste their money any way they choose.

Some kids will learn best using this method. Money always becomes more important when we don't have any. When we give an allowance with fewer strings attached, kids tend to learn faster than when we attach a lot of rules about how it should be used.

Simply encourage them to "use it wisely and make it last" until next time.

"Son, here's your allowance ..."

Here's how one father introduced the "money minus" approach to his eleven-year-old son, Jacob:

Dad: "Your mom and I have decided to give you an allowance. Allowance is money we will give you to use in any way you want as long as you don't buy anything that is illegal, or that I think will hurt or harm you, or others. I will give it to you each week in an envelope along with a statement with your name on it. If you run out of money before next Saturday, there's no more from us until next Saturday."

Jacob: (looking at Dad with eyes the size of saucers) "I can spend it *any way* I want?"

Dad: "Yes, as long as you don't buy anything that I think will hurt you or harm you, or anyone else."

Jacob: "Like what?"

Dad: "What do you think I will say if you buy a toy that I think is dangerous? Or if you want to buy a video that's PG-13 and you are ... how old? I bet you're smart enough to figure this out as we go."

Jacob: "I'm going to spend *all* of it!"

Dad: "Well, that's one choice. Some kids choose to divide their weekly money three ways—save some, share some, and spend the rest. Your allowance allows you to make your own choices, so you can learn how to use money wisely."

Jacob: "What if I want to spend it all? Every week?"

Dad: "That's one choice. Won't it be fun to find out?"

How many of you might find it a Herculean effort to keep your mouth shut when your child says he or she "wants to spend it all"? Many kids don't learn the value of saving until they first have the experience of being broke.

Remember this Love and Logic axiom: let them make as many mistakes as possible when the price tags are small. Your child will have a better opportunity to learn how to save once he or she wants something but doesn't have the money—and the Bank of Mom and Dad is closed to any further transactions on the account.

The "Money Plus" Approach

Many parents of younger or more inexperienced children like the "money plus" approach better, because they want to include lessons in saving and sharing. This approach encourages kids to divide their allowance into three portions, as mentioned earlier. This is easy for kids to remember as the Three S's—<u>S</u>pend, <u>S</u>ave, and <u>S</u>hare. The amount that you (or you and your child together) proportion to each S depends upon many factors, such as your family values, the age of the child, how much allowance you provide, and how often. (To learn how to set up a 3-S system, see "The Allowance Statement: The Three S's" on the next page.)

Many parents keep it simple by using percentages. For example, some parents give their children allowance with the idea that they will save 10%, share 10%, and spend the remaining 80%. Other families use the formula of saving 20%, sharing 10%, and spending 70%. Any combination of 100% will work as long as the child understands there are only three basic things that can be done with money once they have it: save (or invest), spend, or share.

To adopt the "money plus" approach, use Dad's example above to introduce the basic concepts, with the addition of explaining why saving is important, your family values around charitable giving, and so forth. You will also want to add a section to the allowance statement for recordkeeping purposes.

Plus or Minus?

Notice that regardless of what your child chooses to do with their money, either approach allows kids to experiment with their own money at the same time it teaches that different choices yields different outcomes. And, notice how Love and Logic's principles of control, choices, and consequences are built into the child's relationship to his or her allowance when it's set up in this way.

For example, both approaches offer varying degrees of control. Control is shared by giving children choices—lots of choices about where and how they spend their money, what they can save for, what charity they may want to gift, and so forth. Whenever we provide children the opportunities to share in the monetary thinking and decision-making process, they learn their financial lessons via life's greatest teacher—the consequence of real life experience.

The 3-S part of the allowance process becomes a teaching tool for the parent and a learning tool for the child.

The Allowance Statement: The Three S's

Parents using the "money plus" approach to allowance might want to add a third section to the allowance statement, beyond the income and expense sections, called the Three S's—<u>S</u>pend, <u>S</u>ave, and <u>S</u>hare.

Similar to the income and expense sections of the allowance statement, the 3-S section (see example below) is designed to foster conversations about how the child might want to divide their allowance into other categories besides just spending—for example, conversations about spending, setting savings goals, what to do with gifts from Grandpa, and learning how to share. The 3-S part of the allowance process becomes a teaching tool for the parent and a learning tool for the child.

In brief, the authors of Love and Logic suggest the following fiscal principles to use in discussions with your children:

- Spending—pay it wisely, and in full (more about this in Chapter 7).
- Saving—pay yourself first (more about this in Chapter 8).
- Sharing—pay it forward (more about this in Chapter 12).

3–S Statement

Spending portion: [from "income minus expenses" line] _____

Savings portion: _____

Sharing portion: _____

Completing this section provides a good opportunity to practice math skills at the same time that it provides a written record of the agreements made about what to spend, save, and share. Filling out, or not filling out, the blanks on the statement has benefits, either way. Learning will still take place even if your child fills in "$0.00" in the save section; he or she will realize later that saving money is a good idea for times of need.

Again, it's best to involve your child in as much of the process as possible to make the experience of managing their cash more concrete.

Notice also how the 3-S section mimics the standard paycheck. "Savings" deductions are similar to social security or retirement plans and "sharing" mimics disability insurance and tax deductions. The latter could figuratively be viewed as a form of "sharing" with the government for the benefit of everyone.

Complete Allowance Statement

Once all the basic parts of the allowance statement are assembled, it should look something like this:

Complete Allowance Statement

Date: _____

Name: _____

Allowance amount: _____

Other income: _____

Total income: _____

Expenses: _____

Total expenses: _____

Income minus expenses: _____

Grand total: _____

Spending portion: [from "income minus expenses" line] _____

Savings portion: _____

Sharing portion: _____

Final amount after deductions: _____

The 3-S section of the allowance statement provides the verbal and, even better, the written foundation to start many conversations about money with your children. The beauty is that either a complete or an incomplete allowance statement still fosters money talk. Week by week, or however frequently you issue an allowance, using these statements provides concrete, personal examples about the money matters of day-to-day life.

Kid-Sized Bills

Remember the story of Emily, the girl who didn't want to clean her bedroom in Chapter 2? Allowance has some hidden benefits for parents, too. Emily's story is an example of how parents might see the value of allowance in a very different way than their children do. Sometimes, allowance has the ability to motivate.

For kids like Emily, the allowance envelope may contain three things—money, an allowance statement, and … a bill.

Types of Bills

There are lots of situations that will arise whereby "billing" your children for goods and services will come in very handy. There are several types of bills. There are bills for services, bills for things, and bills to pay off a debt for services or things.

The most common type of bill charges for household "services" that you or other people did for the child. These are bills for the chores that your child did not do. Reimbursement to you for a lawn service you hired on the child's behalf when he "forgot," or charges for cleaning the child's room are examples of a bill for services. (Emily's story provides an example of how allowance and bills work together; see "Money Back Guarantee Options" on p. 41.)

The second type of bill, for restitution, is used for payment of "things." A restitution bill could charge for repair of a neighbor's broken window from an errant baseball, for example, or for sports equipment the child has lost repeatedly. (For a fun look at how to handle a child who chronically loses or forgets things, see "AAA Rating: Allowance Added Advantages, or How to Make Forgetfulness Pay" on p. 83.)

The third type of bill is for paying off a loan or an ongoing financial obligation. Use this type of bill when your child is in debt—for example, when you have lent your child money for some sort of worthy cause. Or, it could be used for installment payments for computer software purchased by the parent, or for reimbursement for a special travel or recreational experience.

The chart below summarizes the different types of bills:

Types of Bills

Services	Paying for work performed by others.
Restitution	Paying for repairs and replacements.
Debts	Paying off a loan or an ongoing financial obligation.

Billing for Services and Restitution

The way you bill for services and restitution depends upon your parenting style. One mom I (Kristan) know simply went to the local office supply store and bought a set of generic invoices, which she filled out with her child's name and address, plus the date, description, and cost of the services provided. Once her child paid her, she marked the bill "PAID," including date of payment, and handed him a receipt with the encouragement to keep it for his records.

The following sample bills for services and restitution can provide a formal system, or can be modified to suit your parenting style.

Bill for Services

Date: _____

To: [child's name] _____

Service provider's name: _____

Service provider's address: _____

Service provided for: _____
[lawn care, room cleaning, babysitting, etc.]

Date of service: _____

Cost of service: _____

Amount due: _____

Bill for Restitution

Date: _____

To: [child's name] _____

Restitution for: _____

[replacing a damaged flower vase after roughhousing, a sibling's toy broken on purpose, a library fine, etc.]

Amount due: _____

Paybacks Are How Much?

You may be wondering how much to bill. Adult wages require adult pay. That means minimum wage or more, depending upon the number of hours the adult works. Kids can then use their allowance (or use savings and earnings) to pay back bills they have incurred. (For an example of how one parent handled billing her daughter, see "You're a bargain, Mom!" on p. 84.)

But what if your child's allowance and other discretionary income do not cover the current bill for services or things? Parents have several options, depending on the age of the child and the size of the balance.

Ideally, kid-sized bills should be paid by the end of every week. Why? Because allowing a child to get behind on payments often negates the value of an allowance. In a short time a child may come to think, "What's the use? If I don't worry about the allowance, I don't have to worry about the bill."

Some parents allow a manageable balance to roll over into the next billing statement. This mimics the real world, where payments may be made on bills that cannot be paid in full, on time. Other parents ask their child which jobs or which chores they are willing to do *for* the parents as payment for what is owed.

Hands-On Payments

Invite your child to "do the math" if they are paying a bill with their allowance. Then, allow the child to hand the allowance money back to you as repayment. Why? Because it is the actual experience of giving the money back that cements the teaching. (A mixture of paper bills and coins is a good idea, so that the child can pay you back in "exact change.")

Resist the temptation to simply deduct the amount from the bill. Wise parents understand that the act of giving back cash to pay a bill makes for a concrete learning experience and an impressionable consequence.

One dad said in response to this idea, "But my child can't read." No problem. For younger children, read and explain what the bill means just as you would when helping a child interpret anything else. The value of the lesson is still just as powerful.

By requiring a child to tangibly hand the money back for repayment, we are holding the child accountable for his or her choice. As in the real world, a bill is a statement of what is owed as a result of a choice.

As in the real world, a bill is a statement of what is owed as a result of a choice.

Parents who use money cards for allowance can "put the card on hold" until it can be "reissued" with the reduced amount (i.e., allowance minus what is owed). A money card "on hold" becomes a double consequence. The first consequence is less money to enjoy. The second consequence is having to wait until the Bank of Mom and Dad has time to make the necessary subtractions before reissuing a new prepaid allowance card.

"I can't pay that much …"

What if the child cannot pay the "amount due" with their current funds? It becomes a financial obligation that will need to be repaid with installments. The bill now becomes a loan.

There are a variety of ways to bring an account back to zero if allowance doesn't cover the immediate debt. Kids can earn money by doing your jobs or your chores, or they can forfeit toys or possessions of an equivalent value.

Some parents use a combination package. Kids can use some of their allowance cash, plus possessions, to pay the bill. Possessions can be held as collateral, equal to the balance due. Kids can earn their possessions back over time to bring the account balance back to zero, or forfeit them, without return, for their cash value.

A bill for debts can be set up as in the example on the next page. Many parents use this type of bill as great conversation starter about responsibility and fiscal obligations, wants before needs, and delayed gratification.

Bill for Debts

Date: _____

To: [child's name] _____

Initial amount due: _____

For: _____

Previous balance: _____

Payment today: _____

  • cash amount _____

  • list of possessions forfeited (and monetary value) _____

  • list of possessions taken as collateral (and monetary value) ___

  • list of contributions or jobs (and monetary value) _____

New balance due: _____

Develop a workable plan for repayment with your child based on their age and income. Wise parents involve their child in the decision-making process about how much each installment should be and how often. Many parents pencil out a variety of scenarios, so that their child understands how to make a good choice based on the circumstances. (For more information about how to set up repayment plans, see "Loan Considerations" on p. 289.)

All Systems Go

In summary, you are ready to go with allowance when you have decided how much and how often, and when you have the following:

- The money
- An envelope or other method of storage
- An allowance statement
- Bills for services, restitution, and debts, as appropriate

Many parents computerize their statement and billing system to make it easier. They find that a computerized version saves time, helps with record-keeping, and can easily be expanded to meet changing needs. It also makes a series of statements and bills easier to track for you and the child.

Computers, of course, are not necessary for successfully teaching your kids about basic money management skills. The pencil-and-paper system works well, too! But the very best choice is the one that engages your children in the process.

Once you have establish the recordkeeping details of giving an allowance—computerized or not—you have all "the raw materials" to begin teaching some of the basics of money management.

In Chapter 4, we'll take a look at the different types of money tools to use with children, beginning with cash.

AAA Rating: Allowance Added Advantages, or How to Make Forgetfulness Pay

One dad was sick and tired of his son forgetting one thing after another for soccer practice. Dillon would forget his shoes one day, and his kneepads the next.

No more lectures, warnings, or empty "The next time you forget …" threats. Dad was ready to make a change. Instead of simply going back home to retrieve the forgotten item, Dad was going to hand the problem back to Dillon. How?

He developed a tier of consequences:

- Pay for mileage.
- Pay for mileage and Dad's driving time.
- Pay for mileage, gas, and driving time.
- Pay for a taxi.

Dad knew exactly what he needed to do the next time Dillon forgot something: bill him for "services" at allowance time.

Sure enough, on Saturday morning, the opportunity presented itself. On their way out the door, Dad asked Dillon if he had everything he needed for practice. "Yep," said Dillon, with the confidence of a kid who had double-checked his packing list. So off they went.

Then Dad heard Dillon rummaging through his sports bag in the back seat of the car:

Dillon: "Dad! I forgot my shoes. Would you take me back home so I can get them?"

Dad: "Oh, bummer. Forgot your shoes. I'll be glad to return to the house for the things you want, if you want to pay me for the round trip in mileage. It's up to you."

Dillon: "But I'm going to be late for soccer practice."

Dad: "I know … what a drag. I'll pull over here while you decide."

Dillon: (hemming and hawing) "How much does a round trip cost?"

Dad: "I don't know, it depends on mileage, but I charge fifty cents a mile."

Dillon started to say something, but then stopped, because he had learned that whining and arguing don't work. With a big sigh, he said reluctantly, "Okay, let's turn around and go get them. The coach won't let me play without my cleats." Dad replied, as he switched the blinker on before pulling away from the curb, "I'll set the odometer to zero."

Will this help Dillon remember next time? Maybe, maybe not. But he's faced with a consequence no matter which way he decides. He'll either pay in mileage or pay in sitting on the sidelines at soccer practice. (Dad may need to tip off the coach to be sure he or she supports Dad's strategic "spring training" session.) Notice how Dad let him make the decision by offering a choice. (Kids could also pay you back in "drive time" by doing your jobs or your chores.)

Should Dillon forget again, Dad can move down the tier to the next consequence on the list: "I'll be glad to return to the house if you want to pay me for mileage plus driving time."

Notice how it's going to get more expensive each time Dillon forgets. Dillon is learning what adults already know: forgetting something important, especially once you've already left the house, has its price.

 Bottom Line: Wise parents teach their kids to "not leave home without it" by holding them accountable when they forget.

"You're a bargain, Mom!"

I (Kristan) received an e-mail from a parent who had tried to bill her fifteen-year-old daughter, Jamie, using the prevailing minimum wage. She wrote: "I charged my daughter seven dollars to clean her room, and when I told her the amount, she thought it was a pretty good deal. Now what should I do?" she asked. "It didn't work."

Love and Logic parents know that a little tweaking might be all that's needed to render a strategy effective again.

I asked her, "What do we do in the real world when someone tells us we're not charging enough for our product or service?" "Charge more," she offered. "Exactly," I said, "so here's how you can do it."

Let's fast-forward to Thursday night, when it's time to think about the upcoming weekend:

Mom:	"Jamie, do you want to clean your room this Saturday or pay me to do it?"
Jamie:	"You do it."
Mom:	"No problem. My fee this week is sixty dollars."
Jamie:	"What?! Last week you only charged me seven dollars."
Mom:	"I know."
Jamie:	"That's way too much!"
Mom:	"I know."
Jamie:	"But why are you doing this?"
Mom:	"It took me longer than I thought to clean your room last week, so I'll need to charge more for my time."
Jamie:	"But that's not fair!"
Mom:	"I bet it feels that way. Of course, if you're not happy with my price, you have the choice to hire someone else."
Jamie:	(petulantly) "Who?"
Mom:	"Well, some kids hire their brother or sister. How would that work for you?"
Jamie:	"That's stupid. Joey is too young."
Mom:	"Other kids look up cleaning services in the phone book, call them, and ask what their prices are for cleaning rooms. How might that work for you?"
Jamie:	"Well, maybe."
Mom:	"Other kids decide to do nothing and see what happens. How will that work?"
Jamie:	"I don't know."
Mom:	"Well … I'm sure you'll figure something out. Please let me know what you decide by Saturday morning so that I can make my plans."

What does Jamie decide? She decides that Mom's prices are too high. She decides that saving her allowance for a pair of new skates that she wants for her next big competition is more important than spending her allowance on a clean room. So she chooses to clean her room, and save her money. Good choice, Jamie.

But let's say Jamie decides to do a little comparison shopping. She wants to find someone else to do her cleaning for her. So she looks up "cleaning services" in the phone book and calls around to ask for prices. What do you think she finds? Is Mom's price comparable? You bet. Based on the same half-day rate ("Mom, it costs more than a pair of skates!"), Jamie cleans her room. Again, good choice, Jamie.

CHAPTER 4

The Exchange of Money

Tools of the Trade

Money comes in different shapes and sizes, requiring different degrees
of knowledge, skill, and responsibility. This chapter covers the best way to
introduce the tools of the trade to your children—from paper money to
plastic money.

Paper or Plastic?

The basic tools used to exchange money are cash, personal checks, and a variety of wallet-sized plastic cards. Most kids learn best when concepts move from concrete to abstract. In the case of money, that means from paper money (paper bills, including coins, and checks) to plastic money (prepaid cards, gift cards, store cards, debit cards, credit cards, etc.).

How do you know which money tool is right for your child? And how can you teach your child how to use it wisely?

The answers lie in education and experience with each tool in a sequence that builds on responsibility. Cash should be your child's first experience with money, regardless of their age, prior to the introduction of any plastic money cards. Once you are confident that your child can manage cash with responsibility and respect, they are ready to graduate to using more abstract money tools.

No Fool with Money Tools

Some parents may be tempted to skip cash in favor of plastic. Plastic money cards, in particular, are becoming more and more commonplace as the preferred means of monetary exchange. "Preferred," however, does not necessarily mean "wise." Unfortunately, while popular, plastic money cards tend to encourage kids to indulge in impulse buying and overconsumption if they are not first grounded in experiences with the concrete nature of cash.

Using plastic also requires a certain level of maturity. Many types of plastic money cards require "deferred" payment, meaning that kids are one or more steps removed from the consequences of a purchase with plastic. Deferred consequences are not preferred if we're going to educate our children about the basic cause and effect of sound fiscal management.

A child's lack of willpower, coupled with the technical ability needed to make and track purchases, means the child is at risk for not developing the fiscal skills necessary to manage money responsibly. We need to choose our money tools carefully if we are to have any hope of imparting the fiscal basics to our children.

As the expression goes: A fool and his money are soon parted.

Make Cash Register First

It's best to begin with cash. Paper and coins are the "truer" version of money; plastic is, well, plastic. Plastic should be introduced only after your kids have mastered the basics using their cash allowances. It's only logical that if they can't demonstrate competence using cash, they don't have the experiential foundation to demonstrate competence with plastic. While it may be tempting to start your tween off with a debit card, using plastic before cash is like introducing your kids to adding and subtracting without ever letting them count their fingers.

EXERCISE 4.1: Making Change Count

At one time, some of us were lucky enough to learn how to count change backwards. When was the last time a clerk counted out your change for you instead of just giving it to you and saying, "Have a nice day"? Why do you suppose companies had to start buying cash registers that computed the change?

Due to the popularity of plastic cards, and advances in retail technology, this important step to understanding what transpires in a cash transaction is lost. One way to give children lots of practice with cash transactions is to "pretend" to buy things. Many younger kids love to play "store." Parents can use play money to experiment with the exercise of counting change backwards. For example, if your child "buys" something for $3.59 with a $5 bill, you would gather the change (in this case, one penny, one quarter, one dime, one nickel, and one $1 bill) and hand it back to them while counting aloud, "Three sixty, three eighty-five, three ninety-five, four dollars, five dollars. Thank you and have a nice day!" (Most toy stores carry an assortment of play money, or use the supply from your favorite board game.)

For older kids, you can go catalogue shopping or online shopping and teach the same concept using play money, and add in taxes, shipping, and handling. The pretend-to-purchase idea is a great way to illustrate the realities of any type of spending transaction.

Cash is tactile and the exchange is immediate. When it comes to making or receiving change, teach your children how the whole is always the sum of its parts.

This type of exercise and other real life experiences with cash provide lessons in real time with real objects. Give your children lots of experiences in learning how cash works in the marketplace, both real or imagined, to prepare them for the responsibility that comes with the next level of exchanging money.

Bottom Line: Wise parents understand the importance of giving kids lots of experience practicing with the concrete nature of cash *before* introducing the abstract nature of plastic.

Prepaid, Debit, or Credit Cards?

Once your child has attained the basic skills and knowledge necessary for paper money—learned through plenty of practice and plenty of mistakes—you may want to consider graduating to plastic money.

There are essentially three basic types of money cards—prepaid, debit, and credit.

- *Prepaid cards:* Entitle the cardholder to make purchases based on pre-paid funds, not to exceed the amount on those funds. Banks, retailers, restaurants, and other businesses issue this type of card.
- *Debit cards:* Link to a bank account, typically a checking or savings account. The funds are automatically withdrawn when a cardholder makes a purchase.
- *Credit cards:* Activate a temporary bank loan whenever the cardholder makes a purchase. The bank pays the vendor and then bills the cardholder, usually monthly, with an interest penalty if not paid in full.

The chart below shows the basic similarities and differences between the three types of cards. Notice how the last row of the chart suggests that experience with a prepaid card is the foundation for experience with the other two types.

Money Cards

Prepaid Card	Debit Card	Credit Card
Cardholder makes purchase.	Cardholder makes purchase.	Cardholder makes purchase.
Funds paid in advance. Cost deducted from balance at time of purchase.	Funds are automatically withdrawn at time of purchase.	Funds are loaned to cardholder for a limited amount of time.
Linked to personal bank account that will, by account holder's request, transfer funds to reload card once the money has been spent.	Linked to a checking and/or savings account.	Linked to a commercial lending bank or institution.
Prerequisites: Lots of experience developing competence with cash and understanding allowance statements (income, expenses, reconciling mistakes, etc.).	Prerequisites: Prior competence with a prepaid card, and gift cards, plus an introduction to understanding debit bank statements.	Prerequisites: Prior competence with a debit card, plus a history of borrowing money from parents and repaying it in full and on time, in preparation for obtaining a credit card at legal age.

Note: Card features vary. Check the details with the issuing company carefully before selection.

Let's examine the advantages and disadvantages of each type of plastic card in more detail.

Prepaid Cards

The authors of Love and Logic suggest that if you're going to introduce your children to plastic money cards of any type, you should begin with prepaid cards. Why? Because it's the closest thing to cash. Cash and prepaid cards share a common denominator, an essential prerequisite to managing the rest of the plastic world wisely: if you don't have it, you can't buy it. Once your kids have had lots of experience with cash, the transition to a prepaid card is easier.

Prepaid cards have other advantages. As with gift cards, if you don't have the full amount needed to make a purchase, you have to make up the difference. Kids learn that purchasing those jeans comes at a price beyond the tag—it forces the choice to forgo other desired items at that time, or ante up. It follows the "no pay, no possession" lesson that all kids need to experience if they're going to learn how to stay out of debt.

Show your children how to keep track of the balance on their prepaid cards. Teach them to request a printed receipt at the time of purchase from the vendor. Most cards can also be scanned at the time of purchase to determine the balance. Teach your children how to check and compare their balance against card receipts and statements.

Many parents like the convenience of purchasing a supply of prepaid cards in advance of allowance time. This saves them from needing to have the correct amount of cash in bills and coins on-hand. Other parents simply transfer funds from their personal bank account to reload the card as needed.

A Note About Gift Cards

Gift cards are like virtual money. But they do expire, unlike cash. What are the chances that your children will be prepared to spend Grandma's gift cards wisely if they've had lots of practice with cash or its cousin, the prepaid card?

The proper use of a gift card lies in the holder redeeming its *full* value. Teach your children how to use the complete value of a gift card by holding them responsible for understanding hidden fees and stipulations, and for spending the full amount by the expiration date.

Debit Cards

Debit cards logically follow prepaid cards as the next level of money tool. Debit cards are not much different from cash, except that the transaction is electronic.

Use of a debit card automatically triggers a withdrawal from the account it's linked to.

A debit card allows purchases to be automatically deducted from the cardholder's (meaning the parent's) bank account. After all, the funds need to be "debited" from somewhere.

Once you decide to provide a debit card to your child, he or she automatically becomes your financial partner via a custodial bank account. (Financial institutions require custodial joint accounts for children under eighteen years old.)

A debit card in the hands of an irresponsible kid is not an asset to anyone: the kid, the bank, or you.

Using a debit card is much like co-signing a loan. Even though it is your child who co-signs, you will logically and legally want a co-signer who is fiscally responsible. Many people have learned the hard way to never co-sign on a loan unless they are prepared to take over the entire debt. The bank goes after the easiest money when there is a problem. This means that when the other person loses their ability or motivation to pay, the person with the deepest pockets pays.

A debit card in the hands of an irresponsible kid is not an asset to anyone: the kid, the bank, or you.

Setting Debit Card Limits

Wise parents discuss and set limits with their child before handing over that first debit card. Introduce the debit card to your new joint account cardholder the same way you have introduced allowance. This reinforces the same basic and most essential money management lesson: once the money's gone, it's gone.

With the introduction of a debit card, parents need to teach kids how to understand the numbers associated with credits and debits. This includes familiarizing them with online bank statements or paper copies, so that they can learn how to track their deductions and understand cash flow.

Keep it as simple as possible. Some parents open a joint checking account with a companion debit card and then deposit an amount equal to their child's allowance. Other parents open a custodial savings account with a companion debit card, sometimes without a minimum balance requirement, and make routine allowance transfers.

Search for a financial institution that offers kid-friendly features—low fees, no overdraft charges, a widely accepted card, and easy electronic transfer between accounts.

This is important because debit cards can activate hidden fees, potentially create overdrafts without protection, and damage the cardholder's credit rating if used unwisely. That's a big price to pay for a small account.

As one parent found out the hard way: "Don't mix your own bank account with your child's. My child's debits became my debits." Overdrafts are expensive and often must be paid back with interest.

Securing the necessary protections as a primary account holder can mitigate some of the downside of an overactive debit card. But the very best insurance is providing your kids lots and lots of opportunities to practice with cash and its prepaid cousin before they ever lay their hands on their first debit card.

Credit Cards

Dad: (teasingly) "Have you made your list for Santa?"

Brianna: "Santa's for kids, Dad. I'm ten years old. I don't need to make a list this year. I just want one thing."

Dad: "*One* thing?!"

Brianna: "Yep!"

Dad: "Well that's really admirable! Especially in these materialistic and gluttonous times. What's the one thing?"

Brianna: "A credit card!"

Ever notice how credit card companies promote all kinds of reasons to sign up for their "rewards" programs—from cash back to discounts on travel, vacations, and other gift perks? Their motive is based on you using your card so often that your debt becomes their asset. That minimum "amount due—$10.00" is deliberately deceiving when the bill is actually $376.23.

Here's an eye-opener. Let's assume you have a credit card balance of $3,900 at 18% APR (APR means annual percentage rate, the amount the credit card company charges you on an unpaid balance). If you paid only the minimum each month, it would take you thirty-five years to pay off the balance and you would end up applying over $10,000 in interest alone!

Credit cards can become the crutch for a lifestyle built on a house of cards, *literally.* The sheer number of people in debt today is a testament to the credit card companies getting the better end of the deal.

Not to Our Credit

The authors of Love and Logic think that it is not a good idea to teach kids how to spend money they don't have. A credit card is an implied agreement that payments for purchase will be made at a future date. A purchase made with a credit card is essentially a loan, which when not paid back in full, can cost far more than the original purchase in interest charges, late fees, and poor credit ratings.

Parents must co-sign when opening up a joint bank account, including credit card and personal checking accounts, for any child under eighteen years of age, as noted earlier. (For information about how to introduce the use of personal checking accounts, see "Checks and Balances: Your Child's First Checking Account" on p. 97.) Note that the authors of Love and Logic strongly advise parents not to co-sign for credit cards, or to allow children to use your own credit cards, until they reach the legal age to have credit cards of their own. Introduce your kids to cash first, followed by prepaid and debit cards, as training wheels for a credit card.

While parents can set spending limits on credit cards and add other controls, the wisest of parents give their kids a foundation of fiscal experiences. Only when you have given your kids given lots and lots of practice borrowing and paying back their loans, in full and on time, will you have prepared them for the fiscal responsibility that comes with having their own credit card. Kids will get those kinds of learning experiences that lead to becoming credit card–wise if we allow them the chance to both succeed and fail with money tools that don't carry the risk of "yes to possession now, but pay more later." (For more information about how to give kids the kind of practice that will prepare them for wise credit card use, see "Loan Consequences: Default, Credit, and Repossession" on p. 296.)

Fiscal responsibility is what our children shouldn't leave home without!

Choose wisely for your children now, so that they can choose wisely for themselves later. After all, wouldn't you prefer that, when your college-aged son or daughter is approached by a credit card recruiter, he or she has a solid understanding of what credit means and how to use it? (For tips about preparing children for the use of credit, see "Credit Card Tips: When the Time Comes" below.)

Credit Card Tips: When the Time Comes

That time will come … so here are some tips to help you prepare your children for the use of credit cards when they leave home:

- Be sure your children have mastered their use of the other types of "safer" money tools before you dedicate or authorize a credit card for their use. Otherwise, it's like giving a child seeds to plant without soil, or a teenager a car to drive without lessons.

- Use a stack of play or real money to dramatize how quickly late fees and interest add up when paying only the minimum balance. Explain how this is wasted money that your kids could otherwise have access to if they were to pay off their balances in full. Dramatize the waste by saying, "It's like putting all the potential purchasing power into a paper shredder unused!"

- As an intermediate step, invite your children to practice applying for a personal credit card at their favorite clothing or electronics store. The charge cards issued by retailers are usually easier to acquire than general-use credit cards, and provide the kind of "pay as you go" experience important to acquiring other types of credit cards.

A Creditworthy Score Card

Once your child has obtained a credit card, explain how his or her fiscal actions are the basis for their credit rating, for better or for worse. Explain how they can establish good credit, if they pay off their balance each month, which means lower interest rates and the "credit" ability to make larger purchases in the future. Invite your child to research the cons of poor credit and report back to you.

EXERCISE 4.2: The "T" Chart

A simple but effective way to teach children how to make good decisions is to teach them how to make a "T" chart. To begin, draw a big letter "T" on a sheet of paper, dividing the page into two columns, labeled "Pros" and "Cons." Then have your child fill in all the positive and all the negative reasons associated with a particular decision.

This simple exercise can be used to weigh the advantages and disadvantages of all kinds of decisions, from having a good credit score to deciding which job or college course is the best choice.

Pros	Cons

###

When it comes to credit cards, wise parents avoid the financial temptation to encourage premature sophistication without mature responsibility.

The shortest distance to obtaining a good credit score is to charge a small sum and pay off the balance each month. For this reason, some parents add their children to their own credit card account to help them establish a credit history. Wise parents should consider this only if the child has first demonstrated financial responsibility with spending and borrowing. This has the potential to satisfy the goal of establishing good credit as long as the parent holds the child accountable for full paybacks month to month.

Once your child has some verifiable "credit," teach them the importance of tracking their own credit report. Show them how to secure a copy of their report, how to interpret it, and how to correct any mistakes.

When it comes to credit cards, wise parents avoid the financial temptation to encourage premature sophistication without mature responsibility.

Summary of Money Tools

It's best to use these money tools in the following order:

1. Cash
2. Prepaid card
3. Debit card / personal checks (for children of age)
4. Credit card (for those who have attained an adult level of fiscal accountability with the first three tools, and a clear understanding about the rules of borrowing)

Once your kids have demonstrated *sustained* fiscal responsibility at each level, you are ready to introduce them to the next tool. Abstract follows concrete, and responsibility follows accountability. Each one builds on the other—success with plastic builds on success with cash.

It is suggested that you follow this order regardless of your child's age when you begin introducing money tools. Even if your son is fifteen years old, and he tells you that all of his friends have credit cards, resist the temptation to give him one. Shortcuts can be costly.

Return to cash, if necessary. Let him know that you won't allow him to have a prepaid bank card until he first demonstrates responsibility with his cash allowance. In this way, the consequences of not using the tools wisely are built right into the pyramid of choices.

How do the principles of Love and Logic apply? The most effective tools are those that share control while also providing choices. That's because parents can choose which tools, how much, and how often to make them available. And, kids have the opportunity to practicing using the tools by making lots of spending choices.

When parents choose their fiscal tools progressively, they maintain the control they need, and give away the control they don't need. As for your kids? They have a fighting chance to become penny-wise first, before ever becoming plastic-foolish.

When parents choose their fiscal tools progressively, they maintain the control they need, and give away the control they don't need.

Checks and Balances:
Your Child's First Checking Account

Todd, seventeen years old, learned the hard way what happens when you bounce a check. One night, while trying to be a big shot entertaining his friends, Todd wrote three super-sized checks.

Dad learned later, after questioning Todd about what happened, that his son truly thought that as long as he still had checks in his checkbook, he still had money in his account!

While plastic cards are becoming the norm, personal checks still have their place as a financial instrument. Checks are written promises that mean, "I will pay such and such an amount." Personal checks are another money tool parents can use to teach fiscal responsibility. An ideal time to introduce the checking account concept is when your child gets his or her first paycheck, or if not then, certainly before they leave home.

The rule of thumb for most banks is: no checking account until the person is eighteen or older, depending upon the state's legal age for minors. Financial institutions, banks, and credit unions require an adult's name on the account because minors cannot be held liable to a contract.

If your child already has a custodial savings account, adding a checking line is a natural extension. Most banks tie savings and checking accounts together, which allows customers to transfer funds between accounts and write checks from the balances. Go with your teen in person to your local bank to figure out what the best service is for his or her financial needs. Your teen will not be able to do this alone.

Check Instruction

If your teen qualifies for a checking account (because of a joint account established on their behalf), provide instruction before its use. Teach them how to make deposits—electronically, manually, or directly through an employer—read balances, and write checks. Show them how to "initial" any mistakes they make while filling in the details. Show them how to balance their account against paper statements (i.e., they should save ATM receipts; record debits, check amounts, dates, and check numbers; label expenses; etc.). Teach them how to reconcile a mistake if there is a discrepancy between the bank statement and their own records. (Your child will already have numerous examples of many of these steps if you have introduced check writing as a way to pay the family's bills.)

Be sure to emphasize the importance of signing their checks and the legal agreement it represents—and vice versa, that an unsigned check received from someone else is invalid.

Once your teen knows the responsibilities and legalities of check writing and checking accounts, he or she will be better prepared to recognize the validity of any check received; and to make that first, coveted paycheck deposit!

Overdraft, Not Overprotect

Some parents might be tempted to set up overdraft privileges to prevent problems. An overdraft is a temporary bank loan, with interest, to cover an overdrawn amount on a check until the account holder makes a deposit. Besides the initial amount of the check, banks may charge interest and overdraft fees. Sometimes the penalties can exceed the amount of the check!

It's a good idea to protect yourself and others with overdraft privileges on any joint account, especially while your teen is still learning how to use checks. But like any wise joint account holder, parents make it clear that the person who incurs bank charges is the one who is responsible for their restitution. If your child bounces a check, review the bank's statement with your teen so that he or she understands what happened and how. Then require them to pay you back through jobs, garnishment of their paychecks, and so forth. Wise parents hold their children accountable for any problems for as long as they are joint account holders.

The authors of Love and Logic advise that setting up a joint account with a child, of any age, who has not established a good history of responsible behavior or paying back loans, is an unwise decision and usually creates more problems than it solves.

Bottom Line: Wise parents, when their children come of age, teach them about responsible use of checks and checking accounts before they leave home.

CHAPTER 5

Contributions

The Currency for Teaching Responsibility

The first part of this chapter covers how to introduce a family-friendly way for everyone to get his or her fair share of the household chores completed. The second part uses the "ABC" formula for raising successful household contributors: "A" covers a list of age-appropriate contributions; "B" covers the importance of basic training; and "C" covers how to hold your kids accountable for doing their chores when cooperation wavers.

Gillian's Story: A Mini–Me, Me, Me!

Glancing at the digital clock in the darkened bedroom, Mom watches the numbers flip to 12:22. Where did the evening go? Holding her breath, Mom gently rises from the rocking chair, carrying her newborn across the room to the bassinet. Inhaling deeply to release the tension in her neck, she places her son onto his side, propping him up with blankets wedged gently behind his back. She stumbles back to her bed, sighs deeply, and closes her eyes.

For a minute … no, a second.

"Mommy! Mommy!" Mom's nanosecond of peace is disturbed by Gillian, her four-year-old daughter. The voice is coming from Gillian's room down the hall.

Staring at the ceiling, Mom hopes that Gillian's just talking—okay, yelling—in her sleep. Swinging her legs to the side, Mom props herself up on exhausted arms, her ears straining for other sounds from her daughter: soft sounds, sleeping sounds … Perhaps Gillian will give up and go back to sleep if there's no response.

"Mommy!"

Mom staggers down the hallway to her daughter's room. "Coming, pumpkin … Mommy's coming …"

Turning the corner into her daughter's room, Mom sees Gillian sitting up in her bed, clutching her blanket to her chest and staring at DaDa, her stuffed animal on the floor in front of her … exactly where she dropped it.

"Pick it up, Mommy. *Please*, pick DaDa up," pleads Gillian, staring plaintively at Mom through big blue eyes, moist with sleep and tears. "I love you, Mommy …"

Mom's anger, her exhaustion, her frustration melt in the face of such devotion. She falls to her knees, picks DaDa up, and hands it to her eldest child before kissing her and tucking her in again. "Here, sweetie, Mommy loves you too."

Back in her own bed, her thoughts whirl as she realizes that somehow, without even knowing how, she has created a big problem for herself with her daughter—a four-year-old who can dance and draw, kick a soccer ball through narrow goal posts, dress and undress her dolls, best her mother in her favorite video game, but can't pick up the stuffed animal she drops regularly at bedtime, or change her clothes in the morning, or remember to get to the potty in time on a shopping trip. At home, she leaves her jacket on the floor in the exact spot where she takes it off, yet manages to find her very own hook at preschool among all the others on the wall.

The numbers on the clock flip again, 12:42. Tossing, turning, flipping, flopping, Mom can't seem to get comfortable as distracting thoughts intrude on her

At home, she leaves her jacket on the floor in the exact spot where she takes it off, yet manages to find her very own hook at preschool among all the others on the wall.

desire to "sleep fast." Mind racing, she acknowledges she has a problem but doesn't know what to do next.

"No, *you* do it!"

It was easy for Mom to justify doing everything for Gillian when she was a baby; she was helpless and required Mom to supply her basic needs and be there for her daughter whenever and wherever needed. However, one day at a time, Mom has become her dedicated, loyal, and ever-obliging servant.

Mom attempted to shift some responsibility to Gillian as soon as her second pregnancy was confirmed. But her attempts were met with more resistance than the Great Wall of China.

"Gillian, please put your toys away in the box when you're finished playing with them," Mom would say in light, cheerful tones while pointing to the color-coded storage system she had painstakingly developed.

"No, *you* do it," Gillian would respond.

"Okay, let's take turns," Mom would suggest, forgetting completely that a child who can negotiate so well must also be able to pick up her toys all by herself.

The memory makes Mom smile, but doesn't change the situation: Mom needs to change what she's doing. Now that the new baby is here, Mom realizes it's going to be even harder.

Mom's last thoughts as she drifts off to sleep, for the third time, come in the form of questions: *Where do I start? How do I get her to contribute more as a member of the family? How do I overcome her resistance?*

Bryce's Story: Resistance Increases with Age

Bryce chose to live with his Dad when Dad and Mom divorced. Two years later, fourteen-year-old Bryce has his father right where he wants him.

It never occurs to Bryce to give his father a hand and help out. During the tension-filled years prior to his parents' divorce, Bryce was not required to help out around the house. Today, Dad tries all kinds of ways to motivate or punish him, but Bryce just stares at his computer, playing the latest video game, ignoring everything else around him.

As a single parent, Dad is responsible for the household chores previously taken care of by his wife. After repeated efforts, he's concluded that it's just easier to take care of everything himself than to nag, lecture, bribe, punish, and argue.

* * *

Gillian's mom and Bryce's dad are not alone. However consoling this thought might be, it's not very useful when we try to expand our children's job descriptions.

We *know* our kids should be helping out more, but at times it's more of a chore to get them to cooperate than do the chore!

Let's look at some important considerations to help parents raise responsible contributing family members no matter how old they are when they start. We'll look at the benefits of using chores to teach responsibility first, and then cover how to set up and introduce a simple system that you can use to help reduce control battles in your family over who does what, and when.

Contributions, Not Chores

Chores. Now that sounds like a lot of fun! But really, who can blame children for not wanting to do chores when chores are so "un-fun"? Chores conjure up images of dread and drudgery. Some kids even claim "torture." Unfortunately, the power struggles in getting kids to do chores have become legendary in many a home.

So for starters, let's change the name to something that sounds a bit friendlier, and definitely more interesting. How about "contributions," since chores have gotten a bad rap? Isn't that what chores really are—contributions to everyday family life? Wouldn't you rather have your epitaph read that you "made a contribution" instead of that you "did your chores"? Just sounds better.

Now some parents may argue, "You don't know my kid, changing the name won't make a difference! He still won't do his chores—oops ... contributions!" Not to worry. This will change once you learn how to hand the problem back to him. That falls under the category of what to do when our child's willingness and cooperation wavers, which is covered in the second part of this chapter.

What? Chores Can Be Crossed Off the List?

"Chores"—commonly used to describe everyday household tasks—are very unpopular. For kids, chores conjure up the attitude, "Oh no ... I have to do *this* before I get to do *that*?" And for parents, the word *chore* has become synonymous with nagging, lectures, reminders, threats, and arguments. It has a sketchy history, one that rarely works for adults or children.

So, let's drop the word *chore* altogether. A cursory glance at *Webster's* definition reveals meanings like "routine," "unpleasant," and "hard." Doesn't sound like much fun, does it? While contributions and jobs can sometimes be a chore, we'll probably have better results using *chore* as an adjective—"Whew! That was a chore."—rather than a noun—"Do your chores! Now!"

Chore Heaven

One parent used this idea of switching "contributions" to chores with her first-born, and was delighted with the results. She was in the kitchen one morning when her son, Lucas, three years old, burst into the room. "Mommy, Mommy, come look!" "What?" asked Mom, as she dried off her hands to follow him. Grabbing her hand, he pulled her into the laundry room, and pointed to Rover's food bowl.

She noticed that the food and water bowls were neatly placed beside each other on top of the floor mat. And that a few more dry kibbles had made it into the bowl than out of it. "Look!" Lucas proudly stated as he smiled at Mom, "I made my contr'bution."

"Thank you, Lucas! Your contribution is very important to our family!" Mom responded, and enveloped him in her arms for a special snug hug.

As they went back to the kitchen to eat breakfast, Lucas asked her what he could do "to contr'bute." Does this sound like utopia? Not in this family. This is a true story as told by a very proud mommy!

We Feel Good When We Do Good

How do you think Lucas felt when he showed his mother what he did? Important or unimportant? Good or bad? Happy or sad? This simple story illustrates one of the best reasons why we need to provide opportunities for our children to make contributions to family life. Simply put, we feel good when we do good. Kids are no exception. A genuine contribution has its own reward. (For a look at the Love and Logic perspective about rewards, see "Stars, Hearts, and Sticker Charts" on p. 104.)

Bottom Line: When we change the name from "chores" to "contributions," and do not attach a monetary value, we give more significance to the meaning and true value of being helpful.

What Money Can't Buy

There are other reasons why a name switch from "chores" to "contributions" makes sense. A contribution is simply a voluntary (unpaid) gift of your children's time and effort for the good of the whole family.

While some parents pay children to do their chores, it's not advisable (as discussed in the story of Emily in Chapter 2). That's because money can never equal the true benefits kids receive from doing their contributions. Why? Because of a fundamental truth of basic human nature.

People are born with an innate desire to belong and to feel needed. When kids make contributions to family life, they become a part of something bigger that adds to their sense of importance and connection to others. They receive unstated messages, such as: "I am a part of my family because my family *needs* me" and "I am valuable."

Think about this: Feeling we are needed in the world inspires most adults to get out of bed each morning. The need to be needed gives us meaning, purpose, and significance in our life. We can accomplish wonderful things when we feel valued and valuable. Most adults meet this basic need by being helpful to someone, by donating time or money to a good cause, or by contributing energy and effort to something or someone bigger than one's self. For a child, his or her reference is their family.

Unfortunately, if those basic needs are not met at home, kids look outside the home, often with unfavorable results. The desire to belong and to feel needed is the gap that unsavory peers and gangs can fill when those essential needs are not met at home or at school.

Requiring your children to make household contributions is one of the best antidotes to reducing the risk of them being led astray by negative influences. So, regardless of what your children say about chores being unfair or that none of their friends have to do chores, children need to contribute to the welfare of their family.

Let's not make the mistake of buying our children's willingness to contribute by paying them to do their chores. The price will never be worth the cost.

Regardless of what your children say about chores being unfair or that none of their friends have to do chores, children need to contribute to the welfare of their family.

Bottom Line: Wise parents use family contributions as the foundation to meet their children's basic need to feel valued and become a positive part of something larger than themselves.

Stars, Hearts, and Sticker Charts

"Aren't you going to pay me?" asked Braden, age thirteen, as he entered the kitchen door. He had just finished cleaning out the fish tank in the office without being asked to do so.

Should children be rewarded for doing their household contributions? Many parents ask this question, citing both success and failure with a rewards program of some type or other.

Rewards are highly popular with parents and kids, because they seem like a good idea. Everyone likes to be rewarded, right? Bonuses and incentive packages are great … for a while. But rewards can backfire as soon as they begin to feel like bribes, or as soon as they feel like an entitlement. A wise CEO once said, "After a while, no one can ever pay me enough for doing work I don't want to do."

So how do you know what kind of reward has enough staying power?

Rewards That Stick

The best reward and the one with the highest chance of "motivation longevity" is the one that—and here's the key—allows the person who wants the reward to also be the person doing the rewarding.

In other words, if Josey wants a sticker for sweeping the kitchen floor, then by all means hand her a sheet of stickers to use whenever she feels like she wants to reward herself. It's even better if she can make up her own sticker chart, so that the pleasure of the reward is all hers and not anyone else's.

In this way, the reward for effort is driven from within the child and not from a source outside the child—such as a parent. This is effective because parents avoid coming up with the "wrong" type of reward—"No, not that sticker! I want this one!"—or arguing over whether the child completed the contribution well enough to be rewarded—"I finished it." "No you didn't!" "Yes I did!"

Wise parents remember to use Love and Logic's principles of shared control and shared thinking and decision-making opportunities to reward their children. The key is to *let the child decide* how to reward him- or herself for doing their household contributions (or other achievements), in a way that doesn't involve dependence on you.

If Josey outgrows *her own sticker idea*, invite her to think of another way to reward herself: "What else can you think of that will bring you satisfaction for a job well done?" It can be as simple as asking Mom for a hug, reading her favorite book, or riding her bike to her friend's house to visit.

As for Braden and the clean fish tank? "That looks much better. Do you suppose the fish like it better?" "Yeah," Braden says with a confident grin. "How much will you pay me?"

"How many hugs do you want?" answers Mom with a smile.

Braden's brow furrows as he thinks about it for a few minutes before answering. "How about an extra half an hour on the computer?"

"Sure, whatever works to give you satisfaction for your extra special effort. But I still want my hugs …"

Braden smiles as he gives his mother a perfunctory hug before racing to the computer in the office, the same office where he can enjoy looking at a sparkling-clean fish tank.

We can't always count on others rewarding us, but we *can* count on rewarding ourselves if we choose to do so. When you allow children to reward themselves, then you have also found a way to let the simple sense of inner achievement be its own reward—regardless of any outer expression they choose.

Bottom Line: Teach your children early that rewards are a sure bet in life when they are an inside job.

How to Introduce Family Contributions

Children don't understand all that's required to run a household unless we teach them. One dad shared a funny story about his son who had just started a driver education class at school. He strolled into the kitchen one day and said, "Dad, when will you guys buy me a car?" Dad, with resignation in his voice, said, "You'll have to earn it, son." In a matter of minutes, his son promptly went from room to room and emptied all the inside trash cans into one large garbage bag. He tied it up, dropped it with emphasis in the middle of the kitchen floor, and said, "Now … will you buy me a car?"

EXERCISE 5.1: Family Contributions Balance Sheet

The good news is that parents can introduce "contributions" as a fresh concept, or switch from "chores" to "contributions," at any time, when their kids are any age. Even if you have teenagers, here is a fun and effective way to introduce this concept to your family in three steps:

Step 1: Make a list.
Step 2: Identify the parents' contributions.
Step 3: Identify the children's contributions.

Step 1: Make a list.

Pick a time when you and your family are all in a great frame of mind. For many families, weekend time offers the most promise of relaxation and cooperation. Get some paper and a pencil, because you'll want to write down all the activities that need to happen in order for your household to run smoothly.

Drop the character-building lecture and simply make the announcement to your kids: "From now on, we're going to call the things we do around the house 'contributions,' because 'contributions' is a better word to describe what we do for each other." Title the page something like "What It Takes to Keep Our Family Going."

Begin listing your contributions as parents, to help your kids get an idea of what you're doing for each other and for them. The beginning of a typical list might look something like this:

What It Takes to Keep Our Family Going

Earn the money for the family

Balance the checkbook

Pay the mortgage/rent

Pay the insurance and property taxes

Pay for gas and electricity

Pay the garbage collection bill

Pay the local telephone/cell phone company

Pay cable, Internet, satellite provider

Shop for the groceries

Carry the groceries into the house

Buy and put the groceries away

Cook the meals

Serve the meals

Set the table

Clear the table

Cleanup/do dishes after meal

Clean the kitchen and bathrooms

Change the sheets

Do laundry

Buy clothes

Buy gasoline for the car

Drive to places others like/need to go

Buy toiletries, cleaning products, and other household supplies

Buy pet food

Pay for the vet bills

Feed and care for our pets

Walk the dog

Clean out the kitty litter box

Take out the trash

Do the yard work

Shovel the walks

You get the idea, and so will your kids. As your kids come up with their own ideas, jot those down too. As the list lengthens, your children's eyes may widen. To keep it manageable, some families divide it into categories like food, clothing, shelter, and the like. Naturally, for large tasks, like "clean the kitchen," break them down into smaller, more manageable ones, such as "clean the stovetop," "sweep the floor," and "empty the dishwasher."

This is a brainstorming session, so it is important not to allow "cross talk" between siblings or criticism of other people's ideas. Everyone's input is important, no matter how big or small.

This first step is not about right or wrong ideas, or who is doing what—that comes later. The idea is simply to get a list of all the tasks needed for the household to operate smoothly in the eyes of everyone who lives there.

Step 2: Identify the parents' contributions.

By design, the list will probably begin with at least a dozen items you contribute as a parent.

Once you've come up with a list, you're now ready for step 2. Start at the top again, and go down the list one item at a time. By design, the list will probably begin with at least a dozen items you contribute as a parent. Tell your kids that you're proud and happy to make those kinds of contributions to family life.

Here's how a conversation might proceed after the family's initial brainstorming session:

Parent: "Anyone have any more ideas? Okay. So let's go back to the top of the list. Let's start with the first one. Who wants to take over earning the money for the family?" (the parent uses the child's pause to take the lead) "I want to write my name on that one because I'm proud to be the person who earns the money for the family, and while I'm at it, I'll also keep and balance the family checkbook. Now, number three, how about 'pay the mortgage'? I'll contribute that, since paying the mortgage allows us to live here in this house." (asking rhetorically) "I imagine you like having a roof over your head, especially when it rains or snows …"

Child #1: (nods hesitantly, not sure if the parent is being serious)

Parent: "Next … 'pay the gas and electricity bill.' You like having heat in the winter and air conditioning in the summer, plus use of the computer, television, and all the other electronic gadgets we have … yes?"

Child #2: (sheepishly) "Well, yeah."

Parent: "Okay then. I'll contribute the money for the gas and electricity bill. Next … 'pay the garbage collection bill'—I'll do that, too, because things could get a little stinky around here if we don't pay the garbage collector. Let's see, what's next on the list … 'pay the phone bill' …"

As you continue this process, do you think your kids might be getting the idea that you make lots of important contributions? Do you think they might start to see, with their very own eyes, the difference between what you contribute and what they contribute?

We bet that your kids are smart enough to know exactly where this conversation is headed. They're already thinking that the quality of their life might be in question very soon unless they start doing their fair share. That's all part of the plan.

Finish going down the list and put your name or a "P" (for "Parent") beside all the tasks you willingly do as head of the household. If you want to have a little fun with this, ask the kids if they'd like to do some of the things that you do (and share some control through choices)—things like "pay the bills" and "bring home the groceries." This gives them a chance to say "no" to parts of the list.

Step 3: Identify the children's contributions.

Next it's time to ask your kids about how they're going "to level things out" and "contribute." To differentiate between the parents' contributions, mark a "C" (for "Children") beside all the items on the list that your kids should contribute. Or you could use two columns to divvy up the list—one for the parents' contributions and one for the children's contributions.

Again, this is not the time to get into family arguments over who is doing what. Simply go back over the list and mark which contributions are "C's" and which contributions are "P's." Some families add a third category—"S" for "Share"—for appropriate tasks. Whatever way you choose, wise parents keep the identification process as simple as possible.

As the exercise proceeds, the family conversation might continue something like this:

Parent: "Okay, I think that's everything that I contribute … now it's time to figure out which ones are C's and S's. What are your thoughts about which tasks you kids should contribute?"

Child #1:   "But we don't want to do any of this stuff. We hate stuff like that. Besides, it's not our job. You're the parent. It's your job!"

Parent: (smiling) "Nice try."

Child #1:   (volunteering something easy) "Clearing dirty plates off the table at dinnertime. Yuck!"

Parent: (responding with a smile) "That's a good start. Thanks. I'll put a 'C' next to 'clear the table.' I'm sure you can appreciate that we need to balance out the work a bit more, so what other contributions should you kids be willing to make?"

Child #1:   "Get the newspaper?"

Parent: "And … ?"

Child #1:   (grumbling) "Take the garbage cans down to curb …"

Parent: "… and return the empty ones to their place next to the garage?"

Child #2:   "Hey, wait, I wanted to do that!"

Parent: "We're not deciding who does what now, just whether the kids or the adults should make the contributions, or both. You guys can work that out later. I'll put a 'C' next to 'garbage cans, up and back' … Hmmm, 'clean the house' … what do you guys think?"

Child #2:   "A really big S! P! and C!"

Parent: "I agree. That's a big task. We'll break it down later so it's easier to divide up the work."

And so it goes. Continue this process until everything on the list has been assigned to the parents, the children, or both as shared contributions. The household's division of labor should now appear—at least on paper—more equitable. Once finished, it's a good idea to keep the list as a reference for future changes.

Summary: How to Introduce the Concept of Contributions

Here's a quick recap of the steps to developing your own "Family Contributions Balance Sheet":

Step 1: Make a list of "Everything It Takes to Keep Our Family Going."

Step 2: Identify which tasks are the parents'—the P's.

Step 3: Identify which tasks are children's—the C's.

Now parents don't have to feel guilty about making their kids part of the family.

Congratulations! You've taken an important first step toward developing bona fide contributors to family life. What do you think may happen when contributions are introduced this way?

Could this be an eye-opening exercise in gratitude for some kids? You bet. Many kids, after this exercise, learn that their parents make a lot of contributions that go unrecognized. Most kids have never thought about what goes into the day-to-day operation of a family home, nor will they ever consider it unless we teach them.

Could this be an exercise in alleviating any guilt? You bet. Now parents don't have to feel guilty about making their kids part of the family.

 Bottom Line: When it comes to introducing the need to make family contributions, wise parents balance their P's and C's.

A Tisket a Tasket, Names in a Basket?

Taking the steps to make a list of the contributions needed to keep your family going paves the way for the next step: a selection process based on choices.

Once you have a list of P's and C's, it's time to decide how often each task needs doing and who will be doing it. Wise parents develop a workable "system" ahead of time to reduce the hassles created by temporary "memory loss," last-minute confusion, or sibling squabbles. (For more information about how to handle sibling squabbles over who's doing what, see "It's not fair!" on p. 116.)

Begin by rewriting, or having your children rewrite, the name of each task from the original contribution list on its own piece of paper, index card, or sticky note. *This is a key step, because a flexible system is essential to making sure that your children have choices about which contributions they are going to make.* The goal is for you to prepare a "drawing of individual tasks" for your children to do.

One mom got really creative. She took pictures of her children doing various tasks, glued them on card stock, and then had them write the name of the task below. Her kids loved posing for the camera. Her youngest understood which contribution he selected even though he couldn't read; and Mom was happy because she had as much flexibility as a deck of cards.

Interchangeability among tasks is one of the essential requirements for avoiding control battles with your kids and between your kids. Whichever method you choose, remember to develop a simple but flexible method that's loaded with rotating choices—choices that share control and involve children in the thinking and decision-making process.

EXERCISE 5.2: All Hands on Deck

Once you have your "deck of tasks," here are some guidelines for divvying them up:

Step 1: Sort tasks by frequency.
Step 2: Group tasks for selection.
Step 3: Select the tasks.
Step 4: Keep a record.

Step 1: Sort tasks by frequency.

Identify how often a task needs doing—daily, weekly, or monthly. For example, cleaning up the kitchen after meals and feeding the family pet are daily tasks; taking the garbage cans to the curb for pickup is not. Separate the tasks accordingly.

Step 2: Group tasks for selection.

Some families group tasks together. A set of jars is used for these examples, because it's a simple system that offers the kind of flexibility that makes a system based on choice workable.

You can create jars for the following groups:

- Each child's tasks—a jar for each child with tasks pre-selected according to age and abilities. For example, a child gets to select four contributions among a collection of eight daily tasks. (Of course, true to Love and Logic's guidelines for giving effective choices, wise parents put in more tasks than needed for children to complete, because it provides the opportunity to choose. To learn more, see "Love and Logic Guidelines for Giving Effective Choices" on p. 35.)
- Daily, weekly, monthly tasks—a collective jar that includes all the tasks for selection by all family members based on frequency.
- Common household tasks (meal jar, laundry jar, cleaning jar, pet jar)— each person picks one or more tasks in a "round robin" fashion from each major category as often as needed.
- Indoor/outdoor tasks.
- Upstairs/downstairs tasks.

Or, group the tasks by any other modifiable method that works well week to week!

Be patient; working the kinks out of the system will naturally take some time. Some families use jars or baskets, other families prefer white-board, Velcro, or a computerized chart. Remember, a tisket, a tasket, with names in a basket, helps many families track their tasks without blowing a gasket!

Step 3: Select the tasks.

You are now ready for the selection process—by name and number of tasks. Begin with daily tasks. Many families find that it is easier to pick daily tasks "good for the whole week," because it can be too challenging to keep track of who is supposed to be doing what on a daily basis. (Some families with only two children find that alternating daily tasks each day works just fine. Brother empties the dishwasher one day, sister the next.)

Once you have found a way to select daily tasks that works, apply the same method to selecting the weekly and monthly tasks as well. For example, some families pick the same day every week to do weekly tasks (e.g., Saturday), or the same day every month to do the monthly tasks (e.g., the first Saturday of each month). Other families get together to do their tasks, catch as catch can.

"How many do I ha'fta do?"

How many tasks per child? Some parents divide the total number of C-tasks equally among the number of children. Other parents use the child's age as a guideline (e.g., they add one contribution [or more] per birthday)—an eight-year-old does eight tasks, a twelve-year-old does twelve. In this way, responsibility grows with age and maturity.

Naturally, the younger the child, the more of the task you will be doing with them. Wise parents remember that when their three-year-old draws the task "gather and sort the laundry" from the family jar or share stack, Mom or Dad will be doing the work with their child side by side in "training mode" (more on "basic training" later in this chapter).

Step 4: Keep a record.

Finally, the most effective families use a written plan, or some other way to record the results of the drawing, from week to week. It's wise to have a solid system for tracking "who is doing what" when it involves contributions. In that way, if a disagreement arises, the "plan" becomes "the boss," not a family member.

Once the plan is on paper, created from the suggestions made by each member of the family, keep it impersonal and nonjudgmental. This is important, as it takes the emotion out of the equation. "Go see what 'the plan' says to do, honey" or "Maybe next week you will draw something you like better."

Sometimes the recording process can be as simple as using a paper clip or rubber band to gather the "task" cards for each child each week. Or, you may want to use a chart, bulletin board, calendar, or spreadsheet for tracking. Involve children in this part of the process as well.

Keeping a record of who needs to do what is always more effective in situations with multiple contributors.

How the Smith Family Used These Guidelines

The Smiths illustrate how one family pulled all these ideas together. The Smith family initially identified twenty-two tasks as children's tasks, or C's. Twelve tasks were put in a daily jar, eight were put in the weekly jar, and two were designated for the monthly jar.

Mr. and Mrs. Smith have two children who are both close enough in age that their ability to do the tasks is not an issue. They decided to have each of the kids draw six daily tasks, four weekly tasks, and one monthly task. (If the Smith siblings were further apart in age, the parents would initially need to help them to do the tasks they select, or divide the tasks by age and ability *before* the selection process. Either of these methods makes all the choices acceptable no matter which ones the child draws.)

To prevent any arguments between family members, Mr. and Mrs. Smith treat the selection process as a lottery—it's the luck of the draw. Once the children draw their tasks, they must complete them by pre-determined deadlines.

 It's also important to give children choices about *when* they need to complete their contribution. This prevents the temptation to nag, warn, or argue about when they are going to do them. (For more information about how to set a deadline for completion, see "In a minute … Mom!" on p. 117.)

There was only one exception. The Smith siblings could negotiate a change between themselves. Mr. and Mrs. Smith quickly learned it was best to not get drawn into their children's drama. Better to hand the problem back to its owner for resolution. They wisely adopted the policy to let *their kids* work it out.

The siblings came up with some amazing solutions that even surprised the Smiths. Sometimes they traded contributions just like baseball cards; other times they paid each other to switch contributions. Once in a blue moon they even covered each other during times of school scheduling conflicts or homework deadlines dilemmas.

The parents' rule was: as long as the contributions were completed on time, any arrangement their children made with each other was acceptable. It was understood however, that whoever drew the task was ultimately responsible for its on-time completion, regardless of the "deal" struck between siblings.

One family who used this system shared that their daughter was willing to do two contributions in exchange for the one she never wanted to do. She agreed to clear the table *and* empty the dishwasher daily in exchange for her brother feeding the family dog. Why? Because her brother had no problem doing what she hated to do—going down the basement's steep, dark steps to get the dog's food.

Contributions by Choice

The power of sharing control by giving choices cannot be overestimated when it comes to getting kids to contribute to family life. Choices reduce the likelihood of getting into power struggles with kids, or proclamations of "That's not fair!" When choices are offered, the child has less cause to blame the parents, because *the child* made the choice.

Wise parents remember to give choices about:

- Who does what
- What they do
- When it gets done (deadline)

But not *if* they do it.

In other words, there's no choice about whether or not the child contributes, but there is a choice about what, how, and when they contribute.

Bottom Line: The parents who are most successful at raising willing contributors are those who develop a "system" first—a flexible system that shares control with built-in choices.

Put the *or* in "I'm Bored" to Work

Ever have the experience of needing an extra dose of patience with your kids when the novelty of learning how to do some new chore wears off? Setting the table can be loads of fun … for about ten days, max. Then what happens? Your child becomes bored overnight. No problem if your child has "outgrown" setting the table, or feeding the cat.

A flexible system offering lots of choices can come to the rescue, especially when you have a pool of contributions to choose from. Keep offering choices: Kids can trade with siblings, trade with their parents, hope things turn out differently next selection time, or exchange a task from the leftovers in the basket. For example, parents can say: "You are welcome to accept, trade, choose, or exchange your tasks for one of the extras from the basket." The issue is not about what they do; it's that they are putting in the time and effort into doing *something* to contribute.

"It's not fair!"

It's Saturday morning. Taylor, Tyler, and Tommy have just finished the weekly drawing for their family contributions. Eight-year-old Tyler starts complaining immediately: "It's not fair! Taylor always gets to do the easy stuff. I never get to pick anything I want to do." Taylor, the eldest, chimes in with, "Yeah, but Tyler only has to do eight contributions and I have twelve!"

Very little presses our parental buttons as consistently as the phrase "It's not fair!" And our kids know it. It's very easy to get sucked into our children's claims of unfairness if we're unprepared with an effective response.

Parents can spare their air when it comes to being fair, by remembering that life is not fair. That's why most parents hit the proverbial brick wall when they strive to make things fair between their children. We're trying to make life something it's not.

Ever witness a kid who, after being lectured to about "why it's fair," says, "Thanks, Dad, now I truly understand"? When parents hear, "But that's not fair!" they are wise to drop the explanations, lectures, or the natural compulsion to make things equal. Those types of responses rarely work.

What to do instead? Love and Logic parents remember to neutralize the emotions in the moment by using an empathic one-liner. Here are a few examples to counter the "It's not fair!" refrain:

- "Nice try."
  Neutralizes the child's manipulative attempts to change your mind.
- "Probably so."
  States the truth of the matter—that life is not always going to be or feel equal.
- "I bet it feels that way."
  Validates the feeling of unfairness without inviting further discussion about the issue.

Kids confuse fairness with justice in many a family home. Fairness is really a feeling—a feeling of being "wronged"—when in fact it may just be a situation or circumstance that "just is," or one that's beyond our control.

When Tyler said, "It's not fair!" it's really the emotional meaning he has attached to that particular event, namely not getting his way. Tyler's response is an exercise in trying to gain control of something he has no control over. The result,

Parents can spare their air when it comes to being fair, by remembering that life is not fair.

in this example, is simply the way the world works when it comes to random drawings. We get what we get. It is what it is.

When the "It's not fair!" issue arises, that's the perfect moment for an empathic response such as the ones suggested here. While there's much in life that can't be controlled, we always have control over how we respond.

Even as kids try to argue, some parents find it helpful to say with empathy, "Probably so" or "I bet it looks that way, and what did I say?"

Bottom Line: The most effective responses to the "It's not fair!" refrain are the ones that soak up the feelings of inequality with empathy and show that the parent is not going to negotiate the boundary.

"In a minute ... Mom!"

"Do it now!" To which the chronically resistant Jerrod responds with, "In a minute ... Mom!"

Love and Logic teaches us never to tell resistant kids to do their contributions "Now!" Why? Because we lose control over the situation as soon as we tell a resistant kid what to do—especially when we demand that they do something right away.

What should we do instead? Share that highly coveted control by giving our children a choice about when they complete their contribution. In this way, control becomes a shared venture—there's no choice about whether they do their contributions or not, there is a choice about *when* they do them.

Here are a few examples:

> "Do you want to clean the guinea pig cage out by Friday night, or by Saturday morning at noon?"
> "Would you rather set the table or clear the table tonight?"
> "Do you want to vacuum the rugs or sweep the floors before we leave for Johnny's party?"

Observe that there is a stated time deadline for completion. Inherent in the choices above are the following deadlines: "Friday or Saturday," "set or clear," and "vacuum or sweep."

A predetermined time is important if we are going to hold our children accountable. When a predetermined limit has been set, we have time to plan how we can hold them accountable if they exercise their "right" to forget, dawdle, or get distracted.

Be prepared with a consequence if the deadline passes. Some parents have the neighbor kid available in case the job is not done. Once the deadline passes, it sounds like this: "Oh, no. It's noon already. John will be here in a minute to do the job for you. You can work out payment with him."

Wise parents remember that contributions, choices, and a designated time for completion are a package deal.

Bottom Line: It's far better to give kids choices with a built-in deadline for completion, than to demand they do their contributions "Now!"

Oh, by the way ...

There's one more way that we can sabotage ourselves as parents around contributions: immediately adding more stuff for your child to do upon completion of the original contributions (and agreement).

"Oh, by the way, Jasper, your father ordered a bunch of new computer stuff this week that came with all kinds of packaging material. He made a huge mess in the garage. Would you be a dear and go sweep it up for recycling?"

This is akin to a boss asking you—just after you have finished one project—to do another one, five minutes before you walk out the door to go home. It's discouraging for children to complete their contributions only to be "rewarded" with a request to do more.

What are the chances that your children will learn to dawdle or hide if you have a list that never ends?

Taking the Chore out of Chores:
Using the ABC Formula for Successful Contributors

Once you have a system of selection set up, there are three factors to consider that will help you take the chores out of chores. They are: ability, basic training, and cooperation/consequence, or ABC respectively.

To turn your children into contributors, you need to:

- Match your expectations to your child's <u>A</u>bility.
- Provide <u>B</u>asic training.
- Learn how to gain <u>C</u>ooperation, or deliver a <u>C</u>onsequence.

Here's the basic ABC formula:

Ability + Basic training + Cooperation = Contributing family member

We'll cover the ABC's one at a time, beginning with understanding the need to match our expectations with our children's abilities.

"A" Is for Age-Appropriate Abilities

How many of you have asked yourselves, "What can my three-year-old really do?" Or, "What is reasonable for my ten-year-old daughter and sixteen-year-old son?" Sometimes our expectations are too high, and sometimes our expectations are too low. Remember the story of Gillian at the start of this chapter? Her mom wasn't sure what to expect. (For a more detailed look at what to expect of your children, see "Goldilocks Expectations" on p. 125.)

Ability + Basic training + Cooperation = Contributing family member

The sample lists that follow will get you thinking about what kinds of contributions are reasonable and appropriate for specific ages. As you read through the lists, keep in mind that kids tend to be more capable than we think they are—and more capable than they lead us to believe! Wise parents know that kids are more willing to help them—and here's the caveat—when contributions are not only age-appropriate, but also greatly appreciated. Helping around the house becomes a family value over time when it's reasonable and appreciated, pure and simple.

Read the suggestions that correspond to your child's age, as well as the suggestions plus and minus one year, since children vary widely in development. For example, if your child is five years old, read the suggestions for four-year-olds, five-year-olds, and six-year-olds to decide what is reasonable for your child's capabilities and maturity level.

Begin with the End in Mind

The sample contribution lists are both cumulative and progressive. Cumulative means that a task accomplished at any age is the sum of all the other tasks that precede it. For example, once your child has successfully learned all the steps to loading the dishwasher, he or she will be able to do the entire task. Progressive means that responsibility increases with age. For example, loading the dishwasher is only one of several other tasks a child may do to contribute to cleaning up the kitchen after a family meal.

Notice also that the word *help* precedes most of the suggestions for the first three age groups—meaning the parent's help and supervision.

Wise parents start training early, with three important components:

- The contribution
- The parent
- The fun

Later, as the kids get older and become more capable, you remove yourself and leave the contribution entirely to the kids, whose memories of the fun they had with you will serve as an antidote to drudgery.

At around the age of five, notice that the word *help* is used sporadically in the lists of suggestions. That's because, if shown how, your children will have mastered some tasks and not others. Your kids will naturally continue to need your supervision for tasks until they have mastered them without your help.

The point is to begin with the end in mind. The end result is to teach your kids how to do household tasks without you *or* your help. In this manner, your children become true contributors. For example, every child aged two and older can contribute something toward getting the laundry done, or putting a meal on the table, as illustrated by the sample lists. Notice how every age group includes contributions from among the most basic household tasks—meals, laundry, cleaning, home maintenance, and plant and pet care. In this way, each year adds more responsibility in all areas.

The end result is to teach your kids how to do household tasks without you or your help.

It's easy to confuse ability with cooperation when deciding what contributions children can make. This section is about determining your child's ability to make contributions, not their willingness. Later in the chapter, we'll look at using choices and consequences to help unmotivated children, such as Gillian and Bryce, get into the spirit of cooperation.

Sample Contribution Lists

Two- to Three-Year-Olds

Help put small, nonbreakable groceries away on a low pantry shelf.

Help pour dry ingredients into a bowl.

Help carry small, safe, nonbreakable items such as napkins and spoons to the dining table.

Help gather small items such as washcloths and socks to launder.

Help collect and carry newspaper and magazines to recycle.

Help clean and pick up what they drop and spill (e.g., toys, food).

Help pick up their things and put them in the proper place.

Help scoop and put food into a pet's bowl.

Four-Year-Olds

All of the above, plus:

Help put larger groceries away.

Help mix ingredients together for baking.

Help pour cold cereal into a bowl.

Help with a simple dessert (e.g., top peaches with granola).

Help spread condiments on sandwiches.

Help carry utensils to set the table.

Help clear items from the table.

Help fill the dishwasher with pre-measured soap.

Help pull up covers and arrange pillows to make beds.

Help dust the furniture.

Help carry the mail for drop-off or pick-up.

Help put raked leaves into a bag.

Help change the pet's water dish.

Five-Year-Olds

All of the above, plus:

Help compile a grocery list for weekly meals.

Help with the grocery shopping by looking for things.

Clear items from the dining table and countertop.

Scrape leftovers off plates for rinsing.

Help rinse dishes in the sink.

Help unload utensils from the dishwasher.

Make simple sandwiches or a cold breakfast.

Help measure and mix ingredients together into a bowl.

Sort white clothes into one pile and colored clothes into another pile.

Help sort clean clothes and put them away.

Help make a bed with clean linens.

Help scrub the sink, toilet, and bathtub.

Help collect the garbage from trashcans around the house.

Help clean up debris in the yard (trash, sticks, leaves, etc.).

Help feed pets and water plants.

Six- to Eight-Year-Olds

All of the above, plus:

Help with the meal-planning process.

Write down items for the family's grocery list.

Set the table.

Wash and peel fruits and vegetables.

Help measure, pour, mix, and stir ingredients together for baking or cooking.

Help prepare plates for family meals.

Help load the dishwasher.

Sweep the kitchen floor.

Help cook simple foods (make toast or microwave popcorn, boil an egg, reheat food).

Help prepare their school lunches.

Measure and pour the proper amount of detergent and bleach for the washer and dryer.

Hang up their clothes in the closet.

Gather wood for the fireplace.

Rake leaves and weed flower and vegetable gardens.

Water outdoor plants (e.g., vegetables and flowers).

Take the family pet for a walk around the neighborhood.

Answer the telephone, politely.

Nine- to Ten-Year-Olds

All of the above, plus:

Help make a list of meals, then make a grocery list.

Use the grocery list to begin comparison-shopping.

Prepare baked goods from mixes.

Serve a family meal.

Help serve meals to houseguests.

Help plan special family events (e.g., picnics, holidays, birthday parties).

Sew on a button to repair an item of clothing.

Help change sheets on the beds.

Eleven-Year-Olds

All of the above, plus:

Wash mirrors.

Scrub sinks, toilets, and bathtubs/showers.

Take the recycling/garbage cans out to the curb and return them to the house.

Do a load of laundry.

Make their lunch for school.

Confirm their schedules.

Twelve-Year-Olds

All of the above, plus:

Pack their suitcase for overnights or family vacation.

Read to siblings and tuck them into bed.

Clean the patios and walkways.

Mow the lawn.

Wipe out the refrigerator.

Clean the oven and stovetop.

Wash windows.

Help with some of the family errands (e.g., picking up a repaired item, dropping off a package, etc.)

Thirteen Years and Up

All of the above, plus just about any other task that isn't harmful or dangerous, once the child has been given step-by-step training and modeling about how to do it.

These lists are not meant to be comprehensive. There are literally hundreds of ways children of all ages, at all developmental stages, can contribute to family life.

Two issues come into play as you use these lists. One has to do with capabilities and the other has to do with expectations. Capabilities concern the child's ability to do something; expectations are about what you *think* the child should be able to do. For example, you may find that your four-year-old is capable of doing what's listed for six-year-olds. That's great! (For more information about the importance of seeing our children as capable, see "Will they *ever* be able to do their own laundry?" on p. 127.)

Of course, the reverse can also be true. For example, you may find that your capable thirteen-year-old feigns ignorance when it comes to simple tasks that even his younger brother could complete. He may even try to convince you that he simply doesn't know how. And maybe he does; or maybe he doesn't. If he truly doesn't know how … aaahhh, another teaching opportunity! Now is the time to fill that gap in his education if he hasn't received enough training, so that your knowledge of his capabilities, and your expectations, are a match.

But, if he *does* know how and just *doesn't want to*, there's more about cooperation and consequences in the "C" section of this chapter (see p. 139). Adult expectations and children's capabilities merge beautifully when we remember the importance of building their capabilities and then holding our children accountable.

Capabilities concern the child's ability to do something; expectations are about what you think *the child should be able to do.*

Bottom Line: Wise parents match their expectations with their children's ability, to increase the chances of developing successful family contributors.

Goldilocks Expectations

Expectations can be tricky. Some parents tend to overestimate or underestimate their children's abilities. We need to develop "Goldilocks"-type expectations—neither too high, nor too low, but just right.

Here's an expectation that you can always hold for your children: they can be helpful in some way if they have hands and feet that move (unfortunately, the only body part that moves for many resistant kids is their mouth—in protest).

Naturally, kids can't do many things as well as we can, at first; but with practice they become just as capable as their adult counterparts. One of the best ways to keep our expectations in line with a child's abilities is to provide a step-by-step process of practicing doing the task with them until they can do it on their own.

Let's examine mealtime, a common household event, in the context of adult expectations. Notice how breaking down the task of meal preparation into smaller parts includes children of any age:

At age 2 they can *help you* carry napkins to the table for each person.

At age 3 they can *help you* carry other nonbreakable items to the table.

At age 4 they can *help you* clear the table.

At age 5 they can *help you* rinse the dishes in the sink.

At age 6 they can *help you* plan meals and begin making grocery lists.

At age 7 they can *help you* load and unload the dishwasher.

At age 8 they can *help you* measure, pour, and mix ingredients together, or serve the meal to others.

At age 9 and up, they have all the "ingredients" to plan, prepare, cook and serve a family meal, with your ongoing encouragement!

One step at a time, according to ability, will result in a child who has learned how to prepare a meal for his or her family. Now *there's* some real value, currently and in the future.

Kids tend to live either down or up to our expectations of them.

One thing I (Jim) would do, if I had to do it all over again, is train my children in the complete art of meal preparation by the age of nine. Some parents are shocked at this suggestion. "They're too young" or "They're too busy," they say. But kids tend to live either down or up to our expectations of them.

Naturally, the meal preparation example can be applied to many other tasks. Simply take the age of your child, begin with the first step of the task, and train as far as you can. Younger children may need two months to master a task's first step, but an older child may be able to master a combination of steps in the first few trainings.

Remember, too, in all fairness, we cannot hold our kids accountable for something they do not know how to do. Once we have provided the proper training and modeling—and we know that they *can* do it —only then can we hold them accountable for *not* doing the task.

 Bottom Line: Wise parents tend to avoid expectations that are either too high or too low. Tasks are taught step-by-step so that their children develop their abilities step-by-step. In this way, parents' expectations and children's capabilities find their match.

"Will they ever be able to do their own laundry?"

Our children are our mirrors. In other words, kids tend to see themselves as *we* see them. One of the best gifts a parent can give a child is to see them as being capable of doing something, no matter how small or young. Unintentionally, however, we can undermine our child's ability to contribute day by day when we do things for them that they can do for themselves.

While it can be hard for some of us to accept the fact that our babies are growing up and can do more things by themselves, developing competence and independence is as necessary to their healthy sense of self as eating nutritious food and exercising their growing bodies.

Just for practice, let's figure out how doing the laundry can begin as early as two years old. Notice how capability builds with age:

Whenever you have your children help you, side by side, you model your capabilities so that your children have the opportunity to develop theirs.

At age 2 they can *help you* collect and carry dirty clothes to the laundry room (even if it is only a bath towel they drag on the floor behind them; consider it a lesson in dusting).

At age 3 they can *help you* load and unload the washer and dryer.

At age 4 they can *help you* sort items by dark, light, and colors.

At age 5 they can *help you* measure the soap and pour it into the dispenser, and start the machines.

At age 6 they can *help you* do the entire task above, plus determine the appropriate washing machine settings.

At age 7 they can *help you* put the laundry away.

At age 8 they can *help you* fold the laundry.

At age 9 they will be ready to do a load of laundry, from start to finish, without you!

The word *help* in the above example means showing them how to do each step, defined loosely here because—let's face it—kids are not very much help when they are little. If we disapprove of them for not being able to do it perfectly when they are young, we create kids who do not want to do it (or don't know how to do it) when they are older.

How many grown kids, for example, are still coming home with their laundry bags? Start early if you want to lighten your laundry load now and in the future. Then, you can be proud you have taught your children the life skills they will need once they are independent and living on their own. Even if your children are already teenagers, it's never too late to start! (It's amazing to watch what happens to a teenager's interest in their favorite clothes when we stop doing their laundry.)

Whenever we do things for our kids that they can do for themselves, we have robbed them of an opportunity to discover what they are capable of doing. Parents can set their kids up for success in their later years by showing them how capable they are during their growing years. Whenever you have your children help you, side by side, you model your capabilities so that your children have the opportunity to develop theirs.

Bottom Line: Wise parents recognize and acknowledge the potential in their increasingly capable kids, and then foster those abilities, one day and one task at a time.

"B" Is for Basic Training

If we're going to ask our kids to contribute, then it makes perfect sense to teach them how. Once you've determined which contributions are age-appropriate, it's time to put your kids on a "train to gain" program. When parents train, both parents and children gain!

Ability + **Basic training** + Cooperation = Contributing family member

There are two basic ways for your children to learn how to become contributing members of the family household—the easy way, and the hard way. The first method uses education and encouragement as the teacher, and the other uses life experience.

Both approaches work toward the eventual goal of helping children become future members of Housekeepers of America. The method you select should be consistent with your values, your child's age and temperament, and common sense.

Let's look at the easy way first, through education and encouragement.

Basic Training 101: Progress, Not Perfection

You've probably had the following experience if you're a parent: Your young child is all excited about wanting to do something, but you know he or she really can't do it. They plead, whine, and beg you to give them a chance.

While it's endearing to witness their interest, you *know* they really can't do what they think and say they can do. So you feel conflicted. On the one hand it's wonderful to see their enthusiasm, but on the other hand it's hard to turn them away. So how can we tap into that positive energy called "desire" without dampening their spirit?

Many children learn best by actually doing the task. We tend to show our kids how to do something by asking them to watch us do it and then expect that they know how to do it without ever having done it!

While observation is a legitimate way to learn, it's probably better, especially for younger children, to break down the task into smaller chunks and describe in words what you're doing. Then give them a chance to practice with their own hands, eyes, and feet. That helps the brain connect with the body and lock in the memory.

A Wink at the Sink

Here's an example of how one mom trained her daughter, Megan, age four:

Mom: "Would you like to be part of my super duper clean team?"
Megan: "Yeah!"

Mom turns on some music and heads for Megan's bathroom. Mom has already gathered the cleaning supplies, knowing that one day Megan will be able to do that by herself.

Mom: "We need three things to clean this sink: a sponge, a cleanser, and water. I'm going to pretend I'm sprinkling fairy dust into the sink." (sprinkles a little and hands the cleanser to her child)
Megan: (putting too much cleanser into the sink) "This is fun."
Mom: "That should be enough. Okay, now here's the sponge."

Now Mom demonstrates how to fill the sponge with water, and then squeeze it out. Megan practices filling the sponge with water and squeezing it out, several times.

Mom: "Now you press the sponge against the side of the bowl and rub it back and forth, spreading the cleanser around." (moves the sponge in a fun doodle-like pattern) "Look how the cleanser and the water mix together to create a paste."

Mom demonstrates as she describes, and then hands the sponge to her child. Megan takes the sponge and turns on the water with too much pressure.

Mom: "Here, let's practice turning the water off and on so that it doesn't splash out of the sink."

Now Megan practices turning the water off and on. (Anyone who's ever been a parent knows how much young kids love to play with water. Is Megan having fun yet? Of course!) Remember, as parents we're looking for progress, not perfection. It's the quality of the effort and the time together that really count, not the final outcome.

Mom: "Here, let me show you how to finish."
Megan: "I want to do it!"
Mom: "I'll do half the sink and you can do the other half." (slowly and carefully cleans the sink and hands the sponge to her child) "Your turn."
Megan: (vigorously yet playfully scrubbing the sink) "This is fun."
Mom: "You're really learning how to clean your own sink. Look at how white it's becoming with your help."
Megan: (leaning up against Mom and smiling) "It's getting whiter and whiter."
Mom: (winking back) "It sure is, with *your* help!"

Train and Gain

Effective training includes three important ingredients, from the beginning:

1. Fun
2. The parent
3. The task

Did Megan's mom use this formula? Yes. (For more information about the most effective way to train young children, see "Catch 'em If You Can … When They're Young" on the next page.)

Notice how Mom took a common household task and broke it down into a step-by-step procedure. Mom had Megan practice how to squeeze water out of the sponge, *and* how to sprinkle the "fairy dust" cleanser into the sink, before she ever combined the two.

Big tasks with many steps are daunting for very young children; that's why it's important to break down each task into manageable parts, so that your children experience success each step of the way. If you have either young or enthusiastic kids, you are blessed by their willingness to be with you and learn from you. That's why it's called "the easy way"—with a little education and encouragement, they're on their way.

Older kids will be able to learn multiple steps at once. Naturally, we'll need to show any child the steps as often as necessary, regardless of their age, until we see that they can do it without us.

Bottom Line: Wise parents break down each step and use hands-on modeling and practice so that they and their children will both benefit from basic training, now and in the future.

Catch 'em If You Can ... When They're Young

Every parent knows that young children are mimics in miniature. Young kids love to imitate what their parents are doing. If Daddy washes the car, junior wants to wash the car. When Mom sweeps the kitchen floor, her child wants to be right there underfoot.

Ever notice that the younger the child, the more they want to be with and imitate you? Megan's mom picked an optimum time to teach her daughter the nuances of scouring a sink. The time was ripe because Megan was enthusiastic and developmentally ready to learn.

Supermarkets have adopted a brilliant marketing program based on these very same principles. Ever notice those miniature shopping carts in grocery stores identified as "customer in training"? Chances are, whoever came up with the "smart cart" idea cleverly understood that a trip to the grocery store is easier and more fun when young kids can imitate the adults who take them. They have also figured out that this can generate more sales.

It's training-time heaven when your kids are in that genuine imitation stage! It's that special developmental window of time when they want to be with you and do what *you* are doing. It's the "Me want to do it!" stage, where a little training, extra help, and encouragement go a long way. In fact, when parents can engage their children in harmless imitative behavior, when the time is right, that demanding, sometimes annoying "Me! Me do it!" phrase can turn into a proud "I did it all by myself!" phrase.

You, Me, and the Task Makes Three

Wise parents, if their children are still young enough, use this early developmental training window to their advantage. They capitalize on the child's innate desire to:

1. Be with the parent.
2. Have fun with the parent.
3. Learn from the parent.

Next time you perform your routine tasks and "contributions" around the house or home office, invite your child to "help" you. Hand them a feather duster or dust cloth so that they can copy your dusting methods, following you from room to room. As the expression goes: Imitation is the highest form of flattery.

Many parents find that the younger the child, the better their attitude. With older children, ability tends to go up while attitude tends to go down, so train 'em if you can when they're young.

But there's no need to worry if your children are beyond the cute and curious stage for training, as we'll find out next.

Bottom Line: It's much easier to temper the enthusiasm of a toddler than to breathe life into a reluctant teenager.

Five Steps to Training Success

There are five things that parents can do to be effective "trainers." Any one of these will help, but using all five in combination will make the biggest difference between success and failure:

Step 1: Find your high-altitude attitude.
Step 2: Find the fun.
Step 3: Train when it's sane.
Step 4: Seek progress, not perfection.
Step 5: Use encouragement.

Step 1: Find your high-altitude attitude.

Your attitude about household work is paramount to the success of your child's attitude. If it's a real grind to you and you dread the job, then your kids will mirror that attitude. You want your kids to develop the attitude that contributions are fun, that they are enjoyable because your kids get to be with you, and that, in the end, it feels good to be helpful.

Contributions are always more fun when done as a team effort, and can be a quality source of time together as a family. Find a way to make it fun for everyone, including yourself. Make it a "clean team" dream come true!

This makes your time together count toward bonding and building family relationships. You might as well find a way to make these tasks enjoyable, since you have to do them anyway. Cleaning the toilet can be quality time together, even if it's not necessarily a quality project!

 Bottom Line: Wise parents remember to model and maintain a positive attitude with their children, so their children can mirror the same.

Step 2: Find the fun.

If it's fun for your child, chances are it'll be more fun for you. In the spirit of Mary Poppins, in the Disney classic: In every job that must be done, there needs to be an element of fun. Find the fun, and snap—the job is done!

Turn your trainings into a game. Here are a few fun ideas:

- "I spy with my little eye …" Notice a task that needs doing and preface it with, for example, "I spy with my little eye a toy truck that needs to be put away in the toy box." Repeat "I spy" with each new task.
- Play "I Dream of Genie." Use a quick shake of the head, like a magical genie, in the direction of the task that needs doing. Ask your child to guess what you are thinking. Alternate the role of genie so that your kids get a shake at it too!
- Add mystery with treasure hunts or "Get a Clue." Draw a contributions map to follow (with the promise of a treasure of their own choice upon completion), or hide a note about what the child needs to do to "get a clue."
- Play a version of musical chairs, only it's musical cleaning, or do the "Blitz and Freeze Routine": scurry then freeze; repeat as necessary in timed intervals.
- Personify objects—have those toy blocks grow legs so they can magically walk into their box, or give power to a skateboard so it can mysteriously move all by itself.
- Play music, sing songs, dance together, or play silly games.
- And, take some advice from the beloved Disney characters known as the seven dwarves: *Whistle while you work!*

Or do anything else that invites your children to use their creativity and imagination!

 Bottom Line: Fun gets it done.

Step 3: Train when it's sane.

When is a good time for employers to train their employees—on the eve of a holiday, or on a morning when the day is fresh? Similarly, when is a good time to train your parenting partner in the nuances of taking care of the kids while you're gone—during a time when there are no distractions, or when you're headed out the door for a conference?

Timing is important when it comes to training, for you and for your children. Wise parents of younger children "make hay in the sunshine." They tap into their younger children's enthusiasm when the training window is wide open! Wise parents of teenagers understand that they shouldn't try to plant trees in a tornado. Of course, if your child is interested in learning how, no matter what the age—capture the flag!

As for the trainer? The best time to train any child, of any age, is when you are feeling happy and stress-free. Train during the good times to avoid the bad times. For example, quality time together might only be during weekends; or maybe the best training time is before your kids' favorite cousins come to visit; or perhaps you can schedule "Home Skills Development Days" once a month in advance.

Bottom Line: Wise parents know that *when* they train is as important as *how* they train.

Step 4: Seek progress, not perfection.

Ever notice, when it comes to the household "To Do" list, how your agenda differs from your child's? You want the bathtub scrubbed and rinsed. They want to play with the water. Or you want to get the house picked up, but they want to be with their friends.

Kids play the contributions game with a different set of rules. Adults tend to focus on getting the job done, whereas children focus on what kind of fun they can have doing it (or how to get out of it). Adults are interested in the finished product; kids are interested in the process. That's why having fun and "being with you" are the first two keys to successful contributions training—for most kids it's all about the process, not the outcome.

Here are a few tips to keep the progress flowing:

> *Break the task down.* Every task has its steps. Training will yield better results with any child, of any age, if you break the task down into

While it's fine to see the future potential in our children, we should be careful not to use it as a standard of measure in the here and now.

more manageable parts. Once each part of the task has been practiced to the point of *mastery*, you can move forward. Your children will eventually know what to do to complete the entire task from A to Z.

Offer help when asked. It's perfectly okay to ask your kids if they'd like your help, if they're making an effort to complete the task. Give them a hand as long as—and here's the caveat—*they continue to work at least as hard as you're working.* Parents who do this raise kids who eventually and freely offer their own help—back to the parents!

Say "thank you." For very young children, the effort that goes into making the contribution is more important than the quality of the work being done. Encourage your young child by thanking them for their efforts, even if your young child empties only half the dishwasher. They may have stopped because they weren't sure where to put the next item. The next time they empty the dishwasher, remember that shelving one or two more dishes than last time is *still* progress.

Bottom Line: Wise parents look for progress through practice, not perfection. While it's fine to see the future potential in our children, we should be careful not to use it as a standard of measure in the here and now.

Step 5: Use encouragement.

One of the best ways to get children to do more is to pay attention to them when they're doing it.

Pop Quiz: Encouragement or Praise?

Your child has just finished sweeping the kitchen floor for the first time without your "assistance." Which of the following responses is praise, and which is encouragement?

"Good job!"

"You swept the entire floor all by yourself! And you got all the big chunks!"

The first is an example of praise, while the second is an example of encouragement. While both responses are acceptable, the results of one are far superior to the results of the other. What's the primary difference?

Praise is vague: it doesn't let the child know what he or she did well.

Encouragement is specific: it describes effort with appreciation and detail.

While this may seem subtle, the results of knowing the difference between the two can have a profound impact on your child's self-concept. Praise is a person's opinion of someone else's efforts. Opinion, as we know, is subject to interpretation. But encouragement, delivered specifically and authentically, is a communication tool that parents can us to help the child recognize their *own* efforts. Encouragement can be the "consequence" when your children make good choices. This builds a child's self-concept from the inside out, instead of the outside in.

"But you didn't do ..."

Ever heard the phrase "You get more bees with honey"? Tell your children well if you want them to improve and increase their efforts around the house. Then encourage them to do more of the same.

Some parents tend to see what's incomplete about their children's contributions, instead of what was accomplished. One dad complained that his kid never helped out. Through inquiry it became apparent that when his son mowed the lawn, Dad would ask him why he hadn't also done the edging and weeding. His son became so discouraged that he decided to not do anything, because in his words, "It's never good enough for my dad."

Wise parents drop anything that smacks of "You did this but you didn't do that ..." and "You finally got around to it ..." and "It's about time you did ..." It's best to recognize the child for what they *do* contribute, and make a footnote to yourself to fill in the "training gap" later.

Which parent is going to create a more willing contributor—the one who notices what's right about their child's effort, or the one who points out what's wrong?

Encouragement Is Not Exaggeration

What if the Dad whose son just mowed the lawn said this instead: "Good job! Oh my gosh ... This is wonderful! You're a star! I can't believe you did that all by yourself! Wow! You're awesome!"

That response has its downside, too.

We can make the mistake of going overboard with "encouragement by exaggeration." Exaggeration is phony and therefore isn't very encouraging. The kid may hear your words, but they have little meaning or significance when the tone is embellished, or the words lack specific or unique details.

Kids who are praised excessively, for nothing and for everything, become both fragile and entitled.

Kids who are praised excessively, for nothing and for everything, become both fragile and entitled.

Find the balance in authenticity. Children will be more likely to absorb *authentic* encouragement, because it squares with their experience of themselves in that moment. If children aren't feeling confident about their accomplishments, then a genuine description of their effort gives them a more capable view of themselves—an inner view they can adopt as true about themselves. And that's what developing a positive self-concept is all about.

* * *

In summary, reflect for a moment on your workplace. Which kind of person would you rather have train you—someone who has a positive, fun attitude toward the work, or someone who has a negative attitude? Someone who expects you to do it perfectly, or someone who encourages your progress?

Bottom Line: Use praise sparingly; encourage instead. Wise parents notice their children's effort and accomplishments using descriptive words spoken in a genuine and appreciative tone.

Five Steps to Training Success: Summary

Here is a quick summary of the keys to training success:

Step 1: *Find your high-altitude attitude.* Model and maintain a positive attitude with your children so they children can mirror the same.

Step 2: *Find the fun.* Fun gets it done.

Step 3: *Train when it's sane.* Know that *when* you train is as important as *how* you train.

Step 4: *Seek progress, not perfection.* Look for progress through practice, not perfection. While it's fine to see the future potential in our children, we should be careful not to use it as a standard of measure in the here and now.

Step 5: *Use encouragement.* Substitute praise for encouragement: notice their effort and accomplishments with descriptive words spoken in a genuine, authentic, and appreciative tone.

"C" Is for Cooperation (or Consequence)

Many parents have noticed that somewhere between toddler and teenager, willingness and cooperation waver, or worse, disappear. As one parent stated: "When my kids were young, they were interested but not very capable. Now that they're older, they're capable but not interested." No need to worry. No matter what your child's age, it's never too early or too late to engage them in cooperating on the household tasks.

Ability + Basic training + **Cooperation** = Contributing family member

If your expectations are reasonable, *and* you've provided training and encouragement, *and* your kids are still reluctant to do their contributions, it's time to up the ante. It's time to catch them when they want *you* to make a contribution *to them*. That's the time when some kids might need to learn how to contribute the hard way.

The following story will be of interest to any parent who has experienced a reluctant kid.

"How many times do I have to tell you … ?"

Many parents are all too familiar with asking this question, which ends with "feed the cat," "pick up your things," "clean your room," or any other task their child hasn't completed. If a child is uncooperative or unwilling, then what?

One mom with two tweenage boys came to see me (Kristan) for a consultation because she was sick and tired of doing everything for her kids. Whenever she asked them to do *anything*, they complained so bitterly that it was just easier to do it herself. Asking her tweens to do even the least little bit around the house caused a fight. She was seeking professional help because, as she said, "I've tried everything and nothing seems to work."

Her sons, using guilt and manipulation over time, had apparently convinced her that a request to pick up after themselves, take out the garbage, or do the dishes, was her job. "Mom … You're home all day long. You do it. I'm busy." She would argue, telling them it was *their* room, *their* trash, and *their* dishes. But that inevitably ended with her caving in and doing the tasks for them. By the time she came to see me, she was not only tired, irritated, and resentful, but also very confused. After all, she asked rhetorically, her boys did have a point, didn't they?

Her questions came out between her tears and frustration. "I've tried to be a good mom and do everything for them, but it's backfired on me. If I didn't pick up after them, they'd live like ungrateful pigs." (For the key to teaching children how to be more grateful, see "Teach an Attitude of Gratitude" on p. 144.)

She continued, "Maybe I should pay them to do their chores around the house. Maybe that would help. Am I really asking too much to expect them to pick up their own stuff, so I don't trip over it? How can I make them do what I ask? I can't send them to their rooms anymore—they're bigger than me now."

Let's start with the basics:

*H*er sons, using guilt and manipulation over time, had apparently convinced her that a request to pick up after themselves, take out the garbage, or do the dishes, was her job.

Kristan:	"Andrew and Anthony live in the house with you, right?
Mom:	"Yes, plus my husband—who's a whole different story."
Kristan:	"So your family consists of four people."
Mom:	"Yes."
Kristan:	"That's a lot of work for one person, with daily meals, laundry, and keeping the house clean."
Mom:	"Definitely. I'd be happy to have help for just one of those tasks."
Kristan:	"I call these essential everyday tasks 'contributions.'"
Mom:	"Okay …" (looking doubtful about where I'm going with this) "I like the sound of that. But I just call them 'chores.' How is a 'contribution' different from a 'chore'?"

To help her understand the true meaning of contributions, I asked that, in preparation for our next visit, she put together a list of all the things she routinely did for her kids.

A week later, Mom shared her list with me, in utter amazement at what she'd discovered. "I can't believe it. All the contributions that I want them to make are all things my boys can do for themselves."

She started to explain. "In the beginning, my children were young, of course. It made perfect sense for me to do things that they couldn't do for themselves. As they got older and more capable, I realized that my perspective hadn't changed with their capabilities. They refused to help, and I let them get by with it."

This was her list:

- Pick up your things on the floor in your room and put them away where they belong.
- Make your bed.
- Return your dishes to the kitchen.
- Put your laundry in the hamper.
- Clean your bathroom.

A great start! Then I asked her to make another list, this time expanding her requirements to include the contributions would she would *like* the boys to make to family life. "Seems like an exercise in wishful thinking," Mom said hesitantly, "but I'll give it a go."

A Second Look

Mom's second list built on the first. She included items like "take care of the yard," "care for and feed the dogs and the cat," and "clean up after family meals." She realized that if her kids completed the tasks in the second list, her life would be much more pleasant, and the problem of feeling like "an indentured servant" would be resolved!

Mom: (reviewing both her lists) "But my boys won't even do anything from the first list, let alone the second."

Kristan: "Not a problem. Love and Logic techniques offer a solution without lectures, warnings, or threats. We're going to learn how to make it very compelling for your boys to understand the need to contribute to family life. Would you agree that many of the things you do around the house have to do with your sons' quality of life?"

Then I invited her to notice that, in comparison, her second list expanded her sons' contributions to include benefits to the whole family's quality of life.

Kristan: "The key is to change your sons' perspective about contributions, from 'me first' to 'family first.'"

> This brings to mind John F. Kennedy's famous quote, but with a twist:
> *Ask not what your family can do for you …*
> *ask what you can do for your family.*

Mom: (wheels starting to turn) "But what exactly should I tell them? Should I say, 'If you don't feed the dogs, I won't take you to Joe's house'?"

Kristan: "That approach is probably fertile ground for a control battle. It will probably create more of a mess than it cleans up. You might want to experiment with a generic consequence instead."

Mom: "What's that?"

The Generic Consequence

Kristan: "A generic consequence goes like this: 'I'm glad to do the *things you want* when I feel respected and your contributions are done.' It's a simple statement that sets a limit. Many parents have found it to be very effective for these kinds of situations. I suggest you memorize this statement and keep it on the tip of your tongue."

Mom: "Okay. 'I'm happy to do the things you want when I feel respected and the contributions are done.'" (with a forced smile)

Kristan: "Would you be willing to experiment with this strategy?"

Mom: "Yes."

Kristan: "Here's how it might work in your situation: Wait until Andrew wants you to do something for him. That is key. You'll need to keep quiet until that moment arrives. And remember, when the time comes, lead with "Oh bummer …" or "This is so sad …" before offering the 'I'm glad to do the things …' statement."

Mom: "Got it. I can't wait to see how it works."

The very next day, Mom got her opportunity:

Andrew: "Mom, will you take me to Joe's house? We're going to watch the game together."

Mom: "Oh … bummer" (empathy)

Andrew: (looking a little bewildered) "Yeah, the Reds are playing today. It's the final game of the season."

Mom: "I'm glad to do the things you want when I feel respected and the contributions are done." (consequence)

Will Andrew, or any other typical kid, argue with Mom at this moment? Probably. But you know what to do! Use a Love and Logic one-liner (introduced in Chapter 2)—then go brain dead by repeating that same statement until the child gets frustrated and gives up:

Andrew: "But duh, I'll miss the game."
Mom: "I love you too much to argue, and what did I say?"
Andrew: "You can't do this. This is so stupid. Joe's mom doesn't make him do stuff around the house."
Mom: "I love you too much to argue, and what did I say?"
Andrew: "This is stupid. I'm going to go live with Joe. His parents are nice to him."

Mom shared later: "I felt like Clint Eastwood in the movie *Dirty Harry*: 'Go ahead … make my day,' but of course, I didn't say it out loud. And this time I didn't give up or give in. Nor did I buy into Andrew's excuses and manipulation. He either does his contribution and goes to the game, or doesn't and I don't spend the time and energy to take him."

Quality Life, Quality Lessons

Did Andrew's mom use a simple, everyday request to teach him one of life's greatest lessons? Yes: Andrew does not get, when Andrew does not give.

Mom expected him to do something for the quality of his family first, in exchange for improving the quality of his own life. The good news is that this is not an either-or scenario; everyone can have a good quality of life with a little cooperation. If Mom felt like a "slave," it was because she was a slave—a slave to her sons' desires by treating them as if they were houseguests, not family members.

Who can blame her sons for liking the life of kings? What happens when our homes become welfare states for our kids? They grow up feeling entitled to be taken care of by others. This, in turn, creates an unhealthy and fragile dependency leaning toward an uncertain, unhappy, and questionable quality of life.

Wise parents remember:

> **The contributions kids request of us improve their
> quality of life. The contributions we request of our kids
> improve the whole family's quality of life.**

Love and Logic teaches that children should not be treated as honored guests in your home. They are a part of your family and need to contribute to family life.

Teach an Attitude of Gratitude

Mom arrived at school to pick up Brandi, who greeted her with, "Did you bring me my snack?" Before Mom could even utter a response, Brandi continued, "Did you get the invitations for my birthday party? Order the favors? Did the pony man call you back?"

Mom, feeling drilled by her daughter's rapid-fire questions, paused, looked at her with complete exasperation, and asked, "Do you see the word *SLAVE* written across my shirt?"

Without even filling out an application, Mom had inadvertently joined the ranks of many other parents across America who feel overworked and under-appreciated by their children. It can be a thankless job at times, especially if our children do not understand or share in the day-to-day management of a household.

Little by little, Brandi had picked up the notion that Mom had been placed on earth to serve her and make her happy. How did this happen?

Even at an early age, there are many things kids can do for themselves. It's important that we let them struggle with these tasks, even if the job is not done as well as an adult might do it.

Some kids start to believe that they're not capable when parents do things for them instead of letting them do things for themselves. Others develop the belief that they are so special that others will and should serve them.

We raise kids who feel entitled to more and more whenever we do more than our share of work. Parents often fall into the trap of believing that their kids should be grateful for parental "sacrifices," when most of the time they don't even understand our efforts as sacrifices in the first place.

Time for a Change

This can change once we teach our children the requirements behind our efforts. How can our children learn to appreciate what it takes if we don't involve them in the process?

Take planning a birthday party as a fun example. Let's pick one task among many—arranging for the entertainment. Using the example of pony rides, there are at least four steps:

1. Research and select a name, phone number, and website for someone who rents ponies for birthday parties.

2. Make time to call/contact someone about what you want.

3. Determine if the services you are requesting are a match with the services the vendor offers, at a price within your budget.

4. Make a decision to use the vendor's services. If the vendor is too expensive, repeat steps 1–3 to find someone else. Or change course and decide on some other form of entertainment.

What are the chances that "Little Miss Birthday Girl" would appreciate Mom's efforts a little more if she handed some of those steps back to Brandi, with guidance? Would giving Brandi some of the responsibility also prepare her for tasks requiring planning skills in the future?

Gratitude Is Caught, Not Taught

Genuine gratitude is caught by children when they are either doing something or doing without, *not* when we're doing it for them or when we force them to express their thanks.

By shifting some or all of the responsibility to those who benefit from the effort, genuine gratitude for what others do for us comes more naturally. More than just money, presents, or things, effort inspires appreciation in both directions. The giver and the receiver understand the requirements for each role.

Plus, it sure beats what we tend to do instead: ask for, wait for, or force a "thank you!"

Bottom Line: Wise parents increase the chances that their children will develop the attitude of gratitude by providing real life experiences of effort. Only then can their children learn how to genuinely appreciate the efforts of others.

Lessons with Leverage: The Power of Knowing How

Andrew's mom reported later how pleased she was with the result of her experiment. Once Andrew could see that Mom was not going to argue with him or drive him to his friend's house to watch a game, he actually did his contributions, even though he missed a major part of the game.

In our next session together, Mom wanted to learn how to repeat her success:

Mom: "How do I keep this success up?"

Kristan: "By leveraging what they want from us with what we need from them."

Mom: "And how do I do that?"

Kristan: "Do your boys routinely need something from you?"

Mom: "All the time ... every day."

Kristan: "What kinds of things do they ask you for?"

Mom: "Oh, like ... where's dinner? Or they ask me to wash a favorite pair of jeans."

Kristan: "That's a good thing. That works to your advantage."

Mom: "How?"

I shared the following ideas with her, ideas any parent can apply to getting their kids to do their contributions.

Begin by making a "leverage list" to jump-start your thinking. Make a list of all the things your kids want you to do for them. You might be amazed at its length. For many parents, this is a powerful exercise in reducing any feelings of guilt you may harbor—just in case you ever think you ask your kids to "do too much."

Here are some examples of the day-to-day opportunities parents have to motivate reluctant kids:

Sample Leverage List

Taking them somewhere:

toy store

friend's house

park or mall

Buying something they want:

toys

clothes

electronic gizmos

Providing some sort of service for them:

clean laundry

meals

money

Needing permission to do something:

having a sleepover / play date

going to a party

using the computer

attending a field trip

Asking you to find something that belongs to them:

shoes

backpack

sports bag

Notice that these categories all begin with action words: *taking, buying, providing, needing,* and *asking.* The child wants you to take action, just like you want them to take action. Notice also how many items on the list are *daily* requests. (For more information about how to apply your own leverage through use of the generic consequence, see "Love and Logic's Generic Consequence: Making Your Own Leverage List" below.)

Love and Logic's Generic Consequence: Making Your Own Leverage List

Timing, a little leverage, and a little patience are all that's needed to make Love and Logic's generic consequence effective.

Some parents jot down a few ideas of "leverage moments." They ask: "What kinds of things do my kids ask me to do on a routine basis?" Others keep a list in their heads.

Try to think of things only you can provide for your children: a ride, permission, and so forth. The key is to make sure the items are on *their* agenda, not yours. For example, getting up in the morning for school when they don't want to get out of bed should not be on the list. That's what *you* want them to do, not what they want *from you.* This list should contain only the things your kids ask of you.

Once you have something you can leverage, in mind or on paper, you can use the generic consequence as illustrated by Andrew's story. Love and Logic calls it a "generic consequence" because it can be used for many situations. The first half of the statement—"I'm glad to do the things you want"—can be used for any of your children's requests, since those are the things you *might* do for them.

The remaining half of the statement—"when I feel respected and the contributions are done"—hands the problem back to the child. It is now incumbent upon the child to do his or her contributions if they want to get what they asked for. The consequence is built right into the statement, without lectures, warnings, or threats.

Andrew's mom, for example, used her choice to *not* drive her son somewhere, in exchange for her son's choice to *not* take care of some household tasks. Notice that this technique will not be effective *until* the next time Andrew wants Mom to do something for him.

A repeat of "I'm glad to do the things you want when I feel respected and the contributions are done" will probably trigger an unpleasant memory in Andrew's mind—that arguing and manipulation won't work with Mom. Instead, he'll need to kick up his efforts at home.

All's Well That Ends Well

Want to know the ending to this story? How did the generic consequence work for Andrew's mom in the long run?

In our final session together, Mom reported that things had gotten a whole lot better. She felt both "in power" and "empowered" knowing how to use leverage to motivate her sons. She said, with such relief, "My home is so much more peaceful and calm." Even though her sons don't always immediately do what she asks, just the act of wanting something from her now serves as a poignant reminder to her boys about making their contributions.

Her sons have learned that the overall quality of their life gets better when they contribute to the quality of their family's life.

Such sweet success!

A Menu of Consequences to Choose

Is that the only way to motivate your kids to do their contributions? Of course not. Andrew's mom used a generic consequence, but there are other equally effective methods parents can use:

- Offer a choice to hire someone else to do it, and bill the child.
- Have an energy drain.
- Delay the consequence with "No problem. I'll take care of it" whenever you don't know what to do.

 (For a look at how these consequences can be used, review the example of Emily in "Money Back Guarantee Options" on p. 41. For a step-by-step guide to combining several of these strategies, see "Eight Steps to Motivated the Unmotivated" below.)

Eight Steps to Motivate the Unmotivated

For those of you, like Andrew's mom, who might have missed the magic window of time when your kids want to be with you, and to imitate and learn from you, there's still hope.

Love and Logic recommends an expanded series of steps that may be necessary to motivate the unmotivated. You'll notice that these steps still adhere to the same principles of shared control, choices, and empathy before consequences, but with a few adjustments.

Use these steps whenever a chronically resistant child forgets that—when it comes to contributions—not doing them becomes a bigger problem for the child than just following through on their obligation.

Step 1: In order to create a learning opportunity (and share some control), pick two contributions you are sure your child won't make, and state them in choice form using a friendly voice: "Fred, would you rather clean up after Spot, or mow the lawn?"

Step 2: Don't say, "Do it now." Give the child some freedom by saying, "You don't have to do it right away. Just have one of those contributions finished by Saturday at five o'clock. Thanks."

Step 3: Use a Love and Logic one-liner to neutralize the child's resistance if he or she becomes defiant or refuses. Many parents have found the following one-liner effective: "I love you too much to argue." One-liners reduce the chances that you'll be tempted to lecture, warn, remind, or threaten. Follow the one-liner with: "No problem. I'll take care of it."

Step 4: Hope your child either forgets or refuses. Do not say a word to your child about forgetting. (Additional displays of refusal or defiance can be handled as described in step 3).

Some parents find that their child doesn't act concerned at all. That's because it's not a problem for the child … yet. Chances are that he or she thinks you've forgotten that you'll just do it yourself, or that you aren't going to follow through anyway.

Step 5: Once the deadline has passed, do the contribution or hire someone else to do it. If, or when, your child notices that someone else has taken care of it, say, with empathy, "Remember when you said you didn't want to take care of the lawn, and I said, 'No problem. I'll take care of it'? Well, I had Jimmy next door do it for you."

Step 6: Ask the child how they plan to pay for the service: "Jimmy's coming over in an hour. He'll be asking you how you plan to pay him."

Step 7: If your child gets defiant or argumentative, use the one-liner again—"I love you too much to argue"—and then repeat: "No problem. I'll take care of it."

Pay Jimmy for doing the work, without saying a word to your child. Once again, the child may think they've gotten away with not only not doing their contributions, but also not having to pay someone else to do it. That's all part of the plan.

Step 8: Wait until your next "moment of leverage" and then use empathy followed by a generic consequence. (Your "moment of leverage" is the moment the tables turn. Instead of you wanting your child to follow through on a request, your child now wants something from you.)

When the moment arrives that your child wants something from you, say: "I'm glad to do the things you want when I feel respected and the contributions are done." What's the implied consequence in this statement? The child does not get what they asked you for—whether it's a purchase, a ride, or your permission until restitution is complete. If the child argues, use the same one-liner: "I love you too much to argue."

 If the child continues to refuse, go to alternative step 8 below. (Or, see "How to Ruin the Effectiveness of a Consequence" on p. 298).

Alternate Step 8

When a calm time comes along, tell your child that you paid Jimmy, so now he or she needs to pay you back. You can say, "Oh, by the way, I paid Jimmy for mowing the lawn. How do you plan to pay me back?" If your child continues to refuse, be prepared to take it one step further.

Select one of your child's possessions whose value is equivalent to the cost of the service. Pawn the item, or sell it at the nearest consignment shop, to recoup your money.

Simply say, "This is really unfortunate. To pay myself back, I had to pawn the _____ that I bought you. But here's the pawn ticket with the name of the store, the address, phone number, and the date 'good until' if you want to buy it back." (Pawn or consign only those items that you bought for the child, not items he or she has bought. The most recent possessions work best for both resale value and personal value to the child.)

And should your child still continue to argue with you, what do you say? By now that one-liner is so well memorized it will just roll right off your lips.

Is this akin to a bank asking for collateral to pay back a loan? You bet. Only difference is, instead of you holding the collateral, it's now in the hands of the pawnshop. Does the child have to put in some effort to get their stuff back? Yes. Will it be a hassle for the child to figure out how? Yes. Will the child realize that making the family contributions is a whole lot easier than having to work for the money to buy back their stuff? Yes.

Does your child now have a new frame of reference when you ask him or her to help out? You betcha!

Bottom Line: Teaching personal responsibility is one of our most important jobs as parents. Lessons in learning how to be responsible can be difficult for both the child and the parent. Ask any person who has ever had to repossess something from someone. Better it be you, the parent, than a stranger hired by an impersonal finance company. Taking your child through these steps several times will usually teach them to think that if they don't make their contributions, life gets much harder.

Irritating Children Grow Up to Become Irritating Adults

Ever encountered a sticky mess on the picnic table at a park? Or tripped over something left lying in the middle of the floor? Or found a sour-smelling towel crumpled up in a corner? Presumptuous, arrogant, selfish, egocentric, spoiled, or entitled? Pick one. Children's assumptions that someone else is going to take care of it are irritating. They're also an indication that parents have habitually picked up after their children, effectively training them not to do so for themselves.

You can often tell whether an adult, as a child, was raised with or without expectations of contributing to family life. I (Kristan) was reminded of this one day when I was at the local gym. I noticed a new staff member straightening up the workout area. He was putting dumbbells away, picking up discarded water bottles, and collecting used towels left on the floor.

I introduced myself and told him what a nice job he was doing. Then he said, "It shouldn't be necessary to pick up after others. The mess gym members leave behind … some of these 'adults' are just big kids who were never expected to pick up after themselves while growing up."

I nodded in agreement and he started to say, "My mom …" and then he paused, looked at me, grinned, and said, "You already know my mom, don't you?"

"Well I bet she required you to help around the house."

He nodded again.

"Would you kindly compliment her for me?" I asked with a smile.

As I walked away, I thought to myself: he was one of the lucky ones. Even though Mom's requests around the house probably did not feel lucky for him as a child, the pride in his smile said it all.

Mom's efforts paid off for this young man, for Mom, and for his employer!

When kids are expected to make contributions to family life, they often grow up making positive contributions to the world.

Paybacks Are Heavenly!

What's the payback for *your* contribution of time, persistence, and patience? Contribution "paybacks" provide opportunities for your children to:

- bond with their family,
- learn about cooperation and teamwork,
- develop responsibility,
- practice life skills,
- feel useful, important, and needed,
- gain an appreciation for the kind of work that needs to be done to manage a household, and
- develop respect and gratitude for those who do it.

Will your children presumably grow up to live in a house that has similar tasks to do? Will they learn that there's more than meets the eye to living the good life, besides their own self-centered needs? Will your children eventually be able help you with your household tasks when the tables are turned?

The "ABC" formula for successful contributions applies to life outside the family, too. Using their Ability and Basic training in a spirit of Cooperation (or the spark of a Consequence) will serve your children well, personally and professionally.

 Bottom Line: Irritating children grow up to become irritating adults, unless we teach them to contribute to a world that's bigger than just themselves.

Quick ABC Reference Guide to Contributions

1. Call them "contributions," not "chores."
2. Make a list of all household contributions. Identify which ones are "parent," "child," and "shared" responsibilities.
3. Develop a flexible tracking system of age-appropriate contributions.
4. Stay off the battlefield by giving plenty of choices about which contributions to do, and by when (though there is no choice about whether or not to make contributions).
5. Train, train, and train some more when times are happy, fun, and relatively stress-free.

If it moves from an "I can't" issue to an "I won't" issue:

1. Pick a contribution you know the child doesn't want to do.
2. Give a reasonable deadline: "Just have the living room vacuumed by tomorrow at five o'clock."
3. If the child argues or refuses, choose your favorite Love and Logic one-liner to neutralize the resistance and then say, "No problem. I'll take care of it." Avoid lectures, reminders, or threats.
4. If the child forgets or does not follow through, do the contribution for them after the deadline has passed.
5. Then, let empathy and consequences do the teaching:
   - "Oh no. This is a bummer. I did your vacuuming for you. Now I don't have the energy to take you to your friend's house." (the energy drain consequence, explained in Chapter 2)
   - "This is so sad. I'm glad to do the *things you want* when I feel respected and the contributions are done." (the generic consequence, explained in this chapter)

   If you don't have time to think about what you're going to do, or time to do the task for the child, delay the consequence:
   - "Uh oh. This is a problem. I'm not sure what I'm going to do about it. I need to think about it. I'll get back to you … but in the meantime … don't worry." (the delayed consequence, explained in Chapter 2)

We can inadvertently alter the effectiveness of a consequence without knowing why. For a look at what *not* to do, see "Eight Pitfalls to Avoid When Delivering a Consequence" on p. 298.

CHAPTER 6

Financial Time-Outs

Needs vs. Wants
and Delayed Gratification

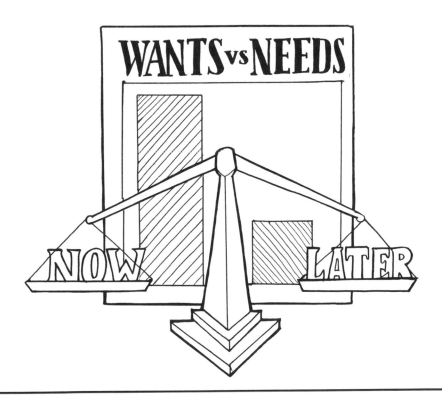

In this chapter, you'll learn how to introduce two concepts to your children that are essential to taking personal responsibility in many aspects of life, not just developing responsible money management skills. You'll discover the difference between needs and wants, and learn how to teach your children delayed gratification.

Waste Not, Want Not?

A mom in the Midwest with two sons, ages five and three, tells a marvelous story about how she seized the opportunity to teach her kids about the difference between needs and wants.

One beautiful summer evening, she decided to picnic downtown at one of the park concerts sponsored by her hometown's business association. After setting up their lawn chairs, she walked over to purchase bottles of water for herself and her kids:

I watched my five-year-old pour his water into his plate and unsuccessfully try to pour it back into his bottle. Needless to say, his bottle of water didn't last him too long, and it was a hot summer night. I knew what was ahead and had already rehearsed it in my head. I was ready!

As he came over with that "I think I could just pass out" look on his face, I asked, "How's it going, Connor?" He immediately began to whine, "Mom, I'm so hot and thirsty and my water is all gone." I responded, "Oh, how sad." He continued, "I was doing an experiment, Mom. I was pouring the water into my plate to see if I could fill it to the top, then I was going to pour it back into the bottle, but when I tried it just spilled all over the grass." I responded, "How frustrating."

Connor continued, "But Mom, now I'm so hot and thirsty and my water is all gone." I calmly said, "I understand." (And now the moment I've been waiting for ...) He said, "So Mom, I need you to buy me a new bottle of water!" To which I responded, "How sad. I spend my money on only one bottle of water for each person in our family." He continued, "But Mom, I'm so thirsty and hot too. And you have more money in your pocket."

At this point I was amazed at how calm I was remaining. I just responded with a quiet, "This is true, and I spend my money on only one bottle of water for each person in our family." He took it up a notch with the added drama of, "But Mom, I'm dying of thirst, I'm going to die, Mom." And with these five words from me, it was over: "Let's pray that doesn't happen." He just stared at me and walked away. It appeared he had so much to think about that he couldn't muster an argument. It was a beautiful thing.

Had Mom given in, Connor would have been ready to try a new water-pouring experiment the next time around, believing that Mom has an unlimited supply of money for bottled water. Her logical consequence, delivered with empathy, gave Connor the opportunity to think about the choice he had made and not depend on Mom to fix things and make him comfortable.

The Power of "I" Statements

Notice how Mom calmly repeated the following statement: "I spend my money on only one bottle of water for each person in our family." That's called a Love and Logic enforceable statement. (For more examples of enforceable statements, see "Love and Logic's Enforceable Statement" on the next page.)

And the epilogue to her story?

I had to laugh when we were at the park the following week. My three-year-old accidentally knocked his water over and quickly picked up the bottle. Connor looked at him and said, "You better put the cap back on that, Danny. Mom's not going to give you another bottle of water if you waste that one!" I felt like someone had handed me a trophy!

This affirmed for Mom that she really had succeeded in helping Connor draw the connection between the choice he made and the consequence of his actions.

When I (Kristan) asked her how she knew she had succeeded, this is what she shared:

Delivering an empathic response to Connor—like "How sad" or "This really stinks"—validated his feelings. It helped him connect his feelings to his actions and then own those feelings. As a mother, using an empathic response reminded me to give the problem back, which in turn just drove home that connection between cause and effect. Finally, and best of all, it offered me a second to take a breath and avoid reacting like I usually do.

So, how does this story relate to teaching kids about money? Kids need to learn how to separate their needs from their wants and how to delay gratification if they are going to learn how to manage their money wisely. Whether it's coins in a pocket or water in a bottle, handing the problem back to them with lots of empathy drives these lessons home. (For more information about teaching kids to set their own limits, see "Needs vs. Wants Starts Early" on p. 159.)

Knowing the difference between our needs and our wants is crucial. If you can't get what you need, you'll never get what you want. If you only get what you want in life, you won't get what you really need.

Love and Logic's Enforceable Statement

Jake was supposed to be earning his spending money for summer camp by cleaning out the garage. When Dad checked up on him half an hour later, Jake was plopped down on his bed, his television still blasting away.

"Jake, how many times do I have to tell you to turn that thing off? If you don't start doing what you're supposed to be doing, I'm going to take that blasted TV out of your room!" As Dad started to leave, he turned back to add: "And I mean it!"

What are the chances that Jake thinks his Dad really means it? Next to none. How many times have we told our children we mean it, but without following through? The "mean it" becomes "meaning-less" each time we say something that we don't enforce or can't follow through on.

Love and Logic has a way with words that allows you to mean what you say and say what you mean (without being mean). It's called the "enforceable statement." It's a way to set limits with your children, financial and otherwise. Rather than tell your child what they should do, you tell your child what you are going to do instead.

Here are a few examples:

> Instead of: "How many times do I have to tell you to turn off that TV?"
> Experiment with: "I'm removing your TV. You can use it again when I no longer have to remind you."

> Instead of: "Behave! What's the matter with you?"
> Experiment with: "You are welcome to shop with me as long as you don't cause a problem."

> Instead of: "Don't talk to me in that tone of voice, young lady!"
> Experiment with: "I charge one dollar per minute to listen to whining."

Knowing the difference between our needs and our wants is crucial. If you can't get what you need, you'll never get what you want. If you only get what you want in life, you won't get what you really need.

Instead of: "I'm not buying you another thing!"

Experiment with: "I buy things for children who show appreciation and take care of what they already have." Or: "When you demand that I buy you things, it tells me you have too much. If you can find a way to earn this, you may have it."

Your children will soon get the point that, when Mom and Dad begin statements with "I"—they *will* and can follow through. Which is better?

"I'm not giving you any more allowance. You've already used it up."

Or: "Oh no … bummer. I give allowance on Saturday."

Enforceable statements tend to place kids in thinking mode, not fighting mode. In the allowance example above, the first statement is more likely to engage the fight-or-flight part of a child's brain, whereas the second response engages the frontal cortex, which is where reasoning takes place. Which mode would you rather deal with?

The power behind every enforceable statement is that it shares control without telling the child what to do. As you begin developing your own enforceable statements, a simple rule of thumb is to begin with "I will" or "I allow." Some parents have also found it effective to use a generic third-party reference to "children" instead of a specific "you" when referring to their child, as shown in one of the examples above, or as in: "I lend money to children who are willing to give up the use of their new toy until they pay me back."

For Jake's dad, things improved as soon as he understood that he could control only himself, and that using an enforceable statement was a way to share control. Either parents share control, or kids will take control.

When we say, "You will …"—we lose control.
When we say, "I will …"—we gain control.

Needs vs. Wants Starts Early

Our Needs Start at Birth

A baby is born with some very important needs, and won't survive if those basic needs aren't met. How do healthy babies let us know when they have a need? They cry and cry and cry. Whether wet, tired, cold, lonely, or hungry, a healthy baby will clearly let us know when things are not right in its world.

From this perspective, one could conclude that babies are born entitled—innocent, but still entitled. They have to be—it's a form of survival. Babies can't verbalize, "Here I am! I need to be held." Yet an up-close and personal experience with a crying baby speaks volumes about their message—"Take care of me ... *now!*"

What happens when we delay fulfilling a baby's need? A baby who will not stop crying is a stressful situation indeed, so we do our best to figure it out as soon as possible. Fortunately, babies are so darn cute that most of us can't help but smile, cuddle, and coo as we look into their beautiful eyes while tenderly embracing their every need.

This is how a cycle of trust and bonding is developed in the first few years of life. The baby has a physical or emotional need; the baby cries; an adult meets the need using eye contact, smiles, and loving touch. When that cycle gets repeated dozens of times over and over again, a bond of trust and love develops.

Naturally, when babies cry about needs, we must meet those needs. We must do whatever we can to help them feel better. In their first two years of life, if we're not sure whether our child is crying about a need or a want, we should always err on the side of nurturing to help them feel better.

Things change for both baby and parents as the second year of life approaches. Developmentally, children grow into a jumbo bundle of both needs and wants.

In their first two years of life, if we're not sure whether our child is crying about a need or a want, we should always err on the side of nurturing to help them feel better.

Wants Kick In at About Age Two

What happens when a two-year-old wants something? The same response. The child cries or whines, only now it might be because they're not getting something they want.

Wise parents start to set limits on these wants as children near their second birthday. Whereas once parents strove to gratify both their infant's needs *and* their wants, *immediately*, things need to change as kids move into their second year of life. Some parents experience trouble at this stage, because they need to shift from meeting all needs and wants, to meeting all needs and *some wants*.

Saying "no" to a want is the source of many a temper tantrum, because it's usually about "I want it and I want it now." That used to work for Mommy and Daddy, but suddenly things are starting to change. When kids cry, pout, or have a hissy fit over a want, they must learn that none of us always gets what we want. The infantile days of immediate gratification are over, in favor of beginning to learn how to delay gratification.

When that time comes, so too comes the need to set limits with children. For example:

> Carrots before cupcakes.
> Practice before mastery.
> Class before recess.
> Earning before spending.

This is where needs and wants and personal gratification intersect with one another. Life requires us to learn how to delay our desires, because we can't have everything we want all at once, all the time. For kids to have happy and responsible lives, we must teach them early that life has its limits—some of which require them to delay their gratification for a time. In short, for children to develop internal limits, they first need their parents to set external ones.

Knowing how to set internal limits—that is, postpone short-term gain for something greater later—affects every aspect of life: health, career, relationships, money, and so forth. It's never too late to start learning to how to set limits with children. Habits formed when they were younger can be changed when we decide to learn how to say "no" effectively.

For children to develop internal limits, they first need their parents to set external ones.

Bottom Line: Wise parents remember that if they don't set limits for their kids early, their kids will have a harder time setting limits for themselves later.

Needs vs. Wants: An Introduction

Kids need lots of experiences figuring out the differences between their needs and their wants. Shopping provides lots of great opportunities:

Krissy: "Can I have this?"
Mom: "You have something just like that at home."
Krissy: "No I don't. This will be more fun."
Mom: (keeps walking)
Krissy: "But Mom, I *need* this one …"
Mom: (looks over her shoulder, smiles, then keeps walking)
Krissy: "Please? Mom? Please? I really, really *want* it."
Mom: (sighs)

Notice how Krissy, age eleven, uses the words *need* and *want* interchangeably. Kids tend to think that they need everything because that's what they're taught through mass media. Everything seems like a need from a child's perspective. Knowing the difference between needs and wants is confusing at times.

EXERCISE 6.1: Needs vs. Wants Balance Sheet

Here's a fun way to introduce the concept of needs versus wants to your children. This process should already be familiar to you and your children if you've completed the exercise about how to introduce contributions to your family (see "Family Contributions Balance Sheet" on p. 106).

To begin, find time, free of distractions, to sit down with each one of your children, individually. Approach this time as special one-on-one time; it should be about fun rather than lectures. Do this exercise separately with each child, because it will vary depending on their age and developmental stage ("needs" will basically be the same for each child, but "wants" change according to age, gender, personality, and temperament).

Step 1: Make a list.

On a computer or with paper and pencil, title the list (substituting the name of your child): "Krissy's Needs and Wants" or "What It Takes to Keep Krissy's Life Going."

Then write down all the things that your child needs, or thinks they need, to live. This is not the time to judge their ideas or be too serious, just let the ideas flow, so the child will get an idea of what you are doing. A typical list might look something like this:

What It Takes to Keep _____'s Life Going

    A place to live

    Food on the table

    Clothing to wear

    Car to go places—school, mall, park, practice

    Toiletries to keep clean

    Books, backpack, and school supplies

    Family vacations, summer camp

    Lessons and equipment for extracurricular activities

    Electronics—computer, TV

    Toys, movies, and games

> Bike, skateboard, scooter
> Snacks, meals at restaurants
> Allowance
> Field-trip money
> Cell phone
> Youth Club dues
> Sports fees

Well, you get the idea, and so will your kids. Let the list flow freely as your child begins to add their ideas. You'll probably find that most of your child's suggestions will relate to fun, friends, and freedom. That's okay. All part of the plan.

This first step is a joint brainstorming effort. This is not the time to dicker over the merits of a particular idea, the difference between wants and needs, or who pays for what. The idea is simply to come up with a list of what you *and your child* think is needed and wanted to keep their life running smoothly.

Step 2: Identify needs vs. wants.

Once you come up with your list, start at the top again, and review each item one at a time. Identify which items are necessities (needs) and which items are conveniences and luxuries (wants). Some parents just mark the needs with checkmarks; all the other items, by default, are wants.

The list will probably begin with a bunch of needs—things you buy that are necessities for your child. Tell your child how proud and happy you are to provide these things.

Step 3: Separate needs from wants.

Create a separate chart, using the same title as before—for example, "Krissy's Needs and Wants." This time, divide the page into two columns, one for needs and one for wants, as shown in the first example on the next page. For older kids, you may want to set up the list using a three-column model, as shown in the second example, to help them understand that there are different kinds of wants. Whichever way you choose, make sure there's a double line between the needs and wants columns. That will come in handy later.

Needs and Wants (for younger children)

Needs	Wants

Needs and Wants (for older children)

Needs *Necessities*	Wants *Conveniences*	Wants *Luxuries*

First, record the items identified as needs (necessities you pay for will rarely be questioned). If your child is old enough, have him or her do the writing. Wise parents do this exercise *with* their children, not *for* them. Then fill in the wants. Involve your children as much as possible in the decision-making process, using the definitions below.

Needs vs. Wants Defined
- Need—a necessity or essential requirement to live.
- Want—a desire, wish, or longing.
  - Convenience—something that makes life easier, faster, better, more efficient, or more fun.
  - Luxury—something wanted because it's nice, enjoyable, or beautiful, or because it brings comfort, satisfaction, or status.

Now go back over the list of wants. For each item, ask your child whether it is a convenience or a luxury—based on the preceding definitions, or based on your own definitions.

Avoid a power struggle if your child gets stuck arguing that he or she "needs" an item versus wanting it. Simply smile, and place a question mark beside that item, setting it aside for the "48-Hour Test" later in this chapter.

Once you've finished, you'll have a list of needs and wants for each child in your family. (For details about how you handle *your* needs and wants, so your children get to see that you don't get everything you want either, see "The Family Budget" on p. 199.)

Invite your child to save this list for future reference, as they may want to add new things.

###

Exercise Summary

Here's a summary of this three-step exercise:

1. Brainstorm all that it takes to keep your child's life going.
2. Identify which are needs and which are wants.
3. Distinguish the needs from the wants in chart form, separated by a double line.

A Need to Notice?

What might your kids notice as you go through this exercise?

Will some kids get the picture that their parents buy them everything they need?

Will other kids get the picture that their parents also buy them many of the things they want?

Will other kids suspect that this exercise is about getting them to pay for more of their wants?

Congratulations! That's the point.

It seems only logical that if you're taking care of all or most of your child's needs, they should start buying some of the things they want. Parents are in a great position to teach their children how to spend, earn, save, and invest wisely as soon as purchases start crossing the double line into the wants category.

How? By giving kids lots of opportunities to buy the things they want rather than waiting in expectation for us to provide it.

How can Krissy's mom use this exercise as a response in the store? It provides the foundation for her to respond to Krissy's pleading with, "Oh bummer, Krissy. I've provided everything you've needed this month, and some of the things you've wanted. It's your turn. Thanks for understanding."

By being given opportunities to practice providing for their own wants, children are being given opportunities to experience the first steps toward financial independence and freedom.

A few parents have reported an even bigger bonus after completing this exercise. Some children will realize that their wants are really gifts from their parents. Not only do some kids become more appreciative of what their parents buy them (the needs), but they also actually become *more willing* to pay for their wants when they see the imbalance. That's because they've been given a new context for understanding the difference.

Bottom Line: Wise parents teach their children the difference between needs and wants so that they'll know the difference as adults.

Crossing the Double Line

Once you've introduced your children to the difference between needs and wants, the next question is: Who's buying? The answer depends on their age and your resources, but here's a simple guideline for starters:

> If it's a need, the parent pays.
> If it's a want, well … that's up for grabs. Lots of options here.

The distinction between needs and wants becomes a good news / bad news scenario for kids. The good news is that their needs are covered. The bad news is that they will have to start paying for some of those wants on their list—that is, *if* we want to give our children plenty of opportunities to practice using money wisely.

Here's how Mom handled delivering the news to Krissy after completing the needs versus wants exercise:

Mom: (pointing to the needs column) "I'll be glad to pay for everything you *need* to keep your life going."

Krissy:	(fidgeting, pointing to the wants column) "But what about these things?"
Mom:	"Well … you'll need to pay for more of the things you want. That's why you have an allowance."
Krissy:	"I don't have the money for all those things."
Mom:	"Then I guess you'll need to find a way."
Krissy:	"How?"
Mom:	"Well … some kids do without. How will that work for you?"
Krissy:	"Bad."
Mom:	"Some kids put those things on their wish list and start saving their allowance. How will that work for you?"
Krissy:	"That takes too long."
Mom:	"Well, other kids earn money with odd jobs. How will that work for you?"
Krissy:	"Maybe … I don't know. That's hard."
Mom:	"Still other kids ask their parents for a loan. How will that work?"
Krissy:	"Well, then I'll have to give up some of my other stuff for collateral. That's no fun."
Mom:	"Some kids put those things on their gift list, and wait to see if they get them on the next birthday or holiday. How will that work?"
Krissy:	"Then I'd have to wait."
Mom:	"I know you've solved problems before … I'm sure if you really want something bad enough, you'll find a way. Let me know if I can help."
Krissy:	(smiling) "You can buy me what I want."
Mom:	(smiling back) "Well … sometimes I will. Other times it will be your turn to buy … if you want it bad enough. But that's up to you."

Notice how Mom used Love and Logic's five-step problem-solving guide in this example. Mom wisely outlined a number of choices about how Krissy could buy the things she wants without Mom's financial help. Notice also how Mom ended the conversation by expressing confidence in her daughter's ability to solve the problem, while still holding her accountable.

Mom also made it clear that, as soon as an item crossed the "double line" into the wants column, there were many options for who does the buying— many of them within Krissy's control. That's the Love and Logic way—control is shared ("I will buy everything you need and some of the things you want") through choices ("You can choose to buy other things that you want with allowance, jobs, and gift money").

Mom wisely outlined a number of choices about how Krissy could buy the things she wants without Mom's financial help.

167

Bottom Line: Wise parents hand many "I want" purchase problems back to their children, to prepare them to handle their "I want" purchase problems as adults.

No Time for Exercise?

You may be thinking that the needs versus wants exercise is too much work:

> "My kid will see right through this."
>
> "My kid won't care."
>
> "My kid thinks all of his 'wants' are 'needs' because all of his friends have that stuff."

No problem. There are other ways to teach the difference between needs and wants. If the easy way—encouragement and education—doesn't work, then perhaps experience will be the better teacher.

Next, we'll look at a sample dialogue between a father and his nine-year-old son over an electronic gadget in the store. This dad hasn't had time to do the needs versus wants exercise, not that his son would even be interested. But he recognized a teaching opportunity when it arrived. He decided to get his son's attention using another approach.

The 48-Hour Test: Good Buy or Good Bye?

"But Dad, I need it. I can't play the game without it. Please … ?!" begged Ethan as he stood holding up the box that contained the next trendy treasure. Dad knew that Ethan had plenty of ways to play his favorite electronic games without another purchase.

Dad:	"Sounds like you think you really need this."
Ethan:	"Yeah. Please please please?"
Dad:	"That's a bummer. Today is not a gift day. But feel free to buy it yourself."
Ethan:	(moans and rolls his eyes)
Dad:	"By the way … can you see your brain when you roll your eyes like that? 'Cause you may need your brain to answer this next question: Do you think you need this, or do you just want it?"
Ethan:	"I want it … No, I mean I *need* it—really, really bad."

At this point, Dad didn't succumb to the temptation to answer with the typical, "You have plenty of toys at home that you never play with." Dad skipped a power struggle in favor of asking Ethan a few questions about the wisdom of his purchasing decision:

Dad: "Do you think that it's a necessity, a convenience, or a luxury?"

Ethan: (sputtering) "Huh? … I don't know."

Dad: "A necessity is something you can't live without, like food. A convenience or luxury item is something you want because it's fun to have."

Ethan: "This is fun!" (fidgeting with the buttons on one of the display models) "It's cool!"

Dad: "Cool?"

Ethan: "Yeah, I could spend hours … me and my friends … playing with it."

Dad: "So, what is it, a need or a want?"

Ethan: "Uh … I don't know."

Dad: "Would you like a fun way to find out?"

Ethan: (stops to look up for a moment) "Sure … I guess …"

Dad: "It's the 48-hour test. If after 48 hours you're alive and well without it, chances are you really don't need it—it's just something you want."

Ethan: "Daaaddd. That's stupid."

Dad: "But don't worry. It will still be available 48 hours from now. You can buy it then—if you have the money to pay for it."

Ethan: (thinking, if I give Dad the answer he's looking for, maybe I can get him to pay for it) "Okay. I guess … I don't need it, but I really want it. And my grades are good, and I do my chores. I don't hit my sister anymore—unless she deserves it. And I call Gramma every Sunday. And I scored two goals in my last soccer game … And I deserve it, right? Now will you buy it for me?"

Dad: "Nice try, son."

The length of this time test can be changed to accommodate your child's age. Some parents of younger children make it a 24-hour test or "the next time we are in the store." It could a 72-hour or even a 1-week test, depending on the age of the child and the item in question. If they survive the waiting period, then the decision to buy or not to buy can be revisited at that time—as *their* want using *their* dime.

Some parents have found success using a combination of time and money. The decision to purchase anything over a certain amount of money is automatically deferred. This provides time to consider if it is still a "want" and still worth the price after waiting. (For example, if an item costs $100, wait two weeks and then see if you still want it.)

One family put this concept into practice using a simple formula that was easy to remember for each child. Anything that was more than the child's total allowance had the potential to be a "cause for pause" with a "wait and see" for the same number of years old as days. (A ten-year-old, for example, would need to wait ten days—or ten hours, or ten "something"—to spend his or her total allowance. Of course, they could earn and save the money in the meantime if they still think they want the item.)

Put It in Writing, Please

Some parents use a variation of this test. One dad of three teenaged daughters grew weary of his heartstrings being pulled when one of them wanted something they "absolutely positively had to have." Using Love and Logic, he simply handed the problem back to them to solve.

He asked them to put in writing all the reasons why they thought it was a "necessity" and then submit it for his consideration. He told them, "I will be happy to pay for anything that you really need, if you have a good reason." This Dad reported that requests for needs were cut in half, and his daughters' purchases for wants increased by one-fourth, using this simple yet effective method.

It Pays to Wait

Whether "in waiting" or "in writing," a "wait to buy" test has several benefits:

- It demonstrates to children that wants are fun to have and to hold, but not a necessity.
- It teaches kids the importance of thinking through a purchase before they make one.
- It gives kids a chance to figure out a plan to pay for what they want.

 Bottom Line: Wise parents use real life experiences to test their children's "needs versus wants" theories.

Mind over Money? Prioritizing Our Wants

Are your children going to want more than they can afford? Will they need some experience in prioritizing their wants? Yes!

Let's revisit the story of Ethan, 48 hours later, to illustrate how his father used real life experience to teach him how to prioritize his wants. Once Ethan realized he couldn't manipulate Dad into buying the electronic gadget, he reluctantly conceded that his desire was truly a want, not a need.

Dad: "So you still want to buy it?"

Ethan: "Yep."

Dad: "Are you saving for anything that's more important than this?"

Ethan: "Nope. This is perfect. I want this."

Dad: "Okay, then. Feel free to find a way to pay for it."

Dad knew something that Ethan had forgotten when he asked, "Are you saving for anything that's more important than this?" Ethan was saving money for his very own baseball glove. Did Dad remind him of this? No.

Dad wants Ethan to learn how to sort out his financial priorities. Having your very own baseball glove is not a necessity, but a convenience. It's Dad's hunch that *if Ethan had thought about it more*, the glove would have taken precedence over adding another piece to his electronic game collection. Dad knows Ethan will learn this lesson best by making mistakes when the price tags are … oh so affordable.

Does Ethan have the choice to return the item (used) if he blows his savings on this gadget? Probably not. It's far more effective for Ethan to discover how to prioritize his wants and delay gratification on his own, as opposed to listening (and not hearing) repeated lectures or reminders. (For a more in-depth look at teaching kids how to prioritizing their wants, see "Five Steps to Wishing Well" on p. 253.)

Bottom Line: Wise parents provide their children lots of opportunities to practice prioritizing their wants. They encourage them to use their mind (and time) over their money before making financial decisions.

Delayed Gratification Games

Ethan's story points out another valuable lesson tied to needs versus wants—learning how to delay gratification. Whenever spending exceeds our income, an opportunity to delay gratification presents itself *if* we do not rescue.

What's more likely to happen to Ethan?

Running out of money?
Running out of things he wants to buy?

Will this be the first and only time he is forced to prioritize his spending desires? Certainly not. (If Ethan thinks 48 hours is a long time to wait, try the experience of waiting 48 years, as is the case for many adults—for example, waiting to have enough money to buy a nice boat, a cabin in the woods, or a dream vacation.)

You are probably getting the sense that, like Ethan, your children need to learn how to delay their gratification more often. No need to feel culpable. It's not helpful to hold ourselves accountable for something we're not sure how to change.

So here is a simple way to begin with your children—play games to illustrate the lesson.

EXERCISE 6.2: The "Now or Later" Game

Start with this "baseline" test. It's similar to adults going to the doctor's office to get a baseline cholesterol test or a baseline mammogram. But instead of a precursory health checkup, it's a "precursory" financial checkup. You want to start by knowing where your kids are on the "gratification continuum," so you'll be able to make adjustments as necessary, and see the progress.

Give your kids a choice: "Would you like to get one dollar this week or two dollars next week?"

While you can use many types of rewards to play the "Now or Later" game, money is an obvious example. Give your kids a choice: "Would you like to get one dollar this week or two dollars next week?" Listen for their answers. Their choices will give you some clues about their current ability to exercise self-control and patience. You want to see if they understand that if they wait, they will get twice the amount next week than if they take the instant one dollar offer.

For older kids, offer more. For example, you may want to offer your tweens or teenagers $10 versus $20. Explain that you know that they'd appreciate some extra spending money, and that you're giving them a bonus as an experiment.

"Experiment? For what?" your teen may ask suspiciously. Just say something like, "I'm just curious to see what you decide. It's your decision. Whatever you decide is fine with me."

Remember that this is just a test. Whichever choice your child makes, accept his or her choice unconditionally. Do not comment on their answer, just make good on your promise by giving them the money. If they take the higher amount, it tells you that there is some work to do to create a better understanding of the value in waiting. If they wait until next week, congratulate them on their self-control and smarts for knowing that by waiting they would double the money.

The promise of money may not work for some kids. That's a possibility for kids who have everything, or kids who are not motivated by money. What is $20 to anyone if they don't need it, want it, or value it? Parents can use other types of rewards, like food or a trip to the park, if they want to use something besides money to "test" their child's ability to delay gratification, or they can play the "Would You Rather?" game described below.

EXERCISE 6.3: The "Would You Rather?" Game

One mother of children aged four, six, and twelve played the "Would You Rather?" game to evaluate her kids' resolve to wait. She gave her children lots of hypothetical situations to consider. For example, she'd ask: "Would you rather have an accent wall painted in your bedroom now, or have your whole bedroom painted next year?" Or, "Would you rather use all of your video time for the week at once, or divide it up over the next couple of days?"

The basic question is: Would you rather have this *now*, or that *later*?

Since these are hypothetical situations, Mom can discuss the pros and cons of her children's decisions without any emotional attachment or without making any critical comments. The very nature of a hypothetical situation makes "right" or "wrong" a moot point.

She invited her youngest child to think of gratification on a time continuum from "this instant" to days, months, or even "when you are seven years old." She drew a line (see below) to help her two younger children, who could point to how close they were to "now" and "later." A calendar can also be used for this purpose.

Instant/Now   *Delayed/Later*

Gratification Continuum

One of the benefits of a baseline test is that you can repeat it at intervals to measure progress. Vary the choices for fun, and move from hypothetical to real decisions.

Here are some more examples:

> "Would you like to go the park for one hour this week, or for two hours next week?"
>
> "Would you like to plan one play date today, or two later in the week?"
>
> "Do you want me to buy you something for a dollar now, or something for three dollars next week?"
>
> "Would you like half your treat now, or the whole treat after dinner?"

 Be sure to follow Love and Logic's guidelines for offering choices (explained in Chapter 2) if you are going to offer your kids "real" versus hypothetical choices. Offer only choices you can live with. You don't want to paint yourself into a corner by offering a choice you don't like, because that's likely the one they'll pick. Over time, their answers will tell you if they are learning the benefits of delaying an instant reward in favor of something bigger or better later.

###

Progress, Not Perfection

Naturally, kids will need plenty of practice learning that there are times when it pays to delay. While they may have learned to delay their gratification around money, they might not be as adept at applying the same principle to other areas of their life. Sometimes older siblings can pioneer the way when younger siblings notice the rewards of waiting.

Here are a few more ways to teach the concept of delayed gratification:

- Don't automatically replace lost items. Have your kids earn them back instead.
- Engage your children in projects that involve planning and delayed rewards, such as planting a garden, saving money for a special gift, training for an athletic event, planning a family outing, developing a hobby, or starting a collection.
- Involve kids in activities that require patience, such as making a pizza instead of ordering out, making gifts instead of buying them, or teaching a younger sibling how to do something.

Delaying gratification is about gaining control over the here and now in order to have more, better, or different choices later. It takes patience, cause-and-effect thinking, and an understanding of time and the future—which only comes through experience. Keep giving them opportunities and use progress, not perfection, as the benchmark.

Bottom Line: Wise parents use everyday opportunities to teach their children how to delay gratification now, so they'll understand its value when they reach adulthood.

PART TWO

Teaching Financial Responsibility

Six Steps to Raising Fiscally Fit Kids

Introduction

If you give a kid a dollar …

He'll want to **spend** it.

If he spends more than he has …

He'll need to **save** it.

If doesn't save it …

He'll need to **borrow** it.

If he borrows it …

He'll need to pay it back.

If he pays it back …

He'll need to **earn** it.

Once he pays it back, and earns more …

He can **invest** it.

When he invests enough …

He can **share** it.

Thus lies the inspiration for the order of chapters in Part Two of *Millionaire Babies*, which cover kid-sized finances and the myriad ways money can be managed—spending, saving, borrowing, earning, investing, and sharing.

Though you can read these chapters in any order and still derive their benefits, spending money is the first thing on the minds of most kids, and sharing it with others is the last.

As in Part One, charts, worksheets, and examples are designed as teaching tools for you and learning tools for your children. The language is deliberately simple so that a parent doesn't have to take the additional step of translating complex financial concepts into kid-friendly language.

Woven throughout the stories and dialogues are Love and Logic's method for instilling the discipline, motivation, and incentives to make teaching money skills a success. At times, you may want to return to sections of Part One to further enhance your understanding of the principles and tools in the context of each new subject.

No matter where you decide to start, starting anywhere is a beginning. Each new day will bring you new opportunities! Take your time and have fun!

If Part One sets the foundation, Part Two is where the fortune lies—because managing money wisely determines much about the quality of our lives.

CHAPTER 7

Spending

Gadgets, Gizmos, and Gigabytes ... Who's Buying?

This chapter is divided into five "option" sections according to *who* is making the purchase: the child alone, you and your child together, no one, you alone, or your child's grandparents. It covers how to handle spending conflicts with overzealous kids, overspending spouses, and overly generous grandparents. Explore, among many other topics, an easy way to set limits, and what to do about unauthorized spending online.

My Parents' Money: MPM Rules!

In my (Kristan's) money seminars, I ask parents what they think their kids know about money. One of my favorites, and one that always gets the audience laughing, is the Dad who complains that the only thing his kids know about money is how to spend *his* money!

There seems to be little problem with spending money, but a big problem with spending money *wisely*. And there's a good reason for that ...

Financial ADHD

Three factors work together to challenge parents in their efforts to teach kids how to spend wisely:

1. Most kids, by nature, are impatient and easily distracted—especially when given the opportunity to shop. This creates a tendency toward impulse buying.
2. Just like adults, kids know that it's satisfying and fun to get what we want, *now!* Delayed gratification is not a strength for most children.
3. Kids don't have any reference point for the time and effort it takes to earn the money necessary to purchase something. They lack not only the experience of earning money, but also the skills and knowledge needed to earn enough money to buy what they beg you for.

When we combine these three factors with the slick lure of child-directed advertising in an overstimulated and consumer-oriented society, we have the perfect storm for developing poor spending habits.

Here's the unfortunate formula for a financial disaster:

An impulsive person ...
wanting to spend for the fun of it ...
without thinking about the time and effort required to earn the money ...
or how they are going to pay for it.

Isn't this a typical profile of many kids in the store? Yes. *But* the eye of the tornado is one of the calmest places to be when teaching our kids how to manage their impulse to spend.

When Opportunity Knocks …

Two of the reasons our children act like "money grows on trees" is that they are not used to making spending and budgeting decisions, nor do they have the objectivity to distinguish between what they need and what they want. Because parents make most of the purchasing decisions for their children, the children lack the experience of doing it themselves.

There are two fundamental questions to ask when thinking about spending money:

> Should I buy?
> If so, what can I afford?

Wise spenders answer both these questions before purchasing something, because they are intertwined. For example, you might have the money, but may not be sure what to buy. Or you might want to buy something, but not have the money.

Notice how the first question concerns becoming a wise consumer and the second question involves becoming a wise money manager. We'll need to teach both sets of skills if our job is to prepare our kids for the financial world of the adult. Both abilities require lots of practice making decisions involving an overwhelming number of good and bad possibilities.

Becoming a wise consumer *and* a wise money manager seems like a lofty and challenging goal for kids. Yet buying things is something we do almost every day, frequently in front of our children. If buying opportunities are abundant, then it follows that teaching opportunities are also abundant.

There are many possibilities when it comes to giving our kids opportunities to practice buying—for example:

1. The child buys it for him- or herself.
2. The parent and the child buy it together.
3. No one buys it.
4. The parent buys it for the child.
5. The grandparent buys it (or another relative, family friend, etc.). That's an easy one: gift a copy of this book to your children's grandparents and godparents, so they can literally get on the same page!

All these options are opportunities to teach our kids how to become wise consumers and money managers—*if* we allow our children to make lots of spending decisions and plenty of mistakes. The first part of the equation is easy: your child wants it. The second part is the challenge: how will he or she pay for it?

This chapter begins with the most effective method—the child buys it. That's because kids learn the most about using money wisely when we allow them to feel the consequences of using it unwisely.

Bottom Line: Wise parents use everyday buying opportunities to prepare their children to become smart consumers and wise spenders.

Kids learn the most about using money wisely when we allow them to feel the consequences of using it unwisely.

Option One: When Kids Buy—Freedom, Not License

The first option for teaching kids how to spend wisely is to give them lots of practice "being the buyer." You'll want to give your kids lots of opportunities to spend, as long as their choices are not harmful. In other words, "You can spend the money anyway you want, as long as it doesn't cause a problem." While you may not agree with many of your children's purchasing choices, agreement and appropriateness are two separate issues.

A basic guideline for teaching kids to spend wisely is to stay out of your child's purchasing decisions, unless it rubs against your values or common sense. In other words, anything that is deemed unsafe, illegal, unhealthy, inappropriate, or immoral, or that in any other way conflicts with your family values, is not acceptable. Remember, you're giving freedom to your kids, not license.

(For more information about how to handle the issues that arise over giving your children opportunities to spend their own money, see "Taking the Slip out of the Spending Slope" on p. 190 and "Unauthorized Spending" on p. 194.)

When the Child Buys: Set Limits, Not Bail

Naturally when kids do the buying, it will be necessary to set monetary limits. The basic lesson is: don't spend more than you have. This is where practice money, or allowance, steps in. We give our children the opportunity to learn from their mistakes when we allow them to buy things with their own money (via allowance, earnings, gifts from grandma, etc.). That is, *if* we don't rescue them.

Your children have already had their first experiences with a spending limit if they are receiving an allowance, along with the unyielding caveat to "make it last."

If not, an allowance offers a good opportunity for their first experience with a spending limit. A true allowance, by definition, *allows* kids the opportunity to practice being the buyer.

Two Types of Spending Limits

To provide kids lots of buying opportunities, parents are faced with how to "distribute the funds." There are two basic approaches—to distribute the funds in one lump sum, or to distribute them based on specific categories.

Some parents like to set specific spending limits for specific purposes. We'll call this the "categorical-limit approach" to spending money. They prefer knowing a little bit more about where and how "their" money is being spent. In this approach, allowance is used as the base amount and expands categorically for a specific purpose as responsibility expands.

Other parents use the lump sum method, because they want to avoid being "nickeled and dimed to death" by their kids. Let's call this the "lump sum–limit approach" to setting spending limits. Allowance is issued as a lump sum and expands as fiscal responsibility expands.

There are several basic differences between the two types of limits. The categorical limit is a methodical, budget type of approach, and the lump sum limit is more of a shotgun approach to spending. The first approach is based on education and planning, and the second is based on laissez-faire, real life experience. The approach you use will depend on the age of your children, their financial know-how, and your family's resources. (For a comparison in chart form, see "Two Approaches to Setting Spending Limits" on p. 187.)

Let's look in greater detail at each approach to setting spending limits.

The Categorical-Limit Approach

Parents who use this approach develop a budget or "spending plan" with preset monetary limits for specific categories. In this way, parent and child determine together what things the parent pays for, and what things the child pays for. With this approach, parent and child work together to set the categories according to the child's want or need. Once the limits have been set, the child is free to spend their allowance on what they categorically want, or not—it's their choice. (For a more detailed look at how to set up spending categories with your children, see "Budget Basics: The Planning Approach" on p. 196.)

One parent, for example, first did the "Needs vs. Wants Balance Sheet" exercise (see p. 162) with her son. Then she told him she would pay for what he "needs" (e.g., books, school supplies, and clothing), and that he would pay for the things he "wants" (e.g., entertainment, recreation, and gifts for friends). How her son divvies up his allowance to buy what he wants in the areas of say, entertainment and recreation, is up to him. When the request for money for

The basic lesson is: don't spend more than you have.

ice hockey skating arises, she'll say, "That's what your recreation allowance is for, dear."

Another family settled on an amount for spending limits "based on need" in a different way. In this family, the teenage son wore the same clothes every day (when allowed to), hung out with his buddies in places that were free, and dined daily at the family refrigerator's door. His older sister, on the other hand, loved shopping for her own clothes, went to coffeehouses with her girlfriends, and had a 24/7 relationship with her cell phone. These parents gave different amounts to their children based on different ages, needs, and lifestyles. Sis got more spending money than her brother, because she was responsible for covering more of her own expenses. Parents who use the categorical-limit approach can be heard saying the following:

"You are welcome to use your allowance for that."
"Feel free to add that category to your budget."
"Feel free to use your money from another allowance category."

The Lump Sum–Limit Approach

Some parents use a broad ground rule for spending. There is no budget or "spending plan," and there are few, if any, categories. This means that if your children want to spend all of their money on clothing and nothing on entertainment, then that's fine. But there will be no more allowance until the next time. Give your kids a set amount for "whatever," minus the expenses you normally cover for them, if this approach appeals to you.

One parent settled on an amount for their tweenage daughter's spending using this approach. Mom averaged a typical two-week period and *subtracted* any fixed items she would continue to pay for (e.g., tuition, health insurance). The amount she gave her daughter was the amount remaining after all these fixed expenses had been covered.

Another parent did just the opposite. She *added up* everything she spent on her sixteen-year-old son, William, for an entire month in order to figure out the lump sum number. She included school supplies, lunches, clothing, and extracurricular activities, and then gave him the full amount, in this case $250, in "discretionary" cash with which to practice. The next month, to further the learning, she taught him how to file an expense report for reimbursement—within limits, of course!

When William complained that his "allowance wasn't enough," she asked him the following question with a smile: "What do you think your boss would say to:

'I want to spend more money, so will you pay me more'?" Should William argue the point, Mom can use a Love and Logic one-liner, such as "Nice try."

Still another parent, one who had "no time for tallies," simply gave each of her children what she thought was a reasonable allowance for their wants, without any categorical references—and said, "Here's what I am willing to pay for each month, and here's what I am willing to give you each week to spend as you wish. Have fun and make it last, because there will be no more money from me until next week."

Parents who use the lump sum spending limit can be heard saying the following:

"Feel free to spend your money for anything you want …
   "as long as it's or not harmful."
   "as long as you have a way to pay for it with your own money."
   "as long as it doesn't cause a problem for anyone else."

* * *

The following chart summarizes the differences between the two approaches:

Two Approaches to Spending Limits

Lump Sum	Categorical
• Uses real life experience. • No spending plan. • Given in a lump sum.	• Uses education and encouragement. • Spending plan. • Specific amounts given by category or need.
If child overspends or spends unwisely, use empathy followed by a consequence. For example: "Oh bummer … I'll be happy to give you your next allowance on Saturday." Or: "How sad. Would you like to know what some other kids have tried when they run out of money?"	

Some parents use both approaches. For example, one mom used the categorical approach for spending weekly allowance, but found that the lump sum approach worked best for special occasions. Whenever the family took a day trip to a theme park or went on vacation, she gave her three children each the same amount of money, in advance of the trip, and said, "Have fun. Make it last." This gave her children experience making all the decisions that go into prioritizing their wants. Mom said, "It brought the pleasure back into a family day together, because a finite limit was set before we ever left home."

Naturally, using the lump sum approach to spending offers more freedom than using specific spending categories. Yet even if you use specific categories, kids still have the freedom to choose how to spend their money within categories, or to exchange money between categories. (For more information about the factors that figure into amounts you give, see "Common Cents Approaches: How Much to Give?" below.)

Latitude is built into whichever type of limit you choose. That's because the outcome is the same, regardless of which type of limit you adopt. Whether categories are used or not, when the money's gone, it's gone.

Notice also that regardless of which type of spending limit you adopt, control is shared by providing kids opportunities to make their own decisions about spending their money. In other words, you share control (you determine the amount and the distribution method), while still giving choices (the child determines how to spend the lump sum or the money within the categories).

 Bottom Line: When parents are clear about their spending limits, then their kids are free to set their own.

Common Cents Approaches: How Much to Give?

There are several factors beyond numerical that should be considered when determining amounts to give. Naturally, the amount of spending money your children receive should be metered out according to age and financial maturity (see Chapter 3, on allowance, for guidelines).

The more responsible the spending decisions, the more responsible the spender. While it might be tempting to give our kids, especially teenagers, more money at the outset, money offers as much opportunity for trouble as anything else … unless we hold them accountable. Let common sense and your fiscal resources be your guide with respect to the actually amount of money you give your children to spend.

If you have an indiscriminate or inexperienced spender, it's probably wise to use the categorical-limit approach, start small, and add spending categories little by little. Start with a base allowance and then add one category at a time. Increase the number of categories and the allowance as fiscal responsibility increases.

If you have a child who is resistant to learning how to budget, or there is no budget, a lump sum might be the better choice. Let real life experience step in. Conversely, if you have a really responsible child, you can give more control and therefore more choices by giving your child all their spending money at once. Either way, parents use the child's allowance as the base amount, and gradually increase the lump sum as fiscal responsibility for covering their own expenses increases.

As your children become more fiscally responsible, you can gradually add more and more allowance using either approach. Once kids get enough practice buying the things they want, you can eventually wean them to buying the things they need—the things *you* used to pay for. In this way, your children gain experience in buying what they both want *and* need ... and learn the differences.

By the way, which kid will be more financially prepared to go off to college—the kid who has had lots of spending experiences, or the kid who is being given spending money for the first time? Wise parents raise their kids to learn how to buy wisely, so that they won't have to "buy out" their kids' financial messes later.

The similarities and differences between the two approaches are summarized in the chart below:

Beyond Numbers: Factors to Figure

Lump Sum–Limit Approach	Categorical–Limit Approach
Use for experienced, responsible spenders, or for a children who are resistant to budgeting.	Use for beginners, inexperienced children, or enthusiastic learners.
Base allowance; no spending plan.	Base allowance, with spending plan categories added as needed.
Amount increases with responsibility.	Amount increases with responsibility.
Covers wants, expands to needs.	Covers wants, expands to needs.

Bottom Line: A gradual approach to spending limits that builds on accountability works best for starters, no matter how old the child.

Taking the Slip out of the Spending Slope

Giving kids freedom to spend their own money seems like a slippery slope indeed. You may be thinking:

> "I can't just stand by and let my kid waste their allowance on something frivolous."
>
> "What if he wants to buy something I don't want him to have?"
>
> "What if she blows her hard-earned money on something I know will break the same day?
>
> "What if he wants to buy something silly, stupid, or risky?"

There are two factors that are bound to come up when giving children some freedom to buy what they want. One is what *we want* for our children—called the "quality assurance" factor. The other is what *our children want*—called the "luxury tax" factor.

As you read through this section, notice the application of Love and Logic's principle of sharing control through thinking and decision-making opportunities. The parent sets the monetary limit based on a standard (shared control), and the child is free to respond in a variety of ways (using choices). For example: they can choose again, do without, save or earn the money, or pay for it themselves.

The Quality Assurance Factor

What to do when your child wants to buy something that doesn't meet your standards for quality or safety? One mom gave her daughter, Hailey, thirteen years old, a spending limit for certain items *she wants Hailey to have and that Hailey wants (and needs)*. For example, Mom and daughter agreed that Hailey needed a new backpack. Mom set a spending limit to cover her own requirements for a backpack—well made and ergonomically correct. It became Hailey's decision to spend her own money if she wanted a higher-quality ("luxury") backpack. Hailey could either accept the limit or spend more of her own money, her choice. (More about the "luxury" scenario later.)

As Mom related this story, she said, "I could see the wheels turning in my daughter's head." When Hailey asked her, "If I find something of equal quality but cheaper, can I keep the difference?" Mom wisely answered, "Yes you can."

This mom knew she was giving her daughter one of her first experiences in becoming a smart consumer. Mom said it worked like a charm, because the incentive to spend wisely was built right into each expense item or category she funded. Mom used this type of spending requirement for back-to-school and seasonal clothing items, "anything with a screen" (video, DVD, computer, TV, cell phone, etc.), and anything else for which value, quality, or a certain standard was important.

She also set a standard for items tied to quality-of-life issues, such as safety and health. For example, Mom required Hailey to spend the entire amount allotted for new shoes, because Mom didn't want Hailey to get cheap shoes in favor of a frilly blouse. Good-quality shoes are important to growing feet.

So Mom set her limit by saying, "I'll put eighty dollars towards your shoes." Then Mom would select a pair to set the standard, and say, "You can buy a pair of shoes like these or better." Of course, if Hailey wanted more expensive shoes of equal or better quality, then she could make up the difference with her own savings or earnings. The choice was Hailey's, as long as Mom approved of the shoes' quality. Anything of inferior quality was met with a smile and an empathic Love and Logic one-liner such as, "Oh, no. Try again."

Parents who set this type of limit can say, "Feel free to spend, as long as it meets my standards for quality and safety."

Seal of Approval

In another example, one parent decided her teenage daughter needed new clothing for school. Mom gave her a seasonal clothing allowance for the beginning of the school year, with one fashion caveat: Mom needed to approve of the outfits. Similar to the "good housekeeping seal of approval," if Mom approved of what her daughter brought home, she could keep the clothes. If Mom didn't approve, she had to return the clothes and the money, or try again.

The spend "no less than the quality standard" requirement should include other items related to your child's physical, emotional, and social safety. These are items whose standard of durability and practicality you care about. Safety devices and equipment for sports, extracurricular, and other related recreational activities, plus items related to your child being near, in, or on wheels, are good examples. Watch for electronic entertainment and techie-type items or services that may lead the child into any kind of "e-trouble" as well.

Parents who set this type of limit can say, "Feel free to spend, as long as it meets my standards for quality and safety." Notice how this falls under the umbrella of spending money "as long as it doesn't cause a problem." The quality assurance factor teaches fiscal responsibility while at the same time sharing control and offering choices.

Quality Assurance Factor: What We Want for Our Children

Parent: Sets a monetary limit based on a standard.
Child: Wants something that costs more than the standard.

    ➡ Child chooses again, or does without.

Parent: Sets a monetary limit based on a standard.
Child: Finds something that meets the standard, but at a cheaper price.

    ➡ Child saves or keeps the difference.

Bottom Line: Wise parents let their children know that purchases related to safety and well-being will be monitored for quality assurance.

The Luxury Tax Factor

The second factor that arises around spending concerns those times when you and your child have different ideas about what to buy. Whereas quality assurance is about what we want for our children, the luxury tax is the opposite: what our children want.

Will there be times, for example, when you want to buy something for your child—like a new bike—but you and your child have a different idea about what to buy? No problem. In comes the luxury tax, by which you set a spending limit and the child can choose to make up the difference between what you are willing to spend and what the child wants. Once you set your limits, your kids are free to make up the difference or not, it's their choice. The luxury tax works especially well if "the difference" is something the child really wants.

Let's say eleven-year-old Hannah wants a new bike. Mom has decided she needs a new bike because she has outgrown her current one. After a little research and commonsense budgeting, Mom sets a spending limit of $150.

Mom and Hannah go to the store to shop for a new bike. Hannah knows ahead of time what Mom is willing to spend. Mom picks out several bikes with her daughter that meet Mom's criteria and that fall within Mom's budget. But Hannah wants the bike with all the latest bells and whistles, costing $200. Bummer for her. That's because she'll need to cough up $50 more for the "luxury" of having what she wants versus having what she needs—a bike that provides a safe mode of transportation.

Here's the math:

Child's choice:	$200
Parent's spending limit:	$150
Luxury tax (the difference):	$50

Hannah is now faced with the real life decision to spring for the difference, or not. She has numerous choices, just like adults do when buying a car. Can she afford the luxury model? Will the luxury model be worth the effort required to pay for the difference? Hannah needs to decide to accept Mom's offer or to earn the difference through jobs, save it through allowance, ask for a loan, wait for Granny's birthday gift, or do a combination package.

The luxury tax is also applicable to kids who want to upgrade their choice based on a brand name. Parents pay for the item, kids pay for the brand. If your budget is $90 for a pair of jeans, and your child wants the ones with the designer's signature-style stitching and logo, the difference is found in the luxury tax. You can say, "You are welcome to make up the difference with your own money. It's your decision."

Notice how the luxury tax teaches personal responsibility while at the same time sharing control and offering choices. Mom gave Hannah choices in several places: Hannah could choose from several "Mom-approved" bikes, *and* she had several ways to buy the one she wanted if she rejected Mom's offer. While it may not feel like it to Hannah, she is in the catbird's seat. She has an opportunity to learn that in real life, every "thing" has its price.

Here's a summary chart:

Luxury Tax Factor: What Our Children Want

Parent: Sets a monetary limit based on a standard.
Child: Wants something that costs more than the standard.

➡ Child pays the difference, chooses again, or does without.

Bottom Line: Wise parents set spending limits to cover their choices and let their children make up the difference for the extra frills.

Unauthorized Spending

What happens when our kids obligate us financially without our permission? If this experience has never happened to you, that's good. Now you can take steps to ensure it never starts. If you're a parent who's had this experience, then you already know the dangers of unauthorized spending.

Spending now comes in flavors other than cash, money order, check, or plastic. Technology has made possible a new form of spending known as "electronic" or "digital" spending. This type of spending is on the rise, and along with it comes trouble— unless we're prepared to avoid becoming our child's indentured "e-servant."

Kids are naturally attracted to all kinds of digital and electronic entertainment. But access has its price. For example, kids can use wireless access to download music and movies on the Internet, join Web-based clubs, send messages to their friends *ad nauseam*, and play video games online, all for fees that can be charged to their parents' credit and debit cards.

You don't need to be your children's pay pals. You just need to know what to do when the charges show up.

With traditional shopping, you normally bring the means (a method to pay for it) before receiving the end (the product or service). But with online purchasing, kids can spend money on things where "charging it" is the *only* choice. No cash accepted. More and more people are buying *on extended time* instead of buying *at the time.*

Electronic and digital shopping wreaks havoc for another reason: "the ends" frequently arrive before "the means." In other words, the service is provided first, then one pays based on usage. That's tough to understand for a "budget-free" mind that knows a lot about fun, but little about fiscal cause and effect.

Does this make a cash allowance obsolete? Or create an accounting nightmare? Not necessarily. Yet parents are finding themselves adding "bill payer or bill collector" to their already long list of parenting chores. You don't need to be your children's pay pals. You just need to know what to do when the charges show up.

How to Keep Online Shopping In-Line

The most effective method to prevent unauthorized spending is to carefully monitor your child's access to any product or service that might obligate you financially. Privilege should always *follow* responsibility.

Numerous opportunities exist for your children to spend money on electronic products and digital forms of entertainment. Products go out-of-date as quickly as the technology. Here are some general rules you can apply:

1. "If you use it, you pay for it."
2. "Let's discuss how you expect to use it, *before* you use it."
3. "If you misuse it, and I know you are misusing it, that would make me an accessory to the problem. That will not work for me, nor will that work for you."
4. "So, let's discuss what you expect my response will be if or when I find you misusing your privileges."
5. "I know that a kid as smart as you can figure out how to manage yourself so that I won't need to be surprised by any unauthorized spending on the computer, your cell phone, or anything else we've discussed."

How would a Love and Logic parent have this discussion with their children? They would develop an understanding with their children that the basic policy is: "Misuse means no use." That's because wise parents know that if you remove access to the object (computer, cell phone, etc.), you automatically remove the problem. (This policy can also be used with lost, stolen, damaged, confiscated, borrowed, or otherwise missing items: if you lose it, you replace it.)

Should that not be practical, for a variety of reasons, children should be accountable for all overages. Again, limit access to the product or cut off the service (the privilege) until the child pays you in full (responsibility).

This policy can be extended to include misuse of private information—yours and your children's. Nearly every website, including kid-friendly ones, is funded by advertising—from banners to pop-ups, from sponsored links to information embedded in the site itself. Some sites even entice kids to enter their personal information to win a prize or to enter a contest. Make your children aware of the importance of their virtual privacy. Once they have an understanding, explain that if your child clicks on ads that contain spyware, then he or she will be responsible for the computer cleanup.

It's never too late to start. A parent can say: "I've decided to set some new rules about the use of your cell phone. I haven't been very clear, so I'm going to change the rules so everyone understands their responsibilities."

Digital Advances of a Different Sort
One mom was completely fed up with—in her words—"digital doling." She tried numerous ways to hold her three sons accountable; none of them worked.

Lectures, warnings, and threats proved ineffective. Then she discovered she could set her limit by saying, "Feel free to [shop online, continue to have a cell phone, etc.] as soon as you give me a cash advance equal to the amount you think you'll spend." In this way, the advance becomes the limit. Any overages are paid in full prior to future use or access.

Restitution and advances can come in other forms besides money. Some kids have forfeited possessions for collateral, performed jobs, or completed their parents' contributions *in advance*, for the privilege of socializing or being digitally or electronically entertained. In this way, control is shared (parents extend the privilege of use on their terms) while still offering choices (the child decides how much they want to spend, and which form of payment they will submit in advance for your consideration).

There are kid-friendly companies that work with parents to provide services that limit or monitor children's spending and types of purchases online. For example, unsavory purchases such as alcohol and cigarettes, and any other objectionable online activities, can be blocked by request. Some companies will e-mail parents with an accounting of their kid's digital transactions tallied in real time. Other companies allow you to prepay or set account limits in advance.

Bottom Line: Wise parents avoid unauthorized spending by setting clear expectations, monitoring accessibility, and then holding their kids accountable for any misuse.

Budget Basics: The Planning Approach

If you choose to set specific limits for spending, then it's time to introduce the power of planning. The principle is simple: knowing that you have a certain amount of money to spend can help prevent excess purchases. The lesson to teach is: don't spend more than you have.

Like many other experiences in life, your children can learn how to spend money the easy way (through education, encouragement, and practice) or the hard way (from mistakes through real life experience). Which way they choose relates to their age and temperament, and their financial know-how.

Let's refer to the easy way as the "planning approach" to spending, and to the harder way as the "no-planning approach." We'll begin by putting a positive spin on the classic planning method known as budgeting.

A New Name for an Old Game

Budgeting is about as popular as "eat your peas" with most people: but budgets have gotten a bad rap. There are more benefits to budgets than meet the eye. Besides, if you think budgeting is hard, try bankruptcy.

So for kids' sake, let's rename the budget. Let's call it a "spending plan" instead. Sounds more interesting and fun. That way we can drop our budget baggage and start fresh, because quite frankly, who *wants* to budget? Besides, of all the things we can do with money—earn it, share it, save it, invest it, lose it, or loan it—spending is clearly the most fun!

So, from now on, think "spending plan." A spending plan is nothing more than a way to gain control over our money so that we'll have more choices. Love and Logic in a nutshell! (For a fun way to introduce the concept of budgeting to your children, see "The Family Budget" on p. 199.)

Categorical Spending

You can introduce the concept of budgeting at any age by giving your children specific amounts of money for specific categories. Most allowance is spent on discretionary wants, because parents buy their children what they need. Budgets can begin to include more of your children's needs and wants as they become more experienced and responsible. Start with a specified amount for a single category—for example, school lunches—if you are just beginning the process.

Let's say Gavin is currently receiving an allowance of $10 per week. School lunches can now be included *as part of* his $10 allowance, or $3 per day can be added to his allowance to cover the cost of his school lunches. (Notice another teaching opportunity here: if school lunches cost $3, but Gavin brown-bags instead, he'll still receive the $3. But if he fixes his own lunch, he can make his lunch for free at home or "buy" his lunch for $1.25 from you, and use the difference for his wants.)

Give kids lots of practice with one spending category before expanding. Later you can add clothing, entertainment, recreation, and gas allowances. As monetary responsibility increases, so does monetary allowance.

The "Needs vs. Wants Balance Sheet" exercise (see p. 162) is one way to help you and your child decide where to begin. Setting up the spending categories is another one of those fiscal activities that you should do *with* your kids, not *for* them. This needs to be a joint, cooperative effort. (If your child is not interested, no problem. See "Allowance Blues" on p. 206 for details about how to handle your child's decision to take the "no-planning approach" to spending.)

Here's a sample list of spending categories that progress through some basic ages and stages:

Sample Spending Categories

Snacks	Clothes
Toys	Communication products and
Games	services (cell phone, computer, etc.)
Gizmos and gadgets	Meals
Entertainment (movies, concerts, etc.)	Vacation fun money
Recreation	Cars (gasoline, maintenance, insurance)

Miscellaneous (for the unexpected)

Notice the last line—the "miscellaneous" line. No matter the age or categories, a miscellaneous spot comes in handy for life's "unexpected" expenditures. For very young children, it's all basically "miscellaneous" anyway!

Wise parents keep the process simple. Some parents just make a list of everything that their kids spend money on, organize and name the categories, and expand the categories and the spending money as their lifestyle and their financial experience expands.

Other parents choose to set up some of the first categories for things that are transitional in nature. Things that are trendy, that the kids will outgrow, and disposables offer excellent opportunities for practice with buying and making mistakes when the price tags are … oh so affordable.

Once the concept of spending categories has been set up, you're ready for the next step—combining the cash with the categories for your child's first lesson in supply and demand.

 Bottom Line: Fiscal responsibility begins with financial planning.

The Family Budget

Our kids frequently witness us spending money in everyday places, such as at stores and restaurants, including online vendors. However, they rarely see us pay the bills. They'll see us *sign* when we buy, but not necessarily *sigh* when we pay.

That's a piece of the puzzle that needs to change if we're going to help our children make the financial connection between what comes in (income) and what goes out (expenses). In order to get an accurate picture of the consequences of spending at the front end, kids need to see the back end—paying the bills.

If kids *do* witness us paying bills, it's sometimes accompanied by a shift in our mood and mumbles of "we have to cut back" and "no more …"

EXERCISE 7.1: The "Money Merry Go 'Round" Game

Here's a budgeting exercise parents can do with their children. It's easy, fun, and an eye-opener for everyone. This exercise teaches the relationship between income and expenses by using the real life example of your family budget.

There are two things you'll need in order to play this game:

1. Play money (use a board game's supply, or purchase it from a toy store; try to find a supply of both bills and coins)
2. All the household bills, organized for the month

Bills can be organized in many ways. Some families arrange and file them chronologically by due date. Other families use a simple foursquare method. The four squares represent the four weeks in a month. Bills are listed in the quadrant they are due. Months with five weeks are "bonus" months, with potential for bonus money. Either method provides a visual picture for kids to see that the bills are a constant and are due at various times throughout the month.

Organizing bills is also a logical opportunity for prioritizing them. It's not uncommon, for example, to have multiple bills due on the same day of the month. Some bills naturally need to be paid before others. This is a good time to introduce the difference between fixed expenses and discretionary expenses.

Basically, fixed expenses are for our needs; discretionary expenses are for our wants. Fixed expenses are a constant and usually don't change much, whereas discretionary expenses are more elective and tend to change with the times.

For example, mortgage or rent is a fixed and necessary expense; allowance is a discretionary, optional expense.

When you have a pile of play money and an organized pile of bills, you're ready to play the "Money Merry Go 'Round" game, which has three steps:

Step 1: Count your income.
Step 2: Pay the bills.
Step 3: Balance the budget.

Step 1: Count your income.

Take the amount of your monthly income and count it out using play money, or ask your kids to count it out for you (if you think that your children shouldn't know how much money you make, you can substitute a hypothetical amount and still teach the lesson).

If you begin with your gross pay, invite your children to make the deductions as posted on the paychecks. (If your children have been making "savings" and "sharing" deductions on their allowance statements, then your own savings deductions, such as for a 401K investment, and your own sharing deductions, for taxes and social security, should begin to make real life sense to them.) Naturally, if you're a dual-income household, combine your earnings into one pile of money. In either case, you now have a corresponding pile of play money that reflects what "comes in"—your income.

Step 2: Pay the bills.

Next, start "paying" the bills, one at a time, by deducting the amount of each bill from the income pile. It's effective to place the play money on top of each bill, so that it provides a visual picture of how much things cost. For example, the mortgage or rent will most likely reflect the biggest pile of money for many families.

Pay the bills in the order that you normally pay them. This illustrates the need to prioritize the more important bills first, should expenses exceed income. Don't forget to include your children's allowance as one of your "bills." Your kids will see that lots of other fixed expenses need to be paid before allowance is issued.

Involve your children in the process, age-appropriately, as much as possible. For example, have *them* count out the play money to pay each bill. Invite them to use a highlighter to mark what each bill is for, its amount, and when it's due.

Ask your children to look for any late fees and share with you how much penalties cost (a great conversation starter about the nuances of financial fine print). Discuss credit card fees and the real cost of not paying bills on time.

If you write checks to pay bills, teach your kids, if they're old enough, the procedure for writing a check. If you pay bills online, teach them how you do it (using common sense: keep passwords, bank account numbers, and money card numbers private).

Once the bills have been paid, show your kids how you keep a record of amounts, methods, and dates. Most people just make a record right on the bill or check stub. The point is to take your kids all the way through the process, from receipt of a bill to payment of that bill.

As one family was doing this activity, Dad heard his son ask, "Who's Bob?" Dad answered, "He's the guy who picks up our trash every week." With a look of stunned disbelief, his son responded, "We *pay someone* to pick up our garbage?!" Dad could see the lights go on in his son's eyes.

Just think … eventually, your children will be able to help you pay the real bills, and they'll be gaining the practice they need for paying their own bills down the road.

Step 3: Balance the budget.

When you've finished paying the bills, see if your budget is balanced, meaning subtract your expenses from your income to see what's left.

If your family has more money going out than coming in, you've gone over budget, and must either increase the income or decrease the expenses. If your family's income and expenses basically even out, or better yet, if you've come in under budget with money left over, congratulations!

###

Have fun with this game. Keep the process simple and repeat it as often as necessary to illustrate the relationship between income and expenses. Kids who are interested can adapt this game to balance their own "budget." (For ideas about helping kids establish their own budget, see "Budgeting: Your Kids' First Lesson in Supply and Demand" on the next page.)

Bottom Line: Wise parents teach their kids the relationship between income and expenses by showing them the real life relationship between spending and bill paying.

Budgeting: Your Kids' First Lesson in Supply and Demand

Help your kids set up a spending plan whereby instead of you saying "no" to them, they learn how to say "no" to themselves.

Want an easier way to say "no" when your children's wants are bigger than their wallets? Help your kids set up a spending plan whereby instead of you saying "no" to them, they learn how to say "no" to themselves.

Here's how one parent introduced the budget idea to his four children, aged five to seventeen. He sat the kids down, allowance envelopes in hand, and said, "Remember the family budget game we played? Well you can do the same thing with your money and set up your very own budget."

Dad continued: "A budget is way to keep track of your spending. Some kids keep track of their money daily or weekly, while others do it once a month. Some kids jot down every penny they spend, while others just eyeball their expenses with an estimate or guess."

He then handed each of them a blank allowance statement that looked like this:

Allowance Statement

Front of Allowance Statement

Date: _____

Name: _____

Allowance amount: _____

Other income: _____

Total income: _____

Expenses: _____
[see back for details]

Total expenses: _____

Income minus expenses: _____

Grand total: _____

Spending portion: _____
[from "income minus expenses"]

Savings portion: _____

Sharing portion: _____

Final amount after deductions: _____

Back of Allowance Statement

Spending amount total: _____

My Spending Plan

[list expense categories]

Toys: $ _____

Snacks/food: $ _____

Entertainment: $ _____

Electronics: $ _____

Recreation: $ _____

Clothes: $ _____

Cell phone: $ _____

Miscellaneous stuff: $ _____

(The allowance statement was first introduced in Chapter 3; the back of the statement can now be added to introduce budgeting concepts.)

Budget or Fudge It?

They each filled out the front of their statement on their own, as Dad continued: "Notice the back of your statement. If you're interested, you can keep track of exactly how you spend your money by writing it down on the back of the statement. If you don't like that idea, some kids label separate envelopes for each category they've chosen— for example, an envelope for lunch money, an envelope for entertainment expenses, and so forth. You just write down how you spent your money on the outside of each envelope, insert the receipts, and tally up the expenses at the end of the week. Other kids decide to lump the receipts all together and stuff them into their allowance envelope and see what happens.

"If you don't want to use an envelope system, that's fine. Some kids who like computers use a financial planning software program with a spreadsheet to keep track of their expenses; others just jot down their expenses in a small ledger notebook with pockets for storing receipts.

"Most kids find that it works best if they keep all their money records in one place. But whichever way you choose, it's up to you. I'm sure with a little practice, you'll each find a way that works for you.

"By the way, if you do decide to keep a record of how you spent your money, it will be easier to find answers to the following questions:

- Where did my money come from? (income)
- Where did it go? (expenses)
- Did I use it the way that I wanted to? (adjustments)

"Some kids keep their allowance statements from week to week to help them understand where their money goes. That way they can make adjustments or changes if they don't like the way things turned out. If you decide not to fill out the back of your statement, or not to keep track of your receipts, that's fine too."

Then he asked his kids to fill in his unfinished sentence: "So kids," he chirped, "when the money's gone …"—and in unison they answered, "It's gone."

With that said, Dad handed his children their allowance envelopes, thinking secretly to himself: "Won't it be fun to see what happens?" He had an inkling that his teenage son, Adam, seventeen, wanted no part of recordkeeping; his attitude was just "give me the money." His tweenage daughter, Lindsay, twelve, who loved anything having to do with the computers, would probably set up her allowance on a spreadsheet in no time flat. And his middle child, Piper, eight, and his youngest child, Kyle, five, might really get into the fun of the learning process.

But at this point, it was all an experiment.

Go Figure

Once you've given your children some ideas about the purpose and how-to's of recordkeeping, you have an educational foundation on which to build. Opportunity is the only thing that needs to be added.

Now, when your children come to you for more money because "I spent it all already," you'll have a conversational reference point. For example, you can boost their understanding by asking, "Where did your money go?" or "How did you spend your money this week?" Or you can say, with a smile, "Bummer. What happened?" You'll probably get an "I don't know" coupled with a blank look (and a blank record).

Here's how this dad responded to Piper, his eight-year-old daughter:

Piper: "Dad, I spent all my money and I need some for the movies today!"
Dad: "What happened?"
Piper: "I don't know. I thought I had enough … but there's nothing left."

*N*ow, when your children come to you for more money because "I spent it all already," you'll have a conversational reference point.

Dad: "Double bummer. Out of money and don't know how it happened? What do you think you're going to do?"

Piper: (shrugging her shoulders) "I don't knowww. Borrow it? … I promise to pay you back …"

Dad: "Let's look at your allowance statement together."

Ever heard of the expression "a picture speaks louder than a thousand words"? Let the unfilled spaces "speak volumes" to the child if the back of the allowance statement is blank. At this point, Dad can help Piper connect the dots between her blank look and her blank spending statement. How?

Dad can use Love and Logic's five-step method for handing the problem back to his daughter. Guess what one of his suggestions is? "Some kids make sure their budget includes a movie!"

Other suggestions include:

"Other kids add up all the things they bought. These are things that they really didn't need. Then they stop buying those things, so that they'll have extra money for what they want."

"Still other kids, if they can't find a movie they want to see, set that money aside for a time when they want to watch more than one movie—perhaps during the winter when they can't go to the movies with their friends because of the weather."

Dad also remembered the fourth step in this method, so he asked Piper, "How will that work for you?" between each idea, in order to generate cause-and-effect thinking. And then, following the fifth step, Dad's last words were: "I know you have solved problems before. I bet you can figure this one out too!"

Notice how Dad's approach to giving his children an allowance follows Love and Logic's principles of shared control through giving choices. (For more details about how to use this Love and Logic method, see "Five Steps for Guiding Kids to Own and Solve Their Problems" on p. 55.)

What if your child runs out of money, but still doesn't want help to figure it out? No problem. Let's use Adam, Dad's seventeen-year-old son, as the next example.

Bottom Line: Wise parents make suggestions to their children, but leave the final decision on developing their own spending plans and recordkeeping methods up to them.

Allowance Blues: The No-Planning Approach

What happens when our kids blow through their allowance before "payday" and then breeze in with a request for more? Well, that's exactly what happened to Adam.

Adam wanted to do it his own way. "I can handle it. Don't worry," he said when Dad presented the option to budget or not. Looks like it's the perfect time for the benefits of real life experience to do the teaching:

Adam: "Dad, I need some more allowance this week."

Dad: "Bummer. What do you think you can do?"

Adam: "I'm doing it."

Dad: "Huh?"

Adam: (grinning) "I'm asking you for more."

Dad: "I'm glad to give you your next allowance … on Saturday."

Adam: "But Daaaddd. I need it now. I'm going out to eat with my friends in a few minutes."

Dad: (smiles sincerely)

Adam: "Daaaddd. Please?"

Dad: (still smiling) "Would you like to hear what other kids have done when they're in a financial jam?"

Adam: (nods reluctantly)

Dad: "Some kids earn the shortfall. I've seen you do that before when you needed more money."

Adam: "That's lame. Matt is coming in a few minutes to pick me up!"

Dad: "I know. And you'll get more allowance on Saturday."

Adam: "That sucks!"

Dad: "I know. And you'll get more allowance on Saturday."

Adam: (stares hard at Dad for a moment, then walks away in a huff, then turns back to argue some more) "Matt's parents would just give him the money. He doesn't have to earn any money in his house. His dad is nice!"

Dad: "I know. How do you think my boss would feel if I acted this way? Do you think he might feel like paying me more, or paying me less? Do your best to resolve this, Adam. I have confidence you'll be able to figure something out."

Fast-forward, ten days later:

Dad: "Adam, are you going out to eat tonight with your friends?"

Adam: (with a puzzled look, like Dad's inquiry came from the nineteenth century) "Are you serious? Going out to eat is too expensive. I'll just download dinner at home and meet them later."

Can you just picture the grin on this father's face?

Real life experience affords parents a wonderful opportunity to teach their children to spend within their means. Notice how Dad did not get sucked into the "whys" and "wherefores" of Adam's request, nor did he resort to lectures about recordkeeping and budgeting. Remember, the delivery of allowance comes with that special tagline: "Make it last." Giving our kids an allowance to practice spending works well, as long as we don't bail them out by giving them more money when they run out, or resort to buying things for them.

To Advance or Not to Advance?

Please, Mom, I won't ask you for my allowance for another month! I promise! Just this one time, please?

One mom thought she'd made a big mistake by advancing her daughter two weeks' allowance for a purse and shoes because they were "on sale for one week only." Mom tried to remind thirteen-year-old Olivia that, in relationship to her resources, she didn't have the money, but Olivia was a sucker for bargains even if she didn't need another pair of shoes. Unfortunately, that didn't work. Olivia bought the purse and shoes on impulse anyway. By the second week, her daughter was griping about not getting her allowance for the week, because now she'd found a shirt "that matched perfectly."

Not to worry. Mom soon realized that another opportunity always comes along, and that the "no reminders, no rescue" policy will probably be Olivia's best teacher. Her daughter was learning the hard way that when we choose the no-planning approach to spending, success is not as predictable.

Discounts That Don't Count

Wise consumers learn that manufactures don't have sales or issue coupons because they care about your budget or want you to save money. They're only useful when they save you money on what you're already planning to buy. "Buy one, get one free," 50% off, and other discounts are irrelevant if it's not what you really need. Research reveals that people who use coupons actually spend more money rather than saving money, because they buy more than what they need or will use. The antidote: make a list and stick to it unless money can be saved for something you really need or want.

The Good in a Financial Fiasco

Some kids are notorious money moochers. Even when our kids try to wheedle and whine their way into our pockets, we need to be sure our wallets and purses stay closed. Nothing will more quickly undermine our efforts to teach basic money management skills than bailing our kids out from under a financial bind.

Kids need to learn to deal with the unexpected so that they acquire the skill of managing risks.

Kids need to learn to deal with the unexpected so that they acquire the skill of managing risks. Pain and misfortune are a part of the human experience, and can teach us about limitations and the fact that our decisions can have negative outcomes. Far better that this happens when the stakes are low and when parents are still around to provide guidance and understanding.

The authors of Love and Logic believe that kids need the opportunity to fail so that they can develop the wisdom to succeed. How many of us have learned more from our mistakes than from our successes? Most of us remember the pain of our mistakes much more than the joy of our successes.

If you have advanced your children money before, no need to worry. The "make it last" lesson is still at your fingertips, if you dole out a heavy dose of empathy before delivering the "no bail" consequence. If we don't teach our kids when they're young, they'll be forced to learn when they're older, with much more serious consequences.

To avoid such misery, wise parents teach their kids what to do whenever their spending exceeds their income. Could Adam and Olivia use a little lesson in delayed gratification? Sure. But Adam wants to learn his own way. Just because we give our kids an allowance doesn't mean they'll know how to make it last.

Practice takes experience, and learning from experience takes patience.

Bottom Line: If you've introduced the idea of a spending plan to your children and they keep falling short before allowance time, hang in there. Resist the temptation to preach and let real life experience be the teacher.

Option Two: Test Before You Invest— When Parent and Child Share the Cost

The second way to teach wise spending habits to children is to share costs with them through a "joint custody" arrangement. This approach helps your children separate what they *think* they *need*, from what they *really want*.

Ever have the experience of being talked into paying for lessons and buying all the equipment, only to find two weeks later your child is completely disinterested?

Eric: "Please, please, please … all my friends are taking karate lessons."
Parent: "Are you sure you want to do this?"
Eric: "Yeah!"

Just last week it was ice hockey, and several lessons and hundreds of dollars later Eric tells you he hates being cold, and oh, and by the way, he prefers in-line skates to ice skates … sound familiar?

Last week's passion is next week's problem. A child's promise is well intended—at the time it's made. However, today's thrill can be tomorrow's tedium. This is natural in the development process for all children. They seek to explore, examine, and try all kinds of things before settling on their hobbies, interests, and passions.

Our job as parents is to create the "pause" between "please, please, please" and the purchase. Children won't know what they like until they try it. This is perfectly normal. Before making an expensive commitment, parents should look for opportunities to encourage their children "to try before they buy."

Testing 1, 2, 3

A cost-sharing arrangement provides financial protection for the parent while at the same time offering financial support for the child. In other words, this is a good option for times when you and your child want the same thing, but you need to "test" their commitment first.

Here are some examples of cost-sharing possibilities:

> Parents pay for the toy; kids pay for the accessories.
> Parents pay for the lessons; kids pay for equipment, uniforms, registration fees, and the like.
> Parents pay for the cell phone; kids pay for its usage.

Notice how control is shared, because the child can choose to earn, pay, or save his or her share. (You might question whether this is their choice, or yours, as a way to spend time, if they choose to do none of the above.)

Notice also how this option teaches a variety of money skills: from using petty cash to saving to paying a bill. Here are some ways children can come up with their portion to correspond with the examples above:

1. The child uses their allowance to pay for the accessories they want.
2. The child saves their money until they can purchase the equipment; then the lessons can begin.
3. The child pays for their cell phone usage when the bill arrives.

With a cost-sharing arrangement, kids will need to be able to come up with their share. Some cost-sharing arrangements use matching funds (e.g., a dollar for a dollar), or some other arrangement—for example, an 80/20 split—whatever seems appropriate for the product or service, and for your child's age and financial experience.

Establish an agreement in advance about who pays for what and how much. As with any good contract, the details of the final agreement should be in writing and signed. (More about matching funds and written contacts in Chapter 9.)

 Bottom Line: Wise parents remember that the best way to teach the responsibility of sharing costs is through sharing control and offering choices.

Option Three: When No One Buys It

 Part of learning how to spend wisely is knowing when *not to spend*. Are there times when "no" means "no"? Absolutely. When your child wants to buy something that's inappropriate for their age or too expensive, or something that conflicts with your family values—then "no" is the best answer. (What if you and your parenting partner disagree about what to buy your children? See "When One Says 'No' and the Other Says 'Yes'" on p. 213.)

The Age-Appropriate "No"

"No" is the only answer for an item of interest that's not age-appropriate. Common sense should prevail with purchases of anything unsafe, illegal, immoral, or ethically unfit for children.

Kids frequently try to push this limit because it's an age-old issue, literally. Most kids just want to fit in. And younger kids want to be more like older kids. Is a PG-13 movie suitable for an eleven-year-old? This is clearly the time to be the parent and not your child's friend. Friends and peers would say "yeah sure"; wise parents say "no."

The ubiquity of technology and consumerism has accelerated access to influences that may be inappropriate for kids. These influences—whether the Internet, peers, or electronic and digital media—have made it even more important to set reasonable limits. The shortest distance between you and your child needs to be the line you draw for anything that's inappropriate.

A simple "no" should suffice if affordability is an issue. If the item is clearly out of the family's financial ability, it's a good time to introduce "The Family Budget" (see p. 199). A budget is a time-tested method for everyone to learn how to earn and save in one area so that they can spend in another.

Bottom Line: Wise parents know when to say "no" based on age-appropriateness and affordability.

The Family Values "No"

Some spending decisions are not as clear-cut because they pertain to our personal values. (If you want to know what people *truly* value, just notice where they spend their money.)

It's not uncommon for family values and purchasing decisions to collide with each other right in the middle of aisle 5 in the store. Every parent knows the drill:

> "Cool! I want that!" quickly followed by, "But everyone else has one."
> "O, wow! I need this!" quickly followed by, "But Jackson's mom lets him …"

You make the substitutions: "But everyone else …"

> "watches it"
> "eats it"
> "does it"
> "plays with it"
> "has one"

What does Love and Logic say? Despite the child's cajoling, begging, nagging, or surprising last-minute promise to do chores, wise parents neutralize the

If you want to know what people truly value, just notice where they spend their money.

news with a simple, repetitive, empathic one-liner: "Nice try," "Probably so," or "I know." (Or, some parents live by the rule that if a child demands an immediate answer, the answer will always be "no.")

It's important to have many "value-able" conversations with your children about how you think and feel—for example, about movies containing foul language and violence, or non-nutritious snacks. In fact, every one of your child's "wants" can be an opportunity for you to share your family values about why or why not to buy:

Nick: "Can I have these?" (holding up a toy weapon and an R-rated DVD)
Mom: (with a smile in her voice) "What do you think my answer is?"
Nick: (sheepishly batting his eyes) "Yes … ?"
Mom: "We've talked many times before about how weapons hurt others."
Nick: "But I won't hurt anybody … I promise."
Mom: "I love you too much to argue."

Saying "no" to your children gives you a chance to share one more example of what you value, including loving them enough to set limits.

Kids, of course, will work very hard at trying to convince us otherwise. Mom could also try the following responses with Nick:

"Who's been making all the choices around here?"
"You can buy anything you want as soon as you are eighteen and financially independent."
"We've talked about this many times before, and you know my decision."

Dollars with Discretion

Parents frequently make discretionary purchases in front of their children. How we spend our discretionary dollars reflects what we value. The expression "put your money where your mouth is" is a good one to keep in mind as we guide our children toward a purchase with "good values."

Courage is a muscle you can exercise when your kids are begging you to buy something. Saying "no" to your children gives you a chance to share one more example of what you value, including loving them enough to set limits. The spending decisions you make, and the ones you don't allow your children to make, will be their model.

What you don't spend your money on is as powerful a lesson as what you do spend money on. Whenever your child lobbies for buying "whatever," be a parent who holds to your principles instead of a politician who waves with the crowd.

 Bottom Line: Wise parents know that one of the inherent benefits of saying "no" lies in its ability to pass on their family values.

When One Says "No" and the Other Says "Yes"

Immediately after eating lunch, a young child whined because he wanted a snack from the vending machine at the airport. Grandpa said, "No, you've just eaten lunch."

So the child went to Grandma and asked her. "Sure, honey," said Grandma, glaring at Grandpa, calling him a "cheapskate" and commanding him to buy her poor little grandson "whatever he wants."

Grandpa followed her orders and off to the vending machine they went. As he and his grandson returned to where Grandma was sitting, their facial expressions told the tale. Grandpa, arms folded across his chest defensively, looked resentful. And the boy? He looked like the cat that swallowed the canary—all smiles and happy again … at least temporarily.

This little boy got what he wanted, but not what he needed. What is missing will turn out to be far more costly than a vending machine snack if this dynamic gets played out repeatedly.

What happens when one parent undermines the other? The child gets to play the divide-and-conquer game, with glee.

What to do instead? Agree that the child needs to get a "yes" from both of you. This gives you time to discuss the matter between yourselves, if needed, so you can deliver a joint decision when ready. That way, a child can't *successfully* play one parent against another, or manipulate the truth.

For example:

Ryan: "Mom said I could buy this movie."
Dad: "She did? Well let's check that out with her."
Ryan: "But she's not here, so can you buy it anyway?"
Dad: "Nice try."

This guideline works like a charm with your parenting partner once you have a solid agreement in place to decide on these types of purchases jointly. The time it takes to make a joint decision provides the "pause with a cause" between impulse and purchase.

Plus it keeps parenting partners from buying something for their child that the other doesn't approve of, and then getting "in trouble" with each other after the fact.

This little boy got what he wanted, but not what he needed.

> If your partner disagrees and one of you continues to buy despite the other one's consideration and caution, your child will have two different role models to choose from—one who makes wise spending decisions, and one who doesn't.

Bottom Line: Wise parents remain united on the "what to buy for their children" front.

Option Four: Parent Purchases

While the parent-purchase option might seem like a contradiction to previous recommendations for teaching children how to spend wisely, it's not—when we remember that kids learn a lot from our example.

Spending money on our children is a common occurrence, because we're responsible for their basic needs, such as food, clothing, shelter, and education. Paying for the things our children need is a fundamental and basic part of our job as parents.

The next level up is what parents pay for because they want their children to have it, experience it, or learn from it. The decision to spend money for "the extras," or what our children want, is more challenging.

A decision about buying our children's "wants" depends on many factors. Some of those factors relate to what we show our children through modeling. Other factors relate to what we tell them. (For a closer look at the factors that play into the purchases we make for our children, see "What We Tell Our Children" on p. 219.)

There are three questions to keep in mind when you are the one who wants to spend:

- Does it have a heart?
- Will it buy happiness?
- Is it really worth it?

Does It Have a Heart?

Most parents have experienced being asked, begged, or even demanded by their children to buy something for them in the store. Does this mean that parents shouldn't buy their children some of the things they want? Sometimes "yes," sometimes "no," and sometimes "maybe." If it's age-appropriate, and fits your family values, then that's fine … sometimes.

Every year, parents and grandparents spend money for gifts on their children's birthdays, holidays, and other special occasions. Be aware of the temptation to purchase what our children want instead of purchasing what you want them to have. Gifts offer a great opportunity to make purchases to influence educational and entrepreneurial experiences—particularly experiences that "grow the child," help them develop, and create lasting memories of the scrapbook variety.

One parent uses the "heart monitor" as her guideline. She asks, "Is the money being spent on something that has 'heart'?" Gifts from the heart usually reflect giving our children something that will help them grow and mature. Let your kids buy the junk and you buy them the jewels that will help them develop good, caring hearts.

Playing interactive family games, getting the whole family together for recreational fun days, and helping others less fortunate are all experiences with people, not objects. In these cases, the "possession" is the memory of fun, service, or being together. The guidelines for determining purposeful loans suggested in Chapter 9 can also be used for determining the best kinds of gifts and purchases for children.

Another parent uses the "relationship value" when deciding to make purchases. He looks for the R-value in the activity. Will the activity be a builder or a barrier to developing a relationship with one's self or others? Of course, the R-value of anything with a screen—such as a television, computer, video game, or cell phone—is suspect when considering the criteria for personal relationship building. While technology appears to connect us, it's missing the vital signs of life that create meaningful face-to-face relationships—eye contact, smiles, and reciprocal listening and conversing.

While technology appears to connect us, it's missing the vital signs of life that create meaningful face-to-face relationships—eye contact, smiles, and reciprocal listening and conversing.

Bottom Line: Wise parents know that the best buys for their children are purchases with "keepsake" meaning and purpose.

Money and the Happiness Factor

Ever heard over the loudspeaker in a store: "Happiness—Aisle 10"? If you think that buying stuff for your kids will create many happy returns, think again.

The pursuit of happiness and the pursuit of money tend to be lumped together as though achieving one ensures the other (Thomas Jefferson declared only the right to *pursue* happiness.) While that is a tempting thought, there is much research (and for many of us, personal experience) to tell us that money in and of itself does not make us happy. It eases life on the outside, but does little to make us feel good on the inside—at least not for long.

Studies reveal little difference in happiness between millionaires and the middle class. In other words, after a certain amount of money beyond the poverty level, having more money has diminishing returns. After a while, the pursuit of money becomes as unsatisfactory as the pursuit the possessions that money can buy.

Possessions can trigger happiness only so long as the experience of having them is new.

Research suggests that the best buys are not always things, but experiences. Possessions can trigger happiness *only so long as the experience of having them is new.* (If you're not sure about this, witness a child a day or two after a birthday party when they've been overindulged with too many gifts.) When the newness wears off, so does the residual interest. "Experiences," on the other hand, offer a bigger bang for the spending buck, because they are longer-lasting.

One grandmother was seen comforting her granddaughter on the way out of the store, after hearing Mom say, "No, you're too young for that." As she wrapped her arm around granddaughter, Grandma said, "Honey, we don't always get what we want, but we always get an experience we can learn from."

 Bottom Line: Wise parents teach their children that money doesn't make them happy, by showing them that the important things in life are not "things."

Too Much Stuff

What happens if we get our kids accustomed to a lifestyle they won't be able to afford as adults? We'll still be buying things for them far beyond the first eighteen years—if we can still afford it—or feel guilty for not doing so.

If we judge others by what they own instead of who they are, we raise children who confuse self-worth with net-worth.

Too much stuff has a dangerous way of becoming a child's identity. "Stuff" becomes a status symbol instead of a means to an end. It makes our children temporarily cool for a nanosecond, instead of permanently who they are for a lifetime. We need to help our children understand that one can't "buy" a personal identity, one must create it. If we judge others by what they own instead of who they are, we raise children who confuse self-worth with net-worth.

Peer pressure is no doubt a pervasive force in our children's lives. It starts early and never lets up (unless we learn to give it up). But what happens when we bow to our children's pressure to buy the latest and the greatest thing in order to fit "in"? We give them the unstated message that what others think and do is more important than what we think and do.

What to do instead? We'll need to stay in touch with what's really important in life if we're to empower our children to do the same. The road to becoming your own person "without external attachments" is paved with personal effort, determination, and achievement, no matter how old you are. (For some Love and Logic suggestions about how to reduce your children's possessions without a power struggle, see "Storage or Standing Room Only?" below.)

In summary, keep in mind the great example you'll set when you are the one buying:

- jewels not junk
- experiences not things
- self-worth not status

Bottom Line: Wise parents are careful not to addict their kids to a lifestyle they cannot afford as adults.

Storage or Standing Room Only?

It's Sunday night. A mother and her six-year-old daughter, Morgan, are trying to straighten up her bedroom before school starts bright and early the next morning. They're surrounded by a roomful of stuff—in fact, it's standing room only. Morgan asks innocently, "How am I ever going to be able to find anything if I have to put everything away?"

When talking to groups of parents, the authors of Love and Logic almost always get questions about kids and their stuff.

Ever forget what color the carpet or flooring is in your child's bedroom? Trip over things on the way to tucking them in? What happens when we buy too many things? We create a storage problem— too many possessions without enough room.

What's a parent to do? You may want to consider the FIFO approach if you haven't yet arrived at the "too much stuff, too little storage" stage. If you're already warehousing too much stuff for your kids, then skip to the PUPA approach.

The FIFO Approach

Some parents adopt the old tried and true inventory system known as "first in, first out"—or FIFO. It's similar to the idea of "out with the old and in with the new."

Naturally, this guideline doesn't have to be taken literally. It means simply that when a new possession comes into the house, another possession goes out of the house. The choice has less to do with equal monetary value, and more to do with adequate storage.

You can begin this policy as soon as storage space for your children's toys and possessions starts overflowing. The FIFO expectation can be stated at the point of purchase—for example, "I'll hold on to your new purchase when we get home, until you decide what you want to part with. Take as much time as you need."

Hold on to the new possession or item until your child has decided what he or she needs to let go or give away. It's wise to stay out of as much of the decision as possible, to avoid any control battles.

With the FIFO approach, you are able to maintain a quantity of possessions that can be manageably stored (shared control), while the kids still have plenty of choices about which possessions get relinquished (shared thinking and decision-making opportunities).

The PUPA Approach

What if you're already overwhelmed by your children's stuff? Enter the "pick up and put away"—or PUPA—method, which has worked for many parents. Tell your kids: "You get to keep the toys you pick up and put away."

While this process may play itself out like a Shakespearean tragedy, over a relatively short period of time you'll find that your children will naturally eliminate the toys they no longer favor. Whatever they choose to pick up and put away will automatically reflect the toys they value and want to keep. To keep the level of possessions relatively constant, new possessions can be kept "on hold" until exchanged for older possessions of equal size (as in the FIFO approach, above).

Of course, part of picking up their possessions means that your children put them away where they belong, not just throw them in a pile behind their door or shove them under the bed.

Some parents use the motto "a place for everything and everything in its place" as a guideline for what "putting away" really means. It's not considered "picked up" if it's not put away in its place. That's the "put away" part of PUPA.

Notice how the PUPA approach shares control while offering choices. The kids choose which possessions they pick up, while you control how much storage you want to provide.

You can begin this policy as soon as storage space for your children's toys and possessions starts overflowing.

Finally, for those kids who need to learn the hard way, a parent can say, "What would work best for you: to give away what you no longer have storage for, or to rent your own storage closet?"

* * *

Now Mom can offer Morgan two choices in answering her question: "How am I ever going to be able to find anything if I have to put everything away?" Mom can say to her daughter, "Would you like to use the PUPA method or the FIFO method?"

Here's a brief summary of these methods:

FIFO vs. PUPA Approaches

FIFO	PUPA
First in, first out.	Pick up, put away.
Kids get to keep the toys they pick up.	Kids can exchange one possession for another possession of similar size.
Use for the "too much stuff" problem.	Use as prevention for the "too much stuff" problem.

Bottom Line: Wise parents hold their kids accountable for the "too much spending, too much stuff" problem by using the FIFO and PUPA methods of inventory.

What We Tell Our Children

Any of the following parental statements sound familiar? They're usually heard in or around the toy aisle or at the checkout stand:

"I can't afford it."
"It's too expensive."
"I've spent enough already."

How many kids have you heard respond with, "Gee, Mom, thanks for sharing" (with an air of sarcasm) or "Oh okay, Dad, now I totally understand"?

Kids are masters at questioning all our responses, all the time. Do explanations or lectures really work? The key for parents is to learn how to respond effectively. How? By learning how to empathize with the child while handing the problem back to them.

Let's look at each one of these common refrains more closely, and then look at how Love and Logic offers a more effective way of saying "no."

"I can't afford it."

A common response when our kids request something is, "I can't afford it" or "I don't have the money." The "can't afford it" response is well intentioned, but probably not quite true. Many parents *can* afford the item, but just don't *want* to spend *their* money in *that* way at *that* time.

It's far better for your children to hear you genuinely say, "I choose to spend my money on something else right now" or "I choose not to spend our family money on this kind of thing. Maybe another time." Once you've introduced the idea of budgeting and wish lists (more about wish lists in Chapter 8), you can say, "That's not in our family budget" or "Feel free to put that on your wish list."

A key word here in Love and Logic's suggested response is *choose*. Kids are given an experience in establishing priorities and delaying gratification when parents respond and model the truth—that the denied request is a choice.

Modeling is one of the best methods for teaching our children to spend within their means.

Take the following response: "I know it's hard to want something and not have it. Feel free to use your own money." Is there an inherent choice here? Note how empathy is followed by a consequence: handing the problem back to the child.

One of two things will happen with this kind of response. Either the child will become involved in the thinking and decision-making processes needed to solve the problem and buy the item, or they won't. If the latter, then the item isn't important enough to the child.

Even if you can afford the item, it doesn't necessarily mean you should buy it. Set the example you want to see. If you need to delay a purchase, it will help the child understand why if they can hear you say, "I think I'm going to hold off buying this new computer until the old one becomes outdated" or "I'm going to cook at home more often so we can save money for vacations." Modeling is one of the best methods for teaching our children to spend within their means.

 Bottom Line: Wise parents remember that they are their children's first model of financial honesty. They demonstrate the truth by modeling the real reasons for making appropriate purchases or not.

"It's too expensive."

It is easier to say "no" to your children when something is too expensive, if your children already have an understanding of a "spending plan." That's because an understanding of *their own* budgetary limitations helps them understand *yours*.

"Too expensive" usually means that something is too expensive based on one's ability to pay. (It could also mean that the price is too high for the quality, value, or design of the item. But regardless of the reason for being "too expensive," there's always an inherent opportunity for kids to learn about spending wisely.)

You can let your kids discover that very same truth with a simple response: "You are welcome to use your own money to buy that" or (asked genuinely), "What do you think? Can you afford that?"

No need for lectures about how hard you work for your money or how money doesn't grow on trees. Just hand the problem back to child by inviting them to figure out their own way to buy it. For example: "Oh bummer. I've already spent all the money I allotted. Feel free to use your own money." Again, empathy followed by the consequence.

Bottom Line: Wise parents know that a "no" based on "it's too expensive" becomes an opportunity to teach kids how to learn that very same thing on their own.

"I've spent enough already."

If you're looking for an argument, the "I've spent enough already" refrain leaves you wide open for many kids. Is there ever enough? (For more information about how to handle kids' over- and underspending, see "Do You Have an Over- spender or an Underspender?" on the next page.)

Parents are often unaware of the number of daily spending activities their kids are exposed to. From toddlers to teenagers, kids frequently accompany their parents on errands, and overhear "spending talk" about the price of this or that.

One of the most effective ways to respond with the "I've spent enough already" scenario is to provide kids the chance to have that very same experience on their own. How? Again, by handing the problem back to them.

Much of what kids see their parents spend money on is for items that are necessities, such as gasoline and groceries. This creates a false impression that money flows freely and that "there's probably more where that comes from" *if I just ask.* That's when kids tend to push our buttons by saying things like, "Why do you work so much if we can't ever spend it?" or "But this toy will make me work harder in school."

Despite the reason for saying "no," whether it's because you really have spent enough already or you just don't want to spend anymore, period, the Love and Logic response teams up empathy with the consequence. For example: "I understand that you'd really like that. I buy extra things for others only after I've paid for everything we need first. Feel free to use your own money." Or: "I've spent all the money I'm going to spend today. You are welcome to save or earn your own money."

What happens when we hand the problem back with empathy? One parent was amused by her daughter's response when catalogue shopping one day. As this young girl was flipping through the pages, she saw an item that she really wanted … until she discovered the price: "Nine ninety-five?!" she gasped. "That's like … ten bucks. No way!"

Bottom Line: The "I've spent enough already" response is best used in conjunction with handing the problem back to the child with empathy, so he or she will have their own experience of "spending enough already."

Do You Have an Overspender or an Underspender?

Most kids don't have problems spending money when given the chance. But what if your kids do just the opposite? What if they hoard their money?

One mom described her first daughter as "a spender" and her second daughter as "a saver": "One keeps her money in a shoebox in the back of her closet and the other one burns holes in her wallet. The spender is motivated by the material gain, and the saver is motivated by financial gain. In fact," Mom mused, "the spender wants to borrow from the saver when she runs out of money."

In this situation, both children have a lesson to learn. The one who overspends needs to learn how to save some, and the one who underspends needs to learn how to "give" or spend a little. Kids will never learn how to spend wisely if they save their entire allowance. And kids will never learn how to save wisely if they spend it all. (For a better understanding of the root causes of over- and underspending, see "'Empty Nest' Kids: The Trouble with More and More Things" on the next page.)

Where's the happy medium? If you have a child who wants to save everything, no problem. One of the purposes of money is to use it to buy the things we need. You can promote "spending experiences" with your children simply by not being the one who buys what they need. Let them experiment.

If you have a child who wants to spend everything, no problem either. Same technique, but this time you can promote "saving experiences" with your children simply by not being the one who buys them what they need. Let them experiment.

In either case, the lesson can be learned using the same guideline:

Give your kids the money you would normally spend for their needs, and let them practice being the buyer.

(Parents normally buy what their children need. This guideline hands the problem back to the children as a learning experience, because they, rather than the parents, are now practicing buying what they need.)

Both "types" of children could eventually run out of what they need, but for different reasons, depending on the results of the experiment. For example, you might give your kids the money you normally spend on their toiletries and school supplies, so that they can get some practice buying those things for themselves. When they discover that they haven't spent money on what they need—such as shampoo, toilet paper, and school notebooks—they'll quickly realize that they do in fact *need* those things to live. The overspender will learn how to *save* for necessities, and the underspender will learn how to *spend* for necessities. In either case, they will learn that necessities are called necessities for a reason.

Bottom Line: Allow your children to buy what they need as practice to self-correct problems with over- and underspending.

"Empty Nest" Kids: The Trouble with More and More Things

People who underspend are just as irrational as people who overspend, and just as miserable.

How does this happen? Chronic overspending stems from trying to fill up one's self with "things." Hoarding, which sometimes manifests as underspending, is the flip side of the same coin, but still stems from the same need to fill up one's self.

Some people grow up without the benefits of having their basic childhood needs met—needs such as affection, control, and a sense of belonging. This creates an empty, hollow feeling inside that triggers a desperate, sometimes lifelong search to fill it up.

Grownup life offers all kinds of promising ways to fill up the emptiness. Some people try to fill up with excessive exercise, some with alcohol. Others use drugs, pornography, or gambling. Other people fill up with food, or conversely, deny themselves food. And some go shopping to fill up on more and more material things.

But kids don't have access to as many ways as adults do to fill up the hollowness they feel inside, at least when they're young. They can't smoke cigarettes, buy drugs, or gamble, and they can't purchase wildly. But they can start to fill up by hoarding, stealing, lying, and overindulgence.

Problems can start to manifest early when young kids are raised without the necessary bonding and nurturance. These are kids who begin life with an "empty nest"—because they lack a foundation of trust and security.

As "empty nest" kids get older, the risk increases as the access to risk increases.

So "empty nest" kids become "higher risk" kids in the only ways they know how. They act out, or fill up on toys and food, or become addicted to anything with a "screen." As "empty nest" kids get older, the risk increases as the *access to risk* increases. Some kids become promiscuous, experiment with drugs and alcohol, and drive recklessly.

This creates a downward spiral, because *we can never get enough of the things we don't really need in the first place.* Emotional holes cannot be filled up with "things."

Saying "I love you"

One woman said that her mother expressed her love by buying her beautiful, expensive clothes. When she realized she was doing the same thing to her daughter, Lynda, she decided she needed to stop and look for better, nonmaterial ways to express her love.

Providing material things in exchange for "I love you" will create a hollow feeling inside Lynda that may one day be filled with an addiction. If Lynda's basic needs for affection, control, and belonging are not met, she is at risk.

If buying stuff is a substitute for love, it's time to start finding it in other ways. Self-confidence and self-respect are the result of struggling to do things you don't think you can do, and prevailing. They don't come from overspending, hoarding, being indulged with excessive gifts, or being treated like you're special.

Bottom Line: "Things" are not, and never will be, the cure for fulfilling our basic physical and emotional needs. Kids want so much more than they really need. But what they really need the most, money can't buy.

Option Five: When Grandparents Buy, or How to Spoil Your Grandchildren Without Ruining Them

This is a special message to the grandparents who are reading this book. Grandparents, understandably, have a penchant for spoiling their grandchildren … it's one of the sweeter privileges of getting older. But did you know there's a wonderful, wonderful way to spoil your grandchildren without ruining them?

Share your "self" with them. Share your wisdom, your stories, and your life experiences. Share your most surprising moments and your most embarrassing, your happiest and your most disappointing, your funniest and your proudest. Take your grandkids to places you frequented as a child or young adult. Do arts and crafts with them, or build something together. Teach them how to open an IRA or other long-term investment. Take photos. Sing, laugh, and dance together. Take walks and have talks.

Even if you're a thousand miles away, take an interest in their activities, ask about their friends, joke with them, mail them stuff about their hobbies, and e-mail or text them to let them know you're thinking of them.

Rather than gifting them with money, make lots of deposits into the relationship account by thinking of ways to engage with them. You can build up your relationship with your grandchildren by keeping the activities people-based, not money-based. For example, take the money you would send to them and use it to go visit! (Remember, kids frequently know what they want—money— but they don't always know what they need or what is best.)

These gifts create the kinds of memories that last a lifetime. There are all kinds of ideas outside the gift box or gift card, limited only by your imagination. Your time is the most precious gift of all, because it's irreplaceable and limited, and the memories are priceless.

Many of today's grandchildren experience an abundance of adult money, but a poverty of adult time. The biggest and best gift you can give your grandchildren is your time. The things money can buy will never be a substitute for your time and interest.

One grandparent gave her twenty-two-month-old grandchild her first dollhouse. She shared that the toddler had no interest in the dollhouse. Granny and toddler played with the cardboard box, for hours, instead.

Many of today's grandchildren experience an abundance of adult money, but a poverty of adult time.

Bottom Line: Wise grandparents "spoil" their grandchildren by giving them lots of time building a relationship, instead of lots of money.

Intergenerational Differences

Whenever one or more generations gather in the family room, conflicts often occur because of differing values and priorities. Most parents are familiar with those awkward moments, because they are the ones in the middle—sandwiched between their own parents and their children.

Intergenerational conflict manifests in a variety of ways. Some parents worry that grandparents are spoiling their kids by giving them too many gifts. Other parents may take the grandparents' generosity for granted and ask for even more. And then there are parents who find themselves in between those extremes.

Regardless of where the conflict falls in the spectrum of possibilities, it can get pretty uncomfortable unless parents learn how to set limits.

Setting Adult Limits

If you're having problems with your own parents giving your children too much stuff, use some of the same principles for setting limits with big folks as you do for little folks.

The best solution for many families lies somewhere in the middle. Parents can give grandparents the satisfaction of gifting their grandchildren while at the same time reserving the right to say, "That's enough." If you're having problems with your own parents giving your children too much stuff, use some of the same principles for setting limits with big folks as you do for little folks. Decide what the limit is, and then ask for their understanding and cooperation.

For Birthdays

Mom, I think twenty dollars is enough money for a child Molly's age. So please limit your gift to that amount. If you want to give her more, we have opened a college fund account and will put the extra money in there. Thanks for understanding.

For Major Holidays

For major holidays (such as Christmas, Hanukkah, Kwanzaa, and Easter), it can be helpful to make specific gift suggestions. Instead of "Shelby likes anything pink," give a menu of specific choices. This avoids the potential for duplicate gifts and disappointed gift-givers. Specific suggestions offered as choices also invite gift-givers to honor your limits and values as you honor theirs, financial or otherwise.

Dad, you asked me what to give the kids for Christmas. I've mailed you a catalogue of educational toys and circled the items I think my kids would like. Please limit your gift-giving this year to one gift for each child. If you don't like the ideas

I've sent, feel free to surprise us! Thanks for everything you do for our children. I appreciate your support on keeping the gift-giving at a sane level this year.

For Special Occasions

Mom, Dad, for Benjamin's Bar Mitzvah, we've decided to limit the amount of cash he can spend. I just wanted you to know ahead of time that once everything has been pooled together, we'll let him keep a percentage and the rest goes into the bank for his education. I trust you'll understand and respect our wishes. Thanks.

* * *

It's important for grandparents to respect the limits that the parents set. After all, the parents will have to deal with the aftermath of spoiled children long after the grandparents are gone. One grandma decided that it would be best to consult with the mom for major purchases, but that small, inexpensive gifts were fine. Besides, is it not true, and our hope, that children can have just as much fun playing with a $7 toy as with a $70 toy?

A few carefully selected gifts that reflect a grandchild's individual personality and preferences will be the most appreciated when holidays, birthdays, and other special occasions arise. Grandparents can gift money for a college education or a down-payment on a home, or simply give the gift of time. (For grandkids that have everything, some grandparents even make a charitable donation in their grandchild's name, along with a small present to unwrap.)

While it's perfectly okay to give your grandkids cash and gift cards, the authors of Love and Logic suggest that monetary gifts be managed just like their allowance. Your grandchildren can be taught to pay themselves first, with savings and investing, and then spend the balance.

Bottom Line: The biggest gift you can give your adult children is not to undermine their efforts to set limits with their own children.

More Gifts, Grandma!

The simple act of springing for a surprise trip to the movies or a spontaneous splurge to the ice cream store delights most grandparents—until their grandchildren expect it or take it for granted.

It's an unpleasant feeling to be taken for granted. If your grandchildren (or adult children) are asking for more, or asking for more than you can afford, then it's time for you to set your own limits. For example:

> "I have a certain amount in mind to spend on Sofia's birthday. Do you have any suggestions of things she might need?"
>
> "I know you suggested the new $500 computer for Trent, but I would prefer to surprise him with a gift of my own choosing."

No Thanks!

Here's how one grandparent handled feeling underappreciated:

Grandparent: "I'm glad to give gifts to your children this year as long as I feel appreciated."

Parent: "What do you mean?"

Grandparent: "I've sent gifts the last few years, but never hear a word back from any of them."

Parent: "I thought they thanked you when you called."

Grandparent: "No, I always have to ask you or them if anyone liked what I sent. How about if I come for a visit instead this year?"

One mom was very embarrassed at how her children acted upon opening Grandpa's generous holiday gifts. Her eldest son leaned over to his younger brother and whispered, "You already have one of those that's way better."

Mom was mortified that her boys acted so ungratefully. So she decided from now on that she would hold on to the gifts until the boys had written a thank you note to PaPa. The policy was: no saying "thank you," no spending or playing with the gift.

Another grandmother asked her grandchildren to let her know when they received her gifts in the mail. Finally, after not hearing from them year after year, she sent just a card; no gift, no money. Guess who called?

Here's what she said to her grandchild:

Grandma: "When I send you gifts and they aren't acknowledged, it tells me that you have too much stuff to keep track of, or that you don't like it or appreciate it. So I'm just going to send you cards for a while.

Grandchild: "Oh Gammy, I'll thank you next time."

Grandma: "Oh good, honey. I'll look forward to that."

The next evening, Grandma shared with the other members of her card club: "I think I'm going to save myself tons of money over the next few years."

Bottom Line: Wise grandparents who feel taken for granted set their own limits.

Eight Ways to Say "No" to "Buy-Buy"

Parents get inundated with daily requests to buy more and more, and their children keep asking for more and more. Kids tend to spend money as fast as they get it, because parents inadvertently become the source of unlimited funds. This cycle gets very annoying unless we learn how to say one of simplest words in the English language: "no." While "no" is only a two-letter word, it's no less challenging to say in the face of our kids' chronic begging, whining, and arguing, or when listening to their endless comparisons of us versus other, more "generous" parents.

What's lacking? Nothing that a little real life experience or education about budget basics, needs versus wants, and delayed gratification can't teach— backed up by a parent who knows the value of a confident "no."

Spending beyond our immediate means is never a good idea. Yet many parents are labeled "mean" when they say "no." Based on what our kids tell us, everyone has the latest-model car or computer. Don't fall into the trap of "guilty giving."

Say "Yes" with Finesse

Woven throughout Love and Logic's solutions to kids and spending is the idea that by saying "no" to buying, we say "yes" to teaching fiscal responsibility. Here's a summary of the possible ways to say "no" by saying "yes"—with finesse!

> "What works best for you: to add a new category to your spending plan, or to do without it?"
> "You are welcome to buy that with your own money as long as it doesn't cause a problem."
> "You may buy anything in the store you can afford."
> "You may choose any acceptable way you like to pay for it."
> "You are welcome to save for that if you'd like to buy it."
> "Feel free to put that on your wish list."
> "I will lend you the money in exchange for an equal amount of collateral. You decide."
> "Feel free to give me an advance in money, or your time."

Notice that the word "no" is not used in any of the above examples. Control is shared by giving the child the choice to buy or not. Each example hands the choice back to the child, so that the child decides whether to buy, not you.

Love and Logic parents know that not teaching their kids how to live within their means threatens the quality of their life as adults.

Love and Logic parents involve their children in as many thinking and decision-making opportunities as possible, so their children *will learn on their own* that something is too expensive, that they have spent enough already and need to save, or that they truly can't afford it. In that way, they eventually learn how to say "no" to themselves.

Some kids will try to convince you that *not* buying them something is "life-threatening." Love and Logic parents know that *not* teaching their kids how to live within their means threatens the quality of their life as adults.

Will your children continue to argue and manipulate? For those who do: go brain dead, be empathic, and repeat your favorite Love and Logic one-liner, such as "I love you too much to argue." Your child will eventually "get" that the decision to buy something or not is their choice, not yours. In that way, your child's poor decision becomes the "bad guy," not you.

 Bottom Line: Wise parents understand that whenever they say "no" by saying "yes," they are giving their children precious opportunities to practice making good and bad spending choices when the price tags are more affordable.

A Means with an End

Setting financial limits is a means to an end. Stating the limit is the "means"; following through with the limit is the "end," because only then does one derive the benefits from setting it. The simple intervention of setting a financial limit has the power to be any or all of the following:

- A want versus need intervention
- A delayed gratification intervention
- A gratitude versus entitlement intervention
- A money management skill practice intervention
- A character-building intervention

That's a sweet spot for any grandparent or parent to be in, all with just a few choice words.

CHAPTER 8

Saving

From Piggy Bank to Promise Ring

This chapter shows you how to get kids interested in saving, and how to inspire them to *stay* interested. Through opportunities to make their own "wish lists," research costs, and "do the math," kids are introduced to setting their own savings goals, prioritizing, and confronting the prospect of their very first withdrawal.

Why Save When It's So Much Fun to Spend?

Saving money. It's like physical exercise. We *know* we should exercise, just like we know we should save some money. Yet many of us don't do either one. Of course we're warned repeatedly that we'll eventually pay the price. One is health and the other is wealth.

Most of us tend to forget the big picture when it comes to saving money— that unseen picture of life down the road. The farther away we are from the horizon, the foggier the image. So it is with the future. Without a clear view of what's ahead, we have to envision our *need* for good health and enough wealth, among other things, by preparing for a future that hasn't arrived.

If it's tough for adults to keep the proper perspective, it's nearly impossible for kids. The causes and the effects are simply too far apart for kids to understand concepts like "saving for the future."

In order to teach our children about saving, we'll need to connect the dots between the causes and the effects of *not saving*. But here's the issue:

We need to *create a need* to save.

The need to save money is a tough lesson to teach kids when so many of them today are *born into* a place of financial security. Many kids, rightfully so, are given what they need. They are financially secure.

Many children today have all the security and freedom that comes with money, without any of the responsibility. What a deal!

On top of that, many kids from affluent homes experience the fruits of financial freedom due to the success of their parents. These kids are given everything they want, and are basically financially free. As a result, many children today have all the security and freedom that comes with money, without any of the responsibility. What a deal!

If you have both financial security and financial freedom, why would your children be compelled to save? Freedom without responsibility, however, creates an artificial and potentially dangerous situation—a financial world that bears little resemblance to the world our children will inherit, and one that does little to prepare kids for the peace of mind that comes with being financially secure for tomorrow and financially independent in the years ahead.

Unless, of course, we teach our children how to create their *own* kid-sized financial security, independence, and freedom. And therein lies the million-dollar question: "How can I teach my kids the value of saving money when there's no immediate or obvious need?"

Let's look at how to how to teach kids to save by combining Love and Logic concepts with some basic financial principles.

Throwing the Book at Travis

Travis, age twelve, has little trouble keeping a detailed account of his expenses over three months. He receives $12 a week and spends $14 or more every week on movie tickets, snacks, and "stuff." His older sister, in exchange for his vacuuming "service," systematically pays him the other $2.

After three months, he presents his calculations to his parents. Trying to contain their laughter, Mom and Dad look up and smile at their precocious son. "Travis," Dad asks, "what happened to the savings plan?"

"It's there … see?" offers Travis, sliding a piece of lined paper from his day-runner across the table toward his father. Dad looks at it for a minute, turns to Mom, and raises his eyebrows in helplessness, before facing his son with a question: "Yes, the plan is here, but where's the money?"

"Uh … I'm going to get around to that as soon as I have something extra to save." He smiles confidently at his parents.

He gets up to leave, but something brings him back to the table. Cocking his head to the side, batting his eyes at his mother, he lowers his voice and says: "Uh … I almost forgot. I … uh … lost my math book and my mean old teacher expects me to pay for it …"

"She does, does she?" Mom responds.

"Uh huh. And those books are really expensive, even though they've been used for years and years …"

"Yes, they are … math doesn't change honey, numbers are numbers," says Dad, reaching for his wallet in his back pocket.

Mom's hand shoots out and grabs her husband's wrist before he can pull the money from his wallet. She turns toward Travis and says, "Honey, it looks like you could use that savings money right now, doesn't it?"

"And how! I can't go to the eighth-grade picnic if I can't find the book or pay to replace it—and I *have* to go to the picnic … Sarah is going to be there …" says Travis, a slight whine coloring his speech.

"That would be a bummer, honey," Mom replies empathically (empathy always precedes the consequence).

* * *

What a great opportunity for teaching kids the importance of saving! Travis is quite fortunate to have created a situation that brings home the point of saving some of his money. While it's unfortunate that Travis will miss the picnic if he doesn't look harder for his book or come up with the money to replace it, the lesson he'll learn will last much longer than the memory of a day at the amusement park.

By Hook or Book: Inspiring Your Kids to Save

Ever notice how many children burn holes in their pockets when it comes to money? Travis's parents watched their son have that experience until they understood how to use day-to-day opportunities, such as a lost math book, to teach the value of saving.

There are several approaches parents can use to interest their children in saving money. One approach uses real life experience ("by hook"), and the other approach uses education and encouragement ("by book"). If we can't motivate our kids through education and encouragement, then we may need to force the issue through real life experience. As in everything else, some kids learn the easy way and some learn the hard way.

Some parents use a combination of education, encouragement, and real life experience. The approach you choose depends upon your family values, your child's financial know-how, age and temperament, and common sense.

Teaching kids to save is a way to wean them from being financially dependent on you now, so that they don't lean on you later. Parents can start this process at any time, with any age, using everyday opportunities.

Here's a look at the "by hook" and "by book" approaches in more detail.

Approach #1: "By Hook"—Using Real Life Experiences

The quickest approach to teaching kids how to save is through real life experiences. Ironically, we can get and keep most kids interested in saving—believe it or not—through having an experience with the consequences of *not* saving.

There are two opportunities that lend themselves particularly well to teaching the value of saving by not saving. They are the "I want a" experience and the kid-sized financial emergency.

Using "I want a" Moments to Teach: To Wean Not Lean

Travis was having an "I want a" moment when he tried to cajole his mother into giving him the money to replace his lost math book. Fortunately, Mom intercepted her husband's natural tendency to rescue and used the opportunity to advance an understanding of the need to save instead.

Travis can either look harder for the missing math book, earn enough money to replace it, or give up on going to that class picnic he so badly wants (or says he wants) to attend.

Do his parents need to worry that Travis doesn't want to save the money? Nope. No problem for Mom and Dad, but an unresolved problem for Travis. Why? Because Travis will continue to experience the problem of not having money to replace the math book … as long as nobody bails him out.

"Doing without" creates the situation for Travis to decide that saving money for life's little ups and downs is a better choice.

The *No* in Knowing

The importance of saving money can be taught the first time your child wants something and you say "no."

What do most kids already know about money?

- They know that money buys them things they need and want.
- They know that their parents usually have the financial power to purchase something for them.

Your best teachable moment arrives whenever you, the financially independent one, say "no" to your child, the financially dependent one. Your goal—in that precious and most teachable moment—is to *transfer your financial independence to your children*, so that they can buy something with *their* money.

Saving money, by its very nature, requires us to delay using our money now, in favor of using it later. What happens if we don't have enough money for our needs and wants (or perceived needs and wants, as is the case with kids)? Financial hardship, frustration, and disappointment. That's exactly the real life experience some children need before learning the value in disciplining themselves enough to save for something they want.

Bottom Line: Wise parents foster their children's independence, so that they can learn to save for and *then* buy their own things. That's why using *their desire* for financial independence teaches the lesson of financial independence so well.

Using Life's Little "Emergencies" to Teach

Another opportunity to use real life experiences to teach saving occurs every day all across America. There's a story in Chapter 7 about Piper running out of money. Piper had a financial emergency that day—at least from her point of view—when she ran out of money and couldn't go to the movies with her friends. She asked her Dad if she could "borrow" the money (along with another empty promise to repay him later).

What would you do if you were Piper's dad? If you want her to learn how to save, the best answer is: do not budge.

Financial emergencies for most kids, like Piper, occur in the marketplace. So they go to the Bank of Mom and Dad for more. Three of the most common financial emergencies for kids are:

Real life "I want a" experiences and kid-sized emergencies are like financial wedgies—they teach the value of saving through the experience of not saving.

1. The parent says "no" to something they want.
2. They lose or forget to bring their money and the parent says "no."
3. They have only a portion of the money to buy what they want, and need more money to complete the purchase.

Whenever any one of these "emergencies" occurs, it's the perfect time to remember that these circumstances are precisely why we give our kids an allowance and a job list.

Notice how all three scenarios force saving (or earning) if the child wants it enough and if the parent does not financially rescue their child. These scenarios allow kids the chance to practice saving money because they get to experience what happens when they don't.

No need to force the savings issue when you are using real life experiences. Simply be consistently empathic while saying "no," and let the consequences do the teaching. Wise parents remember not to rescue their children when they get into a money crunch.

 Bottom Line: Real life "I want a" experiences and kid-sized emergencies are like financial wedgies—they teach the value of saving through the experience of not saving.

Approach #2: "By Book"—Using Education and Encouragement

"What are some incentives I can offer my kids to get them interested in saving, other than experiential deprivation in the store?" asked Marci, mother of three kids, ages five, eight, and fifteen.

Not all kids will need to go to the "school of real life experience" to learn the value of saving. With a little education and encouragement, some kids will "get with the program" early.

Christopher, Marci's youngest child, was that kind of kid. He was interested in watching his money grow from the day he received his first piggy bank on his fifth birthday. He loved to sort Dad's spare change into stacks, and practice his counting. He'd shake the contents of his bank out onto the kitchen table, "match and stack," and then put the coins back into the slot. When Christopher's first piggy bank was full, he wanted to fill up a second one.

To capitalize on Christopher's interest, his parents decided to start him and their other two children with their first allowance, so that they could begin a savings program. Even though Christopher's parents could afford all of their children's needs and much of what their children wanted, they wanted to impart the value of saving to their three children.

Here are some simple ways to get started with a savings program using allowance, along with a little education and lots encouragement. Of course, these approaches are also applicable to learning how to save with earnings and other types of income as well.

Using Allowance to Teach Saving

Allowance is an obvious way to teach kids to save. If we just give our money to kids to save, we miss the step of teaching them how to save their money. There is a difference between "Here's ten dollars to put in your piggy bank" and "How much of your allowance are you going to save?"

Basically, parents can use allowance in one of three ways:

- Automatic allowance deduction.
- Match funds as an incentive to meet a savings requirement.
- No savings requirement. (use real life "I want a" experiences and kid-sized financial emergencies instead—as previously discussed)

You can use one or a combination of these approaches depending upon the age of your child, his or her temperament, and your family values and savings goals.

Marci, like many parents, struggled with the idea of whether or not to make saving a requirement for her three children. Christopher liked saving for a while, and then became disinterested once he understood that he could buy things with money. Her middle child, Paige, liked to save, and embraced the savings idea from the very beginning. But her teenage son, Logan, wanted nothing whatsoever to do with saving his allowance. (For ideas about how to inspire the desire to save, see "Six Keys to Incentive-Style Saving" on the next page.)

To avoid control battles with her two "non-savers," Marci used lots of Love and Logic choices to share control. Here are the options that she tried, along with the choices she used to share control:

- The Automatic Deduction Program
  "You can save one dollar or two dollars a week. Your choice."
- The Matching Funds Program
  "You can save ten percent or twelve percent of your allowance. Whatever you decide, I will match it, dollar for dollar."
- The No Savings Requirement Program
  "You can save, or not save, for anything you want, as long as what you do with your money fits with our family values."

The results of Marci's experiments were predictable based on the age and personality of each of her three children. Christopher decided to save $1 a week when Mom offered him choices. Paige, on the other hand, chose to save the higher percentage—12%—because she liked to watch her savings grow.

As for her teenager? Predictably, he liked the no-savings plan. Notice how Mom did not threaten, lecture, or warn Logan about the consequences of his choice. Mom decided to let the real life experience of wanting his own car (to go with his upcoming driver's license) be the teacher.

What about the "it's not fair" issue among the three children, given that two kids save and one doesn't? No problem. *It's their choice, not Mom's.* Each child can "re-choose" the option that works best for him or her at anytime. Besides, Mom is flexible. She knows that if education and encouragement don't work, the real life experience of "doing without" eventually will.

Bottom Line: Wise parents remember two things when teaching their kids to save: the power of choice and the absence of rescue.

Six Keys to Incentive-Style Saving

Key #1: The Best Savings Advice—Start Early

While there are few absolutes in life, the most common and agreed upon advice about saving is to start early. How many of us wish we had saved earlier in our lives to capitalize on the progression of time without the perspiration of effort? (For details about savings accounts for children, see "When should I open a savings account for my child?" on p. 244.)

Key #2: Fattening the Pig—Make Savings Systematic

Many of us start a savings program but it soon fizzles because we don't save on a recurring basis. Saving money methodically is the key to an effective program. One obvious way to make saving systematic for kids is to make allowance systematic.

Ever heard of the expression "pay yourself first"? That's one proven method for making savings methodical. It means you treat saving money as a recurring expense. Just like paying your monthly bill for utility services, you pay the amount you want to save as an up-front "expense."

Naturally, allowance provides kids opportunities to put this principle into practice. Parents can teach their kids how to regularly "pay themselves first" through an allowance.

Some parents automatically set aside an agreed upon savings amount when giving their children their allowances. Other parents prefer to give their children the money, and then request a percentage back for depositing into the child's savings account. Others combine the two by using the bank's system of automatic withdrawals to set aside savings on a monthly basis.

Whichever way you choose to make saving systematic, use one that provides a visual picture of growth. It can be as simple as a pile of coins on top of a bedroom dresser, like Christopher's overflowing piggy bank; or monthly paper financial statements; or daily financial reports accessed online. A visual picture makes it fun for kids to watch their savings grow.

The issue here is less about how much is being saved, and more about the fact that money is being saved, period.

Eventually, we want our kids to think about the future they'll enjoy from saving some of their money. For instance: "If I save two dollars each week, then in five weeks I'll be able to afford a new necklace." Or: "If I save five dollars each

The issue here is less about how much is being saved, and more about the fact that money is being saved, period.

week, and earn ten dollars each week doing jobs, then in three weeks I'll be able to buy myself some fancy new wheels for my skateboard."

Developing a regular method for saving is an important key to a process for which *the essential requirement for success is the passage of time.*

Key #3: Goals, Not Gizmos—Money Matches

Some parents ignite their children's interest in saving money by offering matching funds. For every $1 your child saves, you might match it with 50¢, or $1, or $2, for example. In this way, you make monetary gifts to your child to support a systematic "savings program."

Many parents choose to match only the savings that their child will use for pre-approved purposes. Naturally, any monetary support should reflect family values. Criteria for a matching funds program might be based on whether the fund will be used for an educational activity or enterprise. Or matching funds can be offered for a major long-term financial goal, such as for college or a car.

This is eventually the solution Marci used with her teenage son, Logan. He wasn't interested in saving his allowance until he discovered that he wanted a car, and that he was going to have to work for it. All of a sudden, saving his allowance became a priority. Mom agreed to support his savings efforts through matching funds.

Money matches can provide the kind of disciplined practice that can turn an action into a habit because it has its own reward. (For more detail about matching funds, see "Partial Loans and Financial Assistance: To Limit, Match, or Grant?" on p. 276.)

Key #4: Use "Interest" to Get Interest

Another way to inspire saving is to use "interest" to get interest. In other words, to get and keep kids interested in saving, introduce the concept of financial interest. Parents can present the concept of simple interest to younger kids, and move into explaining compound interest when they are ready.

Simple Interest

Simple interest is well named. Suppose you or your child puts $100 in the bank and the bank agrees to pay you 5% interest per year. That means the bank pays you a nickel for every dollar each year. After the first year, you will have earned $5 in interest; so now your balance is $105. Of course, the more money you save, the more interest you earn.

Some would say, "That's nothing!" Yet every journey begins with a single step, just as every dollar is the sum of 100 pennies. Wise parents remember that the power of choice is present with savings of any amount. Help your children understand that every penny counts toward a bigger result! Plus, the interest is "free" money!

EXERCISE 8.1: Double or Nothing?

I (Kristan) have noticed that young people often throw their pennies on the ground as they leave a store, concert, or movie theater. How sad. Perhaps this exercise could change their minds about the value of the lowly penny. You'll need a calculator for sure, and real pennies if you want.

Begin with one penny. The idea is to double the number of pennies each day for as many days as you like:

Day 1: 1 penny
Day 2: 2 × 1 = 2 pennies
Day 3: 2 × 2 = 4 pennies
Day 4: 2 × 4 = 8 pennies
Day 5: 2 × 8 = 16 pennies
Day 6: 2 × 16 = 32 pennies
Day 7: 2 × 32 = 64 pennies

Now, 64¢ may not seem like a lot, but see what happens if you keep going. After two weeks you'll have 8,192 pennies, or $81.92, and after three weeks you'll have 1,048,576 pennies, or $10,485.76!

Pennies add up when they are multiplied! Some companies have made millions of dollars with profit margins of only a few pennies.

If an apple a day keeps the doctor away, how about a penny a day to keep the creditors away? Or a nickel, a dime, and so forth?

Compound Interest

There's compound interest, too. That's better than simple interest, because you earn interest on your money as well as the interest you make on your savings—interest on top of interest. Using the same example above: $100 at 5% *compounded daily* yields $5.13 in interest, making the balance $105.13 after one year.

Saving gets more interesting when kids are taught the effects of compounding their savings *over time*. Again, the higher the interest rate, the higher the savings. (For additional information about the advantages of compound interest, see "Win-Win: The Magic of Compound Interest" on p. 246.)

Many financial institutions and their websites publish charts that calculate interest amounts for you. It can be fun to set up hypothetical situations for your children about how much they would earn if they saved *x* number of dollars as opposed to *y*. Invite them to use online interest calculators to explore the possibilities that exist with saving various amounts of money over various periods of time.

Saving gets more interesting when kids are taught the effects of compounding their savings over time.

Parents can also encourage kids to open a money market or other type of financial fund that provides a higher rate of return than a regular savings account. One parent found that her seven-year-old daughter, who put $150 in a bank account, was extremely frustrated that she earned only $4 in interest the first year. So Mom encouraged her to open a mutual fund. Mom found that her daughter's experience turned out to be much more exciting and fulfilling and therefore more of an incentive to save once she could watch her money grow faster.

Of course, the opposite could happen. Your child's account might lose money. Wise parents begin with a savings account, to provide a secure place for the principal amount, and then increase the financial risk with the child's age and maturity. (Teaching kids how to save is the first prerequisite to an investing program. More about investing in Chapter 11.)

Key #5: Keeping Money Safe

Anything we save over time will soon need to be stored. Money is no exception. Parents need to teach their children the importance of keeping their cash, money cards, and financial information safe. This sends the message that money, passwords, and pin numbers are valuable and need to be used and stored with care. It's best to provide a method of storage—from concrete to more abstract—based on the child's age. Most parents begin with a piggy bank or jar, followed by a pocket, purse, or wallet, followed by a bank or other financial institution, as the amount of money increases.

Most adults have had the unpleasant experience of losing money as a child. It's easy to do as an adult, too! Kids need to learn the best places to keep their money safe, inside and outside the home.

One dad who wanted to teach his forgetful nine-year-old son about safekeeping gave him hypothetical pop quizzes. Dad would think of questions to test his son's knowledge about the best safekeeping method. For example: "Where's the best place to keep your lunch money?" "Where's the best place to put your money if your piggy bank is full?" "When you want to buy something at the store, where's the best place for your money?" And the reward for each right answer? A high five and a choice of coins to save!

Another way to teach this lesson is to let your child lose their money without rescuing them. (For an example of how to respond to a child who has lost their money, see "But I lost iiittt!" on p. 71, under the section "Allowance: A Hand-to-Hand Experience.")

Key #6: Money Fun

Finally, parents can get their kids interested in saving by using the same strategy they might use for anything else—make it fun!

Some parents introduce coin collections, while others use colorful piggy banks, treasure chests, and other playful coin holders and sorting devices. Games, toys, "fiscal field trips," and special "money" camps are just a few of ideas for adding fun to your kids' understanding of the importance of saving money.

Fiscal field trips can include educational journeys to the local bank, the grocery store, a favorite restaurant, the consignment store or pawnshop, or the financial section of your local library. The benefits of a "field trip" can also be gained from the comfort of your own home. The kitchen table, your annual garage sale, the solicitation at your front door or in your mailbox, and your investment company's website can all be used to give kids living experiences with the financial side of life.

The Family That Saves Together Plays Together

One of the best fiscal field trips is the trip your family takes on vacation. Many families make saving for their vacation a family project, whereby everyone contributes their fair share. Family vacations, like day trips to theme parks and other recreational and entertainment places, can provide kids an incentive to save money.

EXERCISE 8.2: Family Vacation—All Aboard!

There are three steps to getting the family on board! First, set a savings goal based on total costs, including travel expenses, admission fees, souvenirs, food, and so forth. Second, review the expenses using the same principles presented in Chapter 5, on contributions. Decide who will start saving for which expenses.

(For a parallel exercise, see "Family Contributions Balance Sheet" on p. 106, under the section "How to Introduce Family Contributions.") Third, help your kids set and achieve their own savings goal (using a percentage or sliding scale) based on age, ability, and resources. When a spending decision comes up, so can the discussion about the importance of the expense as compared to the family's savings goal.

Who knows? Some kids may even get inspired to save for their own vacations once they've had a positive experience saving as a part of a family.

 Bottom Line: Use the following six keys to inspire children to save:
1. Start early!
2. Develop a systematic way to save, such as "pay yourself first."
3. Use financial interest as an incentive.
4. Use matching funds to achieve savings goals.
5. Teach safekeeping practices.
6. Make saving fun! (more about that later in the chapter)

"When should I open a savings account for my child?"

At birth. If not at birth, *now* is a good time, as it's never too early to start a savings program (naturally, it will be a joint custodial or guardian account until your child is eighteen to twenty-one years old, depending on the state where you live).

Regardless of when you start, you don't have to be the only one saving for your child's future. Wise parents save for their young children until their children are in a position to join in and learn how to save for themselves. The first savings lesson can be introduced as early as the first allowance.

Two Types of Savings Accounts
Many parents develop two types of savings accounts: "revolving" and "fixed." Some parents set up both types of accounts. Other parents start with the revolving type and graduate to fixed savings. In either case, notice how the two types of accounts fit with Love and Logic's principles—a fixed savings account shares control, and a revolving account offers choices.

Revolving Savings Account
A revolving savings account allows your children to practice how to spend savings wisely. Younger children can "raid and replace" their piggy bank or wallet. For

older children, a custodial account with a bank or credit union provides supervised practice for real life banking, because of deposit and withdrawal privileges.

Allowance from the Bank of Mom and Dad and job earnings are the basic funding sources for the revolving savings account. Regular statements (either the home allowance statement or the bank's), detailing the increase or decrease in money, will provide an excellent introduction for children to analyze their monthly decisions to spend or save.

Fixed Savings Account

The fixed savings account is set up on the child's behalf for long-term goals such as college or retirement, with limited or no access and few withdrawal exceptions. Many parents use growth-oriented investment vehicles, such as mutual funds, for such purposes, because of the long-term horizon and higher rate of return.

Parents, grandparents, and other relatives may fund fixed savings accounts either through matching funds or through dedicating a percentage of money gifts toward savings. A multigenerational approach to saving for college and other large endeavors can be a very smart idea to counteract increasing costs and inflation.

Divide and Conquer

Whichever method is chosen, it's important to set up a simple savings system with your child that's easy to track. Many parents find that subdividing the savings portion of their child's allowance works well. One portion of the savings dollar goes to the revolving account for spending on short-term wishes, and the other portion goes to a fixed "hands-off" account for long-term goals.

One father, for example, gave his son Justin a monthly allowance of $40. Of the $40, they agreed that Justin would save 20% and share 10%, and that he was free to spend the balance as he chose.

Of the $8 he saved monthly, $4 was dedicated to his college fund (which his parents matched at a 1:5 ratio). This was Justin's fixed savings fund. The other $4 was put into a revolving account for all other saving and spending purposes.

Here's the breakdown on Justin's allowance statement:

> Allowance: $40
> > Save: $8
> > > Fixed savings account: $4 toward college fund (5:1)
> > > Revolving savings account: $4 toward current savings goals and spending wishes
> > Share: $4
> > Spend: $28 (or save more)

Notice in this example how a fixed savings account with a monthly match helps both parent and child save for a college education. Once the savings amount gets large enough, or your children "outgrow" the system set up at home, open an official savings account with a bank or other financial investment institution for safekeeping.

Most community banks will allow children to initially open a savings account with a low minimum deposit under your guidance. A "passbook," issued by some banks, is a record of deposits and withdrawals, and offers a visual picture of progress. If a passbook is not available, use the monthly bank statement, on paper or online, as the learning tool for discussing your children's fiscal decisions.

Show Your Kids How: The Application Process

Resist the temptation to fill out the application for your child; instead, walk through the process with your child.

When you open a savings account on your child's behalf, involve him or her in the process of filing out the application. Take them with you on a financial field trip to the local bank, credit union, or other financial "house," or to the computer for online applications.

Resist the temptation to fill out the application *for* your child; instead, walk through the process *with* your child. Teaching a child how to open a bank account is part of the process of training him or her to be "a saver." In this way, whether the experience is online at the computer, or "in line" at a bank, children experience what it takes to open various types of financial accounts—basic savings, CDs, savings bonds, mutual funds, and so forth.

May their first experience with you be one of many positive savings experiences in a lifetime!

Win-Win: The Magic of Compound Interest

The time you take to explain to your children the results of compound interest over time is absolutely, positively priceless! The most powerful way to teach the combined advantage of time, money, and interest is with a simple mathematical example.

Start with $10. Pick an average rate of return—let's say 8%, which is more than a typical interest-earning investment, but less than the historical return on stocks.

Tell your children they have two choices with earned interest. They can spend the interest they earn, or they can automatically reinvest the interest, known as compounding.

What difference does this decision make over time? Not very much ... at first. Both investments return 80¢ in interest in the first year (for a balance of $10.80

246

each). But in the second year, whereas the uncompounded investment would return 80¢ again (for a balance of $11.60), the compounded investment would return 86¢ (for balance of $11.66).

Big deal, right? That 6¢ advantage doesn't even buy a handful of peanuts! But watch how this small advantage grows. After five years, the uncompounded investment has earned $4 (80¢ × 5). The compounded investment, however, has earned $14.69—an advantage of $10.69. The advantage further increases as follows:

Over 10 years: $21.59
Over 15 years: $31.72
Over 20 years: $46.61
Over 30 years: $100.63
Over 40 years: $217.25
Over 50 years: $469.02
Over 60 years: $1,012.57

And this is only starting with $10 *without* adding another dime! Imagine the advantages with $100, $1,000, and $10,000. If you had invested $10,000, the advantage would be 1,000 times the above amounts (for example, after two years, an advantage of $64 for $10,000 versus an advantage of 6¢ for $10). For $50,000, the advantage would be 5,000 times those amounts!

Here's an analogy that may help the youngest of minds to understand: Remember the story of the tortoise and the hare? Who wins the race? In the world of compound interest, the hare and the tortoise each have an advantage. The hare is a symbol for our money's ability to multiply, and the tortoise is a symbol for the slow and steady nature of compounded earnings. Both factors are needed to finish the race, because each brings one of the qualities needed to win the savings game.

Bottom Line: Interest your children early in the magic of compound interest, so that they may take full advantage of their enchanting time horizon.

Toy du Jour Desires: Keeping Kids Interested in Saving

Remember the story of Marci, mother of three? Teaching her children to save was received with mixed reviews, depending upon their ages.

Her youngest, Christopher, at age five, had a ball playing with the coins in his piggy bank, matching stacks, and practicing his counting. It's a year later. Guess what? He's lost interest in saving his money. Getting kids interested in saving is very different than keeping them interested.

Christopher now wants more than a second piggy bank. He wants to buy everything he sees in the toy store. "Can I have that?" he asks repetitively, with an annoying innocence.

Christopher doesn't like the idea of saving anymore, now that he knows money can buy things; all he wants to do is spend, spend, spend. Christopher's parents are wondering, what now? Giving Christopher a choice to save is no longer working.

So how do we keep kids interested in saving? Give them lots and lots of reasons to save.

So how do we keep kids interested in saving? Give them lots and lots of reasons to save. First, make sure you are providing them plenty of opportunities to gain their own financial independence by not buying them everything they want.

A strong unwavering desire for the "toy du jour" usually gives kids the most immediate reason to save. Many kids need time-sensitive experiences to learn, especially in relationship to long-term lessons such as saving.

Second, turn their desire for the toy du jour into a savings goal. Kids tend to be more vested (and invested) when they have come up with their own reasons to save. This can be as simple as creating their very own wish list.

The Secret of the Proverbial Wish List

Want an easy way to say "no" the next time your kids want something? Encourage your kids to start a wish list.

As adults, what do we do when we want something, but don't have the means? We have to initially chalk it up as a wish. Your kids can be taught to do the same. (Your children may already have a head start on a list of wishes if you've completed the "Needs vs. Wants Balance Sheet" exercise on p. 162.)

A wish list is simply a piece of paper with "My Wish List" or "Abigail's Wants" at the top. Items and their prices follow underneath. Your children can fill it out, or you can if they're not yet writing. Younger kids can use pictures to make a collage of their wishes. Then, wherever you're in a store, online, or at a friend's house, and your child has an "I want a" attack, you can say, with empathy, "Oh bummer, honey. Today is not a gift day. But maybe you want to add that to your wish list."

For practical purposes, younger kids may need your help with identifying the essential information, such as price and item number at a store. Older kids can track the necessary details for keeping their own wish list.

As an added benefit, a wish list can double as a gift list whenever someone wants to find out what to give to your child for a present.

Your Child's First Financial Plan

A wish list is effective with kids of most any age, because it visually depicts a "present" wish for more money—with saving (or earning) as solutions. It also serves as your child's first financial plan. If kids are going to understand the real value of a savings program, then making a plan and achieving their own goals can be a way to keep them invested. That's because they will experience the fun of using the money they have successfully saved.

Learning how to save for the things we wish for in life is the first step to knowing we can obtain them.

What do you think is going to happen when the Bank of Mom and Dad is closed to your child's random wishes? Or when the child's desires chronically exceed their means? Many kids have a shorter or more reasonable wish list when they know that they are the ones who have to fulfill it.

It's a challenge not to succumb to giving our kids everything they want. Yet learning how to save for the things we wish for in life is the first step to knowing we can obtain them. The confidence of setting and achieving a savings goal is a luxury we all want to be able to afford. No one said preparing our kids for the real world would be easy, but kids will surely recognize it when they leave home.

Wish, Phish!

Invite your children to make another type of list if they are in a chronic state of not being able to fulfill a wish or two on their list. Have them list how much they spend for snacks, entertainment, recreation, and other items on a weekly basis. If their income is greater than their expenses, revisit the benefits of saving at allowance time. A visual picture that the child creates may help drive home the need to make a fiscal change. (For more information about how to talk to kids about the importance of saving money, see "Five Kid-Sized Reasons to Save Money" on the next page.)

Whenever your children want something and "it's not a gift day," suggest they put it on their wish list. No need to argue. Instead of pulling out your money, pull out your favorite Love and Logic one-liner, such as "I love you too much to argue," followed by, if necessary, "And what did I say?"

Bottom Line: Keep your kids interested in savings by giving them lots and lots of reasons to save. That way they will learn how to turn their wishes into goals.

Five Kid-Sized Reasons to Save Money

Many kids don't want to save *any* of their money. Other kids want to save *all* of it. How does one establish a middle ground between the miser and the spendthrift?

Both types of kids have something to learn. The child who hoards money needs to learn how to enjoy it, and the spendthrift needs to learn how to save it to enjoy it later. Setting goals will help both hoarders and spendthrifts learn to save and spend wisely.

One parent—when her spendthrift stepdaughter popped the question "Why save?"—used a variation of Love and Logic's five-step problem-solving method to plant the seeds for saving and spending wisely."

Here's how Mom handled this situation:

Ella: "So why should I save my money? It's more fun to spend it."

Mom: "Well, I know what some kids have done when they choose to save. Would you like to hear their ideas?

Ella: "Yeah, maybe."

Mom: "Well …

> Some kids save because their parents say 'no' to buying them something … but you already know about that, right?
>
> Some kids save to take a trip with their friends, or to have more spending money to buy fun stuff on vacation.
>
> Many kids know that their parents cannot afford another car for them to drive, so they start early to save money to buy their own vehicle.
>
> Others save to get a head start on paying for college.
>
> Some kids save to buy a special gift for a friend or family member.

Give it some thought. I'm sure you'll come up with your own good reasons."

Notice that Mom didn't ask for an answer on-the-spot. The reason to save needs time to germinate for some kids. See if one or more of these ideas hooks your child, and then invite them to create a personal goal.

Do the opposite if your child tends to hoard money. You can use the examples above for inspiration, and invite your child to come up with ideas that make spending money fun for him or her. (Some parents of hoarders have also found success by giving their kids "family" money—for example, have the child select groceries from a list and handle the payment transactions to practice and to experience the enjoyment that comes with spending.)

Bottom Line: Many kids have a tough time appreciating the value of saving money until given a good enough reason to do so. Once they create their own reason, they tend to take ownership for setting and achieving their own savings goal.

Egads! Fifteen Wishes?

It's a rare child who has only one wish at a time. What do you do when your child has big dreams and multiple wishes?

Maria, nine years old, was so excited about receiving her allowance for the first time that she could hardly stand still. Shaking her head up and down, she shifted her weight from one foot to another, clasping her hands behind her back in an apparent effort to control herself. Maria's smile widened in anticipation as her mother patiently explained the purpose of allowance and how the enclosed statement worked.

Once Maria realized her newfound purchasing power, she thought, "When my parents tell me 'no,' I'll just buy it myself!" She felt *sooo* empowered.

Maria couldn't stop talking about all the ways she wanted to use her money. She followed her mother around the house and wanted to know if and when Mom could take her to the store … Today? Tomorrow? How about now?!

Maria's parents now have the perfect recipe for creating a need to set savings goals:

- Maria's desire
- A want
- A little parental encouragement

"Can we go to the store right now? Please, please, please, please?" Maria pleaded as she tried every kid trick in the book to persuade her mother to put her day on hold and take her shopping right this minute:

Mom: "Sorry, sweetie, but I've got a few things to do before I fix dinner."
Maria: "But …" (shoulders sagging, lips quivering, shaking her head in disappointment)
Mom: "Do you know what you want to buy when we do go?"
Maria: "Fun stuff."

Mom: "Why not make up a wish list? That way you'll know exactly what to shop for when we do go."

Mom helped Maria find some paper and pencils from the kitchen drawer and invited her to sit at the kitchen counter to begin her very first wish list. Maria jotted down a few items and then looked up at her mother and smiled. "I can have everything I write down, right?"

Now it was Mom's turn to shake her head. She placed a loving hand on her daughter's back and said, "Well … you can *wish* for anything your heart desires … won't it be fun to find out?"

Check Mate

What are the chances Maria will need not only a price check, but also a reality check? And what are the chances that her wants exceed the amount she has to spend when they do go to the store?

Maria's list was fifteen items long. Some wishes were small, inexpensive items like gum, a movie, a bracelet, and hair clips, and others were more expensive. A pony, a hand-held electronic game, and a swimming pool topped the list.

After she read them back to her mother, Mom asked Maria to number her wishes according to their importance to her. Mom noticed the numeral 1 next to "swimming pool" as she glanced over her daughter's shoulder.

No need for Mom to dash her daughter's wishes just yet. Because Mom is using the Love and Logic principles of shared control and shared thinking and decision-making opportunities, Maria will be able to figure out the relationship of wishes to money all by herself, either on their first trip to the store or by learning how to turn desire into decisions, as described next.

And what if Maria comes up with a wish that rubs against family values? Mom can simply say, "Feel free to put anything you want on your wish list as long as it fits with our family values."

 Bottom Line: Wise parents test the strength of the child's desire as a prerequisite to the effort required to make it come true.

Turning Desire into Decisions

Wouldn't it be cool if every amazing idea that came into our heads magically happened? We wouldn't have to do a single thing except think, "I want … a swimming pool … a new cell phone … a new TV and computer!" That's how many kids think. Adults know, however, that there are many things that need to happen between each one of those dots.

Simply wishing for something doesn't make it so, as Maria finds out—but setting realistic goals sure helps. It's our job as parents to help our kids connect the dots between their wishes and monetary reality.

EXERCISE 8.3: Five Steps to Wishing Well

Here are five action steps to take when your child's wishes are bigger than their bank account:

Step 1: Make a wish list.
Step 2: Prioritize the items.
Step 3: Research the cost of each wish.
Step 4: Assess current savings.
Step 5: Estimate the time, do the math, and plug in the numbers.

Step 1: Make a wish list.

Begin by inviting your child to write down his or her wishes if they haven't already done so. Coach them, as necessary, to jot down what they want "to be," "to do, and "to have" in life. Committing their dreams, wishes, and ambitions to paper helps kids clarify what's important to them. (For some tips about how to be your child's dream coach, see "Too big for your britches!" on p. 255.)

Step 2: Prioritize the items.

Once your child has developed a wish list, ask them to number each item according to its priority. Most kids won't have trouble picking the most important ones first; but, since not all goals will be immediately attainable, kids will need to be coached into numerically choosing one over another.

Like Maria's mom, wise parents use a written plan and ask lots of questions to encourage the child's thinking—so that *the child* discovers whether his or her priorities are fiscally logical.

Step 3: Research the cost of each wish.

Next, encourage specifics. This step is a fact-finding mission. Ask your child to estimate or research the approximate cost of each goal.

Step 4: Assess current savings.

Assess how much money, if any, your child has already saved, and how much they want to apply to their wishes. This determines how much money they'll need to have to achieve each goal.

Step 5: Estimate the time, do the math, and plug in the numbers.

Encourage to your children to:

- Set a date for achieving each goal.
- Calculate how much money to put aside for each planning period (weekly, monthly) to reach that goal by the desired date.

Here's each step in chart form:

My Wish Worksheet

Wish/Goal	Estimated Cost	Current and Future Money [savings, job earnings, etc.]	Total Amount to Be Saved	Periodic Amount to Be Saved [weekly, monthly, etc.]	Target Date

The Way to Wishes

Some parents go through these steps one wish at a time. Other parents encourage their children to group like items together (inexpensive versus expensive, immediate versus long-term, etc.).

This step-by-step process teaches children how to make smart financial decisions based on realistic goals. What you choose to do will depend on the age of the child, the number of items on the list, and the child's financial know-how. Adapt as necessary for the particular circumstances.

Parents who use this method report that each new wish-of-the-day gives their kids another opportunity to practice finding out if their wishes and their financial realities are a match. Instead of feeling like shopping with your child is a curse, it becomes a blessing. Many parents have found freedom from the tyranny of begging by smiling and using this one-liner: "Feel free to put that on your wish list."

As for Maria and her number one wish for a swimming pool? She quickly changed her priorities after discovering how much a pool costs—a swimming pool on a $7 weekly income? "I don't think sooo, Mom!" she quipped. Once the swimming pool was out, the bracelets automatically moved up the list.

Notice how Mom avoids having to struggle to say "no" or argue about the impractical nature of the wish. No lectures or fights are necessary. And if Maria tells Mom, "*You* can afford a pool!" Mom can answer with confidence, "Sweetie, it's not in my budget either"—something her daughter is learning the meaning of firsthand!

Parents who use this method report that each new wish-of-the-day gives their kids another opportunity to practice finding out if their wishes and their financial realities are a match.

Bottom Line: Wise parents set up the situation so that their children work out the plan!

"Too big for your britches!"

Ever notice how children want to be a firefighter one day and an astronaut the next? Or they want to have a drum one day and a string instrument the next? These "wishes" stimulate their imagination, creating positive energy toward achieving their goals.

Kid-size dreams tend to be big—super-sized in fact. That's because kids feel their potential long before they know how to realize it. Well-intentioned adults, however, tend to bring children back to reality in ways that can crush a young and tender dream.

Try not to dash their fledgling desires with a "realistic" response when kids are making and sharing their wish list with you. No matter how far-fetched or impractical their ideas seem, encourage their dreams. Perhaps what they suggest may not be possible today or even tomorrow, but *it may spark something that is.*

Here are some typical reactions to kids' schemes and ideas:

Child: "Mom, I want to babysit."
Parent: "Honey, you're not old enough yet to take care of anyone else's children. I doubt anyone would trust or hire you."

Tween: "I'd like to repair other kids' bikes."
Parent: "You can't fix your own bike, let alone anyone else's."

Teen: "I've decided what I want to do to earn some extra money."
Parent: "What?"
Teen: "Seal driveways with that black paint stuff."
Parent: "*That's* not going to happen if you don't start exercising and develop some muscles. You're not strong enough to carry those buckets."

These parents are well-intentioned: they don't want their children to fail and feel the disappointment of life's harsh realities. But the discouragement that children sense, because the parents don't believe in the visions the children hold for themselves, is more damaging than allowing them to discover the merits of their ideas on their own.

Turn Well-Meaning into Well-Being

What can you do instead? Ask lots of questions. Encourage a dialogue to find out what interests the child about the idea. There's something swimming around in their growing mind that needs cultivation, not deprivation. After all, it's only a thought, with the potential for many variations.

Better responses are:

"Oh? Tell me more about that."
"What interests you about that idea?"
"How can you find out how much money you'll make doing that?"
"What can you do to find out if that's possible?"

The key is to keep the field of dreams and possibilities wide open with active questions that promote thinking. Questions that begin with "What" and "How" engage children more than questions that begin with "Could you," "Have you," "Should you," "Can you," and so forth. The latter foster passive answers such as "yes" or "no," whereas "What" and "How" questions are more conducive to an interactive conversation.

If your children answer with "I don't know," invite them to research the feasibility of an idea. Send your children on a fact-finding mission to test the seriousness of their commitment to their goals and ideas. In that way, children become the creators of their own source of joy (or disappointment), and learn from it.

Wise parents resist the temptation to protect their children from many of life's failures and disappointments. They encourage their children to discover what is appealing about their dreams, thereby allowing the potential of their ideas to grow along with their children.

Bottom Line: While our kids' britches may be too big at first, and their minds limitless, our job as parents is to allow them to discover and grow into their dreams in their own unique way.

Dreams and Schemes: The Real Cost of a Pet

Wise parents use their children's wish lists and the "My Wish Worksheet" as learning tools for teaching their kids how to set realistic financial goals. Regular use of these steps helps children get lots of experience with what it really takes to turn a desire into a dream come true. Let's look at how one dad used his daughter's wish du jour as a teaching opportunity.

Ten-year-old Chloe was focused on wanting only one thing on her wish list— a puppy. She suddenly became enthralled by the same special breed of dog that her favorite movie star owned, and while she had other things on her wish list, a new puppy jumped to the top.

Dad invites her to research how much a puppy of this breed will cost, as well as the costs of caring for and feeding the puppy. Dad agrees to cover the mainte- nance costs (food, vet and kennel care, etc.) *if* she buys the dog and *if* she takes care of the dog every day.

It's Sunday evening. Dad and Chloe are sitting at the kitchen table with pencil, paper, and a blank wish worksheet. Dad uses this worksheet to guide his daughter's decision-making process. Using the results of her research, he shows her how to plug in the numbers to reflect the facts of her findings.

Here's what Chloe figured out:

Chloe's Wish Worksheet

Wish/Goal	Estimated Cost	Current and Future Money [savings, job earnings, etc.]	Total Amount to Be Saved	Periodic Amount to Be Saved [weekly, monthly, etc.]	Target Date
1. Puppy	$400	$150 saved, plus my job earnings of $20 per week	$250	$20 weekly	12 and a half weeks

After charting her course, Chloe can see that she has some saving to do. She is very surprised! She remarks that she'll be eleven years old by the time she saves enough money!

Instead of Dad telling her that a puppy might be really expensive and that it will take her a long time to save enough money to buy it, Chloe discovers for herself what her wish for a special dog will really cost.

Benefits of a Cost Analysis

Wise parents, like Chloe's dad, encourage a process by which the child gets to make the discoveries that the parent probably already knows. What would be better: telling Chloe that purebred puppies are expensive, or having her learn that on her own? Chloe's dad does her a big favor by allowing her the opportunity to research and explore, firsthand, the cost of fulfilling her wish.

Once Chloe developed her own "cost/benefit analysis," she was more open to Dad's idea of considering a dog that looks like her favorite breed—at the pound, for free. A puppy saved is not always a puppy earned!

Notice how Dad shared some control by giving her the opportunity to re-search her wish; the choice, however, was still hers. (Dad is unconcerned at this time with the responsibilities of owning a pet. Kids' ideas change as often as the weather; besides, it's a moot point until she makes her decision.)

Research and Destroy, or Research and Enjoy?

Did Dad proceed to tell Chloe all the reasons why an expensive and popular breed of dog is probably not a good idea? Or that taking care of a puppy is more work than it seems? No. Dad used the simple strategy of asking lots of "What" and "How" questions.

To fill out the wish worksheet, Chloe had to find the answers to:

1. What she wants.
2. How much it costs.
3. What has been already saved that can be used for the purchase.
4. When she wants to buy it.
5. How much she needs to save incrementally over time.

The answer to the last question is where the rubber meets the road. At this point, some kids decide they don't really want their wish as they thought they did; others become even more committed once they understand and see that it's achievable.

Chloe, for example, realized that she would have to save her entire allowance for three months straight, and work at jobs every week, to earn enough for her "celebrity" pet.

Most wishes involve a financial factor, which children don't consider or understand unless we teach them. An important step for turning wishes into possibilities is to research and analyze the reality of making their wish come true.

Children receive important lessons in how to make realistic financial decisions—with lifetime benefits—when they are given the "job" to search for their own answers to those time-tested questions, and are able to examine them from a financially sound and factual perspective.

Bottom Line: Wise parents remember that desire is a powerful motivator for changing wishes into goals.

Savings Withdrawals: The Case for Financial Planning

Let's say Chloe has decided she still wants a purebred "celebrity" dog in spite of the price. She's been saving for several weeks and then along comes another compelling desire. At a recent sleepover at her best friend's house, she discovers she wants a mural painted on her bedroom wall, just like the one in Kayla's bedroom.

Kids' wishes can change by the day, or the hour. This can be fertile ground for arguments, and a potential minefield for parents who don't have a financial plan. A written plan, such as Chloe's wish worksheet, provides the groundwork for judging the financial merits of one wish against another. It also comes in handy later, when it's time to reprioritize or to consider spending money.

Let's see how this might work. Here comes Chloe, bounding into the living room, front door slamming behind her:

Chloe:	"Dad, you should see Kayla's new bedroom. There is this beautiful mural right above her bed. It's a picture of her chasing butterflies. It's so cool!"
Dad:	(looking up from his newspaper) "Sounds pretty!"
Chloe:	"Yeah. I want one. Really, really bad."
Dad:	(smiling) "Oh … Really? I suppose personalize murals on girls' bedroom walls are free …"

Chloe approaches Dad and throws her arm around his shoulders, cocking her head to one side and smiling:

Chloe:	"No … not free … but Kayla's aunt is a professional painter and she did that for Kayla as a gift, so I know she'd do one for me."
Dad:	(nodding) "For free?"
Chloe:	"Uh … probably not … for free …"
Dad:	"Okay. Then how do you plan to pay for it?"
Chloe:	(tentatively) "You could buy it for me … ?" (looks to Dad, but he just smiles and returns his attention to the sports page) "Or, I could take it out of my savings … ? But I don't have enough …"(still searching for any loophole, but then arrives at the right answer) "Or, I can save for it."
Dad:	"Saving might work. How can you find out more about that option?"
Chloe:	"I don't know … Get out my savings plan?"
Dad:	"Yep. Let's see if you need to rethink this … between a dog and a mural, what's more important now?"

Chloe:	"A mural. Definitely."
Dad:	"Okay. How much does it cost?"
Chloe:	"I don't know."
Dad:	"How can you find that out?"
Chloe:	"Call Kayla?"
Dad:	"Sounds like you have some research to do. Let me know what you find out."

Chloe heads back out the front door and bounds off to Kayla's house again.

A few hours later:

Chloe:	"Dad, her aunt usually charges over a thousand dollars to paint a mural! But she said she would do it for only six hundred!"
Dad:	"So now what do you think?"
Chloe:	(looking down at her wish worksheet, pausing thoughtfully) "I don't think I have enough money to save for both. Besides … I think I want a dog more."
Dad:	"Well, it's your choice. You don't have to make your decision today. If you just continue to save each week, you'll be able to eventually reach your goal for whatever you want at that time."
Chloe:	(starting to pout) "But Dad. This is so lame. None of my friends have to use a savings plan. Their parents love them. And besides, Kayla says that it's the parents' job to buy nice things for their kids."
Dad:	"Nice try, Chloe. Maybe you could get Kayla's parents to adopt you. Then you could forget about savings plans."
Chloe:	"Oh Daaaddd!"

A kid with a savings plan takes the monkey off the parent's back, because the plan either supports or denies the child's financial reality, not you.

The beauty of a written plan with specific goals is that no matter what Chloe decides, her choices to reprioritize or spend money become clearer.

The wish worksheet, for example, will help Chloe figure out that if she switches gears to save for a mural, it will delay her saving for what she really wants more—a dog. A kid with a savings plan takes the monkey off the parent's back, because *the plan* either supports or denies the child's financial reality, not you.

Bottom Line: Wise parents let their children's own financial research and planning be the "prioritizing and withdrawal boss," not them.

A Means to a Dream

This chapter's stories about Travis, Maria, and Chloe illustrate several important points about our children's perceptions of their money and our part in guiding them to responsible money management.

Making our dreams come true requires financial planning—even if it's just remembering to bring our money to the store. Wish lists, reserves for the unexpected, changing priorities, and experiencing the reward of buying something we've saved for are all part of the fun of having money.

Most of us can agree that it's difficult for kids to plan how to use their money in the future when they can't see beyond the present. Our job is to provide opportunities for our kids to practice planning and setting financial goals, and then allowing our children to realize the consequences of their decisions—both positive and negative. Those actions are an essential first step toward the kind of financial future we want our kids to have as adults—a future characterized by financial security, independence, and freedom.

While our children lack the maturity to think in those terms, wise parents keep the big picture in mind. Smart saving is an essential skill for a more fulfilling life. That's the basic reason to teach children how to save, no matter how much or how little they can afford.

 Bottom Line: Wise parents use real money, real life experiences, and real world lessons to teach their kids how to save.

CHAPTER 9

Borrowing

Here's to Your Credit

This chapter shows you how to use loans, grants, and matching funds to teach your children financial responsibility. It covers the reasons to loan, types of loans, how much to loan, repayment plans, and the consequences of not repaying a loan.

The Love and Logic of Loans: Hero or Zero?

After what seemed like the 100th run down the ski slopes, Brittany, thirteen years old, eyed a pair of "spectacular" sunglasses in the ski lodge gift shop. She spontaneously decided she just *had* to have them as part of her eyewear collection. One slight snafu … she didn't have any money with her.

So Brittany did what most children do: she asked for a loan. "Dad, I promise to pay you back. I really, really will …" she pleaded, flashing the very same eyes she wanted to decorate.

Dad thought, "Uh huh, right! Just like you did the last time and the time before that." Then Dad did the usual: "How much do you need?" he asked with resignation, handing her a couple of bills.

This scenario is a daily occurrence in many shopping malls throughout America. Kids ask for money from their obliging parents, with lots of promises to pay them back. Meanwhile, those same kids are pretty confident that Mom and Dad will either forget or at least not collect.

Many of us feel as if we're in a double bind when our kids ask us for money.

Like Brittany's dad, many of us feel as if we're in a double bind when our kids ask us for money. On the one hand, our failure to recoup our cash leaves us feeling like we're not doing our job teaching them about the rules of borrowing. On the other hand, collecting a few measly bucks feels like taking on the role of a knee-capping hit man or nasty loan shark.

Most kids don't make it any easier for us either. They grumble, gripe, or try to manipulate their way out of their fiscal obligation. Sometimes it's just easier to do what Brittany's dad did—give, but don't ask your kid to pay you back. Then we promise ourselves (and threaten our kids) that we'll *never, ever* lend them money again unless they pay us back.

One forgetful mom, reluctant to ask for her money once she remembered weeks later, said, "It gets really nasty for both me and my kid, because the joy of the toy has passed and the promise to repay has been forgotten."

That is, of course, unless we learn how to effectively handle our kid's requests for money.

A Gift or a Loan?

Loaning money to kids can be confusing. Was Brittany's dad being a hero? Or was he being a zero by giving her money for sunglasses without requiring repayment? Was the money a gift or a loan? The answers lie in what happens when Brittany and her father return home.

It's a gift if the money is not repaid. It's a loan if it is. What's the difference?

A loan is a lending hand, a temporary use of money as a service to another in need or want.

A bona fide *loan* ends with repayment.
A bona fide *lender* requires repayment.

A gift, on the other hand, does not require repayment. In Brittany's case, unless Dad sets it up as a gift ahead of time by *telling her it's a gift*, then it's technically a loan. Notice how giving kids money automatically *becomes a gift by default* when we don't require repayment.

What's a Dad to Do?

So, standing there in the ski shop, Dad was faced with three basic choices:

1. Give her the money without requesting repayment.
2. Be empathic, followed by "No."
3. Loan her the money and require repayment.

Let's briefly look at the pros and cons of each choice.

By giving Brittany the money to purchase the sunglasses without expectation of repayment, Dad missed an opportunity to allow his daughter to gain some important money management experience. Instead, Brittany had another fruitful experience in how to manipulate her way toward entitlement. The financial policy of "can't pay for it, can't have it" apparently does not apply to Brittany.

Another choice would have been for Dad to refuse. He could have said, "Bummer, honey. Those sunglasses look really, really nice on you, but I'm all out of loaner money today." If Brittany had continued to plead, he could have calmly replied, with a smile, "Nice try" (or some other Love and Logic one-liner) to neutralize the arguing. (For more ways to say "no" to your children, see "Eight Ways to Say 'No' to 'Buy-Buy'" on p. 229.)

There's only one good choice that Dad could have made to teach Brittany the rules of borrowing: loan her the money and require repayment. Otherwise, in his noble effort to be a hero, he has zeroed out the potential for Brittany to pay a visit to the BRME—the Bank of Real Money Experiences.

One could argue that giving Brittany money to buy sunglasses is no big deal. What's the harm? No harm done *unless* we understand the value in using everyday opportunities to teach our kids fiscal responsibility. Wise parents take advantage of such opportunities when the price tags of making mistakes are more affordable. They know the importance of using real life experience to teach real life financial lessons.

It's okay to give kids spontaneous gifts of money as an occasional surprise, but not when they beg, demand, or act entitled. (For more information about the importance of teaching your kids how to borrow money, see "The Dangers of *Never* Giving Loans to Kids" on the next page.)

"Okay, Brittany, but ..."

So let's say Dad decides to loan her the money. Here's what he could say, standing there in the store: "Honey, I will loan you the money to buy your sunglasses, but how do you plan to repay me when we get back home?" Then, he'll need to listen for a workable plan, and follow through by requesting a direct cash repayment or a signed I.O.U. No plan, no pay, no sunglasses.

What might Brittany learn if Dad requires repayment? An experience that helps her understand and think: "I'd better remember to bring my money next time—just in case I want to buy something. Plus, when Dad lends me money, he respects me and himself enough to back up his words with actions."

Dad teaches an important lesson in honesty, too. By requiring Brittany to follow through on their mutually agreed upon repayment plan, he encourages her to put her money where her mouth is. Integrity grows each time she makes good on her promised payback—just as she'll need to do with any bank loan. Not a bad payoff for a single transaction.

Rescue or Repayment?

Love and Logic parents know that rescuing kids by loaning them money is rarely a good idea except in matters of life or limb, or to teach a lesson. While it may appear that we're heroes when we give money to our kids, we can also be rescuers. The real hero is the parent who understands that when we rescue kids from having "financial experiences," we rob them of some very important opportunities to be accountable for their choices.

Parents who rescue their kids usually want to "save" them from disappointment, dissatisfaction, or any experience of being unhappy or uncomfortable. Save them instead by holding them accountable for repayment.

Rescue teaches entitlement. Repayment teaches character.

If we're going to bankroll our kids, we need to learn how to "qualify" our loans; otherwise we're faced with the same problem as the bank—bad debt ... in more ways than one. Brittany's desire for a new pair of fashionable sunglasses does not "qualify" as a learning opportunity *unless* Dad requires Brittany to develop a plan and then follow through on the repayment process.

Let's look at how to loan children money using the principles of Love and Logic.

The Dangers of Never Giving Loans to Kids

This title must be a mistake. Shouldn't it read, "The Dangers of *Giving* Kids Loans?" Actually it's just the opposite. With easy credit, easy mortgages (low or no down payment), and easy virtual money transactions, today's financial reality dictates that there is a risk in *not* giving your kids loans for practice.

Many affluent parents want their children to take advantage of every opportunity available to them and are willing to endlessly "fund their fun." But just because you *can* afford it, doesn't mean you *should* pay for it. While you might *want* to give your kids everything *because you can*, the wisest parents exercise fiscal restraint in their children's pursuit of happiness. As discussed in many places throughout this book, "too much take and not enough give" raises entitled kids.

Less affluent parents also want their kids to have things and be happy. These parents still want to buy whatever they can afford, instead of loaning their children money for practice.

Regardless of your socioeconomic situation, the issue is never how much money to loan, but that money *gets loaned for practice*, period. A bone fide loan holds kids accountable because it requires them to give back. They learn how to become fiscally responsible now, just as they'll need to be later as adults with families.

Few of us can go through life without borrowing money at one time or another. Wise parents give kids plenty of opportunities to experience borrowing and repaying, because ...

Regardless of your socioeconomic situation, the issue is never how much money to loan, but that money gets loaned for practice, period.

Fun requires funding. Life requires funding.

Instead of funding *all* their fun, loan for fun instead. If the child wants money for something you approve of, it's "Eureka!"—a perfect opportunity to provide a loan with the kind of value that can last a lifetime.

When to Loan

Lenders use the term "qualify" to describe the overall ability of the borrower to repay a loan. You receive money if you "qualify."

But what does it mean for a parent to "qualify" their child for a loan, when the child has no real financial history, no collateral, and no credit score?

Kyle: "Mom, can I borrow twenty bucks?"
Mom: "No."
Kyle: "How about thirty bucks?"
Mom: "Kyle, if I won't lend you twenty dollars, what makes you think I'll lend you thirty?"
Kyle: "How about fifty bucks?"

Do you think that this teenager's use of the term "borrow" is suspect? Are you thinking that Mom should ask: "What for?"

Here are a few "qualification" guidelines to help with the "to loan or not to loan money" decision. One guideline considers values; the other considers the purpose of the loan.

Loan with True Value

Values—yours and your child's—are the first guideline to use when deciding to loan money.

Family Values

Wise parents decide to loan or not to loan money based on their family values. For example, you may want to lend money for a fruit salad, but not a candy bar. Or you might loan money for setting up a tropical fish tank, but deny a request for an objectionable video game.

The point is to use "lending money" as a way to *teach your values*, not contradict them. As long as lending money to your children doesn't compromise your family's core values, a chance to practice borrowing money flexes their financial muscles while it builds their credit and character.

Child Values

Some parents lend money to their kids for something *they* want them to have, as a way to get them motivated. Guard against becoming a lender when your child does not want to be a borrower. One parent loaned money to his capable but unmotivated child—for a math tutor! Paybacks can have their drawbacks.

When adults need a loan, they go to the bank, the bank doesn't come to them. And so it goes for kids.

Err on the side of lending, therefore, only when your child asks to borrow. It may be hard to collect if you want to loan money to your child for something *you* want them to have versus something *they* want. For inexperienced borrowers especially, make sure that the decision to borrow money is your child's.

> **The loans with the most value are the ones where the *decision to borrow* is child-driven, and the *decision to lend* is parent-driven.**

Notice how this guideline fits with Love and Logic principles. Control is shared through choices. The parent can control whether to lend money or not (based on family values) and the child can choose to borrow money for what they want, or not. If they choose to borrow, they can also be given choices about how to repay the loan.

Loan with True Purpose

Purpose is the second guideline to use when deciding to loan children money. The authors of Love and Logic recommend that parents loan money to their children for two basic purposes:

1. To practice the cycle of borrowing and repaying loans.
2. To educate or invest in oneself.

The best loans are the ones that give kids plenty of practice with the policies and procedures of borrowing and repaying money, while also giving kids a chance to invest in themselves. As with all good opportunities, the goal is learning with a purpose—the type of learning that prepares our children for the financial realities of becoming happily self-supporting.

Notice how the two reasons to loan money to your kids—to practice and to invest/educate in oneself—work well together. It's a loan that repays twice. Kids can learn all about the rules of "the loaner" and "the loanee" while also developing their interests, hobbies, and education about life.

Let's take a closer look at loans for practice and loans for education and investment.

Loan for Practice

Kids need lots of practice feeling both the affects and effects of borrowing money now, and paying it back later. Loans for practice are usually small in amount, repaid quickly, and offer a good foundation for the second type of loan—loans that advance educational or entrepreneurial endeavors.

Understanding the cycle of borrowing and repaying requires repetition, as with learning any new skill. Wise parents allow their kids the opportunity to borrow small amounts of money on a fairly regular basis, one loan at a time. It's best to refrain from issuing another loan until the first one has been repaid in full, to establish creditworthiness. Then—and only then—are they ready for more significant loans.

What better experiences to offer children than those that require time and effort, while investing in an education about self and life?

Loaning money to our children for practice makes the price tags for "mistakes"—literally and figuratively—more affordable. Kids who have had these opportunities before they ever sign their first car loan have an enormous advantage over other kids whose parents have never given them a chance to experience the cycle of debits and credits.

Loan for Education and Investment

The second purpose of loaning children money is to support educational or entrepreneurial experiences. What better experiences to offer children than those that require time and effort, while investing in an education about self and life?

From a lender's perspective, a loan is an investment—an investment in the person and the person's ability to repay the money. It's really an exchange of the borrower's time, energy, and effort for the lender's money. When you invest in someone who is willing to invest in him- or herself first, it increases the likelihood of being repaid, because the investor decides that the potential reward of helping someone outweighs their risk.

There are several factors to consider when making investment-type loans to kids. Your answers to the following questions should help you decide:

- Will the loan advance your child's personal growth and character development?
- Is the loan for an educational or entrepreneurial purpose?
- Will the opportunity be a learning experience?

 You've made the first cut in the decision-making process if you can answer "yes" to any of these questions. The second level of decision making is: "Exactly what for?" (For a list of investment-type loans, see "Loan Opportunity List" on the next page.)

Loan Guidelines Summary
- Fits with your family values.
- Decision to borrow is the child's.
- Offers opportunities to practice.
- Offers opportunities to invest in oneself.

Loan Opportunity List

Joshua: (sauntering into the kitchen) "Dad, can I have some money?"

Dad: "What for?"

Joshua: "Oh just 'cuz ... I ... uhm, just need to borrow it ..."

Of course, lots of situations will come up in a parent's life that will test the use of these guiding principles.

To keep it simple, loans for education and investment fall into three categories—a person, place, or thing. In other words, loan your kids money for educational or entrepreneurial opportunities

- with special people,
- in special places,
- for special things.

Let's look at some specific examples.

Why Loan?

Educational/entrepreneurial experiences with special people:
- Field trip with school class
- A mentoring experience in a field of your child's interest
- Religious or charitable mission trip

Education/entrepreneurial opportunities in special places:
- Specialized summer camps—gymnastics, water sports, horseback riding
- Tuition to support your child's special interest—vocational, hobby, or recreational opportunity
- Capital for a lemonade stand or startup equipment for a lawn service business

---

> **Special educational/entrepreneurial things (to advance educational goals):**
> - Games
> - Software
> - Books
> - Electronics or digital items that educate
> - Sports/vocational/extracurricular activities—equipment, lessons, services

Use your family values as a guideline for what constitutes a special person, place, or thing. For example, a decision to loan money to your child to buy a new bike may reflect the value you place on health and recreation. Or a decision to not loan money for a collector's series of video games may reflect the importance you place on quality social time with friends outdoors.

This list is not comprehensive, of course; adjust it to fit the unique circumstances of your family.

Qualified Loans Are Quality Loans

Note how all of the loan opportunities in the previous list satisfy the guidelines for selecting a "qualified loan." In other words, the loan is automatically a quality choice on two different levels—values and purpose. This reduces conflicts about what you will or will not lend money for. When selected in this manner, your loan has the wonderful potential to advance *your child's* personal growth and character development while maintaining *your family's* value system.

These guidelines are not meant to imply that the only way your children will experience any of these opportunities is to borrow money from you. But these are the kinds of loans that often bear the most fruit.

Isn't it true that the people who have the best chance of paying you back are the people who have learned how to invest their time, abilities, and energy wisely?

Types of Loans

Let's say your child asks you to loan him or her some money. The purpose of the loan qualifies as practice or education and it fits with your family values. The next question is: How much?

There are several factors involved in determining how much money to lend. Part of the decision depends on the child's financial know-how, and the amount of money in question. The other part involves the type of loan—such as full versus partial, and short- versus long-term. Let's take a look at several factors to consider when providing any kind of "financial assistance" to our children.

Full or Partial Loans?

Parents can choose between two basic types of loans: for the full amount, or for a partial amount.

A full loan needs no explanation. The lender lends and the borrower repays the full amount of the original loan. Loans for the full amount are a good choice when the amount is small, and the borrower is inexperienced and needs practice. Many parents understandably are not inclined to loan their child larger amounts of money, for a variety of commonsense reasons.

Partial loans lend only a portion of the amount. A partial loan is a good option if:

- family funds are limited
- you want to offer an incentive to earn or save
- there are concerns about the child's ability or resolve to repay

There is an important distinction to make between loaning the full amount and loaning only a portion of the full amount. As stated before, a bona fide loan can be for any amount of money (full amount or part of the full amount). It's a temporary use of money as a service to another *with the expectation of repayment* for the amount of money loaned.

Partial loans, on the other hand, mean that some of the money is borrowed and the rest of the money needs to come from somewhere else. Matching funds, donations, and certain types of grants and scholarships are all examples of "permanent but partial" *gifts, without the expectation of repayment.*

Full vs. Partial Loans

Full Loan	Partial Loan
Full amount borrowed.	Partial amount borrowed.
Temporary use of monies.	One portion is borrowed. The other portion provides permanent use of monies, which come from grants, gifts, matching funds.
Monies repaid in full.	Only borrowed monies repaid in full.

Let's say your child wants a special piece of sports equipment. You can loan him or her the full amount. Or you can offer partial funding in one of two ways:

- Offer to loan a portion of the money for repayment.
- Offer to match, grant, or gift "up to" a certain amount.

If the sports equipment costs $100, for example, your child could repay the full $100, repay $50 because you gifted $50, or earn $1 for every $5 you will match until the total is reached.

Short- or Long-Term Loans?

Loans are either short-term or long-term debts. Wise parents save the long-term loans for those special opportunities and lessons that might not otherwise happen unless the costs are shared. (For a look at when the parent and child share the cost of something together, see "Option Two: Test Before You Invest—When Parent and Child Share the Cost" on p. 209.)

Short-term loans are exactly that: they are loans kids pay back *in full* within a week or two. Long-term loans are for more experienced borrowers who can handle a lengthier repayment of a larger amount. The basic differences between short- and long-term loans can be found in the chart below:

Short- vs. Long-Term Loans

Short-Term Loan	Long-Term Loan
One to ten days.	Ten days or longer.
Beginner or inexperienced borrower.	More experienced borrower.
Small amounts.	Larger amounts.
Repaid in full.	Repaid in installments.

Here's a simple guideline to decide between short- and long-term loans: do not extend any new loans until outstanding loans have been repaid. Give your children lots of borrowing and repayment practice with small, short-term loans now, so that they'll be prepared to handle longer, and larger, obligations in the future.

Bottom Line: You want to determine the best type of loan for the circumstances—partial or full, and short- or long-term. Wise parents remember to find an appropriate match between their child and the type of loan they issue.

Kid-Sized Loans: How Much?

Wise parents consider two other factors when determining how much money to lend. One relates to proportion and the other concerns manageability.

Let's look first at the easiest guideline, proportion, since it's a practical matter that combines simple math with common sense.

Loans and Proportion

Loan amounts are typically based on the borrower's ability to repay. Wise lenders use a reasonable "debt to income ratio" to determine how much money to loan.

Wise parents begin with a one-to-one loan ratio (1:1). This means that one dollar is loaned for every dollar earned, saved, or collected in jobs, allowance, or collateral, or a combination thereof. Some parents experiment with higher or lower loan ratios depending on the child's borrowing experience and resources.

The 1:1 ratio has several benefits. It's simple for inexperienced borrowers to understand. And it helps to keep loans timely, short-term, and age-appropriate.

Of course, ratios are not necessary for every loan. Just keep in mind that it's important to loan an amount proportionate to your *child's* income, not *your* income.

For example, you may think that $30 isn't a lot of money, but it's huge, percentage-wise, when your child's allowance is $10 per week. A 3:1 ratio is three times their ability to pay with current income, unless they are highly motivated enough to repay quickly and have the resources to do so. After all, would it be wise to get a loan that would consume three consecutive weeks' worth of your income?

The debt-to-income ratio can increase as the child's age and income increase. For example, you can loan your gainfully employed teenager $5,000 toward the purchase of a car, because their ability to earn money and repay you over time has increased. For your six-year-old, however, whose "income" is basically an allowance, lending $3 for the week is more appropriate.

Loans and Manageability

The second factor concerns the relationship between manageability and motivation. We improve the chances that our children will be more motivated to follow through on repayment if we give them loans that are manageable.

Ever dangle a carrot to entice a horse toward you? The carrot factor encourages a loan opportunity close enough to be doable, but not so far away that the goal becomes discouraging or overwhelming. This is important because

Keep in mind that it's important to loan an amount proportionate to your child's income, not your income.

275

the younger or more inexperienced the child is, the more likely their interest, patience, and ability to repay may become compromised.

Bottom Line: Choose a sensible ratio when figuring the actual amount of money to loan to your child. The key is to keep the amount of the loan *relative to the child's income and ability to repay*, so that it's manageable *for the child*.

How Much to Loan: Summary

The basic qualifier for kids is the same as for adults: don't lend more than you will get back! Or conversely, don't borrow more than you can pay back!

Wise parents set up the loan based on shared control: what the parent can afford and what the child can realistically repay. Wouldn't you want your bank or lending officer to do the same for you?

Partial Loans and Financial Assistance: To Match, Limit, or Grant?

Partial loans are one way to make a loan more manageable for the child and still offer much needed borrowing practice, incentive, or both.

Partial loans are for those parents who are asking:

> "What if my kid wants one of those special things, but they, or I, can't afford it?"
> "What if they want something, but repaying such a large amount is out my child's reach?"
> "What's the best way to go about loaning or assisting them with a portion of the money?"

In fact, partial loans and other types of financial aid are a good choice when you want to encourage your child to pursue one of those special educational or entrepreneurial opportunities suggested in the "Loan Opportunity List." Lending a portion of the cost becomes an incentive, as mentioned earlier. While it may be daunting for your child to earn and save $1,200 for the down payment for something special, meeting them halfway monetarily becomes more enticing.

There are a variety of ways to issue a partial loan. Some parents use the matching funds concept. Some parents provide a limited assistance amount. Other parents provide a grant or scholarship as seed money. All should require the child to develop a plan that qualifies their intention to repay you in effort—that is, in time, possessions, money, or a combination.

Let's examine each kind of assistance in more detail.

Matching Funds

Matching funds typically use a set ratio. A common ratio is 1:1, meaning that for every dollar your child earns or saves, you will match it by gifting a dollar. Other common ratios are 1:2 (i.e., 50¢ given for every $1 earned or saved) and 2:1 ($2 given for every $1 earned or saved). In any case, use a ratio that allows the child some choices — depending on their effort and determination—to reach their goal.

Matching funds are a good option when you want to help your child reach a savings goal for a big-ticket item, provide startup capital for an entrepreneurial enterprise, or encourage a hobby, recreational, or educational opportunity.

Matching funds usually work well for both parents and kids, because they share control while at the same time encouraging choice. Kids get to choose their level of effort, and parents get to choose their level of expenditure. Similar to riding a tandem bike, matching funds have a built-in test that measures the determination to keep in balance with the incentive to keep on pedaling.

Similar to riding a tandem bike, matching funds have a built-in test that measures the determination to keep in balance with the incentive to keep on pedaling.

Limited Financial Aid

A variation of matching funds is the concept of limited financial aid. It's quite simple: the parent's side of the ratio remains fixed. In other words, the parent donates "up to" a certain number of dollars toward their child's goal.

For example, let's say Noah wants to go to a day camp that specializes in tennis. Having already foot the bill for his usual two-week summer camp (which, by the way, already includes tennis activities), his dad decides to offer him up to $150 more toward his summer camp experiences, period: "Noah, it seems like you want to play lots of tennis this summer. I'm glad to pay for all your basic camp expenses, but you'll need to come up with the difference for any other extracurricular expenses."

Thus, if Noah wants to play more tennis at camp, he'll need to come up with the difference. Like any good investment in others, the best way for Noah to secure Dad's assistance is if Noah demonstrates his willingness to assist himself.

Grants and Scholarships

A grant or scholarship—a.k.a "The Benevolent Foundation of Mom and Dad"—is another way to provide financial assistance to kids. Grants usually have stipulations and are most often connected to a worthwhile cause or humanistic endeavor. Funds are typically granted to artists, scientists, inventors, and writers to support a specific altruistic or enterprising purpose.

Grant and scholarships can be a partial gift or the full amount of funding based on a variety of factors beyond financial. Grants are usually awarded on the merits of a submitted proposal, the availability of funds, and whether the potential recipient's purpose and values match the Foundation's mission. Once the money is granted, the "grantor" typically holds the "grantee" accountable using follow-up measures to confirm that the money has been used wisely and for its intended purposes.

The Benevolent Foundation of Mom and Dad should mimic the requirements of other typical foundations in as many ways as possible. Wise parents require their children to research and submit a sound written proposal as a test of sustained interest and perseverance. You will not be able to justify your monetary assistance if your child is unwilling to justify his or her idea.

The Application Process

One parent was wise enough to use this idea before providing "seed money" to her son, Jeremy. She knew Jeremy had not thought about the concept of a lawn service business nearly enough to make granting him the money a good investment. So she asked him for a grant proposal in writing.

She kept it simple by coaching him to begin a business plan using the Five W's:

- Who?
- What?
- Where?
- When?
- Why?

To her amazement, Jeremy persevered. He researched the topic online, talked to the local gardeners and nurseries, visited hardware stores, and lastly, surveyed the neighborhood for potential customers. He even put his conclusions down on paper in a fairly organized fashion! Jeremy and Mom discussed his plan, including the risks and the rewards, and agreed that it was a viable possibility—at least initially. But Mom could see there was more work to be done. Time to get more specific with the how-to's.

So Jeremy went back to the drawing board to continue his research. He put together a more accurate budget and estimated the amount of "seed" money needed to finance his initial efforts. Mom encouraged Jeremy to "present" these additional financial details to her, together with his answers to the following questions:

- What equipment and materials do you have and what equipment and materials do you need?
- How much money is needed to fulfill the initial startup costs?
- What will you need to do to get a loan (i.e., determine amount, repayment plan, and collateral)?
- How will you let people know about your new lawn service?
- What kind of services will you offer? At what price?
- What days and hours will you be available?
- What will you need to do to be accountable? To your customers? To your "loan officer" (Mom)? To your school and home life? What about any follow-up?

With some additional coaching and discussion, Jeremy came up with a final plan, which Mom agreed to fund through grant money. Mom knew that by granting him the money to start his project, she was giving him the unstated message that she had confidence in his budding talents as a new business owner.

Notice how Mom's decision fits the guidelines for loaning money for educational and entrepreneurial opportunities. Notice how she served as a Love and Logic consultant to Jeremy as he worked out the details of his business plan. And notice how she shared control and offered him plenty of choices by giving him the ultimate responsibility to demonstrate his abilities and test his determination *before granting him the money*.

The Foundation of Mom and Dad

The value of this kind of experience lies in the process. A process that gives kids unparalleled opportunities to make decisions at a time in their life when exploring a direction in life or making a change is simple and the cost affordable. Allow your kids to invest in their own "research and development" as often as possible. Even if Jeremy had decided to change or drop his plans, he still would have learned some valuable lessons about himself and the world of business through researching and developing his own ideas.

The quality of our lives has a lot to do with the decisions we make. What we do today shapes tomorrow. Practice in thinking and decision making is exactly what kids need, to develop the skills for making future quality-of-life decisions.

Practice in thinking and decision making is exactly what kids need, to develop the skills for making future quality-of-life decisions.

Wise parents give their kids lots of opportunities to make good and poor decisions so that they can learn from them.

**The Foundation of Mom and Dad meets
the Foundation of Childhood Endeavors. What a grand
investment in the futures of both parent and child!**

Making a Note: After the Quote

After the decision to loan, and the transfer of funds, it's time to "pay the piper"—it's time to set up a plan to collect.

One wise dad, a banker by profession, was inspired to use the same principles utilized in his own industry. He used the following financial formula when loaning money to his kids:

$$\text{note} + \text{collateral} = \text{loan}$$

Let's look at how to apply this formula successfully at home.

Take Note

All good lenders need a record of the loan, commonly known as a "note." There are several ways to record a lending transaction. Naturally, smaller loans require less-complicated records and repayment plans than larger loans. Wise parents keep the record process as simple as possible in the early stages, and expand as the child matures (and loan size grows).

Parents of young children begin with a simple I.O.U. Wise parents make it official by putting the "I owe you" in writing. They include the date, the amount, what the loan is for, and then ask the child to sign it as a pledge to repay. Just like in the adult world, a legible signature is not really necessary. Scribbles will do! (For a look at teaching your children the meaning of their signature, see "'X' Marks the Spot" on p. 283.)

Small Loan Notes

One mom uses a cashier's receipt as a record of any loans she makes to her school-aged child. She asks the checker to scan the child's item separately. This isolates the expense from her other purchases and creates a separate receipt. The receipt, which automatically prints the date, the amount, and a description of the item, becomes the official record for repayment. She then asks her child to sign the receipt, often right on the spot. Mom calls it her "on-the-go" note.

Below is a sample loan note that includes the basic essentials. Notice how there is no entry for a "balance due," only "loan due by." That's because keeping a balance is not suggested for small loans to inexperienced borrowers. For I.O.U.'s and receipt-type loans, the "loan due by" date should be within a week.

Small Loan Note/Record

Date: _____

Lender's name: _____

Borrower's name: _____

Total loan amount: _____

Amount due: _____

Loan due by: _____

Signature: _____

Date: _____

Wise parents remember to keep basic loans small and week-to-week, so that their children learn to pay off loans in a timely fashion. This means that the "total loan amount" and the "amount due" need to be the same number, to give kids lots and lots practice at becoming responsible borrowers.

Larger Loan Notes

Once children have demonstrated mastery with a simple I.O.U., they'll require larger loan notes as they become more experienced borrowers. Officially called a "promissory" or a "security" note, this type of note is especially useful if the terms of the loan become more complex. This happens as larger amounts of money are loaned over longer periods of time.

Terms for larger loan amounts include:

- Time: The length of time the lender is loaning the money (two weeks, thirty days, etc.). There are long-term loans and short-term loans.

- Payment plan: A timetable whereby the borrower sets aside money at intervals for the gradual repayment of debt.
- Collateral: Sequestered items that at resale will equal the value of the loan.
- Down payment: Usually a percentage of the loan.

It's important to discuss and negotiate all these terms before you agree to lend your child "long-term" money. Realistic terms, agreed upon in advance, improve the chances that your child will be successful and pay off the loan within a reasonable period of time.

Below is a sample note for larger loans that builds on the practice provided by I.O.U.'s and receipts (samples of more official loan documents can be found at office supply stores, online, or at your local bank). It has the basics of an I.O.U. note, but with additional terms to consider and negotiate (added in italics). Notice how control is still shared and choices are still offered by virtue of the negotiation process.

Large Loan Note/Record

Date: _____

Lender's name: _____

Borrower's name: _____

Total loan amount: _____

Down payment: [if applicable] _____

Collateral:

[list of sequestered items equal to the value of the loan]

1. _____
2. _____
3. _____

Amount due: _____

Loan due by: _____

Amount due now: _____

Balance owed: _____

Signature: _____

Date: _____

* * *

Keep in mind that kids should have a lot of practice honoring I.O.U.'s and signed receipts before the first promissory note is ever issued. Wise parents begin with small, manageable loans first, even for teenagers if they are inexperienced, to set the tone for the more complex requirements of larger loans in the future. For a summary of the differences between note types, refer to the chart below:

Small vs. Large Loan Notes

Small Loan Note	Large Loan Note
Signed I.O.U. or receipt.	Signed security or promissory note, or other proof of intent as an agreed upon contract.
Beginner, inexperienced borrower.	More experienced borrower.
Small amounts, short-term.	Larger amounts, long-term.
Repaid in full.	Repaid in installments.

Bottom Line: Whichever type of record you choose—an I.O.U., a cashier's receipt, or a promissory note—the recordkeeping method should match your child's "fiscal" maturity to the amount and significance of the loan.

"X" Marks the Spot

"It's a deal!" the car salesman says as he points to a line at the bottom of the page. "Just print your name, then sign here."

How you ever signed a piece of paper without paying attention to the details? The consequences for adults can be devastating. Credit ratings get ruined, cars and homes are repossessed, and prenuptial agreements surprise spouses in the face of a divorce.

Wise parents teach their children what their signature really means. How many kids who sign their first check or credit card receipt fully understand that their signature is a tacit agreement to pay the merchant the stated amount?

And, taken one step further, how many kids understand the financial consequences if they don't honor their agreement?

Our signature is important. Signing our name means that we legally agree to do whatever the written contract states. Teach your children to never sign any contract that they do not fully understand, including any loan, safe driving, or behavior contracts you establish with them. Suggest that they ask another trusted adult's opinion (a third, unbiased party) about the terms of the agreement. Encourage them to ask as many questions as necessary until they understand the complete ramifications of not following through on the agreement.

Three Easy Steps

It is the salesperson's job to make the process seem easy: "Just sign here." It sure gets harder, however, if we don't teach our children early to apply the following three-step process to every piece of paper requiring their signature:

1. Read.
2. Understand.
3. Sign wisely.

And, of course, make and keep a copy.

This is one of those "priceless" lessons for your children to learn when they are young. If they don't follow through on a loan contract, for example, use the "No Pay, No Play" policy described on the next page.

While children are not legally accountable until they are eighteen years old, parents can teach them the difference a birthday makes by holding them accountable before they turn eighteen.

Better *you* be your child's first "lawyer" than anyone else.

**Wise parents teach their children to
learn what the financial bottom line really means
before they sign on the dotted line.**

Collecting Collateral

Once you have a note, or record of what is owed, you're ready for the next step—you'll need collateral. For most loans, if you're going to "hold paper," then you'll also need to "hold possessions." Collecting collateral is the next step for holding borrowers accountable.

$$note + collateral = loan$$

Collateral comes in many forms. The best, most effective types of collateral are goods that can be easily sold for the amount equal to the loan.

Collateral, once secured, is a way to insure that the lender will not lose his or her money. Most collateral is acceptable as long as it retains its value for the life of the loan. Should the borrower default on the loan, the lender can still theoretically "cash in" the collateral to recoup their money.

Before credit cards became popular, many department stores offered something called the "lay-away" plan. You chose something you wanted to buy and the store would hold it for you until you paid for it in full. Essentially, it was a "no pay, no possession" policy.

No Pay, No Play: Collecting Tangible Collateral

The "no pay, no possession" policy can be adapted as a very effective way to collect collateral from your children. This is simple to do with tangible, retail items, because the item *is* the collateral.

With a signed receipt or an I.O.U. in hand, keep the purchase *in the bag or box unopened* until your child has repaid the debt. Pay before play, period.

Your "note" is the I.O.U. or receipt, and your "collateral" is the item you bought for them. It's yours to have and to hold until they repay you: "I'll be glad to hand you your new game as soon as I'm repaid."

Wise parents hold on to their collateral, despite any begging or pleading, until their child pays them back in full. That's because the lay-away plan is valid insurance that the item will not be used, broken, or lost, and therefore will still be equal in value to the loan amount. Plus the consequences of not paying the parent back are built into the plan: no pay, no play.

Wise parents hold on to their collateral, despite any begging or pleading, until their child pays them back in full.

This policy is also effective to motivate children to overtly express their gratitude to others' for their gifts (i.e., no gratitude, no gift). This is explained in more detail in "More Gifts, Grandma!" on p. 227, under the section "Option Five: When Grandparents Buy, or How to Spoil Your Grandchildren Without Ruining Them."

Return Policy

There's another advantage, besides convenience, to using a receipt as the loan note. Many stores and vendors print their return policy and the corresponding "return merchandise by" date right on the receipt.

This allows parents to automatically use the date on the receipt as the term of the loan. Some parents come up with their own term, usually repayment within a week or two. Wise parents choose a length of time that corresponds with their child's age and ability to repay, and with the store's policy—otherwise, they're left literally holding the bag.

Due Date

For simplicity's sake, write the due date on the I.O.U. or receipt at the time of purchase. Make sure your child has the opportunity and access to the resources to pay you back via his or her allowance, or a job list, or both. Once you have shared potential ways to repay you and by when, and any other terms of your agreement, sit back to see what happens.

If the child pays you back on time, congratulations to both of you. If the child doesn't pay you back on time, the item, sadly, gets returned. Wise parents remember to use a heavy dose of empathy before delivering the "no pay, no play" consequence.

You may be thinking that your child will forget about it—an out-of-sight, out-of-mind situation—or might even change his or her mind about paying you back. No problem. Just return the merchandise quietly *without saying a word*.

If, or when, the child remembers, wise parents have their empathic response right on the tip of their tongue, as with Hunter's mom in our next example.

Hunter's Lesson About Loans

Here's an "empathy before consequence" conversation between a mom and her son when he's forgotten to pay her back:

Hunter: "Mom, where's my toy I got the other day?"
Mom: "What a bummer, son. When I was out running errands the other day, I returned it."
Hunter: "You *what*?!"
Mom: "I know … this is so sad. I only loaned you the money until Saturday. You must have forgotten about it."
Hunter: "But I remember *now*!"
Mom: "I know …"
Hunter: "You can't do that!"

Mom:	"I know … but I did. I noticed that you didn't make any effort to repay me, so I returned the item to the store. That was our agreement. But don't worry. I'm sure the store probably has another one, if you want to try again."
Hunter:	"But you didn't tell me you were going to return it!"
Mom:	"I know … and that was part of our agreement."
Hunter:	"It was my most favorite toy of all!"
Mom:	"I know …"
Hunter:	"But … I didn't even get a chance to play with it—not fair!"
Mom:	"I know it's disappointing, and I love you too much to argue with you."
Hunter:	(sputtering) "But … but …"
Mom:	"And what did I say?" (walking toward the kitchen)

Will this increase the chances that Hunter will pay more attention to the terms of his loans in the future? Most likely, especially if he really wants the item as much as he proclaims.

What does this kind of response teach? It creates a circumstance whereby *the child's poor decision to not repay or to forget* becomes "the bad guy," not the parent. How? By following through on one of Love and Logic's most basic principles: use a heavy dose of empathy (in this dialogue, it was Mom's repetition of "I know …" followed by, if necessary, the question: "And what did I say?") before delivering the consequence.

Accountability is best taught by showing children, not telling them, how debt can affect their life.

Accountability is best taught by showing children, not telling them, how debt can affect their life.

No Fund, No Fun: Collecting Collateral for the Intangible Things

What about loaning kids money for items don't come in a box or a bag? These are things one cannot secure "tangible" collateral for as easily, such as a class trip or ski lessons. How do you handle collateral for loans that are not retail-type purchases or not "returnable"?

The "lay-away" policy applies here as well. The only difference is that possessions already in use by the child are secured, rather than a new possession. In other words, kids can use their current possessions as collateral for repayment until the debt is paid off.

Here's how to collect collateral for intangible opportunities. Ask the child to collect or come up with a list of items that would equal the monetary value of the loan. For example, if you loan your child $100, ask him or her to collect enough of their possessions to equal $100. Collateral might include electronic or computer-related items, bikes, or other recreational equipment.

The best items for collateral are the items your kids value the most—which usually works out to be the items you purchased most recently anyway. Recent possessions are an excellent choice, because they tend to be worth more to your children and to a buyer. Plus, kids usually want to earn their most recent possessions back as soon as possible.

It's perfectly normal if your child suggests or brings you items that do not hold any personal value to them anymore. Some kids will try to manipulate you into thinking that their abandoned and broken possessions make for mighty fine collateral.

If this happens, wise parents simply respond with a grin and a calm "Nice try," or lead with empathy and say, "That's so sad. This doll without a leg is not going to work, because I won't be able to collect enough money for it. Try again."

Just apply the Love and Logic rule of thumb: don't do more work than the child does when it comes to collecting collateral.

Your goal here is to make sure the list reflects—as closely as possible—true value in the marketplace. Invite any child who is skeptical to negotiate the value of the collateral using a third party, such a pawnshop or consignment store, to establish present worth. Or contact your neighborhood's garage-sale maven for advice on the worth of "used" items. No need to get into an argument. Just apply the Love and Logic rule of thumb: don't do more work than the child does when it comes to collecting collateral.

Once the correct value of the items has been determined to your satisfaction, secure those items in your possession, or establish a way for those items to be "out of commission" until the loan is paid. You may notice that your kids are less likely to ask for loans that require collateral if they know that they'll have to give up some of their favorite things until they pay you back.

Put on Hold or Sell?

One dad, when his son started to complain about not being able to use his "laid-away" skateboard, explained it this way: "Well, it's up to you to decide if you want to pay me back. I will need to hold on to your skateboard to be sure it retains its value while you are making the payments. If something should happen to your skateboard, then I have no way to recover the money I've loaned you."

Apply the "no pay, no play" policy if your child defaults. Sell the items to recoup your money. Remember, empathy precedes the consequence.

This Dad might say, "I know. What a bummer. I had to take your skateboard down to the pawnshop … but here's the ticket. Looks like you still have time to earn the money to buy it back. But that's entirely up to you."

Should we defend our actions if the child argues and gets mad? Wise parents, like Hunter's mom, default in their own way. They go right to neutralizing the emotion in the moment by using a Love and Logic one-liner—such as "I love you too much to argue. And what did I say?"—and then walk away.

To demonstrate how the policy you adopt corresponds with the type of collateral you will need to collect, refer to the summary chart below:

Collateral and Policy Differences

Loan Policy:	No pay, no play	No fund, no fun
Use for:	Tangible items (e.g., accessory, game, toy).	Intangible items (e.g., anything that can't be boxed or bagged).
Type of collateral:	Sequester the new possessions.	Sequester slightly used possessions of equal value to the loan.
Default policy:	Return the item for a refund.	Pawn, consign, sell, or repossess possessions for a refund.

Bottom Line: Wise parents know that holding collateral until a loan is paid in full teaches kids how to hold themselves financially accountable.

Loan Considerations:
Down Payments, Extensions, and Interest

Down Payments

"You mean I have to give *you* some money?" Charles asked as he and his father walked around the showroom floor of the local car dealership. "Dad, you don't understand. I want you to give *me* some money!"

Is a down payment a good option? Yes. Down payments are another form of securing the loan, and holding a borrower accountable. Larger loans naturally lend themselves to a down payment because it reduces the lender's risk. The amount of the down payment is based on a percentage of the loan amount.

Again, when it comes to providing larger loans, consider if your child has a good track record of repaying smaller loans. If not, securing a down payment becomes even more necessary to insure your risk. A down payment is also a measure of the child's true intention to repay the loan.

Here's a basic guideline about whether to require a down payment or not: the higher the risk, the higher the need for a down payment. To secure the loan, use an adaptation of the original loan formula:

$$\text{note} + \textbf{\textit{down payment}} + \text{collateral} = \text{loan amount}$$

Using this formula, the collateral will be equal to the value of the loan's balance, minus the down payment. For example, let's say the original loan is $500. If your child gives you $100 as a down payment, then the value of the collateral will need to equal $400. This is just in case cashing-in becomes necessary to recover your loss.

What about loaning money for a car or some other big-ticket item? The "no pay, no play" policy might get tricky. Surely Charles should have the use of his car at the same time he is paying off the loan, particularly if the repayment plan includes the means (transportation) to an end (getting to a job to earn the money for repayment).

Once more, let's go back to our original goal of preparing kids for the real world. Ask yourself how a real bank would handle this. Wise bankers, like wise parents, hold the title of the car in their name until the loan is fully paid. (For more information about teenagers, cars, and ownership, see "Hormones, Wheels, and Deals" on p. 293.)

Payment Plans

Installments are another good option for big-ticket items and more experienced borrowers. If installments are appropriate, some parents simply use the bottom section of the allowance statement as the record of repayment. Other parents enclose payment coupons, similar to enclosing bills. Still others go to their local office supply store and purchase a loan template to complete.

On the next page is a sample loan contract, including a sample payment coupon. Notice that once you have developed a loan contract, much of the information is fixed (shown in italics). This includes devising a payment schedule that lists dates and amounts due, with payments incrementally leading to a zero balance.

The information for the payment coupon should be carried down from the information on the loan contract. To help make the repayment of the loan even more concrete week to week, involve your child in as much of the recordkeeping and remittance calculations as possible. Some parents involve their child in the process of designing their own payment coupons. Once the coupons have been completed, they can be enclosed in the allowance envelope or issued separately for payment.

Loan Contract

Date: _____

Lender's name: _____

Borrower's name: _____

Total loan amount: _____

Final due date: _____

Down payment: [if applicable] _____

Terms of possession or use during loan period: _____

Collateral:

[list of sequestered items equal to the value of the loan]

1. _____

2. _____

3. _____

Balance: _____

Payment Plan: _____

Payment 1: _____

Amount due: _____

New balance: _____

Payment 2: _____

Amount due: _____

New balance: _____

[etc.]

Account balance: $0

Signature: _____   _____

Date: _____

Loan Coupon

- ✂ -

Payment Coupon #1

Today's date: _____

Amount due now: _____

New balance due: _____

Next due date: _____

Grace Periods

Wise parents agree in advance what will happen if their child gets behind on payments, and the length of the grace period—that is, the exact number of payments before the loan is in arrears. For example, if your child stops making weekly payments twice in row, write what will happen under "terms of possession or use during loan period."

Our children are "borrowers in training." It's best to keep the grace period short, so that the child more quickly experiences the consequence of not keeping up with their payments. This gives them the best incentive to "catch up." Allowing them to slip too far behind may overwhelm and discourage the child.

Don't give in to the temptation to just forgive the loan either. If we do, then we have forgotten our most important purpose—to teach our kids the real life rules of successful borrowing. It's only through the process of holding our kids accountable via repayment that they will understand exactly how being in debt affects their cash flow.

Loan Extensions

Should you extend the terms of the loan if your child doesn't meet the deadline? Extensions are rarely necessary, but consequences are, even as your child tries to negotiate one exception after another.

If the item was bought in a box or bag, quietly return it. While that's sad for the child, the item, or one similar, will still be at the store if he or she wants to try again. Use lots of empathy, followed by the "no pay, no play" consequence.

It's also sad for the child if he or she misses meeting the payment plan for nontangible items, such as the enrollment fees for a sports camp to be attended with a best friend. Opportunities with special people or in special places have their deadlines. Extending the loan undermines the reason for providing the loan in the first place. Again, lots of empathy, followed by the "no fund, no fun" consequence.

In short, wise parents do not offer loan extensions except under the most extenuating circumstances. Wise parents remember the importance of letting their children make as many mistakes as possible when the price tags are affordable. Sometimes what seems like the wrong thing to do in the short term (not rescuing a child for their mistakes) is the right thing to do in the long term (allowing the child to learn from their mistakes).

Remember the moral of the "Hero or Zero" story?

Rescues teach entitlement. Repayment teaches character.

An Exception to the Rule About Rescue

The authors of Love and Logic believe that rescuing a responsible child is not usually a problem. It can, in fact, reinforce our relationship with him or her. It also raises the odds that he or she might do the same for us in the future. However, rescuing an irresponsible child only leads to more trouble and entitlement.

What About Interest?

Some parents consider adding interest to their principal loan as a real world lesson. Interest is money paid for the use of another person's money. The authors of Love and Logic invite you to tread lightly in this situation. Loans between parents and their children are best offered interest-free as a demonstration of support and recognition of their role as learners.

Wise parents use experiences with *saving and investing money,* versus borrowing money, to teach lessons about how interest can work in their financial favor.

Hormones, Wheels, and Deals

Driving is an important rite of passage for teens. Possession of that permit gives teens entrée into adulthood and independence … and egress from you.

Most parents vacillate between pride, fear, and panic when their child returns with a big grin after taking their driving test. While one hand is waving

Sometimes what seems like the wrong thing to do in the short term (not rescuing a child for their mistakes) is the right thing to do in the long term (allowing the child to learn from their mistakes).

the temporary license in front of you, the other is outstretched for your car keys.

Unfortunately, we have no control over the importance other drivers place on safety and responsibility. However, we *do* have control over the importance we place on safety and responsibility, which *should* determine whether our teenagers drive or not.

While life holds no guarantees, one way to increase your teen's awareness of the "safety factor" is to hold them financially responsible for *what* they drive. We can never be sure *how* they drive unless we're with them, but we do have control over whether they drive at all and whether we provide them with a car or not.

Once your teen has a learner's permit, and passes the necessary driving tests, they'll be ready to go, go, go—along with their friends, music, and cell phones as passengers … oh my! The question becomes: Are you, the parent, ready to let them go?

Accountability Builds Responsibility

While your teen *wants* the keys to the car, what they *need* are the keys to safe driving. One essential key is developing accountability.

There are numerous choices parents face when teenagers and cars intersect. The following four options move from holding the teen most accountable for his or her driving, to holding the teen least accountable:

1. Require the teen to earn and save all the money to buy their own car.
2. Loan them all or a portion of the money.
3. Allow them to use the family car.
4. Buy them their own car.

Option One

The wisest of parents invite their teenager "to buy whatever you can afford." It's called, "We want you to go first-class on your own money." Sound too harsh? Not when you consider that, according to research, this option has the highest chance of increasing overall safety. Kids tend to take much better care of something when the equity used to buy it is their own sweat.

The basic Love and Logic principle applies here: if you want it, you pay for it.

Option Two

Wise parents can also issue a full or partial loan as a variation of the first option. Your teen still needs to earn it, but with a little financing help from you. Again, if your teen wants to drive it, they'll need to pay for most, or all, of it first. All car loans should include the same bells and whistles used by banks—down payment, default clause, collateral, and the like.

Option Three

The third option is the teenager who wants to use the family car. But how can you protect yourself against the financial risk of lending *your* car?

The same rule applies, with a slight adjustment to cover your risks and increase the chances that your teen will take driving more seriously: "If you want to drive my car, you'll need to come up with an amount of money equal to the premiums and deductible on the insurance policy, plus pro-rated expenses." This money is deposited in the parent's bank account, not in the child's.

Paying their share of the insurance deductible, in particular, serves as an important cash reserve should there be any mishaps. Gasoline, repairs, maintenance, license fees, and all other ongoing costs associated with operating a vehicle can be pro-rated and paid monthly according to use (usually based on mileage). Invite your teen to use an automobile club as a resource to research the real costs of driving a car.

It seems perfectly logical that if your teen cannot be responsible for the costs associated with owning and operating a vehicle, then they are not ready for the privileges associated with driving a car. If your teen does follow through with loan payments or the insurance requirements, the car keys are your collateral.

Option Four

Finally and sadly, some parents buy their teenagers their own cars outright. The authors of Love and Logic do not recommend this approach, for the reasons already cited. The higher the "endowment," the higher the risk that your teenager will not "take care" on many levels.

You might wonder: "What about good grades as a way to earn a car or driving privileges?" The authors of Love and Logic do not recommend this approach either. These are desperate attempts to motivate kids that do not work. (For a look at the relationship between grades, driving, and money, see "Pay for Grades?" on p. 355.)

It seems perfectly logical that if your teen cannot be responsible for the costs associated with owning and operating a vehicle, then they are not ready for the privileges associated with driving a car.

Bottom Line: When it comes to the privilege of a car, wise parents of teenagers raise the odds for driving responsibility through the sweat equity of "earned" ownership.

Loan Consequences: Default, Credit, and Repossession

What if your child stops making payments? Some children will already know that defaulting on a loan has its own set of natural consequences, if they have had an experience or two of not following through on their financial commitments. Either the item gets returned, or that special experience does not happen.

The "no pay, no play" and "no fund, no fun" consequences are built right in. The child's failure to put forth the necessary effort to earn something he or she wants, *combined with* losing some prized possessions as collateral, is usually a memorable enough consequence.

But there's another consequence to consider when your child defaults on a loan: he or she is now a poor credit risk. As in the real world, reducing the available credit from the Bank of Mom and Dad should pinch your child's ability to "score" when applying for another loan.

Kid-Sized Bankruptcy?

If we give our children one loan on top of another, we have created a situation whereby our kids are technically in debt.

Parents can do several things to teach their children how to become more creditworthy. First, do not issue any more loans until your children repay all previous loans. If we give our children one loan on top of another, we have created a situation whereby our kids are technically in debt. Second, if your child defaults on his or her loan, you can reduce the amount of each loan payment and extend the time period. Third, the less creditworthy the child, the more important that other terms of the loan become, in order to increase the chance of success.

Parents who choose to restructure the payment plan and terms of the loan can mitigate a kid-sized "bankruptcy." Here are a few suggestions to help your children ante up:

- Secure and sequester enough collateral.
- Require a higher down payment.
- Ask the child to rewrite their repayment plan to include a description of "how" they will repay you as well as "how much" for each installment.
- Renegotiate a default period of ten, twenty, or thirty days.

Wise parents understand that the higher the credit risk, the more important it is to negotiate the terms of the loan contract prior to issuing the loan. Renegotiate the terms using some or all of the terms set forth above if there are problems with repayment.

Giving Kids Credit

For a child who has questionable "credit," some parents loan only as much as the child earns or saves first. This puts the onus on the child to put forth the initial effort, and reduces "your risk" altogether. You will not meet your fiscal responsibility until the child has met *theirs first*.

Let's say your child wants to borrow $50. A parent using this approach can say, "As soon as you earn or save fifty dollars, I will loan you fifty dollars. Once you pay that back, you can renegotiate again for another loan." Start small and build on the child's success to reestablish his or her creditworthiness.

Some parents choose a more structured approach. They set up the terms for their child to pay them in full in advance. A payment plan is established incrementally, and once fulfilled, the money is issued. This gives the child practice paying off a loan before receiving the money. There is no need for collateral, since payment is made in advance of purchasing the product or service. A parent using this approach can say, "I will be happy to give you the money you want just as soon as you pay me in full."

The real world of borrowing uses collection agencies to collect for nonpayment. Wise parents help their kids become creditworthy by not extending more credit than they can handle. (For more information about how to prepare your children to become creditworthy before they leave home, see "Credit Card Tips: When the Time Comes" on p. 94.)

Repossession

Actual repossession is not necessary in most circumstances if you collect and hold collateral. This is based on the assumption that if the loan goes unpaid, the possessions you set aside get returned or sold. In this case, possession is nine-tenths of the law. That works, of course, unless the loan is for a big-ticket item that's *in use* before the loan has been paid in full.

A car is a good example. Should your teenager get behind on his or her car payments, wise parents repossess the keys until he or she gets back on schedule with payments. (One parent, faced with this circumstance, used the following enforceable statement: "I will be happy to put the tires back on your car just as soon as you catch up with your payments.") In this case the car takes a permanent parking spot in the family driveway until further notice. Of course, all of this has been explained by you, the primary lender, and understood in advance by the child according to the terms of the loan note.

And yes, repossession is always a sad time for the borrower. So lead with lots of empathy and hold on to the keys until your child can come up with the money. When you follow through using empathy and then the consequence, you'll be the parent who had the wisdom to trade the temporary use of a car for a lasting experience of becoming more responsible. Isn't that worth the exchange?

Repossession is never fun, but for kids who need to learn the hard way, it may be just what the self-discipline doctor ordered. Wise parents repossess if necessary to avoid the potential for any "collateral damage" in the future. (For more detailed information about how to use repossession as a consequence, see "Eight Steps to Motivate the Unmotivated" on p. 148, and "How to Ruin the Effectiveness of a Consequence" below.)

How to Ruin the Effectiveness of a Consequence

Economic laws have their own way of delivering natural consequences without much intervention. If we spend more money than we have, our credit suffers. If we forget to balance our accounts, we are charged management and overdraft fees. If we don't pay back our loans, our possessions get repossessed.

Many of the stories and examples used throughout this book illustrate the benefits of allowing your children to experience the natural consequences of their monetary mistakes. In many cases, the "no bail, no rescue" and "no fund, no fun" policies are the most effective financial teachers. Just use a heavy dose of empathy, or sadness, for the child, and let the "economics" of the consequence take its course.

 (There are other times when more than empathy is needed and a logical consequence may be necessary. Love and Logic uses several types of consequences. See p. 153 for examples of the delayed consequence, the energy drain consequence, and the generic consequence. These are consequences whereby kids can use their money, their possessions and toys, or their time and energy to make restitution in exchange for your worry, energy, or inconvenience due to their poor choice.)

Eight Pitfalls to Avoid When Delivering a Consequence

Just as there are effective and ineffective ways to deliver empathy, there are several ways to undermine a consequence's effectiveness, regardless of which type of consequence you choose.

Try to avoid the following tendencies when delivering the consequence to your children:

- Talking or explaining too much
- Feeling sorry and giving in
- Using the consequence as a way to get even
- Lecturing, moralizing, or threatening
- Rescuing, warning, or reminding
- Displaying anger or disgust
- Telling the child ahead of time what will happen
- Saying, "I told you so" or "This will teach you a good lesson"

Above all, remember to use a heavy dose of empathy when your children make poor choices, and words of encouragement when they make good choices! After the empathy (or encouragement) opens the mind to thinking, let the consequence of the child's decisions do the teaching.

Staying in the Loan Zone: Steel or Steal?

One mom and dad experimented with the "no fund, no fun" policy even though it was hard for them to stick to their guns. Their son, Jonathan, announced that he would like to go on the school trip to Washington, D.C., next spring. The cost of the trip per student was $1,000, with the money due by January 31.

His parents decided that this would be a great opportunity for Jonathan to practice meeting a financial goal. They told Jonathan that they would be willing to provide half of the cost and he could earn the other half through jobs around the house or neighborhood. The choice to go or not to go was up to him; but they made it clear that if he wanted to go, he needed to earn $500 by the deadline.

Jonathan agreed. Mom and Dad assembled a job list and posted it on the refrigerator. They placed a big clear jar in the kitchen for him to visibly see his money grow. And they showed him how to keep a running total on a piece of paper inside the jar.

It didn't work. Day after day, Jonathan found something else to do instead of earn the money for his trip. To his parents' credit, they decided to let him experience the consequences of his poor choices without lectures, reminders, warnings, or threats "that January 31st is around the corner." They had to "steel" themselves to not say anything to Jonathan, so that they wouldn't "steal" a valuable lesson from him in financial responsibility.

To their silent dismay, Jonathan did not make his goal and therefore stayed behind while the majority of his classmates tripped off to D.C. Because Mom and Dad did not get angry, Jonathan was left holding a half-empty jar as the unpleasant result of the choices he had made.

If you think this would be hard to do as parents, imagine how hard Jonathan's life will be down the road if he doesn't learn to follow through and take responsibility, financial or otherwise.

To sustain their resolve and summon their courage, Jonathan's parents had to keep reminding themselves of the answer to a very wise question: How will Jonathan have the preparation and character traits he needs to reach life's larger goals without prior experience reaching smaller ones?

Ease builds entitlement. Effort builds character.

Bottom Line: Be a Home That Loans

Imagine the difference between children who grow up in a home that provides loans for practice, versus a home that doesn't. Would you rather your child have their first experience defaulting on a $5 toy loan, or on a $15,000 car loan? How about repossessing their skateboard versus the bank repossessing their car, or foreclosing on their home?

Will the children who grow up in a home that loans have a much better chance of understanding the real deal on buying their first car or home on credit? You can bet your money on it. They understand how to avoid the real cost of debt, while their uninformed or entitled counterparts risk experiencing its devastation.

When kids pack their bags from a home that loaned, they'll have a smart start for understanding the real life cycle of lending and borrowing.

Loan Summary Chart

Reminder: Wise parents do not extend any new loans until outstanding loans have been repaid.

Borrower's Experience	Size of Loan	Length of Loan	Amount Loaned	Repayment Terms	Collateral	Default/ Consequence
Beginner, regardless of child's age.	Small amount.	Short-term (week to week).	Full amount.	Simple note (I.O.U. or a signed receipt).	For tangible items. Keep new items in box or bag unopened.	Use the "no pay, no play" policy. Return the item.
More experienced.	Larger amount.	Longer-term (two weeks and up).	Partial amount (grant, scholarship, limited assistance, matching fund).	Written promissory note, business plan, or other proof of intent.	For intangible items. Sequester and hold lightly used possessions equal to the loan's value. May also add a down payment, or earn matching funds.	Use the "no fund, no fun" policy. Sell, pawn, consign, or repossess.

CHAPTER 10

Earning

Jobs and Pay Daze

This chapter discusses a variety of ways children can earn their own money, beginning with jobs they can do at home. You'll learn the difference between a contribution and a job, and how to teach your children the reality of prices, wages, and earning abilities.

You'll also find answers to how much to pay, how to develop work values and skills, and what to do about allowance and paychecks once children start earning their own money. Self-employment and the special issues that arise with teens and employment are explored.

An Education in Earning

Six-year-old Rebecca overheard her mother tell the sales clerk in the clothing store that she didn't have enough money to buy the dress she wanted for her friend's wedding. Her daughter tugged on her blouse and said: "Mommy, Mommy! Why don't you just go to the bank and get some more money?"

A father surprised his son with box seats to the opening game of the baseball season. They had lots of fun, sitting right behind home plate in an action-packed game. On the way out of the ballpark, K.C. looked up at his dad and said: "I had so much fun today! I'm going to buy season tickets with my next allowance!"

Montana, fifteen years old, wanted to go on a mission to Africa with her church youth group. Between airfare and other travel expenses, she needed to save $3,000 for her share of the costs before the end of the school year. Her parents offered to match $5 for every $1 she earned; but they made it clear that if Montana didn't make her goal, she would not be able to go. She responded: "Fine. I'll just work a few hours every week because ... you know, like ... I still want time with my friends, time to hang out and shop ... you know, like ... I'm not worried ... I have lots of time ..."

Many kids grow up before having any real life experience earning money.

Out of the mouths of babes comes a fundamental lack of understanding about the reality of earning money ... unless, of course, we teach them. How can Rebecca, K.C., and Montana's parents make earning money more "real"? Give them real earning experiences.

Many kids grow up before having any real life experience earning money. They miss an important piece of financial reality if we don't teach them what their labor and their earned dollars are worth. But parents can begin to prepare kids for the realities of earning money before they join the adult world of work, by beginning their earnings education at home.

 Bottom Line: To make earning a real experience, wise parents give children real experiences to earn.

Firsthand Job Experience

One of the best ways to give our children earning experiences is to give them a job. There are three basic types of jobs:

- Jobs at home
- Self-made jobs
- Jobs for hire

Kids can be given lots of opportunities to earn money as gradual preparation for the world of work as adults. Depending on their age and abilities, they can begin with either household jobs or self-employment jobs and eventually move into jobs-for-hire by an employer.

Earnings come in several varieties. There is earned income, derived from jobs people do for payment or compensation. That's the type of income we will be discussing in this chapter. And there is passive income, derived from the income earned through real estate and other investments—that is, when money *works for you* instead of you working for money. Naturally, making money without having to work for it sounds pretty inviting to most people, including kids. More information about investing in Chapter 11.

Objection: Jobs for Kids?

You may question jobs for kids as these parents did at a recent workshop that I (Kristan) conducted:

> "My kids have the rest of their lives to work. Let kids be kids."
> "My kids are busy with schoolwork, sports, afterschool stuff, and of course their everlasting friends. There's no time to add work to their already crammed schedule."
> "My kid only has time to study for a scholarship, since she can't throw a football for a full carry to the university."

Parents, particularly of teenagers, are often faced with this decision. The authors of Love and Logic recommend that your kids should at least be given a flavor and feel for earning money so that it's not a foreign concept when they leave home. The issue is less about the amount of money earned, and more about the opportunity to experience the value and meaning of doing work. Job

The issue is less about the amount of money earned, and more about the opportunity to experience the value and meaning of doing work.

experiences at home offer the kind of practice that improves the chances of success for jobs outside the home. (For a look at the importance of preparing our children for the competitive marketplace, see "Earn Local, Think Global" below.)

Unless your kids are going to be independently wealthy or dependently supported by you for their lifetime, give them lots of opportunities to earn before they *have to* earn. Better to learn in the more forgiving atmosphere of a home than among the unfamiliar pressures of the workplace. By gradually exposing your children to the values and skills required to earn a living, you are providing

them with an essential foundation for their future. (For more information about how to help your children develop a set of work ethics and skills, see "Learning to Earn" on p. 319.)

Bottom Line: By giving our kids lots of job opportunities at home, we prepare them for the land of future job opportunities.

Earn Local, Think Global

What's your dream for your children? Do you dream that they'll go into the world of work prepared for its competitive realities, or do you dream that you'll outlive them so that you can always be there to provide a safety net?

Here's a sobering thought: today's kids spend 500% more than their parents did at the same age, adjusted for inflation. Where is the money spent—on basic necessities, conveniences, or status? And what percentage of the money spent on conveniences and status is actually earned by today's kids? Many of today's kids have no idea how much work and self-discipline it takes to earn the money for these things.

As we move toward a more global economy, your kids are going to have to compete for jobs with kids in other countries, kids who are hungry right now. These are kids who have learned that the path to success is self-discipline and hard work, not entitlement.

If your kids are not earning the grades they get, the car they drive, the things they want, and the privileges you give them, then their economic future is

at risk. (For Love and Logic's recommendations about children earning their grades and their driving privileges, see "Pay for Grades?" on p. 355.)

It's entirely possible that a child from a developing country, who is starving today, may be the one competing for your kid's future job tomorrow, and may well be the one who earns it.

Bottom Line: Earn local, think global. When it comes to preparing our children for their economic future, there is no better time than now to teach them all that it takes to earn their own "things."

First Day on the Job

> Peter's dad proudly waved to his teenage son as the boy backed out of the driveway on his way to his first day at work. "Bye," his father said. "Enjoy your day."

Our child's first day of work is a rite of passage for them, but it's also a rite of passage for us—similar to that day not so long ago when we kissed our child goodbye on their first day of school. Of course, neither day stands alone.

Our child's first real job becomes the acid test of our efforts to instill in them the values associated with a good, solid work ethic—one that will stand up to the rigors of the first job, and the rigors of many workplaces thereafter. Those are the times when parents, like Peter's father, hope they've done all they can to prepare their kids for the real world.

Part of the preparation is the example we provide. Chronic conversations about how mean or incompetent the boss is, or how much you hate your job, don't make the work world a very compelling destination for our children. We need to set a good example for our children that being productive can be enjoyable and fulfilling. Adopting the habit of talking positively about your work and your accomplishments—while your kids can overhear you—will pay dividends in many ways.

Many teens can be overheard saying, "Why should I work hard in school to get a degree and a job, just so I can be as miserable as my parents? I'm going to have some fun when I grow up." Then they practice having fun at school instead of working hard for their grades and their future success at life's other endeavors.

The example we set as adults is one way of preparing our children for the world of work. The other part is experience.

For Pete's Sake: A Foundation That Contributes

Peter's preparation for his first day on the job began as soon as his parents taught him to pick up after himself, mow the lawn, or vacuum the car out.

Preparation was built into all those times when his parents kept their eyes open and their mouths shut (choosing empathy instead of lectures, warnings, or threats) as Peter dawdled when taking out the trash, or forgot to feed the dog. Peter's parents knew that the training and experience he gained while doing his household contributions and jobs were the same training and experience that would develop his work values and skills. (For a look at what types of work kids should be paid to do, see "Job or Contribution? The Difference a Dollar Makes" on p. 313.)

Research tells us that kids who are required to do work at home have a higher chance of being successful working outside the home.

Kids who are trained and required to do household contributions and jobs learn how to do the task, put forth effort, and persevere to complete the task. In the process, they also learn how to motivate themselves in the face of distraction, and how to keep their agreements. These are identical to many of the requirements for mastering entry-level jobs in the workplace.

Research tells us that kids who are required to do work at home have a higher chance of being successful working outside the home. If you have not turned your children into honored guests at home, then they will not act like honored guests on the job. The ability to work well, to be part of a team, to tolerate frustration, and to accept responsibility just doesn't happen on its own—it takes parental time and attention. Wouldn't it be nice if your kids recognized this experience called "work" on their first day on the job?

Bottom Line: Wise parents provide a "working" example for their children. They provide plenty of experience with household contributions and jobs as their first introduction to developing a set of skills and values suitable enough to take to work.

Jobs at Home

Jobs at home are the first way parents can provide practice earning money. The authors of Love and Logic recommend that your child's first experience with "being hired" be at home, regardless of their age. Even if your teenagers are employable now, it's best to provide them job opportunities at home so that they can learn some of the skills and qualities required for basic employment—such as punctuality, reliability, follow-through, and teamwork.

This step requires parents to define and create a list of jobs.

Defining the Job

Developing a job list begins with a clear definition of "a job." Jobs are tasks that parents give their kids to do for the family, or tasks that parents don't want to do themselves.

What? Give kids *your* jobs? Well, isn't that how it works in the real world? In the adult world, when we pay someone else to do our household work, aren't we actually paying someone else to take care of the hassle for us? Either we don't want to do the job, or we don't have time to do it ourselves. So we hire someone else when we can afford it. Those are the perfect tasks for your job list.

The authors of Love and Logic use the word *jobs* as opposed to *chores* to describe tasks children can choose to do for payment. This includes any of *your contributions* you want to pay your kids to do for you.

Creating a Job List

The parent creates the job list, usually without the child's input (unless you have an earnest child who wants to suggest his or her own jobs). Have some fun with the title. One parent named the household job list: "Ten Super Duper Ways to Find a Job." Other parents use the title: "Your Parent's Most Hated Jobs." Some parents personalize the title: "Andrea's Extra Special Ways to Earn Essential Cash." Once the list has been developed, post it in a conveniently public place. Then, kids are free to choose what jobs they have an interest in doing to earn extra money.

Your list should offer reasonable and age-appropriate choices. Here are some examples:

Sample Job Lists by Age Group

Preschoolers
This is generally too young an age for kids to be able to understand that jobs are a way to earn money for things they want. It's best to hold off paying very young children for jobs until they reach school-age.

Start with mini tasks you want them to learn how to do for you, like gathering and putting away all the stray shoes in the family room, and begin to train your child in small steps. When you teach them how to pick up the family room, you are also teaching them how to pick up other rooms, too. Good deal. That's because when they are older and no longer need to be supervised, not only will they be able to earn money doing your jobs, but they will already be trained!

School-Age
Any of your contributions you want to pay your kids to do for you, plus household jobs such as:

Pick up sticks in the yard.

Organize the junk drawer.

Throw out old magazines and catalogues.

Sweep out the garage.

Clean out the garage shelves.

Polish or wax special household items.

Clean parents' bedroom.

Clean parents' bathroom.

Stack firewood.

Tweens

All of the above, plus any of your contributions you want to pay your kids to do for you, plus household jobs such as:

Specialized outdoor projects such as planting bulbs, removing dead bushes or brush.

Remove cobwebs from indoor corners or outdoor eaves.

Wash the car.

Clean the patio (wipe down furniture, sweep, etc.).

Edge the lawn.

Weed the flower beds and gardens.

Vacuum and clean the inside of the car.

Clean mirrors and windows.

Outdoor plant maintenance.

Disinfect and clean out the garbage and recycle cans.

Shovel snow.

Jobs in the neighborhood (at this age, an ambitious child may want to branch out into the surrounding area to earn money—jobs in the neighborhood are similar to other jobs in this list, only the neighbor is paying the bill; or they may be job opportunities not otherwise available at home).

Teenagers

All of the above, plus any of your contributions you want to pay your kids to do for you, plus household jobs such as:

Wash and wax the car.

Run errands.

Rake the leaves.

> Provide childcare for siblings.
>
> Clean out the gutters.
>
> Jobs in the neighborhood (see above).

Notice that "your contributions" is listed each time as a potential job choice. Parents' contributions are on the job list because they fit the definition of a job—tasks you may not want to do yourself. These are tasks that you want to gradually pass on to your kids, once they've been sufficiently trained in those areas to begin receiving wages.

Notice also that "jobs" tend to include occasional or seasonal tasks. Your list will naturally vary, because each household is different, and each child is unique. Children differ widely in both ability and experience, so pick and choose jobs that make the most sense for you and your family. The important part is to make the list available so that your kids will always have the *opportunity* to earn extra money at home first.

Wise parents do not pay their children to do anything that might be considered one of the child's contributions down the line. That could be confusing later when you want them to contribute to doing the family laundry for "free." We need to be careful about habituating our kids to being paid for jobs that they should be able to contribute later. (For a list of job versus contribution examples, and guidelines to determine whether to pay your children or not, see "Job or Contribution? The Difference a Dollar Makes" on p. 313.)

Remember: Only pay children to "help" you do *your* jobs and *your* contributions, not *their* contributions. Even though it's tempting to pay your child for helping you carry the laundry to the laundry room, don't.

Job List Variety Is Key

Keep in the mind that the purpose of a job list is to give kids opportunities to earn enough of their own money to buy something they want. You'll want to provide a long enough list, with enough choices, to allow your child to successfully earn enough money to make their own purchases. If your child wants to buy a toy or an electronic gadget, for example, make sure that he or she would be able to earn the total price of the toy or gadget from the options listed. Variety in tasks, and in the amount kids can earn, shares control and offers choices—two keys to engineering the situation for kids to earn money successfully. (To see how one father introduced and used a job list, see "Introducing a Job List" on p. 317.)

Of course, a job list could collect dust very quickly. How? If you forget that the only way it will ever get used by your kids is if you keep your wallet open for payroll and closed for purchases.

 Bottom Line: Wise parents post an age-appropriate job list for their children so that they'll always have the choice to earn their own money.

For jobs that are done together for the good of the whole family, payment comes in the form of connection, not coins.

Family Jobs

What about family jobs? Should parents pay their kids to do jobs the entire family can do, like working in the yard or cleaning out the garage?

Let's take the example "rake the leaves." Is that a job that can be completed alone? Yes. So, is it a family project with no pay? Or is it a paid job for your teenager? That depends on whether raking the leaves is a job that creates family bonding—an opportunity to have fun together and work as a team toward a common goal. Maybe the family should do it together if they all hate doing it, so no one gets stuck with doing the whole job.

Or, perhaps raking the leaves would be a great job for your teen because you don't like to do it or don't have time this particular autumn. If your teen wants some extra cash due to a special circumstance, then paying him or her to do it is fine.

Family jobs, especially when two or more people are required to do the job, provide opportunities for children to feel needed. The best kind of family projects are basically home improvement projects that *require* "four hands or four eyes," such as putting in fence posts, stringing holiday lights and decorations, holding the ladder, and "lifting a finger" to help tie a ribbon around a package. While kids may grump and complain about it, being a helper in joint projects is an important part of being a family member. (For more information about how to create more family bonding experiences, see "Making a Family Match" on p. 422, under the section "A Heritage of Helping.")

For jobs that are done together for the good of the whole family, payment comes in the form of connection, not coins. Use your family values, the unique situation, and common sense as your guide.

Job or Contribution? The Difference a Dollar Makes

Randy has been chronically late getting ready for school because he couldn't find what he needed when it was time to go. Mom was getting tired of hearing every morning, "Where are my shoes?"… "Have you seen my backpack?"… "Mommm, I can't find my jacket."

So one rainy Saturday, Mom decided to spend the whole day with Randy organizing and sanitizing his room so he could find what he needs for Monday morning and every morning thereafter. Together, they sorted things into piles, labeled bins for all his toys, added a new laundry hamper and trash can, and installed clothing hooks for his convenience.

"No more excuses now," Mom thought as she surveyed the day's work. As an incentive, Mom decided to pay him $5 per week to keep his room looking "just like this." Randy was cool with that until the following Saturday when he wanted to go play with his friend instead of earning $5 to clean his room. What do you think will happen this Saturday and all the other Saturdays thereafter? Will it cost Mom more than $5 and even more in time and energy?

Kristy, a single parent, was sick and tired of constantly nagging her girls to help out at home. With two part-time jobs to try to make ends meet, she found it difficult to do it all on her own. Now the holidays were fast approaching and her parents were coming to visit. Her girls needed to consolidate their bedrooms into one room to accommodate their grandparents.

She began by asking politely, followed by repeated reminders, warnings, and finally threats. When none of that worked, in frantic desperation, she offered to pay them to help get the house ready for the rest of their family. What do you think will happen the next time Kristy needs a spare bedroom for houseguests? Will it cost her not only more money, but also more time and energy? Is there any possibility that she will experience some type of extortion from the girls later on?

These two examples are among hundreds that illustrate the confusion parents have about whether to pay or not to pay their children for doing things around the house. Parents often ask, "Should I pay my kids to clean their room? Do the dishes? Empty the trash? What about washing my car? Or mowing the lawn?"

One factor that differentiates a contribution from a job is based on the "self-interest" principle. The second factor has to do with the nature of the task.

The confusion disappears once a distinction is made between what tasks are contributions and what tasks are jobs. Once that distinction is clear, then the issue of paying or not paying automatically becomes clear.

Bottom Line: Wise parents know the difference a dollar makes in their children's character development when they are able to distinguish contributions from paid jobs.

The Self-Interest Principle

Some of us grew up with parents who gave us an allowance for doing chores around the house. Our parents may have tried to motivate us to take out the trash, make our bed, or clean our rooms for money. This creates an unfortunate result.

"Would my child's future spouse pay him to do what I'm asking?"

Parents who pay their children money for doing everyday housekeeping tasks create entitled children. Those kids are not so lucky, since they develop the expectation that they should be paid for doing even the most essential tasks. Can you imagine your child's first experience away from home? Might they wonder why their college dorm-mates are not paying them to take out the trash?

Love and Logic teaches that children should not be paid to do anything that contributes to the quality of their lives. One of our jobs as parents is to help our kids understand that making contributions to family life *is* in their own self-interest, because it improves *their* quality of life, whether they are five or fifty-five years of age.

One parent asked herself a simple question as a guideline to determine self-interest: "Would my child's future spouse pay him to do what I'm asking?" If her answer was "no," she put that task on the contribution list. If "yes," then she added it to the job list.

Bottom Line: Wise parents know that one way to differentiate contributions from jobs is to use the self-interest test.

The Nature of the Task

The second way to differentiate a job from a contribution is related to the nature of the task. Contributions are defined in the Chapter 5. To review briefly, contributions are day-to-day tasks that contribute to the everyday flow of family life. Tasks such as taking out the kitchen garbage, emptying the dishwasher, or pet care are necessary tasks required by any group of people who share living space together.

Other tasks are more occasional and sometimes seasonal. Those tasks are jobs that kids can do to earn extra money. Jobs such as weeding, sweeping out the garage, or vacuuming the inside of your car are optional, non-essential tasks that can be categorized as above and beyond what is necessary for everyday housekeeping.

Many of the tasks listed in the jobs category are tasks adults might hire and pay someone else to do for us. Window washing and seasonal yard work are good examples of typical jobs we might pay someone else to do. Many parents keep a list of these so that their children will always have a way to earn extra money.

Some might argue that since adults get paid to do their jobs, kids can get paid to do their jobs, too. But adults really get paid to do other people's jobs— jobs that others want done or jobs that others don't want to do themselves. Those are exactly the kind of jobs that *kids can choose to bid on* when they're interested in earning extra money.

The operative words here are *choose* and *jobs*, used in the same sentence. In other words:

- The tasks your kids choose to do to earn extra money for "payment" are jobs.
- The tasks your kids do to contribute "without payment" are contributions.

In short, pay your children for jobs; don't pay your children for contributions.

Here are some examples to help clarify the differences between jobs and contributions:

Jobs vs. Contributions

Examples of Jobs

$ Sweep out garage.

$ Wash the car.

$ Wash the dog.

$ Clean out the garage shelves.

$ Organize the junk drawer.

$ Weed the flower and garden beds.

$ Rake the leaves.

$ Clean out the inside of the car.

$ Babysit a sibling.

$ Clean mirrors and windows.

(For a list of jobs based on age-appropriateness, see "Sample Job Lists by Age Group" on p. 309.)

Examples of Contributions

Set or clear the table.

Collect laundry for laundry basket/hamper.

Vacuum.

Dust.

Sweep the kitchen floor.

Pick up things in the living room.

Bring the dishes to the kitchen sink.

Help carry in and put away the groceries.

Take the garbage cans to the curb and return them to the garage on
trash pickup day.

Feed and clean up after pets.

Notice how the jobs are preceded by dollar signs, but there are no dollar amounts listed. Set job fees are problematic. The prices should be negotiable, for several reasons. Age, ability, experience, training, motivation, and attitude are all factors that pertain to job performance. Your child may do a job worth $10 one day, but that same job, through extra effort on the child's part, may be worth $15 on another day. Or the reverse may be true. (More about negotiating wages with your children later in this chapter, under "How Much to Pay?")

So what difference does a dollar really make to parents raising their children? Should Randy be paid $5 to clean his room? Should Kristy's daughters be paid to help their mother get ready for company? You're on the right track if you answered "no" to both questions, because both scenarios fall under the category of making a contribution to *their* family life.

Bottom Line: Wise parents differentiate between jobs and contributions based on the self-interest test and the nature of the task.

Jobs vs. Contributions: Similarities and Differences

The differences between jobs and contributions can be confusing, because there are also similarities, as summarized in the following chart:

Jobs vs. Contributions

Jobs	Contributions
Similarities	*Similarities*
• Age-appropriate. • Task matched to child's ability.	• Age-appropriate. • Task matched to child's ability.
Differences	*Differences*
• Money is earned. • Begin once child has desire to earn extra money, varies with age. • Basic training required to get paid. • Optional. • Child bids among list of jobs.	• No money given. • Begin as early as two years. • Progressive training opportunities increase with age. • Required. • Child chooses among list of contributions.

Introducing a Job List

Once you've created a job list, it's time to make an introduction. Here's how one father introduced a job list to his two boys, Mason, ten years old, and Blake, eleven and a half. Dad began by explaining the purpose of a job list:

Dad: "Boys, I have put something together that I want to show you. It's a list of jobs. You can choose any of the jobs on this list if you ever want to earn extra money. These are all jobs that you can eventually do by yourself after you have learned how. Some of these are jobs I don't like to do and will pay you to do, after I've showed you how I expect the work to be done."

Mason: "How much will you pay me?"

Dad: "That depends on the kind of job you do."

Mason: "What do you mean?"

Dad: "It depends on lots of different things, like how well you do the job and how much effort and time you put into it. There are no dollar amounts next to the jobs because I want you to tell me how much you would like to be paid to do a certain job. Then we can negotiate back and forth. But if your price makes sense to me, you might get to do the job."

Blake:	(acting very bored) "Can I go now?"
Mason:	(eyes lighting up) "Sounds good to me."
Dad:	"So next time you need extra money, check this list for job opportunities at home. If you don't like the jobs on this list, I'm open to your suggestions. Once you practice these jobs at home, if you want to earn more money, you can always ask our neighbors if they have any jobs for you to do."
Mason:	(hesitantly, unsure why Dad is explaining all this) "Okay. Thanks, Dad."
Blake:	(unimpressed) "Can I be excused?"

Two Different Children

This dad is wise. He's unconcerned about Mason's "not sure why you're telling me this" demeanor, or about Blake's blasé attitude. Dad knows that it won't be until his boys ask him to buy something that the true value of the job list will strike home.

A few days later, Dad and Mason are in the store. "Hey Dad, look at this!" says Mason, noticing a gadget he saw advertised on TV recently. He picks up the gadget and begins pushing its buttons. "This is so cool … Can you buy this for me? … Oh look … Cool! This was on TV … Please … ?"

Like many kids, Mason's first effort to get what he wants is to beg and whine for the money. It has worked in the past, but to Mason's surprise, it doesn't work this time. That's because Dad is ready. He has discovered a new ally—the job list—for such an occasion. The only buttons Mason will succeed in pushing today are the gadget's buttons.

The Value of a Job Referral

With his new strategy in place, Dad calmly walks up to his son and says, "Mason, wouldn't it be great to have that … Feel free to buy that gizmo yourself."

Predictably, Mason looks confused and whines, "But I don't have enough money."

"Oh … what a bummer," Dad says with heartfelt empathy, "maybe next time." With this one simple statement, Dad has calmly handed the problem back to his son. Mason can choose to resolve the problem, or not.

When Mason doesn't have enough money, Dad can be truly empathic (having had that experience himself). And the consequence? The same one adults experience when don't have a way to pay for something they want—no money, no purchase.

Dad is learning to allow Mason's desire for something do the teaching. Mason is now faced with the problem of how to get the money to buy it himself, if he wants the item bad enough. Dad has strategically provided Mason a job list as the perfect referral to use in the land of materialistic desire. Out steps the once reliable Bank of Dad and in steps the new job list and an earning opportunity.

Should Mason continue to plead, beg, or argue in the store, Dad is ready. He can use his brain dead yet empathic tone of voice to restate the limit: "Please feel free to buy that gizmo yourself," followed by, if necessary, "And what did I say?"

Once Mason knew his father was *not* going to buy it for him, he started to ask about a few of the jobs around the house on their way home from the store. Dad knew that if Mason wanted that gadget enough, he would need to earn it.

And that is exactly what Mason ended up doing, as you'll discover when we pick up the story again later in the chapter.

Dad has strategically provided Mason a job list as the perfect referral to use in the land of materialistic desire.

Learning to Earn

There will come a day when your child, like Mason, wants some extra money. What's next? Learning how to earn money.

Learning how to earn involves two factors. One is values and the other is skills. Work values are taught through putting in the effort to achieve something for oneself and for others, and appreciating the results. Work skills are taught through training, education, and experience.

Fortunately or unfortunately, depending on one's perspective, there is no getting around developing a set of work values and skills except through actually doing work. Experience is by far the best teacher when it comes to work.

Let's examine how to develop a set of values and skills that will serve our children well.

Developing a Work Ethic

The collective values one places on doing work are sometimes known as a "work ethic." For those of you unfamiliar with the term "work ethic," America was founded on the Puritan work ethic. The Puritans were the people who wore pointy hats, large white collars, and frowns on their faces. They believed that "idle hands were the work of the devil."

So they kept very busy … working very hard, as the expression goes, pulling the plow. As farmers, whose lifestyle required them to be self-reliant, they did whatever they had to do, because if they didn't, they didn't survive. They developed the inherent values of all hardworking people as a result—perseverance, determination, and struggle—and did whatever it took to get the job done. They were the original 24/7 folks, minus Sundays and today's technology.

The work ethic has evolved over time, fortunately. At least, there are fewer pointy hats and collars and hopefully a few more smiles. Unfortunately for some, however, a work ethic of any type is unfamiliar or underdeveloped. Today, in many cases, the silver spoon has replaced the shovel, and entitlement has replaced effort.

Entitlement—the silver spoon—places little value on the shovel—effort, struggle, and perseverance. Entitlement is about: "I want what I want because I want it"; instead of an ethic of effort: "I want what I want so I will work hard to earn it." Entitlement is a direct contradiction to the timeless and traditional values of a work ethic.

Bottom Line: We give kids the gift of developing a healthy set of work values by providing them opportunities to learn what it takes to earn the things they want.

The children whose parents teach them to be workers and achievers are much more likely to inherit the keys to the kingdom than the kids of parents who allow them to grow up as watchers and waiters for the kingdom to be handed to them.

> ### Lucky or Unlucky Kids?
>
> Giving kids things, without requiring them to make the effort to earn them, robs kids of the opportunity to develop *their own understanding of the value in work.* We actually give our children an opportunity to try when we *deny.* It's a gift of experience in effort, instead of an expensive experience in entitlement.
>
> Kids born with silver spoons in their mouths are not as lucky as one might think. They miss valuable character-building opportunities to develop values relating to future achievement. While we might think that "rich kids have it made," Hollywood headlines are a poignant reminder of what happens when we treat our children like princes and princesses.
>
> The children whose parents teach them to be workers and achievers are much more likely to inherit the keys to the kingdom than the kids of parents who allow them to grow up as watchers and waiters for the kingdom to be handed to them. Let's raise the next generation to become creative problem-solvers, instead of complainers who blame others for their lack of achievement or success, and who would rather settle for less than face adversity and persevere.

Developing Work Skills

The second part of the learn-to-earn phase is developing work skills through experience. A household job list offers a wonderful opportunity for parents to begin this process at home.

If we're going to offer kids a list of our jobs, it makes sense that we provide on-the-job training. When we hire household help, don't we like to hire people who are fully trained and who won't need our supervision? Otherwise we just end up doing the job ourselves. It works the same way when we hire our children. We train our kids how to do the job first, and then offer the job for hire.

Once children are properly trained, they can be a marvelous source of affordable labor. If your only choices are to pay someone else to wash your windows, or do it yourself, consider a third option: pay a "willing-to-earn-extra-money, specially-trained-by-you" child.

On-the-Job Training and Benefits

On-the-job training for household jobs works the same way as on-the-job training for contributions, as explained more completely in Chapter 5. Training includes a step-by-step process—with you—in a fun, happy atmosphere until the child is able to do the job by him- or herself. (For more information about how to train your children, see "Basic Training 101" on p. 129.)

Wise parents keep expanding the job list via a continuous job-training program. Training your child is like training an employee. While it's an initial investment in time and effort, the payoff comes later. Train up front to get benefits at the back end. That way, more jobs can be added to the list as your child is able to complete more tasks without your supervision.

Training your child to do the job right will also pay off when he or she goes outside the house to perform jobs for others in the neighborhood. Jobs practiced at home build skills, competence, and confidence for tasks outside the home. As the child's first "employer," parents have an opportunity to shape positive attitudes toward work that can be transferred from home to neighborhood to career.

Jobs practiced at home build skills, competence, and confidence for tasks outside the home.

There is another benefit to training kids to do household jobs. Wise parents know that someday their kids will not only need to do those very same jobs in their own household, but will also be able to help them when they are older. That is, unless they grow up to earn and manage their money well enough to pay someone else to do all their own (and eventually their parents') housework for them!

On-the-job training benefits both parent and child, now and later. Wise parents know that the jobs their kids do as children will prepare them for the jobs they do as adults. There is much wisdom to starting early.

Bottom Line: Wise parents know that at-home job opportunities are a way to prepare their children for developing both work skills *and* work values for jobs outside the home.

How Much to Pay?

Kids can be unpredictable in terms of job performance. Some may start a job but not finish it, while others may do an even better job than expected. It's best, therefore, to come up with a system of pay that can be adjusted according to accomplishment. Negotiation fits the bill.

Why Negotiate?

You may wonder about the reasons behind the suggestion to negotiate wages. Why not say to your child, "I will pay you twenty dollars to weed the flower beds"?

Negotiating the price on a job-by-job basis has several benefits. Negotiation offers choice and flexibility for both parties, which tends to reduce potential control battles. You will be able to restate the standards you expect for a finished job, and your child will be able to tell you what he or she thinks their time, skills, and effort are worth.

Negotiable pricing also helps with age and ability differences among siblings. For example, what you agree to pay your teenager to wash your car unsupervised should be very different from what you agree to pay your six-year-old "in training" who *helps* you wash your car.

In truth, negotiation honors the truth of the process—that wages vary from job to job and from person to person.

How to Negotiate with Your Child

There's an art to negotiating that you can use with your children. Always put the other person in the position where they have to come up with the first amount. In other words, children can make the first offer and the child decides if the amount the parent counter-offers is worthwhile or not.

To begin the negotiation process, ask your child to name a price for a job they have selected from the list, then negotiate up or down from the starting point. You may need to prompt inexperienced or young children to "make me an offer," together with some reasonable suggestions, saying, "Some kids suggest three dollars for vacuuming the inside of the car, other kids suggest four." Older children may have a tendency to see how much they can get away with by naming a high price. This is a good time to use the Love and Logic one-liner: "Nice try!"

Your children need to learn about a "free market economy." Should your child's offer be too high or unreasonable, you can suggest that you'd be willing to offer the job to someone else, such as the neighborhood kids.

In either case, high or low, the parent negotiates with a counter offer, or their idea of a reasonable amount of pay for the job. This, in turn, *allows the child to decide* if the parent's final offer is worthwhile or not.

Wise parents resist the impulse to lecture, warn, remind, or cajole if kids do not complete the job. The natural consequence is that your child—your "employee"—does not earn what he or she wanted to earn. They learn that there's no pay for an incomplete job … and parents don't have to say anything beyond an empathic word or two.

Notice how Love and Logic's principles correspond with the nature of the bidding process:

- Does the bidding process share some control?
    Yes, because kids have a choice of jobs to bid on from a list of options.
- Does it offer choices?
    Yes, because kids can choose to accept the parent's counter offer or not.
- Are the consequences built in?
    Yes, because it's the kid's good or poor choice to do a good or poor job that ultimately determines whether he or she receives wages. Just remember to add in the empathy if the job experience doesn't turn out well for the child, and encouragement when it does.

Pay and Training Factors

Naturally, level of training and level of pay are linked for jobs that kids do: skill, experience, and performance determine payment, just like in the real world. What you decide to offer depends on the age and ability of the child, but generally speaking, children should be paid children's wages for doing children's work (up to the adult minimum wage). Level of pay should be reflected in a child's increased effort and ability as they become more skilled and experienced. (For an exercise to help children understand how earning money is related to effort, see "Easy Money: Turning Depreciation into Appreciation" on p. 330.)

Here are some commonsense guidelines:

- Pay the full amount for a complete, satisfactory job.
- Pay more for exceptional work.
- Pay justly, not excessively. (Too much money for too little work breeds a false sense of what the effort is worth. Pro-rate the hourly minimum wage to accurately reflect a portion of an hour's work.)

It's unwise to pay an amount higher than what you would pay an adult, or a neighbor kid, to do for the same service. Why? Because unless your children live on another planet, real world living requires a lesson in real world wages—wages that are based on training and experience, and that are commensurate with the geographical area.

With or Without Supervision?

The amount of supervision and training needed is also a factor in determining wages. There are "regular" wages for kids who can do the task unsupervised; and there are wages for "on-the-job training," whereby the parent pays the child for his or her "side-by-side" assistance.

Regular wages are basically a minimum hourly wage. Regular wages should be reserved for kids who can do the job without your help. If your child completes the job well, then he or she has earned full pay (i.e., the hourly minimum wage × the number of job hours). Or, if the job is completed in under an hour, pro-rate the wage to a portion of the hour. For example, if the wage is $8 per hour and the child completes the job in forty-five minutes, the wage is $6.

Training wages, on the other hand, should be commensurate with helpful effort. Naturally, training wages are *a portion* of what the child could earn for the same job without training (i.e., between zero and the hourly minimum wage—think partial amounts). Use the amount of time and your child's effort as your gauge, eventually increasing the amount to a full hourly wage as described above. Using the same example above, if the wage is $8 per hour and you and your child work side by side for forty-five minutes to complete the job, the wage is "shared"—thus $3 ($8 divided by two workers = $4, which pro-rated at forty-five minutes = $3).

Here's a chart that should help you determine wages based on training and pay levels:

Wage and Training Levels

	Training Wages	Regular Wages
Level of Training	Supervision required.	No supervision required.
Level of Pay	A portion of minimum wage.	Minimum hourly wage not to exceed "adult wages."
Based on hourly wage of $8:	Child-in-training works two hours with supervision. Wage: $8	Child completes a two-hour job without supervision. Wage: $16
Based on child's earning goals:	Negotiated, less than full wage.	Negotiated, full wage.

Wise parents develop a wage system that is simple. Some parents stick to round numbers to make calculations easy to understand. They use the same hourly wage for everyone in the family, but make different adjustments based on age and the amount of training and time worked. Other parents simply negotiate a kid-sized wage that is reasonable based on the child's earning goals, as shown in the next example in our continuation of Mason's story.

Bottom Line: Wise parents negotiate job wages according to level of training and real world economics.

Mason Negotiates for a Car Wash

Let's return to our story of Mason, to learn how a job list, wages, and an eager kid work together to teach a valuable lesson.

The dialogue between Mason and Dad continues a few days after Dad didn't buy that gizmo for his son in the store. Of course, without any money, neither did Mason. In steps Mason's first experience with negotiating payment for a job.

It's a beautiful summer afternoon. Here he comes, bouncing into the kitchen:

Mason: "Dad, I want to earn some extra money."

Dad: "That's great. What are you going to do?"

Mason: "I want to wash your car. It's on the job list, remember?"

Dad: "Yes. And how much do you think the job you will do is worth?"

Mason: "Ohhh … fifteen dollars!"

Dad: "Well, I'm willing to pay you ten dollars to wash my car."

Mason: (plaintively) "Ten bucks?! Uh, um … okay" (heading toward the garage)

Dad: "Mason … oh Mason … please come back. What's your understanding of a complete car wash?"

Mason: (turning to face his father) "Well … Get the car wet with the hose, wash the outside all over with soap, rinse the car all over, and then dry it with some rags."

Dad: "Good. That's my understanding, too. We've done it together many times before, so you should have a good idea of what a complete job looks like."

Mason: "Yep!"

Dad: "Well, that's the kind of job I'll pay you ten dollars for. And, what's your understanding if you don't complete the job?"

Mason:	"I won't get ten dollars."
Dad:	"Good. Have fun!"
Mason:	"Okay!" (runs off toward the garage to get started)

Notice how Dad clarified what kind of job Mason needed to do to earn $10. Mason was able to describe the work that needed doing when Dad asked him, "What's your understanding of a complete car wash?" That's an important step in the process, because it prevents misunderstandings and is the sign of any good training supervisor. It also encourages kids to use their own words to describe the job, which helps the child's brain lock in the sequence of action steps.

In this case, agreement about what needs to be done was reached easily. That's because Mason has had lots of side-by-side car wash training over the years. At least Dad knows Mason is *capable* of doing a job worth $10.

Up Front and Personal

Be sure to negotiate the price and what the finished job will look like, up front. No pay until the job fits the description of the finished job.

Dad anticipated the potential for this distinct possibility with Mason. Thus, to prevent any misunderstandings, he asked, "And, what's your understanding if you don't complete the job?"

Some kids may need to write down the description of a finished job before they begin. Then the parent can just point to the child's description and ask, "You said the finished job looks like this. Does it look like that yet? Not to worry. I'll be paying you as soon as the job is finished."

Some parents set up a more formal contract that they agree to in advance and keep on file, complete with photos! Other parents invite their children to draw up their own contract for each job, stating the specifications for a finished job. These parents make the contract the "boss" if the job is not done to these specifications. Then, they use the enforceable statement: "I'll be paying you just as soon as the job is finished."

Only Half a Job?

Will Dad have a clean car by the end of the day? Maybe. Maybe not. That's the beauty of a job list. It's optional, and consequence is built right into the child's choices. One of the following will happen:

- Mason finishes the job and gets paid.
- Mason never starts the job. (He was merely daydreaming about buying his gizmo.)
- Mason starts the job but doesn't finish it.
- Mason does a lousy job but wants to be paid anyway.

The first two consequences are clear-cut. For workers: "Congratulations! Here's ten dollars." For daydreamers: "Bummer. Maybe another time."

For a child who never starts the job, wise parents pick their battles. Mason's dad chooses not to teach the lesson "you should do what you say you're going to do" at this time. That's because he understands that Mason's poor choice can do the teaching. How?

By using the benefit of time. The most teachable moment—for learning the importance of following through on earning his own money—will occur during Mason's next trip back to the store. Or perhaps when his best friend brings the same gizmo to school. Or maybe not. But Dad knows that if it's not *this* gizmo, it'll soon be something else. The act of letting Mason continue to *want* something builds a strong case for putting in the effort required to earn it.

Negotiate Down

Let's look at the third and fourth possibilities:

- Mason starts the job but doesn't finish it.
- Mason does a lousy job but wants to be paid anyway.

Should Mason make either of these two choices, he'll learn that an incomplete job results in not getting paid. Because Dad wants to avoid any kind of a power struggle, he remembers to share control through shared decision-making opportunities. How? By using a Love and Logic combination of choices, empathy, and consequences.

If Mason comes to collect his money for an incomplete car wash, Dad will empathically offer Mason a choice: "You can finish the job now or finish it later. You decide."

If Mason tells Dad he got "tired," Dad can say: "Oh Mason, what a bummer. Looks like you've changed your mind about needing ten dollars." The problem is handed back to Mason because his poor decision may result in him being $10 short of buying something he wants. In this way the "no work, no pay" consequence can be delivered empathically without anger or lectures.

The most teachable moment—for learning the importance of following through on earning his own money—will occur during Mason's next trip back to the store.

What should Dad do if Mason argues? Dad has learned how to neutralize his son's complaints with an empathic one-liner—such as: "I know. What a bummer."—to short-circuit the whining.

As for the fourth possibility—Mason does a poor job but expects full payment anyway—Dad should treat that situation like Mason is still "in training." He can say: "Payment will be made when the job done matches the specifics of our agreement." No need to argue. Just use your favorite Love and Logic one-liner—such as "Nice try."—followed by, "And what did I say?"

Negotiate Up

In the world of free enterprise, bidding and negotiations can go either up or down. Unfortunately for Mason, the negotiations in the above scenario didn't work in his favor.

But what if your children want more money for a job well done? Again, we will draw our inspiration for solutions from how the real world works. How do adults get paid more? We usually put in extra effort.

Let's say Mason really *really* wants to earn $15 so that he can buy that highly coveted gizmo. Dad's handy job list offers him a couple of choices. Mason could peruse the neighborhood, bid on another job on the list that will pay him $5 more, or negotiate an increase for a more deluxe car wash.

Let's pick up the story again from the beginning, only this time the conversation shifts because Mason doesn't want to settle for Dad's original counter offer of $10:

Mason: "I want to wash your car."

Dad: "Okay. And how much do you think the job you will do is worth?"

Mason: "Ohhh … fifteen dollars."

Dad: "Well, I'm willing to pay you ten dollars to wash my car."

Mason: (plaintively) "Ten bucks?! But I really, really, really need fifteen. Pleeezzz?!"

Dad: "Hmmm. Well, what kind of extra effort are you willing to put forth to turn a ten-dollar job into a fifteen-dollar job?"

Mason: "I could polish all the trim?"

Dad: "And what else?"

Mason: "I could scrub and polish the hubcaps extra good, too."

Dad: "Okay. So tell me again the complete job you will do for fifteen dollars."

Mason: (reiterates correctly everything the fifteen-dollar job entails)

Dad: "Okay, Mason, sounds like we have a deal. That's the job I will pay you fifteen dollars for. Anything less than that …"

Mason: "I know, I know … I won't get paid." (starts out the door, but pauses and looks back over his shoulder) "What if I detail the inside, too? Is that worth more?"

Dad: (smiling) "You catch on quickly, son."

What is Mason learning? Among other things, he's learning how to manage his time and energy while at the same time learning how to earn some money. Mason is also learning the rewards of keeping his agreements, to himself and to his dad.

Not bad for getting a deluxe car wash.

Household Jobs Summary:
Key Points for Being Your Child's First Employer

Pay them to do only your work, not theirs.
Once you pay your children to do something, they will probably expect to be paid in the future. For that reason, remove any confusion, now or later, by not paying kids to do their contributions. Remember, you can pay your children to do *your* jobs and *your* family contributions, but not to do *their* family contributions.

Use the train-and-gain method.
A job list will only be as functional as the training you provide. Remember, the whole reason to hire out a job is that we don't want to be bothered with doing it ourselves. It would be like hiring a window-washing service and then paying the washer to allow you to help.

Supervise and train only as long as necessary for children to learn how to capably do the job without supervision; otherwise it defeats the purpose of offering them the opportunity to do the job in the first place.

Match the job with ability.
Job offers should be appropriate to the age and ability of your children. The success of your children's effort at completing the job will build confidence and capability. We learn more from our failures than our successes. Allow the job to stretch your children's ability without overwhelming them by impossibility.

Match payment with performance.

- A good, completed job results in full payment.
- An incomplete job results in no payment.
- "On-the-job training" pays less than unsupervised work.

We do a disservice to our kids when we either deflate or, more commonly, inflate their pay. Children are aware of the truth. The payment needs to be the result of effort to be meaningful. Keep to a kid-sized pay scale no matter how much more children say they need or want. Invite them to bid on more jobs if they want more money. In this way, pay is realistic because it increases with age, experience, and ability.

Easy Money: Turning Depreciation into Appreciation

Sydney:	(running into the kitchen) "I hear the ice cream truck coming! Yippee! Yee haw! Dad, can I have a dollar?"
Dad:	"No! I've already given you money every day this week for ice cream. It's time you learn to earn some of your own money. Money isn't that easy to come by, you know."
Sydney:	"Aw please?"
Dad:	"No!"
Sydney:	"Pretty please!"
Dad:	"I said, *no*!"
Sydney:	(starting to pout) "But all the other kids on the street are getting an ice cream." (getting on her tippy toes to look out the window) "I'm the only one who'll be left out."
Dad:	(giving her his "stern look" while reaching into his pocket) "Oh, all right ... here's five dollars, but this is the last time ... and I mean it!"
Sydney:	"Cool! ... Can I have another dollar to get a drink? Ice cream always makes me so thirsty ... and five dollars won't be enough ..."

While this is a probably a pretty typical summertime scenario among many families throughout America, there's one line that should catch all our eyes and ears. It's when Dad says to Sydney: "Money is not that easy to come by, *you know*."

Trouble is, this child *doesn't know*. Money is always easy "to come by" when all we have to do is beg and it's handed to us. What can Sydney know about the reality of earning money unless it's taught?

There's a disconnect for many of today's kids between what one earns for their effort and what it will buy. Sydney, like many children, knows a lot about the pleasures of spending, but little about the perspiration of earning.

EXERCISE 10.1: The "Price to Earnings" Game

There is a fun and informal hypothetical game you can play to give children the experience of what it takes to earn "real" money. The game consists of a series of fill-in-the-blank questions. Many of the questions are designed to be conversation starters about the relationship of effort to earnings.

To begin, you'll need some "fake" money, which you can borrow from a board game, such as Monopoly, or buy at your local toy or game store.

Is the Price Right?

You can approach this exercise several different ways, depending upon the age of your child and their financial know-how. Some parents accept their children's answers at the outset, and only comment or provide information when invited. This is the "wait and see" approach. It works well for parents who want to hear how their children connect the dots between what they want and what they'll need to do to earn it.

Other parents play the game with a more studied approach. They invite their child to research their answers first and come back to the table with their findings. Or, they answer the questions together and stop to discuss the pros and cons of each answer with the goal of filling in the blanks more realistically.

Regardless of the approach you use, the goal of the game is to develop your child's understanding that, to get what they want, they'll have to work a certain number of hours at a certain number of dollars per hour.

"Price to Earnings" Questions

Step 1: Ask your child about something they would like to buy with their own money—something they need to earn *because you are not buying it for them*. (If your child has created a wish list, you can use it as a starting point—see "Toy du Jour Desires: Keeping Kids Interested in Saving" on p. 247.)

Item: _____

Step 2: Ask the child how much the item costs. Invite them to research the price if they aren't sure. Have them count out the amount in play money.

Price of item: $ _____

Step 3: Ask them what they *think* they could earn as a child on an hourly basis. Again, count out the amount on the table.

Hourly wage: $ _____

To illustrate the visual difference between steps 2 and 3, you can encourage your child to make a pile of money to reflect the item price and another pile to reflect their hypothetical "earnings." Then, ask your child to compare the two piles and figure out the difference.

Notice that these first three steps are designed to get your child to define what he or she wants and what they think he or she will earn if they go to work for it.

Price Check, Please ...

Step 4: Next, ask the child how many hours they would need to work to buy the item. Do the math together as needed.

To figure the number of hours, take the price of the item and divide it by the hourly rate. For example: If I earn $5 an hour, I will need to work two hours to make $10. You may want to round the figures up or down for simplicity's sake.

Price of item: $_____ ÷ Hourly wage: $_____ = Number of work hours: _____

Step 5: Use questions to help the child draw their own conclusions when you finish plugging in the numbers. For example, ask:
"What have you learned?"
"What's the difference between the number of hours you'd like to work and the number of hours you'll *need* to work to buy what you want?"
"What could you do if you wanted to earn more money?"

Some kids will need help interpreting the results in order to concretely combine the two concepts. Other kids get the picture right away. In either case, look for their basic understanding: earning money requires effort.

###

If Dad were to play this game with Sydney, what would she discover? That $5 for ice cream and a drink is not so easy if she has to earn it!

The Conversion Formula

Once you've played the "Price to Earnings" game, you have a child-friendly example to illustrate a basic economic principle—that wants have a cost. Next time your children ask you for money, invite them to plug in the numbers so that they can convert their effort to earnings.

Here's the basic equation that your children can use whenever they want to find out what something really costs in time and effort:

Price of item: $_____ ÷ Hourly wage: $_____ = Number of work hours: _____

Honey and Money

But what if you're in the store, without pencil, paper, and time to do this exercise? One parent, when she's out shopping with her child, has found magic in a simple phrase: "You're welcome to find a way to earn your own money, honey."

Why is it magical? Because it hands the "to earn or not to earn" problem right back to the child, kindly but effectively. She shared that nine times out of ten, her child responds with resignation by saying, "Never mind." That's because her child knows something we all know: Isn't it always easier to spend someone else's dime?

Bottom Line: Wise parents use the conversion factor to bridge the cognitive chasm between being given money and earning it.

Jobs: Self-Employment

Another way for kids to earn money is to become "self-employed." These are jobs kids create for themselves.

They can be jobs they find in the neighborhood, such as watering lawns, caring for pets, babysitting other children, shoveling snow, or washing cars. Or they can start up their own business out of the home, such as online sales and marketing, website creation, or data input.

Your first clue that your child is interested in becoming "self-employed" might be when he or she brings you an idea. Some of your children's ideas will naturally have a better chance of success than others. It's important to encourage children to experience the difference between working for others and working for oneself. This is a perfect opportunity for consultant parents, as they can serve as guides in the process. (For a description of the consultant-style approach to parenting, see "Behind Door #4: The Consultant Style" on p. 32.)

The best ideas *for your child* are the ones that combine their natural abilities with their interests. The best ideas *for earning money* are for products and services that meet a need or solve problems for people. The most successful self-employed people are the ones who combine the two—they choose to do something they are really passionate about, and then work to meet a need in the marketplace.

Darlene is a good example.

Ideas to Love

While the lemonade stand is the proverbial symbol for entrepreneurial kids, one creative eight-year-old girl lived on a dude ranch located across from a large camping and family resort RV park. Guests would walk over to the ranch after dinner to pet the horses and feed them apples and carrots. One summer night as she sat on a bale of hay, Darlene decided to share her passion for horses with the ranch's visitors.

The first summer, she baked a bucket of "sweet lumps" and sold bagfuls, with instructions on how to feed her horses, for $1 each. The next summer, responding to some requests for souvenirs, Darlene borrowed her father's digital camera and sold snapshots of the "dudes" standing next to their favorite horse for $2 each. The third summer, she did both of the above, and in addition, collected all the old, discarded horseshoes around the ranch, hand-painted them with bright colors, and sold them for $5 each as paperweights.

Each summer after that, Darlene's business continued to grow, because she was satisfying the need to capture sweet summer memories for vacationing families. From one "sweet lump" in the first year came a business that yielded enough money to pay for a fancy new saddle.

Planning: The Mother of Every Good Invention

Ideas for earning money are limitless. Some kids will be able to come up with their own ideas; others may need help. With children, we can turn "necessity as the mother of invention" into planning, brainstorming, and trying something just for the fun of it. Kids can come up with some of the most amazing projects. Ideas that prompt adults to ponder: "Why didn't I think of that?" A better mousetrap gets reborn again!

Parents can develop their children's entrepreneurial muscles by asking them what interests them enough to want to do it for others. Does your child love to build things? Does he or she have a passion for theatrics? Music? Cooking? Is your child good with younger children? Is he or she a techie type? Help your children incubate ideas long enough to turn their heads *and* their hearts.

Being self-employed requires a variety of characteristics. Is your child imaginative? Creative? Energetic? Determined, disciplined, and organized? Those are some of the most important qualities necessary to being our own boss. Of course, these qualities can be cultivated in children in the *process* of learning what it takes to provide a product or service to others.

In short, the initial step is to help them match their abilities, interests, and passions with marketable ideas.

Parents can develop their children's entrepreneurial muscles by asking them what interests them enough to want to do it for others.

Research and Development

Once your child has an idea that "feels right," encourage them to research it. Is there a need in the marketplace? Who will buy their product or use their service? How much will they charge? How will they tell people about it? What materials do they need to get started? How will they pay for it? Is anyone else doing the same thing? (For more information about helping kids research a business idea and develop a kid-sized business plan, see "The Application Process" on p. 278.)

Parents can encourage their children's entrepreneurial spirit by inviting them to do "field" research as well. Some parents help their child arrange an interview with a person who is doing the job or providing the service they are proposing. Other parents set up an opportunity for their child to "shadow" a mentor to explore an idea's potential. Still other parents help their children explore an apprentice or internship opportunity.

Regardless of the resources children use to research their ideas, whether writing up their own proposals or shadowing someone else's, they all provide opportunities to test your child's true desire to be their own boss. Or, perhaps, it may be an opportunity for them to discover that self-employment is not for everyone, or at least not for now.

While parents may have misgivings at first about kid's ideas, be careful not to dampen your child's enthusiasm with an excessive dose of reality. Let your child's investment in writing their business plan, or their real life experiments with "field" research, do the teaching. Remember, too, that our expectations for financial success may be very different than our children's expectations. A lemonade stand that makes a $5 profit may be enough of a thrill to be stamped a "success"! (For more information about encouraging your children's enterprises, see "Too big for your britches"! on p. 255.)

Bottom Line: Wise parents encourage their children's "inner entrepreneur" by offering guidance and support to research, plan, and develop their own ideas.

Laurie Goes Door-to-Door

Laurie is ten years old. She has expressed a repeated interest in publishing and selling a neighborhood newsletter. After much research and discussion with her mom, and a "pre-approved" written business plan, she determined she needed $50 in startup costs for her new business.

With Mom's permission, she canvassed the neighborhood to solicit personal-interest interviews, took photographs, and put together a newsletter from a computer template. She then printed copies and sold them for $1 each.

Laurie's mother, wanting to support her entrepreneurial spirit, decided to pay for some of the more expensive startup costs. This decision was based on Laurie's research into the project, a viable proposal in writing, and her enthusiasm. The seed money was designated to cover the initial costs of using Mom's color toner cartridge and the first ream of glossy heavyweight paper.

Laurie worked diligently and successfully delivered the first issue on time. Experiencing a sense of achievement, she honed her creativity and computer skills even further by coming up with more ideas.

Need Capital for a Capital Idea?

Laurie: "Mom, can I have more money? I need to buy some card stock and stickers for my greeting card idea."

Mom was now faced with the financial decision about what to do when Laurie expressed a desire to expand her product line with greeting cards. Should she give Laurie more money, loan it to her, or require her to earn it?

Mom provided the initial funding to Laurie based on her idea, her efforts to develop the idea more fully, and her enthusiasm and follow-through. As for expanding her business, Mom decided that the experiment in entrepreneurship was not realistic unless Laurie used her own money. So Mom gave her two choices: to borrow or to reinvest.

Mom: "I'll loan you some more money if you like, or you can reinvest the money you have already made."

Laurie chose to reinvest her earnings. She now has a great opportunity to learn how to invest by reinvesting in herself. Laurie is learning what all successful self-employed businesspeople know—that reinvesting profits has its benefits. Reinvestment is a gift that gives twice, because it contributes to the business owner's character and product development.

What would have happened if Mom had kept giving Laurie money for each new idea? Laurie would have experienced all the joy of being creative without any of the effort of earning her success. By suggesting that Laurie use the profits from her newsletter to expand her business, Mom taught Laurie an important lesson: being your own boss requires wearing all types of hats—from bookkeeper to CEO, from fundraiser to artist and photographer, and from salesperson to inventory manager.

If Laurie chooses to take Mom's offer for another loan and "refinance," Laurie would need to go back to the drawing board to "requalify" for the additional amount.

Reinvestment is a gift that gives twice, because it contributes to the business owner's character and product development.

How Much Funding?

Where should parents draw the line for funding their children's enterprises? Part of the decision is related to needs versus wants.

In the beginning, Mom understood that in order for Laurie's idea to work, she needed money for startup materials whose prices would be quite daunting to cover on her own. So Mom decided that these items were *needs*, meaning that Laurie would not be able to succeed with her initial idea without them.

Then, success happened and Laurie decided to expand. Laurie's mom used the guideline of *wants* in her offer to loan her the money for additional supplies.

In this way, Mom taught Laurie about the difference between needs and wants—even in business.

Mom's decision sent the message that she supported Laurie's creative endeavors, but that her daughter needed to continue to work and support her own efforts, too.

Some Capital Guidelines: Need or Want?

Here's a simple guideline to use when funding your children's enterprises:

If it's a need, a scholarship or startup gift can often be the best answer for many parents. Grants or matching funds also have inherent incentives for the child as long as he or she is held accountable.

If it's a want, then an outright loan is often a better answer. That's because once the basic need for supplies and materials has been met, additional funding for business expansion becomes a want.

Examples: Parents pay for the ingredients; kids make and sell the lemonade. Parents buy the equipment or materials; kids provide the labor. Parents loan the initial costs; kids reinvest the profits.

The important point to remember is never work harder than your child on their business ventures. (For more guidelines about funding your children's ventures, see "When to Loan" on p. 268.)

Of course, the exact amount of money offered will vary according to the business idea. The capital needed for a lawn-mowing or window-washing business may be very different than for a pet-walking service. Turn your children back to the planning table whenever they ask you for more capital. Funding should be based on a purpose and a need versus want assessment regardless of whether it's a gift, scholarship, grant, or loan.

Encourage your kids to start small and build on their successes gradually. Wise parents know that their children will profit far more from encouragement than from overfunding.

Laurie's Postscript

There's a P.S. to this story. Mom was worried that her daughter might be preying on the friendship of neighbors for repeated purchases—first a newsletter, then greeting cards.

Is this a good time for another growth and character development opportunity? You bet. Mom could invite Laurie to reinvest in herself once again by expanding her services (and her earnings) beyond her own neighborhood. Isn't that what the best of life is all about—nurturing our passions while providing a service to others?

Bottom Line: Wise parents use a little education, a lot of encouragement, and progressively accountable funding whenever they want to motivate their children to explore the world of self-employment.

Jobs: Employment and Teens

Mom #1:   "Where's your daughter?"
Mom #2:   "Oh, she's at work. She started a job at that new clothing store downtown. You know … Lula-belle's."
Mom #1:   "How's it going?"
Mom #2:   "Good. She seems to be enjoying it a lot. You know, she's always been a fashion bug, ever since she was little."
Mom #1:   "My girl isn't interested in working. But that's okay with me. She has the rest of her life to work."

The third way for kids to earn money is through real world employment. Whether you allow your teen to work or not while in school is a personal decision involving many factors. Federal child labor laws, family values, and financial resources, as well as your child's academic standing, temperament, and motivation, all play into the decision.

Which way do you see it? Here are a few pros and cons to consider.

Cons

Working a job while going to school is always a challenge, at any age. Parents who say "no" to their teen who wants a job may worry about undesirable side effects when balancing school and work at the same time. Grades may begin to suffer, contact at home may become less frequent, and the stresses of a work schedule may result in poor decisions about how to manage it. Some research reveals that drug and alcohol use and other types of risky behavior may increase for kids who are working too many hours.

Pros

On the other hand, balancing a work and school schedule gives children the experience of how to get and keep a job, how to manage their time and their paycheck, and how to get along with other people.

For kids who are not academically inclined, or who may not go to college, employment will give them an early boost in the labor market. For other kids, who may be tempted toward negative influences, a part-time job may keep them out of trouble. Finally, for some kids, their first sense of being capable comes through a job. For them, the job experience is even more valuable than what is happening at school.

The pros of teenage employment include real life workplace experience, which is desirable to employers after graduation, a chance to be successful outside of school, and a head start on career exploration before it really counts.

Balance Between Pros and Cons

If your teen is begging you to allow him or her to work, one potential solution is to experiment during a vacation period, since there's no conflict with school.

The need for more freedom—which additional spending money provides—is the main thing that motivates teens to look for a job. If your teen is begging you to allow him or her to work, one potential solution is to experiment during a vacation period, since there's no conflict with school.

Few teenagers are going to know what it is like to balance a school and work schedule until they are actually doing it. Balancing acts are easier to juggle with less to balance. Teens can always practice with their vacation or summer schedules by starting with jobs at home before taking jobs for hire outside the home. In this way, parents and their teens can experiment with the upside of employment and minimize the down side.

Ease-In or Ease-Up Jobs

Even a few hours each day or a few days each week should be enough of a trial run. A limited work schedule will give your teens practice showing up on time, staying on task without loafing, and working with co-workers and customers. Even getting fired for lack of performance can be a wonderful real world experience if it happens early in life … and before there is a family to support. Limiting working hours is also a good compromise between family time, friends, and extracurricular activities.

Most of the work opportunities available to teens are seasonal or part-time anyway. This makes the nature of teenage work opportunities compatible with the benefits derived from doing it. In other words, there is just enough time to get started on developing good work habits without too much time to become consumed, bored, stressed, or overwhelmed.

If your teen is able to handle part-time employment during "vacation periods" successfully, then perhaps continuing to work during the school year is a viable option. But if you see signs of it not working for them, such as tardies, absences, or lower grades, use a Love and Logic enforceable statement such as, "I'll be glad to let you experiment again next summer."

Whatever you decide, Love and Logic parents share control by limiting the time of year and number of hours their children work, while still giving choices about what kind of work they do.

Bottom Line: Small doses of work may yield the biggest benefits to preparing our children for their future work life.

When the Parent Isn't Ready

What if you don't want your teenager to work? Or what if your teen complains, "All my friends have jobs" … "I don't have enough money" … "You never let me do anything I want"?

If your teen begs you to work and you're still not a fan of an "early work release program," you can say, "You may feel ready to work, but as a parent I'm just not ready for you to have a job." If they badger you for more allowance, "Because, duh … you won't let me work," you can always fall back on the technique of neutralizing the issue with a Love and Logic one-liner, followed by, "And what did I say?"

Or, you can invite them to volunteer.

The Validity of Volunteering

Many opportunities abound for kids to volunteer in the community. Working in the local museum, hospital, nursing home, or childcare facility may offer even more responsibility and leadership opportunities than a paying job.

These types of extracurricular activities have value beyond a job in several ways. First, volunteering feels good. Volunteering is often work with a heart—the mercenary nature of being paid to do work is different than doing it for free. With volunteers, it is presumed that you *want* to do the work instead of that you *have* to do it. This builds up your children's character, because the rewards are internal.

Second, volunteering is altruistic, and therefore is seen as a positive factor on a résumé for future employment and on college admission applications. A volunteer job can be a source of job references, and indicates a developing work ethic, and a willingness to serve. Third, if the position does not work out for your child, it is much easier to make a change than if they are being paid.

Money or time? When invited to volunteer, some teens will say, "But I want the money!" If money is the reason that a teen insists on a paid versus a volunteer job, some parents waive the allowance sharing requirement as an exchange for their teen's time and effort. For example if your teenage son is sharing $10 every month from allowance for charity, then perhaps he would like to *work* for his favorite charity and keep the money. (For more information about the exchange of money for time, see "Ways to Waiver" on p. 421, under the section "The Three T's: Time, Talent, or Tithe.")

Bottom Line: The benefits of learning what work requires come in many forms.

Jobs as Career Exploration

Jobs, volunteer or otherwise, offer wonderful opportunities to explore careers. One of our jobs as parents is to see what our children do well, and then help them find out how to make a career out of it. Our children have a good chance to enjoy their work, instead of just endure it, if we can help them link together the things they are good at, with a way to get paid. Plus, if they enjoy it, we are less likely to have to nudge them out the door to do it.

Most jobs for teens are in the retail, hospitality, and leisure industries. Entry-level positions in restaurants, offices, grocery stores, movie theaters, baseball parks, amusement parks, and gasoline stations are the most common (and legally acceptable) forms of employment for young workers.

Invite your children to research their employment and earning options. Some states require teens to get a work permit. Age, hours, and types of work are all legislated under child labor laws. Be sure to check your state and federal regulations for the latest requirements. (For a look at helping our children understand the reality of wages, education, and lifestyles, see "A Wage Against Reality" on p. 344.)

Pay Is Not the Only Thing That Counts

Some kids have found that the most valuable jobs are not the ones that pay the most, but the ones that teach the most. Those jobs tend to be the ones involving small businesses, sole proprietors, or family-owned companies. Instead of just doing one task repetitively, like flipping burgers, kids who work in small shops or businesses learn how to multi-task at a variety of functions quickly.

The intimacy of spending time with the owner of a business will give kids an up-close and personal perspective that's hard to find with large franchises and corporate conglomerates. Rather than being just one cog in a system of activity, working for a small business develops several skill sets. This kind of experience also exposes the teenager to a variety of tasks, some of which he or she will enjoy, some of which he or she will detest. Those job experiences can be very important to influencing career decisions in the future.

One teen, who worked several summers in a row for a special events organizer, ordered flowers, rang up sales, and calmed brides-to-be all in one day! Having learned many of the nuances of "a day in the life of a small business owner," she went on to successfully open her own wedding-planning business after she graduated from school, named "Your Wedding, Your Way!"

Family-Owned Business Jobs

What if your child wants to go to work for you in the family business? Some parents who self-employ their children require them to go through the same application, interview, and hiring process as anyone else who is seeking a job in the company. If they get the job, those same business owners should expect the same, or more, than they expect of any other employee in the same position. That's because it prepares them to work their way up to filling your shoes, or bigger shoes someday if they so desire.

Some families prepare their teens to work in the family business as soon as they are able or willing. One grandfather who owned a golf course hired his grandson, fourteen-year-old Skip, to work at a putting green. He was hired as a cart boy and ball washer during the summers, and later became a caddy. Skip's duties expanded to management once he graduated from college. The other nonfamily employees respected Skip because he had worked his way up through the ranks of responsibility and intimately understood the requirements of the employees he now supervises.

Other families prepare their children to inherit the family business by inviting them to work—not for them—but for someone else in the same business. That way their children can learn the ropes on someone else's dime and time. Kids come to understand the commitment that is required through the experience of doing it. When kids work for someone else in the same business, they can make a more informed decision about all that is required to be a part of the family business, without the emotional weight of being a family employee.

When kids work for someone else in the same business, they can make a more informed decision about all that is required to be a part of the family business, without the emotional weight of being a family employee.

When to Step In and When to Step Out

On a sad note, there's a young man who works for his parents in a business where I (Jim), as well as other customers, have seen him steal from the cash register. This has gone on for several years. His parents are aware of this but have not stepped in and fired him for theft.

What is this teaching this young man? The consensus of the customers who know about this is, "We hope his parents outlive him. He could never make it in another business, nor would he be able to take over the company when his parents get too old to provide a job for him."

Let's remember that it's the kid's job, family business or otherwise. It's time to step out whenever you find yourself working hard to motivate your child, or whenever you find yourself working harder than your child.

One parent found himself getting up two hours earlier each day to try to wake his sleeping son. When asked why he did this, he responded, "If he's late delivering his papers, he could lose his job."

The authors of Love and Logic believe that losing a low-paying job due to irresponsibility at age fifteen might be the experience that teaches how to keep a higher-paying job later in life.

A Wage Against Reality

Mia's parents told her they would pay for her tuition, room and board, and books when she left for college, but she would be responsible for everything else. Here's how the conversation went about how Mia, eighteen years old, was going to handle earning her spending money:

Mom:	"So Mia, what do you plan to do for your spending money at college?"
Mia:	"That's not a problem. I'll just get a job."
Mom:	"How much will your job pay?"
Mia:	"I don't know … Maybe nine dollars an hour?"
Mom:	"How many hours will you need to work at nine dollars to earn the first hundred you want to spend?"
Mia:	"I don't know! Mommm! This is so stupid … I can't wait to be on my own!"

Mia needs to understand that her "skills basket" is not as large as her shopping basket.

Ask most anyone the following question, and you would likely get the same answer: If you want to earn $60, would you rather work six hours or twelve hours? Six hours, of course!

Mia, like many kids, does not understand the reality of wages. Nor does she understand that earnings are frequently related to job training and education. Part of our job as parents is to give our children a basic primer about the relationship of education to earnings.

Would it be helpful, for example, to learn that $60 can be earned in one minute, ten minutes, six hours, or twelve hours, depending on the education and experience of the worker?

EXERCISE 10.2: The "Education to Earnings" Game

Here's a variation on the "Price to Earnings" game" introduced earlier in this chapter. The "Education to Earnings" game helps children understand the relationship between earnings, education, and lifestyles. Play this game when you have a child who, like Mia, needs a little lesson about the relationship of earning to education.

Step 1: Ask your child about something they would like to buy with their own money—something they need to earn *because you are not buying it for them*—and how much it costs. (If your child has created a wish list, you can use it as a starting point—see "Toy du Jour Desires: Keeping Kids Interested in Saving" on p. 247.)

Item: _____
Cost: $ _____

Step 2: Ask your child what they can earn as an hourly wage right now.
Actual hourly wage: $ _____
To keep it real, coach your children to use no more than the amount of the current minimum wage. Minimum wage is subject to change and varies from state to state, so invite your child to research the current amount. Most kids can only earn the minimum wage, based on their abilities and level of experience.

Step 3: Ask your child what they would *like to earn* on an hourly basis as an adult.
Desired hourly wage: $ _____
If you get "I don't know" for an answer, this is a great opportunity, for older children especially, to research job and career options, educational qualifications, and salaries.

Use this exercise with children of all ages. Encourage them to take what they learned one step further by inviting them to come up with a plan to earn the money for the item they want, as listed in step 1. Determine a realistic hourly wage (from 50¢ to minimum wage) and then invite them to have fun earning the money to buy what they want.

If you've been providing allowance practice, your children will be familiar with making their own buying decisions. Only this time, their decision is another step closer to understanding what it takes to earn what they want to purchase. Rather than buying something based only on the number of dollars, the decision is also defined by the number of hours they will have to work to pay for it.

One dad skipped the official exercise and, just for fun, used piles of play money to develop an understanding of the relationship between education, earnings, and lifestyles. He and his teenage daughter researched the average salaries of a high school dropout, a high school graduate, a college graduate, and someone with a postgraduate education. They counted out four piles, one for each level of education. No need to explain here: the difference an education makes was clearly visible in those piles.

Rather than buying something based only on the number of dollars, the decision is also defined by the number of hours they will have to work to pay for it.

To Study or Not to Study?

Once your child has completed the steps, have them compare the two hourly wages for a reality check. Ask them a few questions such as the ones below, and discuss their conclusions.

> "What's the difference between what you would like to make as
>   an adult and the amount of money you can make now?"
> "Which wage will allow you to buy what you need or want easier
>   and faster?"
> "What will it take to make up the difference?"

Nine times out of ten, the difference is one, or a combination, of the following three factors:

- Education
- Job experience
- Job demand

While job demand fluctuates with the economy, the correlation of higher wages to higher-level education and job experience is steadfast. Advanced levels of education and experience give people more independence and freedom to pursue more career and lifestyle options. (Of course, there are always exceptions to the rule. Some people can develop an idea and then, with "street smarts" in addition to regular attendance at the "school of hard work," earn plenty of money, even millions of dollars.)

An Even Quicker Study

What if the lure of immediate income tempts your reluctant student to quit high school prior to graduation? Then perhaps a real life experience with the purchasing power of minimum wage will be more effective.

One dad took his sixteen-year-old son, Austin, who was not doing very well in school, on a fiscal field trip. Dad decided it was time that Austin learn about a few of life's financial realities.

On their way to the restaurant for dinner, Dad handed Austin some money (one hour's minimum wage) and said: "You are welcome to spend as much or as little of this money as you need for your meal. And, I'll even let you choose the restaurant, as long as it doesn't involve golden arches, a bell, a king, or a cute redheaded girl in pigtails." Eyes eager with anticipation, Austin smiled and mentioned a sit-down chain restaurant in the neighborhood.

After sliding across the banquette seat, Austin grabbed a menu and started browsing. A few minutes later, a frown replaced the smile and, eyebrows raised, Austin looked up from the menu to his father. "Dad, I need a couple bucks. My favorite meal costs twice what I usually get … Jeez! Is this some kind of a joke?"

Sustainability in school becomes much more important when it strikes in the stomach.

One Caveat

Education, in and of itself, does not automatically equate to earning potential. While this exercise may imply that if you're not earning a lot of money, you're not doing anything worthwhile, we know that this isn't true. Teachers, ministers, police officers, social workers, and other service professionals may not earn a lot of money, but all require more than a high school diploma, and often require a college education, to do their jobs.

Education and satisfaction can correlate, with or without money. Education and service to others can also correlate, with or without money. But it's important to help our kids understand that, in general, the more money they desire, the more education they'll need.

Bottom Line: Love and Logic parents are careful not to addict their kids to a lifestyle they cannot afford. Instead, they help their children connect the financial dots between education and earnings so that they can afford the lifestyle of their own choosing.

Top Ten Job Search Tips

Parents can provide job search guidance and supervision in a number of important ways. Some kids may want your help with their job search. Other kids may want to find their own help (some high schools offer job counseling).

Here are ten tips for assisting your teen in their search for a job:

1. Help them make a suitable match between who they are and the job.
2. Help them develop a résumé, if relevant to the job they are seeking.
3. Teach them how to fill out a neat and complete application.
4. Role-play to teach them *how to talk about* their accomplishments, interests, hobbies, or school activities. Practice with question and answer sessions. For example, you or a business friend might do a mock job interview with your teen to help them sell themselves to a prospective employer. Hone examples of their strengths (e.g., honor roll student, fast learner, involved in extracurricular activities, maintains good grades, manages time well).
5. Practice eye contact, posture, how to shake hands properly, and how to address the interviewer (Mr., Ms., Dr., etc.).
6. Discuss appropriate job interview attire.
7. Coach them to develop and ask questions before they are hired:
   "What kind of training does the company provide?"
   "Do I have to work a minimum number of hours?"
   "Do I have to work at certain times, like at night?"

> "Are the hours flexible, in case I have a big exam or need to rehearse in the school play?"

8. Practice how to ask about "the next step" once the interview is over. For example, "When would you like me to follow up?" or "When would be a good time to check back to see if you have made your decision?" Most teens will not think to do this unless they are trained in the benefits of closing the interview with an agreed upon future action to take.

9. Discuss the importance of thanking prospective employers in writing, as well as thanking family and friends who provide referrals, regardless of the job search outcome.

10. Once a job is secured, discuss what happens to allowance and how the paycheck will be used, preferably long before it gets cashed. (See "Allowance, Earnings, and Paychecks" on the next page.)

Staying "On the Job"

It's important to stay tuned to your child's life at work, in case any problems arise. Just because they are old enough to work doesn't mean they are old enough to figure out everything they will encounter in the real world.

Some teens may be tempted to rationalize their low pay and lousy hours by dipping into inventory or into the till. Talk to your teen before he or she starts their first job. Unlike teachers, coaches, and family friends, your teen's first employer may be the first adult that doesn't necessarily have a stake in your child's development.

Tell your kids the importance of talking to you about work, especially if something goes wrong on the job. Kelly, seventeen years old, had just gotten his first job as a convenience store cashier. After several weeks of successful employment, he was accused of stealing money when his cash drawer was short. When Kelly flagged the problem to his manager, he was told that the amount would be deducted from his paycheck if he couldn't "figure it out." He came home very upset.

After talking it over with his mom, Kelly remembered that a video camera was trained on the cashier and register at all times. As it turned out, someone had scammed him by distracting him with so much "friendly" conversation that he gave that person their change—twice!

If your teen has been hired to open or close a business, for example, set up hypothetical examples of situations and talk about the best way to deal with them: What if a T-shirt is missing from the stock room? What if the store was

Unlike teachers, coaches, and family friends, your teen's first employer may be the first adult that doesn't necessarily have a stake in your child's development.

broken into overnight? By placing your teens in hypothetical "role-taking" situations, you have set the stage for an appropriate response should they need one.

Finally, beware of Internet scams by unsavory people trying to lure unsuspecting teens with offers of easy money, such as: "Do you want to be one of the many kids who make millions of dollars from the comfort of their own bedrooms?" Teach your kids that if any offer—especially involving money—sounds too good to be true, it is. Nearly all websites, including kid-friendly ones, are funded by advertising—from banners to pop-ups, from sponsored links to information embedded in the site itself. Talk to your teens about advertising gimmicks, what to avoid, and why.

 Bottom Line: Wise parents encourage, support, and stay closely tuned to their children's work life.

Allowance, Earnings, and Paychecks

Some parents believe that an allowance is the first step in learning how to manage money. Others feel that an allowance should be associated with "chores"—do the chore and receive the allowance, or don't do the chore and receive nothing. And still others desire to disassociate an allowance from the money their children earn.

Regardless of which category fits your point of view, the issue remains: What should happen to an allowance once children begin to earn their own money? Should parents continue to provide an allowance, or should they cut it off once their kids begin making money?

There are three basic approaches you can adopt, depending on the age of your child, your financial resources, and your values. One approach encourages saving and the other two encourage earning. Two approaches encourage progressive financial gain and the other encourages progressive financial freedom. All three approaches acknowledge the changes that employment brings, while still benefiting the child:

- The "what they earn" approach: allowance is matched to earnings.
- The "what they save" approach: allowance is matched to savings.
- The "from wean to lean" approach: allowance is gradually reduced.

(There is another approach, which is status quo: allowance remains the same. This approach is a good option for parents who do not want their children to work because it would conflict with their family values—for example, their children are earning scholarships, volunteering, taking an extra heavy college prep course, or involved in demanding extracurricular activities.)

There is always the no allowance approach, too (see "When Allowance Doesn't Allow" on p. 26). It's important to remind our children that extenuating circumstances may preclude whatever arrangements you make with them regarding their allowance and earnings. A sudden death, divorce, or unemployment can trigger a change in the family's economic situation that will require their understanding and support.

The "What They Earn" Approach

Match whatever your child *earns* dollar for dollar (or some other ratio) and place it in a savings or investment account. As your child's earnings increase, so does his or her savings.

The "What They Save" Approach

Match whatever your child *saves* dollar for dollar (or some other ratio) and place it in a savings or investment account. The more the child saves, the more you save on his or her behalf.

If your kids have developed the habit of saving their allowance, then saving a portion of their earnings is a natural extension of the "pay yourself first" habit.

If your kids have not developed the habit of saving (and want to spend every penny, as so many of us are tempted to do), one option is to find a bank that will automatically save a portion of your teenager's paycheck through automatic deductions. (See "Avoiding Paycheck Battles" on p. 353.)

What if your child earns more or less than their allowance? Some parents may need to set limits if their financial resources are limited. In other words, they will "match but not exceed" their child's allowance. Other parents use a ratio or percentage as the way to either cap or expand their contribution.

The "From Wean to Lean" Approach (Without Being Mean)

Some parents want to stop their children's allowance once their kids begin to earn their own money. A gradual weaning process is an option if this is the case.

The weaning approach reduces a child's allowance month to month through incremental deductions. This is designed to encourage your child to gradually begin paying for more of their own needs and wants with their money. By transferring the "power of the purse strings" from your hands to theirs, you are expressing your self-confidence in them while also giving them a sense of independence.

Parents who use this approach can say, for example: "Once you are sixteen and are able to work, I'll gradually reduce your allowance each month so that you have an opportunity to learn fiscal responsibility while also enjoying the benefits of earning your own money."

This is an effective approach to use for kids who are capable of working on their own but may want to lean on us financially longer than we like (some teen-agers may not want to work if their allowance does the job). You can explain it as an "inalienable teen right": they may earn as much or as little money as needed for the things they want … provided they take care of their primary responsibilities first. That means family obligations, school or vocational training, and whatever else is part of your value system.

The "wean to lean" approach is also effective if your kids need to work because you are no longer willing or able to support them, or they are struggling just to get through high school (see "Whose Problem *Will* It Be?" below). Notice how this approach supports Love and Logic's rule: "Be prepared at eighteen years of age to continue your education or to be totally self-supporting."

Bottom Line: Wise parents restructure their child's allowance by offering benefits and incentives to fit his or her special earning and employment opportunities.

Whose Problem *Will* It Be?

Some parents may think: "Why should I make it my child's problem if I don't make enough money?" Other parents may think: "Even if I do make enough money, why should I make it my child's problem to earn his or her own money?"

Parents' income aside, the answer is the same either way. Because that's the very same problem your kid will need to solve for him- or herself some day. Here's the story of one parent who understood that preparing her son for the working world was the key to preparing him for his future.

Try It with Wyatt

One high school teacher, the mother of a reluctant and unmotivated student, had tried everything to encourage his education. Nothing worked.

She knew he was capable of good grades, but he just didn't care enough to want to work for them.

So she decided to teach Wyatt everything she knew about the skills necessary to run a household. She taught him to be a jack-of-all-trades, since he was not interested in becoming a master of even one subject at school. Mom figured she had better prepare him for entry-level employment, since he was totally disinterested in getting his education as preparation for a career.

After school each day, Wyatt made the rounds with Mom. She taught him how to cook, clean, and do laundry, as well as how to do maintenance and repair work. He actually became more enthused about his housework than his homework.

One night Mom sat down with Wyatt and played the "Education to Earnings" game with him (see p. 345). He wanted to buy an ATV, and had started to save for it. This led to a discussion about his limited earning potential without a high school diploma. He could expect nothing more than minimum wage. Unless, of course he were to continue his education, academic or vocational, become creatively self-employed, or get a job managing others who flip burgers.

As of the time of this writing, Wyatt plans to open his own household cleaning and repair business, just as soon as he graduates from high school.

* * *

A child's introduction to the world of employment can determine his or her future success in the real world, providing that you, as the parent, help prepare them for the real world environment of opportunities and expectations. This is one of those places in life where preparation meets opportunity, if encouraged. The issue is not about the amount of money earned; it's about providing the opportunities and preparation to learn how to be part of the future world of work.

The issue is not about the amount of money earned; it's about providing the opportunities and preparation to learn how to be part of the future world of work.

Avoiding Paycheck Battles

Ahhh … the first paycheck. And the first taste of financial freedom! Once your teen earns their first paycheck, it will be easy for them to think, "Now I no longer have to listen to my parent's stupid rules about what I can buy or how I spend my money!" Wrong.

It's much easier to pedal forward than it is to pedal backward. To avoid the typical refrain of: "It's my money! I can spend it any way I like!" the authors of Love and Logic suggest you talk about that first paycheck well before it ever gets issued.

Jonathan was thrilled when he received a call telling him he got the job on the maintenance crew at the local zoo. Here's how his father approached the issue of spending his earnings:

Dad: "Congratulations on getting your first job. That's terrific! What do you plan to do with your first paycheck?"

Jonathan: "Spend it …" (rolling his eyeballs)

Dad: "Well, then I'm glad we're having this conversation."

Jonathan: "Why?"

Dad: "Because you can spend your money any way you like as long as it doesn't cause a problem for anyone else."

Jonathan: "What! That's stupid. It's *my* money!"

Dad: "I know."

Jonathan: "You can't do that."

Dad: "I bet it feels that way. But until you are eighteen years old, I'm still legally responsible for you. As long as it fits with our family values and you can afford it, feel free to spend your paycheck as you like."

Jonathan: "That's not fair!"

Dad: "I know. I bet it feels that way. But as soon as you are eighteen or living in your own home, whichever comes first, you can spend your money any way you choose."

Once the spending limit of "as long as it doesn't cause a problem" is understood, additional conversations can occur about the types of incentive programs you offer (to match their earnings or savings, or to gradually wean them from yours).

What if Jonathan's spending causes a problem? The previous conversation has already set the foundation for the next:

Dad: "Well, son. This is really unfortunate." (empathy) "I've learned something disappointing."

Jonathan: "Hey! What are you talking about? I didn't do nothin'."

Dad: "Your spending has caused a problem. I can't actually control how you spend your money, but I would feel awful if I were part of the problem. Providing allowance money that contributes to this kind of spending is part of the problem."

Jonathan: "What's that supposed to mean?"

Dad: "It's very simple, Jonathan. When you don't get an allowance this week, I'm sure you'll understand." (consequence)

Once more, we see that the empathy is expressed first and the consequence second. Love and Logic teaches: lock in the empathy before delivering the consequence.

Bottom Line: To avoid power struggles over how their teen spends their paychecks, wise parents set clear expectations before that first check is cut—in more ways than one!

Pay for Grades?

Paying kids for good grades is a dicey deal. It falls under one of those desperate attempts—along with lectures, warnings, and threats—that parents use to motivate their kids. How does paying your kids for grades square with Love and Logic's basic principles?

The authors of Love and Logic believe that kids should not be paid to do anything that is in their own self-interest. Naturally, a good school record (and a good driving record) falls into that category.

Whose Grade Is It?

Why is it so easy to fall into the trap of wanting to motivate our children by paying them to learn? People tend to try to control others when feeling powerless. That's understandable. It is a natural way to deal with the fact that we are fundamentally not in control of many things in life. One of the facts of life is that we cannot *make* kids learn.

Have you ever known someone who simply refuses to eat her vegetables, do his homework, or get up on time to catch the bus? Or how about a teen who, trying to prove who's really in control, fails an entire grade at school, gets involved with drugs, or runs away from home?

The Impermanent Nature of Rewards

I (Jim) know of a father who learned that a short-term fix can make things worse in the long run. When his son Marc's grades began to falter, this father started to pay him a certain dollar amount for any A's and B's he brought home. Each year, his son wanted more and more money for his efforts. So each year, Dad was in a bind when his son raised the bar. Finally, Dad felt like he had no choice but to agree with Marc's offer of good grades for a car. As you can guess, the grades improved just long enough for his son to get the car, and then they fell again.

Now Dad was faced with an additional problem. When he tried to take the car away, Marc threatened to quit school. The system, begun long ago with the first cash reward, grew to the point that his son was able to extort and keep a car he had never earned in the first place. While this may seem extreme, sadly enough it's one of many stories I hear about daily in my business.

Stated or Unstated Message?

We send two messages to our children when we pay our kids for grades. One is stated and the other is implied.

Here's an example of a stated message:

> *Jasper, I will pay you ten dollars for every A you get this year.*

Here's the unstated message:

> *I know that your grades are not important to you, but they are so important to me that I'm willing to reward you (or is it bribe?) for the effort you put into school. While you are also growing socially, emotionally, and physically, I will only reward you for your intellectual efforts. Of course, if I thought those other things were as important, then I would pay you for every new friend you make this year or pay you for being the best player on the team.*

Our subconscious mind is a magnificent computer. It has the ability to cut right through the stated message and hone in on the unstated message. When your mother used to say, "What's the matter with you?" you knew that she wasn't seeking information. You also knew that when she said, "How many times do I have to tell you?" that you'd better not answer, "I think that seven times should be just about what I need."

**Our unstated messages are much more powerful
than our stated messages.**

Learning as a Chore or a Joy?

Being "paid to learn" turns your child's school experience into a cash transaction. As Marc's dad learned the hard way, the essence of the relationship changes when we pay kids.

> **Instead of it being a relationship between school,
> the student, and learning, it becomes a relationship between you,
> your child, and your idea of what their grades should be.**

Paying kids to learn devalues a unique, and hopefully, lifetime process that allows our children the opportunity to reach their fullest potential. As hard as it is for us as parents, let's remember that we can't make kids learn, but we can influence their motivation to learn. A focus on how to influence kids to motivate themselves is a far better focus than the short shelf life of rewards or bribes.

After all, should learning be a *chore* that we get paid for, or should learning be a lifetime *contribution* we give ourselves and then share with the world in our own unique way? (For educational materials about practical solutions for underachievement, check with the Love and Logic Institute.)

Bottom Line: Wise parents are careful not to get trapped into paying their kids for anything that good solid lessons in perseverance and accountability will do for free.

No B's, No Keys? Driving and Grades

These same principles can be applied to driving. A good driving record is clearly in your teenager's own self-interest. The essence of the relationship changes, however, when we try to bribe kids to drive safely using grades or other incentives as the rubber stamp.

> **Instead of it being a relationship between the child, the car,
> and driving responsibly, it becomes a relationship between you,
> your child, and your *hope* that they will drive responsibly.**

While many of us want to believe, including insurance companies, that there is a correlation between good grades and good driving, it's still a risk (it is assumed that if a child is responsible enough to earn good grades, he or she will be responsible enough to drive safely). Maybe, maybe not.

Regardless of the reality for your child, the outcome of a mistake on a test versus a mistake on the road is clearly, sometimes irrevocably, not the same. If you have any doubt whatsoever about how your kids follow the rules of the road, restrict their driving until you no longer have any doubt about safety. Lives are at stake.

Bottom Line: Wise parents see to it that their teenagers understand the inherent reward in learning how to drive safely, uncluttered by money, good grades, or other incentives.

What About Blasé Blake?

Remember the father who introduced his two sons, Mason and Blake, to a job list? Dad's denial to buy Mason the latest and greatest gizmo brought his son face to face with the prospect of earning his own money to buy what he wanted, or doing without. In this case, Dad's denial sparked Mason's desire.

But what about Mason's brother, Blake? How does a parent motivate a child who doesn't seem to want to earn any of their own money, even when they say they want something?

Could it be that Blake has TMTS (Too Many Toys Syndrome)? In this type of situation, it creates kids who end up thinking: "Why earn my own money when I can manipulate, cajole, or extort it from my parents?" If a child has too many toys, then we may need to inspire *more* desire in our children using some real life experiences.

If this is the case, parents can use the same principle that Mason's father used. He let the *desire* of not having something play itself out long enough to encourage his son to want to work for it. In other words, we can take the phrase "play itself out" literally, because it may take a while to create motivation if the child has too many toys in the first place.

Or, if not TMTS, could it be that Blake is not interested in earning his own money because he's not interested in material things? If that's the case, Blake could become the poster child for all the other children who want to surround themselves with too many toys and possessions.

But perhaps what's really going on is that Blake hasn't discovered what he wants intensely enough to be willing to work for it.

If you have any children like Blake, who don't seem interested in earning their own money, perhaps it's time to encourage their *desire* by helping them discover something they are so passionate about that they'll want to work for it.

Yearn, Learn, Earn

Two realities must work in tandem if money is to be earned successfully. First is a yearning to earn (desire), and second is learning to earn (doing). If kids are not motivated to earn money, then the first reality, wanting to work, undermines the second reality, the discipline to learn how.

It's a fundamental formula that has stood the test of time:

$$\text{motivation (yearn)} + \text{discipline (learn)} = \text{achievement (earn)}$$

While achievement comes in many other forms—such as recognition, personal fulfillment, and service to others—*if earning money is the goal*, it must be preceded by the desire to learn how.

Finding Your Inner Earner

For the kid who may be a Doubting Thomas about the "yearn, learn, earn" theory: Ask your child to research the life of one of their heroes or heroines (or piggy back on an already completed biography project from school). It has to be someone who has contributed to society in a positive way. Invite them to search for those three factors—yearn, learn, earn—in their hero or heroine's life story. Whether in the field of sports, arts and entertainment, or education, your child will discover that all of their heroes are very familiar with this fundamental principle of life.

Inspire or Desire?

Motivation comes from doing without, not from getting something handed to you. When we provide our children a variety of opportunities to work for what they want, we give them a gift—a gift of meaningful work that creates a sense of satisfaction and the pride of achievement. An experience that says: "I earned this all by myself!"

In order to motivate kids to develop a "yearn to earn," we need to find a way for them to earn money that provides meaning for the child. How? Find what "hooks" them. One way, as noted earlier, is by not buying them everything they want. Another way is to encourage them to pursue their interests.

Bobbi's New Hobby

Hobbies are a good way for parents to inspire their children's desires enough to want to earn money (and learn at the same time). For example, one mom complained that her daughter, Bobbi, never seemed interested in earning any money. But one day, when Mom went to pick her up from the afterschool program, she was surprised to see that Bobbi had learned how to knit. Bobbi couldn't stop talking about what she needed Mom to buy to "help her out."

She needed yarn, needles, scissors, and patterns … and oh yes, a subscription to the monthly magazine for junior knitters. Praying that this new passion would last, Bobbi's mom said she would buy the initial supplies, and after that, she would provide ways for Bobbi to earn the money to buy whatever else she wanted to continue knitting.

Mom's prayers were answered. Bobbi was so jazzed about making her first scarf that, when she saw "the coolest yarn in the whole wide world," she asked Mom what she could do to earn extra money. In this case, Bobbi's "hook" was knitting!

Most kids are naturally curious about life. Wise parents use their children's innate curiosity to discover how to get them motivated. Make them aware of the many opportunities to satisfy their interests through personal investment or "ownership." Financial ownership, in particular, allows children to explore the object of their interest with the type of self-respect and satisfaction that develop from the feeling of "I got this all by myself!"

 Bottom Line: One way to give kids the gift of motivation is to help them discover something they are interested in enough to want to work for it.

Patrick and the "Twice Bike"

Here's a different kind of "yearn, learn, earn" story about the positive results of not giving someone everything they really wanted. It's about Patrick, who wanted a new bike when he was seven years old. He'd hoped for one on his birthday, but it didn't appear. When he asked for one, his older brother gave him his "twice bike." It had been handed down from his older brother, who had received it from an older cousin. Naturally, after the third owner, it was missing its handlebar grips and fenders, and the drive chain drooped like a noodle. The paint was gone, leaving rust in its stead.

Patrick climbed aboard, and soon realized the bike was too small for him. There was no point in asking his parents for a bigger one, because they would tell him he already had a bike. But, of course, it was not the one he wanted. He learned that if he was going to get a new bike, he was going to have to earn it.

One crisp fall day, he saw an advertisement in the back of a children's magazine. He could sell personalized greeting cards door to door, and make 50¢ on the dollar. And that is exactly what he did. He sold enough greeting cards to buy himself a brand new shiny bike at the local discount department store.

The Gift of Opportunity

Patrick was lucky. He had parents who, by design or circumstance, did not give their son everything he wanted. By not giving him a new bike, Patrick's parents created the opportunity for their son to learn how to give *himself* what he wanted.

The delay in gratification—that period of time *between wanting and having to wait for something*—is what creates the motivation to work for it. Without the desire, the opportunity to learn the value of effort and perseverance gets lost.

While he would not have appreciated this as a young boy, owning a new bike was secondary to the primary gain. What else did Patrick gain by this experience besides a new bike? He learned that big dreams take big desires. On the outside, he got a bike he wanted. On the inside, he learned he had the courage and determination to try something new. He experienced, firsthand, his own ability to have a desire, persevere toward a goal, and fulfill his dream.

Patrick was fortunate to learn this lesson early in his life. He not only felt good about himself, but he also learned that earning money gave him a tremendous sense of freedom and independence. He didn't have to manipulate, negotiate, beg, or borrow from anyone as long as he was willing and able to earn his own money.

Patrick's parents gave him a real gift. More than the temporary gift of a bike, which he would outgrow, his parents gave him the gift of opportunity with the potential to last a lifetime.

Without the desire, the opportunity to learn the value of effort and perseverance gets lost.

Depression Turned Impression

I (Jim) was lucky enough to be born during depression times. My parents couldn't make the mistake of giving me very many of my *wants*. I was even luckier to have parents who said, "The world doesn't owe you anything, but you can have what you want if you are willing to work for it."

When I saw other people who had things I wanted, my father would say, "You can have that too. Work hard and be creative." These two components, not having something and having parents whose message was, "You can earn it," went hand in glove.

What if they had told me that I was some kind of a victim because we were poor? Wouldn't that have been a disaster? Most of my success and happiness is rooted in the early messages of two very poor but very wise parents: the poor person is not the one without enough money, but the one without a dream.

The Value of an Education in Earning

Earning money requires us to wrestle with economic reality. Earning *enough* money requires us to wrestle with our dreams. While it's okay to start life bald, helpless, and broke, it's not the way we want to end our lives.

Ensuing conversations with your children should create a better understanding of the relationship between wishing for something and working for it, and help them bridge the gap between realities and their dreams.

As one wise financial advisor said, "When you find too big of a difference, you'll need to either adjust the work or adjust the wish."

Bottom Line: Wise parents prepare their children for their future by giving them lots of opportunities to learn how to earn money. In this way children can discover the positive values and meaning found in work.

The World's Best Job Benefits Package

What gives kids opportunities to:

- Earn money?
- Learn the difference between their needs and wants?
- Learn time and money management skills?
- Learn to delay gratification?
- Learn gratitude?
- Learn a new skill set?
- Develop a work ethic?
- Learn the "education to earnings" difference?
- Learn the "price to earnings" difference?
- Learn the "hours to income" index?
- Explore career options or volunteer?

Jobs! Looks like a list of benefits too good to be true, yet it's quite possible to enjoy these benefits once we understand the importance of providing job opportunities to our children.

It starts with the introduction of a "job list" at home. Kids can bid on the parents' jobs or get paid to do their parents' contributions. They can canvas the neighborhood for jobs, or they can try their hand at self-employment. Or, once old enough, they can seek jobs with an employer outside the home. Any of those choices work toward the child's goal of earning extra money, and toward the parents' goal of teaching their children the meaning of responsibility through work.

Is It Material?

What's the number one mistake parents make to sabotage the benefits package above? Giving their kids everything they want so they rarely have a need for extra cash. Parents who satisfy their child's every materialistic whim will create kids who never have a reason to yearn, learn, or earn.

One divorced single mom shared what happened when she asked her nine-year-old daughter, Rachel, why she didn't want to make any money around the house doing stuff. "'Cuz," said Rachel, looking at Mom incredulously, "Dad pays for everything."

Dad had taken away the "wanting" factor that's so essential to learning that personal effort is required to get what we want. Dad is not doing Rachel any favors by supplying her every "want" rather than supporting the "yearn to earn" concept favored by her mother.

How will our children want to earn money for things if we're always giving them everything they want? Let's transform that wishbone into a backbone. The things your kids need in order to materialize their dream are not necessarily material things. When we give kids more material comfort than they need, they don't develop the chance to want something intensely enough to go after it for themselves. Love and Logic parents encourage them to yearn enough to earn it.

Entitled to Benefits?

Many employers today bemoan their employees' lack of a work ethic, ambition, or drive to succeed. The employees think they deserve a raise or want to start at the top because they started "at the top" without any effort at home.

Those experiences develop the following kind of stinking thinking in our kids: "Mom and Dad bought me everything I wanted, so why should I work for it now?"

I (Jim) believe we actually steal from our kids when we take away opportunities to build their self-concept based on what they have worked for through effort and perseverance:

> Purchase without performance …
> Attitude without gratitude …
> Work without genuine effort …

How will our children want to earn money for things if we're always giving them everything they want?

all can be summed up in one word—*entitlement*. You can keep your kids out of the entitlement trap when you set up the conditions for them to yearn to earn instead.

Most of us can agree we need to give our children lots of opportunities to prepare them in many areas of life. Two VIP opportunities too important to miss are:

1. Provide opportunities for your kids to earn extra money for what they want.
2. Allow kids many, many opportunities to want something.

You have met one of two conditions necessary to avoid a big part of the entitlement trap when you give them opportunities to work.

The other condition is—you guessed it—not buying them everything they want.

* * *

One just needs to look around to see the variety of ways people can earn money. Self-employment and jobs for hire are a common and an obvious place to start with children and earning. Yet there is another way to make money beyond wages and paychecks, which is the subject of our next chapter, on investing.

CHAPTER 11

Investing

Taking Stock of the Future

This chapter expands on the savings chapter. Using two different approaches to teach kids about investing, it explores stocks, bonds, mutual funds, and the awesome timeline for kids to make money without working for it!

A Zest to Invest

It's Sunday morning. Dad is at the breakfast table reading the newspaper and sipping his coffee. Mom is standing at the kitchen sink. Brent is reading his horoscope while his younger brother, Brandon, is looking at the comics online.

Dad: "The S and P closed higher this week. It's up by twelve percent from a year ago."

Mom: "That's great!"

Brent: "Dad, what does 'S and P' stand for?"

Brandon: "Salt and pepper!"

Dad: (laughing) "It can mean that, Brandon, but in business, 'S and P' stands for Standard and Poor's, an index of five hundred stocks from large companies."

Brandon: "What's a stock?"

Dad: "It's one way to earn money without working for it."

Brent: "That's sounds cool. How can I do that?"

Brandon: "Me too!"

The best time to get kids interested in investing, or anything else for that matter, is when they show an interest. Some kids will naturally be more interested than others. And some kids may never be very interested, but they will need to learn how to be interested. That's because learning how to invest wisely needs to be more than a passing fancy to our children—it needs to be cultivated as a lifetime interest. If we're going to prepare our children for their financial future, then investing needs to be a part of it, too. (For a look at the critical importance of teaching your children how to invest in their future now, see "Investing in the Next Generation" on p. 404.)

Theoretically, investing combines the concepts of "earning" and "saving" at the same time. In other words,

> we need to earn enough to save
> save enough to invest, and
> invest enough to earn more!

Once we have enough money saved to invest, then we are free to do what Brent and Brandon want to learn how to do—"earn money without working for it"!

A New Dimension

Learning how to invest adds a whole new, more sophisticated dimension to your child's understanding of money. It is recommended that you give your children lots of practice at saving money before they actually "invest" money.

Practice at saving money lays the foundation for investing by teaching kids how to delay gratification, determine needs versus wants, and prioritize limited resources. Wise parents build on their children's understanding, practice, and successful use of savings before introducing the concepts of investing. Return to the exercises and activities in Chapter 8, as necessary, to lay the groundwork for success in this chapter.

It is recommended that you give your children lots of practice at saving money before they actually "invest" money.

Two Approaches

If your children are already experienced at creating and using wish lists to achieve savings goals, then you are in a good place to introduce the concepts of investing.

There are two approaches to teaching your kids the basic concepts of investing. One approach builds on learning how to save first, through education and encouragement. This approach is more systematic and expands on the concepts of financial planning and goal setting introduced in Chapter 8. The other approach uses more real life practice with investing money. This approach lets experience do the teaching. One is by the seat of the pants; the other is one leg at a time.

Both approaches work to introduce your children to the world of investing, alone or in combination. The approach you use will depend on your child's age and temperament, their financial know-how, and your financial comfort zone.

Let's look at the story of Josh, who has his first kid-sized experience "investing" through saving.

In Case of Emergency: What Would *You* Do?

"Josh!" Mom yelled from the bottom of the stairs. "Hurry up! Mitchell's dad will be here any minute!"

Josh, twelve years old, was scrambling to get himself ready for a last-minute invitation from his best friend to a baseball playoff game. He was so excited he could hardly think. But he knew he wanted to bring some money to buy *something* special—a commemorative item of some sort. But when he opened his wallet, all he saw was two $1 bills staring back at him. "Mommm!" Josh yelled back, from the top of the stairs. "Can I have my allowance early this week?" Total silence. "Mommm?!"

Here lies the tipping point for most parents. Mom has two basic choices—give him the money or not. What would you do? Here's how a conversation might go using the first option—give him the money:

Mom: "What happened to the allowance I gave you two days ago?!"
Josh: "I already spent it."
Mom: "How about the money Grandma gave you for your birthday? Did you spend that, too?"
Josh: "Mommm … I need some money *now*! Can't we talk about this later?"
Mom: "How many times do I have to tell you to save a little money here and there for occasions such as this?"
Josh: "Mommm … come on …"
Mom: (heading toward the kitchen, with Josh now close at her heels) "I'm going to stop giving you an allowance if all you do is spend it as soon as you get it!" (finds her purse, digs around for some cash, and hands it to him)
Josh: "See ya."

Let's compare this to the second option—to not give him any money. Instant replay. "Mommm!" Josh yelled back, from the top of the stairs. "Can I have my allowance early this week?"

Josh pretty much knew what Mom was going to say from the other times he had asked for an advance. Sure enough: "Nice try."

Thinking quickly, he remembered his "cash stash," an envelope he kept in his desk drawer to use in case of an emergency. Opening the drawer, his reserve money was just where he had left it. With a great sigh of relief, he grabbed three $10 bills, stuffed them into his wallet, and bounded down the stairs just in time to see his ride pull into the driveway.

Mom: "What did you decide to do about taking some money?"
Josh: "I grabbed some out of my cash stash."
Mom: "Oh. Well have a fantastic time, honey!"
Josh: "Thanks! Bye!"

Four hours later, Josh bounded back into the house as he waved goodbye to his friends. He couldn't stop talking about who won, how close he was to his favorite players, and the thrill of watching the last inning. He was especially proud of his new baseball cap with its special tournament insignia. It was a fine new addition to his collection of baseball caps. Not wanting to spoil his good time, Mom listened attentively, but didn't mention a thing about him raiding his savings.

That comes later.

Which Option Is Better?

Some parents might think that Josh's mom should have given him a loan or advanced him the allowance. Other parents might think that Mom should have given him some extra spending money, above and beyond allowance, for such a special and unexpected occasion. Still others might think that Josh should not have been allowed to dip into his "savings" at all.

Those scenarios are all possible, but this mom had learned that in situations such as this, kids become their own best problem-solvers when they are not rescued. (In fact, she had developed a motto to keep herself on track. She would whisper to herself: "Rescue now, repent later ... Rescue now, repent later ...") Mom had also learned that kids need plenty of practice using savings wisely (or unwisely) when the price tags are affordable.

Which outcome has the best chance to teach Josh the value of saving his money—the mom who lectures, reminds, threatens, and then rescues at the last minute, or the mom who holds Josh accountable?

Which option is better to prepare Josh to spend and invest his savings wisely:

- To have few or no opportunities to use his savings?
- To have lots of opportunities to raid and replace savings?

Which option shares control? Which offers choices? And best of all: Which option will give Josh the best opportunity to understand the value of saving and financial planning, even if it's a last-minute trip to a special baseball playoff game?

Pre-Qualifying Investors

You may be wondering how Josh's story relates to learning how to invest money. Saving with success is excellent preparation for investing with success. We need to give kids opportunities to practice achieving their savings goals over and over, before they save for multiple goals. As soon as you introduce investing to your child, he or she is faced with adding one more type of financial goal—to invest.

Josh is learning how to save one experience at a time—even if it starts out as an "investment" in sports memorabilia to add to his collection.

Bottom Line: Wise parents give their children lots of practice saving for a goal, and enjoying the rewards of reaching it, as financial preparation for investing.

What Did Josh's Mom Do?

Josh's mom believed in the importance of teaching her son to save for life's unexpected expenses. Josh would *not* have had $30 to spare if Mom had not already taught him the value of saving for a "rainy day" or for an unexpected "emergency." (For more information about how to set up a revolving savings account, see "Two Types of Savings Accounts" on p. 244, under "When should I open a savings account for my child?")

Wisely and purposefully, Mom delayed talking to him about replacing his funds as soon as he got home. She knew that the most opportune moment for teaching him the need for replacing his savings would arrive soon enough.

Fast-forward to Friday—allowance day:

Mom: "Here's your allowance and your statement."

Josh: "Thanks." (eagerly opening the envelope to look at his $12)

Mom: "By the way, how do you plan to replenish the money you spent on your baseball cap?"

Josh: (already knowing that manipulation and arguing won't work) "Oh, uh … I forgot about that."

Mom: "Then you'll need to come up with a plan so you'll have money the next time you need it in a hurry. Let's look at your statement together."

Groaning, Josh sat down at the table and did some figuring. One thing he knew to do, from a prior experience, was to increase his percentage of savings over the next few months from the usual 20%. But after making all of his deductions, he could see that his grand total was *negative* $15.95! Josh was bummed. He was beginning to appreciate the real cost of his new collectible cap.

Josh's Allowance Statement

Date: Friday
Name: Josh

Allowance amount: $12
Other income: $2 leftover in wallet

Total income: $14

Expenses: $29.95 baseball cap

Total weekly expenses: $29.95

Income minus expenses: –$15.95
Grand total: –$15.95

Mom was genuinely empathic. She followed with Love and Logic's process for guiding kids to solve their own problems. "Some kids," she said, "use the job list, while other kids sell off some of their possessions." She continued, "Still others spend less until they have replenished their savings, or do their siblings' contributions to make it up."

After exploring each idea with Josh, Mom helped him work out an acceptable plan of his own choosing to refill his reserve fund. (Mom could also offer a matching fund option—a "dollar for dollar" deal—if she feels it's appropriate under the special circumstance; the more he saves each week, the sooner he'll be back in the black.)

Bottom Line: Wise parents offer their children lots of opportunities to raid and replace their own savings while they are young. Then they don't feel obliged to raid their own life savings or investments for their kids later.

The Invest by Education Approach

Josh's story is an example of the kind of experience that will give kids the foundation to learn how to invest wisely. Savings is the bridge to investing, so there is a common denominator among the strategies and skills used in previous chapters. (For example, setting goals, doing research, and making systematic contributions are all strategies that work with investing, too. Understanding numbers, as well as reading, understanding, and tracking financial statements, are some of the skills utilized by the wise saver *and* investor.)

There are three building blocks that lead one to a better understanding of investing using the educational approach:

- Planning and setting goals
- Understanding the numbers
- Practice

For the purpose of giving kids investing practice, let's examine these factors one at a time.

Investing in Goal Setting

One goal naturally conflicts with the next when there are limited financial resources. Naturally, as your children's interest in fulfilling their financial goals expands, so will their need to make a plan.

To sort out the realities of their investment goals, most kids will need a basic "Investing 101" course to explore the reasons to invest and the purposes of investing, and to decide how much and how long. Financial investing goals can be established on three levels.

There are three basic *reasons* to invest:

- Security
- Independence
- Freedom

These correspond to the three major *purposes* to invest:

- Emergency/reserve
- Larger, more expensive items
- Future

With three basic *timelines* to consider:

- Short-term
- Intermediate
- Long-term

Some parents like to substitute other words for the adult terms applied to financial concepts. Some parents use "safety net" as a substitute for "security," and "choice" and "more choices" as a substitute for "independence" and "freedom," respectively. Use whatever words make sense for your child's age and his or her stage in the financial educational process. The chart below summarizes these concepts:

Investing Goals

Reason:	Security *safety net*	Independence *choice*	Freedom *more choice*
Purpose:	Reserve or emergency (for unexpected necessities and last-minute wants)	Expensive (for wants that require a longer time to save before purchasing)	Future (for wants that require the longest time horizon)
Timeline:	Short-term	Intermediate	Long-term

Naturally, an adult goal of financial security is very different than a child's goal for "security." The same with freedom. Kids are *not* going to be thinking about their need for a college or retirement fund, but they might be thinking about how to save for the latest computer game.

The story of Josh is a good example of a "kid-sized" goal. Mom gave Josh an opportunity to develop some financial *security* by having a *reserve fund* to take care of a *short-term want*. In this case, Josh had a monetary safety net that allowed him to buy a special memento of the occasion. Josh was learning how to plan and save for the unexpected, at the first level of financial planning.

Bottom Line: Wise parents introduce their children to the concepts of financial planning as preparation for having more than one financial goal in life.

* * *

Practice with setting multiple goals is an important factor in teaching our children how to become wise investors. Let's look at these concepts in more detail using some kid-sized examples, so that we can give our children opportunities to practice meeting these types of goals.

Kid-Sized Financial Goals:
Security, Independence, and Freedom

We'll need to introduce our children to the concepts of financial "security," "independence," and "freedom" in a kid-friendly version; otherwise, understanding the importance of these concepts may get lost in translation. Here are some general ideas to get you started.

Kid-Sized Security

Josh, at least in his mind, had an "emergency" on his hands that day, until he was able to lay his hands on his own money on the way out the door.

Of course, financial emergencies for kids are not real emergencies. However, we are remiss in our parenting duties to deny our children the experience of unexpected financial events and their consequences.

Examples of kid-sized emergencies include:

- Wanting a special item requiring more money than this week's allowance.
- Needing a loan when they forgot their money.
- Repairing their bike after being careless.
- Fixing a neighbor's broken window.
- Replacing eyeglasses or an orthodontic retainer that they've lost for the umpteenth time.
- Bailing themselves out of a library snafu by having to repay a fine before more books are checked out.

Three Lifetime Benefits to Having a Reserve Savings Fund

Among the three types of savings goals, it is easiest to begin with a reserve fund, because it is short-term and doable. A reserve fund can be introduced under many different names, such as a "cash cushion," a "just-in-case fund," or "Samantha's rainy day money." Josh called it his "cash stash."

There are three benefits inherent in establishing a reserve fund. It gives kids practice raiding and replacing savings when the mistakes are affordable, it teaches delayed gratification, and it creates a good lifetime habit:

- First, as with Josh's experience, raiding and replacing savings provides excellent preparation for the inevitability of the financial unknown.
- Second, teaching a child to maintain a reserve fund is a valuable lesson in how not to spend their money as soon as they receive it. This teaches

children fiscal self-control and gives them an experience of delayed gratification. For teenagers, it can also be their first introduction to "deductibles" and the concept of "insurance," because these are designed to cover economic risks and unexpected expenses.

- Third, a reserve fund is a great introduction to the value of having such a fund later in life. Eventually your children will grow up and live on their own, but they will have had the experience of setting aside money in reserve for the "expected unexpected" in life. Those savings will simply be a part of their overall financial picture, a habit rather than a hardship.

One to Six Months

Experts recommend three to six months of living expenses for an adult emergency fund. Some parents translate this amount into three to six months of allowance saved over time. Other parents set up the initial reserve fund for their children and then hold them accountable for replenishment. Still others use the minimum balance required to open their first joint savings account as the source of the child's reserve fund.

Some parents ask their older children to track their expenses for several months to establish average "living expenses." That amount is then multiplied by the number of months to determine the best amount to hold in reserve.

Here's the formula:

(average monthly expenses) × (1–6 months) = amount of reserve fund

Ideally, regardless of how the safety net is established, as soon as the predetermined amount has been put into reserve, your child is free to do other things with his or her money.

Bottom Line: Helping kids develop kid-sized financial security has three benefits—it compels the child to consider needs versus wants, it provides a lesson in delayed gratification, and it helps develop an important lifetime habit of financial resiliency in the face of the unexpected.

Kid-Sized Financial Independence

After your children reach some measure of security, they are ready for the next level—financial independence. A measure of kid-sized "financial independence" can be achieved by saving for items that are more expensive, such as the latest electronics, special trips or concert tickets, tuition for a sports camp or private lessons, or other recreational items. These are intermediate goals for items that children want in the short term (which for kids means the next few weeks or months), but that still require some time to save for before purchasing.

Your children have learned how to save and are ready for the next steps when you see that they are repeatedly able to purchase things, with their own money, that their peers cannot.

Your children have learned how to save and are ready for the next steps when you see that they are repeatedly able to purchase things, with their own money, that their peers cannot.

Kid-Sized Financial Freedom

Once a degree of independence has been established, kids can move toward setting longer-term goals for the future. Long-term goals are for things your children want later, over the next several years or longer: a car, a TV to take to college, signature sporting equipment over the next several years, and so forth. Saving money to begin a business venture, start a college fund, or implement their "to do B 4 I die" list are examples of long-term goals for kids on the early path to financial freedom.

In short, saving on all three financial levels at the same time is ideal but not necessary. Introduce your children to the concepts of savings "goals" and "planning" as gradual preparation for their application to investing.

 Bottom Line: Wise parents help their children understand the idea of setting multiple financial goals on several different levels.

Taking Stock: Charting Multiple Savings and Investing Goals

So far we have looked at goal setting and the importance of giving children opportunities to practice. The second and third factors for raising wise investors are to make a plan for reaching the goals and then put that plan into practice. This includes "playing with the numbers."

Remember the story of nine-year-old Maria from Chapter 8? She came up with more wishes than money. Saving for one thing is doable; saving and investing for a slew of things can be daunting.

How can Maria's mom help her daughter turn her fifteen wishes into realistic goals? And how can Mom show Maria that her wishes are bigger than her bank account, without dampening her spirit? Love and Logic consultant parents let the kid's research and thinking process be the financial planning boss.

Mom invited Maria to complete this research using the "Five Steps to Wishing Well" exercise (see p. 253). Maria determined that she needed to eliminate her number one wish (a swimming pool), because "I don't have the money yet." She decided she was still interested in saving for a bracelet, a gift for her best friend, a pony, and a hand-held electronic game, in that order.

Seems like a tall order for a pint-sized kid. So how can Mom help Maria divvy up her savings dollars? How will her daughter know what to save, earn, or invest for first?

Time to play with the numbers.

Plan Before Purchase

Mom sat down with Maria at the kitchen table and explained the reason for using a planning chart. She explained the purpose behind each column as an important key to helping her reach her goals. (For three tips for setting monetary goals with your children, see "Being Your Child's Financial Goalie" on p. 379.)

Maria's number one priority is to buy that new bracelet she's been eyeing. So she began filling in each of the columns—plugging in the cost, current resources, amount to be saved, and a reasonable time frame. Then she plugged in the numbers related to the other items—a gift for her best friend, a pony, and a hand-held electronic game.

After their discussion, and a little of Mom's coaching about saving for college, Maria completed her saving plan as follows:

My Savings/Investing Goals

Wish/Goal	Estimated Cost	Current and Future Money [savings, job earnings, etc.]	Total Amount to Be Saved	Periodic Amount to Be Saved [weekly, monthly, etc.]	Target Date
Short-Term					
1. Emergency/reserve fund	$80	n/a	$0	$0	Complete
2. Bracelet	$8	$2	$8	$2 weekly	3 weeks
3. Gift for best friend (same bracelet)	$8	$2	$8	$2 weekly	3 weeks
Intermediate					
1. Hand-held electronic game	$30	$0, but I could earn $5 per week	$30	$5 weekly	6 weeks
Long-Term					
1. College education *Do not touch!*	Gazillions	My parents' matching funds (5:1)	$1	Weekly	When I'm 18 years old!
2. A pony	I need to look into that more				

Notice how Maria's desire for a hand-held electronic game, while seemingly *immediate* to Maria, gets bumped to *intermediate* status when it comes to prioritizing multiple wishes. The bracelets (one for herself, and one for her friend) come first, so she'll need to delay the gratification of owning a pony and an electronic game for a while until she saves enough money.

Notice also that Mom has already taught Maria about a reserve fund; now she wants to introduce her to her most important long-term goal—investing for her college education. As an incentive, Mom agrees to match $5 for every $1 Maria saves for her college fund.

Notice how Maria's desire for a hand-held electronic game, while seemingly immediate to Maria, gets bumped to intermediate status when it comes to prioritizing multiple wishes.

The Goal of a College Education

There are many ways to fund your children's education. Financial instruments change quickly. Consult with a qualified financial advisor about the benefits of a savings plan (tax-free growth, high contributions limits, flexibility, etc.), not only for your children but for you as well. Most college savings plans can be used for all types of public and private higher-education institutions in the United States, including junior colleges and technical and trade schools, and can cover a broad range of costs for such things as tuition, room and board, and books and supplies.

As for Maria's pony? Well … that's on the back burner for now, where it needs to be (along with other long-term goals of saving for college), until she develops some appreciation for how saving, investing, and earning the things she wants works in real time.

Planning Chart Before the Shopping Cart

A planning chart for savings and investing goals, such as the one Maria used, helps children to understand the factors involved in making financial decisions based on multiple goals.

Kids will need your help with this chart. It's an expanded version that builds on the same concepts outlined in the "My Wish Worksheet" (see p. 254). Use it whenever your child has multiple competing goals, which happens on the first day that your child wants two or more things that you are unwilling to buy them.

When this chart, or something similar to it, is used as an exercise in financial planning, conversations ensue that are rich in teaching opportunities. For example, if your child wants a new game console plus all the latest accessories, help him or her see how to achieve it by using the chart as the planning tool.

Or, if you wish to open a college savings account with your child, plug in your numbers so that your child is given a *financial* context to appreciate the value and meaning of a long-term investment.

Notice how the Love and Logic principles of shared control and shared thinking and decision-making opportunities come into play. Parents are the consultants, helping their children with the meaning and interpretation of these experiences, but the kids are the final decision-makers based on financial reality.

Like other money management skills, learning how to save for the future takes planning and practice. Use this chart like any of the other charts presented in this book. Apply appropriate sections based on your child's age and financial know-how, and your own family values and common sense.

Bottom Line: Wise parents teach their children financial planning skills so that they will know how to "take stock" before they are allowed to "pick stocks."

Being Your Child's Financial Goalie

Setting goals is an important life skill. Goals are based on one's values—the things that are most important to a person. Goals give direction and meaning to one's life. Goals help us achieve our dreams. Without monetary goals, many people, including kids, feel lost and flounder financially. Here are three tips to keep in mind as you become your child's financial goal coach.

Be Non-Judgmental

Goals change as needs, wants, and circumstances change. While setting goals with your child, don't be concerned if they're only interested in toys, collectibles, and gadgets. It's a learning process. There's enough time to refine the process as your children grow. Kids' sense of what is important to them will mature with time and age. If not, let the reality of the numbers be the one to deliver the "bad news," not you.

Begin Anywhere

Some parents encourage their children to save for the things on their list only *after* a reserve fund has been established. Other parents encourage their children to begin saving based on what goal motivates them the most. And still others encourage their children to start saving for a short-term goal concurrent with investing in an intermediate or a long-term goal.

Age and resources are a factor when considering the best place to start. Parents of younger children may want to begin by encouraging only short-term savings goals, while parents of older children may want to encourage saving and investing for multiple goals at the same time.

Begin Small

Regardless of age, kids who are just beginning their own savings or investing program begin at ground zero. For that reason, it's best to stick to the basics long enough for kids to experience some success at meeting smaller goals before expanding.

Later, as kids gain more respect for saving money by experiencing the benefits, they can begin to broaden their thinking about achieving more of their goals. Eventually and ideally, your children can pursue short-term, intermediate, and long-term goals all at the same time.

Keep in mind that specific goals are easier to meet when we plan for them. Keep the focus on the principle of saving something—anything—and let the rewards of desire and real life experiences provide the teaching. Wise parents encourage their children to learn how to set age-appropriate goals as preparation for developing saving and investing skills for the future.

The Invest by Experience Approach

The other approach to teaching your kids how to invest is through real world experience—to give kids some money and let them run with it. Education and encouragement are still essential parts of the approach, but more emphasis is placed on "buy and see what happens" versus "plan to buy and see what happens."

Here is a story of a grandparent who used real life experience to give her two granddaughters their first taste of investing.

Grandpa's Money Garden

It was a beautiful fall day. Nana had invited everyone out to her house for the annual fall family reunion. It was the family tradition that Nana would sit by the fire after dinner and talk about her own parents during the time when she was growing up. "Those were your great-grandparents," she'd remind her grandchildren.

Nana would tell them stories about how dairy farms used to deliver milk in glass bottles to homes, how there were only three channels on the first television set her family owned, and how things were so different when she was growing up compared to today. Her grandchildren would tease her and tell her she was "from another galaxy."

One of their favorite stories was about their great-grandfather and his "money garden." Nana shared how Great-Grandpa started out earning 75¢ per hour sweeping the factory floor, and how he was promoted from job to job until finally he became the manager of the whole floor. She said their great-grandfather was smart. He saved some of his earnings and bought stock in the company he worked for, and over time, he and the stock grew in value together.

Great-Grandpa had a saying he liked to recite about money: "It's what you do with the money you earn that makes you rich or poor, happy or sad."

"When it was time for Great-Grandpa to retire," she continued, "he had enough money from his investments in the company, and elsewhere in real estate, that I inherited money when he died."

"So," she concluded, "that's what he called his 'money garden' and that's how I could afford this house and property that you and your mom and dad enjoy today."

"How can we do that, Nana?" eleven-year-old Jesse asked.

"Do what?"

"Have lots of money like Great-Granddaddy?" asked Callie, Jesse's twin sister.

"Well, we can start a money garden like Great-Grandpa did … but you have to plant the seeds, water and fertilize it regularly, and then harvest it. In order to have a money garden, I'm going to have to teach you how to become wise money gardeners and give you some seeds to plant. Are you ready?"

Callie and Jesse nodded vigorously.

While they had heard about Great-Grandpa's money garden many times before, they had not heard anything about being given "seed" money to invest themselves. That sounded exciting.

"Mom makes me save my money," offered Jesse. "Is that the same?"

"Well," Nana answered, "the basic difference between saving and investing can be explained like this:

A penny saved is a penny saved. A penny invested has the potential to be a dollar made or a penny lost.

In other words, a penny invested is riskier than a penny saved, because investing can result in gains or losses, whereas savings are generally more secure."

"I want the one where you give a penny and get a dollar!" Callie chirped.

Great-Grandpa had a saying he liked to recite about money: "It's what you do with the money you earn that makes you rich or poor, happy or sad."

Becoming a Stakeholder

"Well," Nana continued, "the first thing to know about true investing is that, unlike saving money, you won't have as much control over the outcome. Sometimes you win; sometimes you lose. But that's all part of tending to the money garden so that you learn best how to harvest what you sow.

"So today, girls, to get started, I'm going to give you some ideas about the pros and cons of different types of investments. I want you to stay in touch with me so that I can help you track your progress.

"Of course, your mother can help you, because I taught her all the same things I will teach you. But please call when you have questions or concerns. Wise investors always ask lots of questions before they make their decisions, so that they fully understand both the risks and the rewards of investing."

After Nana sat down with them and explained the basics, she handed them each a check for $1,000, with the promise that she would stay in touch.

 (You can read about the basics of investing, and how to explain the various investment instruments to children, in "Growing Young Investors: Investment Tips for Parents" on p. 387.)

The Need to Seed, and Weed

A year later, Nana called her twin granddaughters, now twelve years old, to tell them how excited she was about seeing them again at the upcoming family reunion. She asked them to bring along their financial statements and the results of their investments.

The day of the annual family reunion finally arrived. As usual, after supper and after the dining room table had been cleared, Nana sat down with her granddaughters. Only this time, instead of hearing about Grandpa's money garden, Nana was going to learn about her grandchildren's money gardens. She met with Callie first.

Callie had chosen to invest in a mutual fund that specializes in bonds. She discovered that it paid a higher rate of interest than her bank's savings account. She chose to reinvest the dividends and make a small monthly contribution from her allowance. After about three months, she transferred a portion of her savings into her bond fund to increase the principal and interest.

Nana asked her if she was pleased.

"No … not really," said Callie. "I think I should have made more money."

They did some research online and Nana offered her some guidance about how to make some changes to increase her return, and better meet her investment goals.

When Nana sat down with Jesse, she got a very different story. True to life, her granddaughters' personalities were reflected in their investment choices. While Callie tended to be cautious, Jesse was more of a risk-taker; in fact, one of her favorite game shows was *Jeopardy*. Nana learned that while Callie had a steady but perhaps disappointing year, Jesse had an exciting ride of highs and lows.

Jesse chose to invest in stocks. She loved gold jewelry, so she had experienced a year of learning about commodities, especially gold.

Nana asked her if she was pleased.

"Yeah," said Jesse, "but I wanted to sell every time the stock went down. And I didn't have time to check up on it all the time. But I made some good money, huh?"

"Yes you did, but it sounds like unpredictability was a bit of a problem."

"Yeah," Jesse shrugged. "Do you have any suggestions about what I could buy that's ... like ... less random, but like ... will still make me more money?"

As with Callie, Nana did some research with Jesse to help her reassess her investing choices so that they would better suit her goals.

Investing: A Family Tradition

What did Callie and Jesse learn about investing in just one year? And what's going to happen over time to the girls' understanding of investing?

Perhaps they learned that stocks traditionally make more money than bonds but carry more risk; or that adding to the principal increases the fund's value; or that reinvesting dividends is a good idea, particularly with a long-term horizon; or that buying commodities carries higher risks.

While each girl wanted a different outcome, Nana was, quietly, the most pleased of all. This was a golden opportunity for her granddaughters to learn about gaining and losing money without it being too costly. She knew that the value of the experience and the knowledge her granddaughters gained would be worth far more than her $2,000 investment.

Now a new tradition has been added to the family hearth besides telling stories about Great-Grandpa and old times. Each year, time is set aside to harvest and replant her grandchildren's money garden.

Young Bucks

Unlike Nana, most of us don't have very much experience with investing. Don't let that deter you from introducing your children to investing opportunities—a fundamental and beneficial function of money. Help your children understand, as you help yourself understand, that money begets more money over time.

Help your children understand, as you help yourself understand, that money begets more money over time.

Some parents find themselves scrambling for how to invest their children's inheritance from Grandma or Uncle Joe! Naturally, we need to know the value of investing before we can teach our children. No need to worry! You're not alone in your interest to teach your children good money management skills while still working on yours!

If you don't think you are qualified, then how to do that is best left to the expertise of someone who is financially trained. *Millionaire Babies or Bankrupt Brats?* is not designed to teach investing, but to emphasize the importance of introducing the idea of investing to our children.

The benefits of investing, especially early in life, are staggering. The compounding of time and interest is truly the eighth wonder of the world. (For more ideas about how your children can find their own wonders in the financial marketplace, see "So You Want to Be a Millionaire?" below.)

Many grandparents or godparents are uniquely qualified to pass on their financial experiences and perhaps a little seed money to get started. Like the twins' great-grandfather, grandparents can be the generation in their family that starts an investment tradition.

So You Want to Be a Millionaire?

While kids may not have many financial assets, including an understanding of money, they have one financial asset much bigger than their parents'—time.

Picture ten-year-old Brent, baseball cap on backwards, sitting in a chair opposite a financial advisor. His feet are propped up in front of him on the advisor's desk. Behind Brent on a frosted glass door is the inscription: "Financial Services and Investments."

Brent says to the "well-suited" man sitting behind his desk: "I think we need to take an aggressive approach. I save a buck a week from my allowance and I want to retire with a million dollars by the time I'm sixteen."

While kids may not have many financial assets, including an understanding of money, they have one financial asset much bigger than their parents'—time.

Brent must be watching a lot of TV lately. There are a variety of "reality shows" that have made becoming a millionaire seem more possible than ever before. If you can just survive the maze of hoops to get to the top, then you have a promising shot at fame and fortune. Of course, there are no guarantees.

Brent might benefit more, however, if he learns that there is another way to become a millionaire by the time he retires—a time-honored, noncompetitive method that already existed long before the media popularized the concept.

It's called investing. It is a way to make money with money, or having your money work for you, instead of you working for money.

The Three E's of Investing: Education, Encouragement, and Enhancement

So you want to be a millionaire, eh? With a little education, encouragement, and monetary "enhancement" from their parents or grandparents, children have the opportunity to become millionaires by becoming investors—early and often.

Here's a simple example: If you open a tax-deferred custodial account with $500 at the birth of your child, and add $200 annually (just $16.66 a month)—using an average annual gain of 10%—your child will have one million dollars in just under sixty-three years, just in time to start thinking about retirement!

Or how about two and a half million, tax-free? Let's say your sixteen-year-old is gainfully employed, and opens a Roth IRA with $5,000 (the contributions are not tax deductible, but the deductions are at lower tax rates). If your teen earns and deposits another $5,000 per year, from ages seventeen to twenty-one, *and doesn't contribute another dime*, he or she will have over two and a half million (again assuming a 10% rate of return) by the time they are sixty-five! And better still, the money will be 100% tax-free!

If you'd like to develop your own examples, consult your financial advisor or research the Internet for a "retirement income" or "millionaire" calculator and plug in your own numbers. It's fun, and it a great way to set a specific annual or monthly monetary goal.

Using Ample Advice

These examples are for illustrative purposes only. They are not adjusted for inflation or the potential for a change in tax rates, which can reduce an investment's value. But all the more reason to invest early and often as a hedge against both factors.

There are also many variables and assumptions to consider when using investment examples—child's age upon opening the account, rate of return, amount of money invested, changes in government regulation, and so forth. These scenarios are not meant to reflect the performance of any specific investment, nor are they are a substitute for legal, accounting, investment, and other professional advice to suit your personal needs. The authors of Love and Logic recommend that you always consult a competent professional for answers to your specific financial questions.

Now back to Brent: "Well, Brent my friend," says the financial advisor, leaning back in his chair, his hands folded behind his head, "assuming a nine percent rate of return at a dollar a week, you will reach a million dollars in approximately ninety-six years and six months from now."

"You're kidding me, right?"

"Wish I could give you better news. Looks like retirement by the time you are sixteen is out of the question!"

Pausing, the advisor leans forward as though sharing something in confidence, and whispers, "But here's what you can do … You can open a savings account or money market account, and when you earn your first paycheck you can open an IRA … the letters I-R-A stand for …"

IRA's: A Head Start

One of the best ways to get your children started toward financial freedom is to open an individual retirement account, or IRA. There are two basic types of IRA's. One is a traditional IRA and the other is a Roth IRA.

Unlike traditional savings accounts, IRA's "defer taxes"—in other words, the money is not taxed until it's withdrawn at retirement (early withdrawals, however, incur penalties). That's a big benefit, because there's a chance that the tax rate will be lower at retirement age.

The decision about which kind of IRA to open for your child depends on several factors, including the type and amount of income and your child's age. Federal tax and financial laws change with the economic times. Minimum balances, fund objectives, risks, fees, and other variables vary among investment companies that offer IRAs.

Be sure to do your research. Find the product or service that fits your family's needs. Some parents like to contact the company directly for a prospectus (documents that contain detailed information about the investment). They read it carefully and ask lots of questions to be sure they understand everything they need to know to make their decision. Others follow the advice of a financial professional whom they trust and respect to help them make the best investment choices for their family. Still others try it on their own and then, if they are not satisfied with their results, seek professional help.

Be Your Own CEO

By now, Brent's feet are no longer propped up on the advisor's desk, as the conversation continues. "If I open a savings account with my parent's help, what's next?"

"Then you become a CEO," offers the advisor.

"Huh?"

In this case, "CEO" means Contribute Early and Often.

* * *

There are many ways to make contributions to one's investments. Annual contributions, whereby you "invest" in yourself first, will help you meet your investment goals. This is similar to the "pay yourself first" concept introduced in Chapter 8, on saving. Or, consider automatic investing if annual contributions seem difficult. Automatic investing allows you to set up a bank account so that it automatically sweeps a designated monthly amount into an investment account. This reduces the temptation to spend the money instead of invest it.

Automatic deductions have another benefit known as "dollar cost averaging," which means that by buying a fixed dollar amount of shares on a regular basis, you actually purchase a larger number of shares when the price is low and a smaller number of shares when the price is high.

Regardless of which way you decide to contribute, each and every contribution can add up over time. The sooner you get started, the more opportunity your own and your children's savings accounts, IRAs, or other investments have to grow.

The path to financial freedom or to becoming your own CEO, especially for kids, is really that simple: **C**ontribute **E**arly and **O**ften. Investment accounts do not necessarily have equal outcomes, but they are an equal opportunity investment strategy open to anyone.

> *Investment accounts do not necessarily have equal outcomes, but they are an equal opportunity investment strategy open to anyone.*

Bottom Line: Wise parents let their "babies" know that becoming a millionaire is entirely possible. They foster the possibilities by encouraging them to become the CEO of their own finances.

Growing Young Investors: Investment Tips for Parents

Wise parents keep it simple when introducing the concept of investment to their kids. How and when you actually introduce investing to your child should be based on their age and level of interest, and on your own values and financial resources.

Begin by defining a goal or reason to invest as an incentive. Then do enough research so that you can match the goal with the correct financial instrument.

(If you have worked with the "My Savings/Investing Goals" planning chart introduced earlier in this chapter—see p. 377—you already have a good foundation to begin.) There are dozens of factors to consider when developing an investment strategy. Here are six important steps:

>Step 1: Define the investment goal.
>Step 2: Determine the amount.
>Step 3: Choose the objective.
>Step 4: Research and strategize.
>Step 5: Select the investment.
>Step 6: Analyze the results.

Step 1: Define the investment goal.

What would more money allow them to do that they can't do now?

What would interest your kid enough to make an investment? What are their goals in life? What would more money allow them to do that they can't do now? What would they be willing to give up in spending power now, for the potential to enjoy more spending power later?

Keep in mind that the investment goals kids suggest will tend to be short-term. Investment advice differs, but one point financial planners agree about is the need to invest for the long term to reach long-term goals. Of course "long term" in a child's world is a relative term. Teach your children that they need to be in this game for the long haul or they won't be able to watch their money grow as well as it could.

Some parents, who have coached their children to develop a savings goal or wish list, start there. They select something small to begin practicing. Other parents select something on the list that is "large" enough that an investment strategy may be a good focus (e.g., a down payment for a car, extra spending money for a special trip, a dream wedding).

Step 2: Determine the amount.

"What's this?" Darren, sixteen years old, asked his grandmother as he opened the envelope. "A gift card to my favorite coffee shop? Money?" He loved to guess correctly when being gifted.

Grandma: "Well, it's money, but it's not money to spend. It's money for investing."
Darren: "I've heard of that before. What's 'investing' mean?"
Grandma: "Investing is when you use money to earn more money."

Darren: "Cool! Then can I spend it? Like on coffee and stuff?"

Grandma: "No, not this money."

Darren: "Why? What good is it if I can't spend it? … That makes no sense …"

(For a look at one reason why, see "Turning Star Bucks into Big Bucks: The Half Million Dollar Mocha" on p. 399.)

The next step after setting a goal is to determine how much money to invest. That depends on your financial resources and the type of investment you select (initial requirements vary with the investment). Some parents help their children save enough money to make their first contribution and then introduce them to their first investment. Other parents match whatever the child saves to accrue their first contribution. Still others get their child interested in investing through the back door. They gift them a contribution and walk them through their first investment together.

Regardless of the amount, the importance of investing over time is always encouraged. Once the initial investment has been made, invite your children to systematically invest (from earnings, savings, gifts, inheritance, etc.) and to reinvest their dividend earnings so that their investment grows.

Step 3: Choose the objective.

The objective you select is determined by the investment goal. Most investments have three basic objectives:

- Stability—for safety of initial investment and easy access to the money.
- Income—for current potential to earn.
- Growth—for future maximum potential for return.

The objective selected is based on the investor's time horizon, his or her goal, and the amount invested. (Of course, an investment can offer a combination of objectives; for example, income and growth, or stability and income.)

Kids have a phenomenal time frame as early investors. Choosing an investment that has the objective of growth is an obvious choice for opening a child's retirement fund. Choosing stability might be the best choice when saving for a car.

Rate of Return

The rate of return is an important factor that figures into selecting an investment's objective. Do you want a high or a low return: 5%, 7%, or 10%? Of course, if asked, most kids would choose 10% without necessarily understanding the risks involved in higher rates of return.

One advantage of a higher rate of return is that it offers a hedge against inflation. For example, let's say your child put $100 of Grandma's birthday gift into a money market fund with a 5% return. Nothing is added to the account but the interest that accrues for ten years. The return is $162.89. Adjusted for 3% inflation, however, the return is $120.12. That's a difference of $42.77 in buying power.

Here is the same example—$100 of Grandma's money—but with a 10% rate of return. Again, nothing has been added but the interest that accrued for ten years. The return is $259.37. Adjusted for 3% inflation, the return is $191.27. That's a difference of $68.10 in buying power.

The 10% example—the higher rate of return—provides a better gain and a better inflation cushion for the future than the 5% return.

The Rule of 72

To find out how fast your money will accumulate at different interest rates, use the "Rule of 72." When you divide 72 by the interest rate, the answer tells you approximately how long it will take for your money to double. For example, at 12%, your money will double in six years. At 10%, the money will double in 7.2 years. At 8%, the money will double in nine years.

To illustrate this to your children, use a simple $100 example, with play money for fun, or go online and play with the numbers using a financial calculator.

Risk vs. Reward

A discussion about the rate of return is also the perfect opener to have a conversation about risk and reward. The higher the risk, the higher the gain or loss. For example, if you want a 10%, 12%, 15%, or higher rate of return, you will need to pick an investment that has a higher risk. Or, if you want to be more cautious, consider an investment that is more stable and secure, one with a 3%, 4%, 5%, or 6% return.

One way to balance risk with reward is to diversify. Diversification is a time-honored way that uses variety to minimize risks while maximizing return. Wise investors diversify among types of investments (e.g., stocks and bonds), and diversify among assets (e.g., different companies and industries). Many mutual funds are a combination of investments and can be a great choice for kids initially, especially if diversification is one of the fund's primary objectives.

Another way to ease the risk versus reward factor is to follow the advice of experienced investors. They know not to invest any more than they are willing to lose.

Step 4: Research and strategize.

There are numerous ways to research an investment. Here are a few resources:

- Daily newspapers and business magazines
- Prospectuses and annual reports
- Online financial websites (unbiased sites are best for young investors, when the objective is educational and financial literacy)
- Your local bank's investment division
- Financial professionals you trust to give you sound advice, such as investment brokers, accountants, and certified financial planners

Some parents like to show their children how to track stocks and mutual funds in the daily newspaper. Others use their own investments or hypothetical investments as educational "research" opportunities. This allows a child to see the role that various economic factors play on a daily basis, as reflected in Standard and Poor's 500 or the Russell 2000, for example.

Make researching different types of investments a game. Do the research alongside your child. Learn together. Make it fun. Start small. And be the example. While seeking financial information and advice, ask lots of questions so your decision will be an informed one.

Step 5: Select the investment.

Regardless of the type of investment selected, kids under eighteen years of age will need a parent or guardian to make the investment purchase. Many custodial investments accounts that are suitable for children can be opened in person, by mail, by phone, or on the Internet.

To keep things simple, beginning investors can start with one investment. For example, begin with one or two stocks, or a mutual fund that combines stocks and bonds. As children develop more confidence, they can expand to a collection of investments, called an investment "portfolio."

Here's a basic list of investments suitable for getting started in the world of investing:

- Collectibles (e.g., coins, cards, sports memorabilia)
- Money market funds
- Savings bonds
- Stocks
- Mutual funds

Collectibles

Some kids are naturally interested in collecting things. This can be a way to invest, but it takes lots of experience, or luck, or both. The goal here is to collect *things that you like just for fun*. If it yields a little profit over time, it was a good investment. If not, at least the collector had fun playing with things he or she enjoyed!

Money Market Funds

Money market funds are a step up from savings accounts because their interest rates are usually higher than the rates offered by a traditional bank. This is a good choice for the conservative or cautious investor, because while the return is not as high as for other investments, the principal is stable (the principal is the amount of the investment on which the interest is computed).

Savings Bonds

Savings bonds are loans to companies or government entities such as cities, counties, and municipalities. The investor makes money on their principal, plus interest for the loan. Some people give U.S. government and savings bonds as gifts to newborn babies and children for their birthdays. Investors who buy bonds help the country grow along with the value of the bond.

U.S. bonds are considered low-risk. Bonds issued by companies—sometimes newly formed or distressed companies—carry a higher risk than money market funds. While it may take a little sleuthing work, bonds can be a fun purchase for kids if a personal connection can be made to the issuing government or company. Investing in a tax-free municipal bond fund in the child's own state is an example.

Stocks

A gift card from your child's favorite electronics company is nice, but what about buying stock in the company? A stock is a small part, or share, of a company. Once a child owns a stock, they become a part-owner of the company, or shareholder.

Individual common stocks can be real kick for kids! The point of investing really gets noticed when kids compare the value of owning a piece of the company versus just working for the company.

Investors buy stocks for two basic reasons—dividends and value. Dividends are earnings based on a percentage of each share. Wise investors reinvest their dividends to increase their return. "Value," in the world of investing, is based on the company's growth. The more valuable the company becomes, the higher the stock price.

Stock prices go up and down all the time. If your children buy stock in the company and change their mind or want their money back, they will need to sell. If the stock is sold and the price is higher than the purchase price, the shareholder could make money. But if the price of the stock is lower than when you bought it, you will lose money when you sell.

> *The Rule of Two:* Some people use the "2% rule" to determine when to buy and sell, since no one ever knows for sure how the market will perform. This rule means that when a stock loses more than 2% of its value, it's time to sell. Some brokerages make such value-based selling convenient by allowing you to sign up for a "stop loss order" for each one of your holdings, meaning that the brokerage will sell a stock automatically if it loses more than a pre-specified percentage of its value.

Value by a Different Name

Stocks can also be selected based on a different definition of value—value that is personal, not numerical. Coach your children to pick a company that reflects their interests and their personal values. If your daughter is interested in clothing, perhaps a company that is socially responsible and environmentally sensitive is a good choice. If you a have a son who loves cars, then perhaps a car maker who promotes fuel efficiency and biodegradable manufacturing processes is a good choice.

Parents or grandparents can help children select one or two stocks from their favorite publicly owned store, or any company of interest. If they purchase a particular product they like, invite them to research the company to see if they would like to purchase some of its stock, if available (hypothetically or for real).

Because they are minors, kids will need your help in making the actual purchase. You can make your purchases directly through a brokerage house, or through a stockbroker, who can do the buying and selling for you. If you want to

Stocks can also be selected based on a different definition of value—value that is personal, not numerical.

keep your costs low because the purchase is small, you can search for a discount stockbroker or use an investment management company that offers low minimums, account maintenance fees, and commissions.

Once stocks have been purchased, you can help your children track their performance via the money exchanges, such as the New York Stock Exchange and the Tokyo Stock Exchange. While the reports might appear complex, the listings are simply a daily record of the buying or selling of stocks in the marketplace. Kids can be taught to flip to the business section of their daily newspaper or go online to find the current value of their stocks.

Each stock or mutual fund has its own abbreviation. Help your children decipher the abbreviations and make comparisons. Some parents create an imaginary portfolio of stocks and track their progress as a way to practice reading the daily stock report. Which stock lost money? Which gained? Why? Make a graph together to illustrate the difference in performance. One graph can represent a "bull" market (an increase in stock prices), and one graph can represent a "bear" market (a decrease in stock prices). (For more detailed information about teaching your children how to select and track their own stocks, see "Mock Stocks and Investment Games" on p. 400.)

Mutual Funds

Mutual funds are a variety of stocks and bonds grouped together.

When you invest in a mutual fund, you join other investors who also own a fraction of the whole fund collection. Some fund managers pick a cross-section of shares from lots of different industries, such as technology, international, medicine, research, and environmental companies. Other mutual fund managers specialize by buying stocks in lots of companies in the same industry.

If you are interested in a mutual fund, there are two types of particular interest for young or inexperienced investors—a balanced fund and an index fund. A balanced fund does just what its name implies. It balances its investments between cash, bonds, and stocks. Index funds are a type of mutual fund that own fractional shares in a variety of companies or markets. They tend to have lower management and maintenance fees and fewer tax consequences, and their return represents the average growth in the common stock market of companies grouped together.

There are hundreds and hundreds of mutual funds, with varying requirements and risks. Some companies require a large initial investment. Other companies are more suitable for getting started because they offer a low minimum investment, lower management fees, and lower commissions.

As with stocks and bonds, help your child match his or her interests with an appropriate mutual fund. One teen was interested in the environment, so he selected a mutual fund that focused on "green" companies. Another liked all the latest technology, so she picked a mutual fund that specialized in computers and electronics. Like all investments, research the choices and read the prospectuses to make the best match between the objectives and the investor.

Take a Risk? Different Types of Investors

Most investors fall into one of three categories, depending on how much risk they feel comfortable taking:

- Conservative investors—cautious, want to be sure
- Moderate investors—like to balance between risk and return, middle of the road
- Aggressive investors—risk-takers, willing to gamble on a win

---

Help match the investor type with your child's personality when searching for the right investment. If an investment turns out to be too risky, or conversely, not risky enough, select another investment that corresponds better with your child's comfort level. Except for the riskiest of choices, children are likely to achieve some success with most long-term investments, due to their long time horizon.

Step 6: Analyze the results.

Investing can be really fun for kids. Naturally, we hope they will succeed in growing their money. However, if they're not meeting their investment goals, they can choose among several different options:

- Reduce the goal.
- Increase the investment amount.
- Invest for a longer time period.
- Seek professional investment advice from a qualified and trusted financial consultant.

Analyzing the results is an important step. Figure out together how your children might improve their choices over time if they fall short of their goals.

A Family Affair

One dad made a yearly pilgrimage to the safe deposit box to review the family's financial papers. "Kids," he said, "let's add up the assets for this year to see how they grew." Despite the fact that they complained and rolled their eyes, he went through each mutual fund the family owned and reviewed it with his children.

"This is the objective, this is what we have now, this is how we got it, and this is what we need to do to manage it next year." He wanted to involve them in the analysis process, even though they didn't understand everything in the beginning.

Each year, his kids took more and more of an interest in the process and the results as both his children and the investments matured. This was because they understood that they might very well become the future beneficiaries of the family's funds. (Unfortunately, some kids may become interested only if they think they will inherit money—see "Inheritance: Squandering and Squabbling" below.)

Investment Maturity on Two Levels

Kids have an awesome timeline for learning how to invest wisely. Investment activities emphasize discipline, diversification, and a long-term outlook. Once an appropriate investment strategy has been determined, parents can give their children lots of opportunities and choices to "play with the market."

Naturally, learning how to invest is not the first skill that kids will need on the path to financial literacy, but it will make their life easier if they learn how to do it well, early, and often. As kids mature, so can their investments.

Bottom Line: Wise parents walk and talk their kids through the steps to becoming wise investors as soon as they are ready to learn.

Inheritance: Squandering and Squabbling

How do you prevent your adult children or grandchildren from squandering their inheritance? Is the legal age of eighteen or twenty-one a good predictor of fiscal responsibility?

Past behavior is a frequent indicator of future behavior. If a beneficiary is not fiscally responsible today, he or she will not magically become fiscally responsible tomorrow by being given more money. If you're not sure about this, consider the problem many lottery winners experience with their sudden wealth.

Some sad tales have been told of young adults inheriting hefty sums of money and then squandering it with reckless abandon—money that would have been worth millions of dollars later if they had only learned how to use and invest it wisely. Some families have averted this type of financial disaster with wise and thoughtful planning, while others have not been so lucky.

Make That Two Million!

One dad, visiting his eldest daughter's home for Christmas, proudly shared that he had donated one million dollars to his alma mater. His gift, he explained, was going to be used toward a new research building and lab, a portion of which would carry his name.

His children were astonished. But he was even more astonished as he listened to them complain and whine about how they thought that they were going to inherit all of his money. He was secretly heartbroken by their greedy and entitled response.

He called the university president when he returned home and told him he'd been rethinking his donation over the holidays. As he held the phone, the president's heart started pounding heavily because he thought the donor was calling to tell him he had changed his mind. After what seemed like a terminal pause, the donor announced that he would double his gift—and endow the university with two million dollars!

Preparing Heirs to Trust

To avert any inheritance disasters, one affluent family set up trust funds in each of their grandchildren's names. Turning eighteen was not going to be enough to inherit this family's wealth.

Grandpa and Grandma wanted their grandchildren to avoid the traps and trappings of leading a spoiled, entitled, unhappy, and unproductive life. They wanted them to experience their own personal power in the world before they were given financial power. As benefactors, they were faced with several important decisions. Who will be the executor of their estate, and under what conditions will the funds be disbursed?

Grandma and Grandpa decided to hire a trusted and reputable financial firm to be the executor of their wills. While they thought of using a family member as executor, they decided against it, because of the potential for moral and ethical conflicts down the road. (If children are still living at home, the benefactors should name or designate the custodial parents as the responsible party for disbursing funds.)

After many soul-searching discussions, they decided that the "real" legacy they wanted to leave to their grandchildren was:

- To instill a love of learning so that they could pursue their passions through meaningful work.
- To instill the values of a work or service ethic while building their character.
- To instill the values of living within one's means, needs before wants, and delayed gratification.
- To instill stewardship and gratitude through sharing.

Based on those four goals, they stipulated that the following conditions needed to be met before any disbursement of funds:

- Complete your education, or vocational training in a field of your choice.
- Be productive in the lives of others. Work or serve (or raise a family, or both) for at least fifteen consecutive years using your education or training.
- Be debt-free (a house mortgage is acceptable).
- Tithe 10% to a nonprofit charity of your choice.

Once a grandchild met all four conditions, he or she could petition the executor of the grandparents' estate for release of their inheritance. Of course, because the inheritance was substantial, disbursements were metered out judiciously and incrementally based on the uniqueness of each situation.

Notice how Love and Logic's principles apply in this example. The grandparents share control by gifting the money on their terms, while the grandchildren can choose to meet the conditions, or not, to inherit the money.

I'll Match You!

There are many other ways to distribute an inheritance. Another family decided to match earnings to investments. For example, "I'll make an annual disbursement of one dollar for each dollar you earn for as long as the inheritance lasts." If the beneficiary earns $50,000 that year, the estate would grant $50,000. Still another family had seen the damage that a huge amount of money can do to a young person upon the benefactor's passing. So they decided: "No inheritance until each grandchild meets the terms of the trust or turns forty years of age, whichever comes first."

What's the best insurance against squandering an inheritance? Help children capitalize on their human "assets" first, so that they will be ready to handle the responsibility of financial assets later. Benefactors need to protect their financial assets until their children or grandchildren demonstrate they are ready to handle the increase in freedom and responsibility. Seek the help of a professional financial and estate planner if necessary.

Wise benefactors pass on their money to the next generation only after the beneficiaries prove that they can handle the worth. They make character count before money, or find someone who will carry their wishes forward after they are no longer able to manage their own financial affairs.

Squabbles: For Love or Money?

Family horror stories abound about who didn't get "the money" they thought they should get. Siblings are estranged for years, marriages dissolve, and families are torn apart by the decisions of the deceased in a will. Jealousy, resentment, and disappointments ensue, leading family members to sue one another over money. In extreme cases, the family pet gets a higher nod.

To prevent squabbles over money, wise parents and grandparents are clear about their expectations, so that their heirs will be clear about theirs.

Turning Star Bucks into Big Bucks: The Half Million Dollar Mocha

Darren, sixteen years old, begins most of his days with his favorite drink—a triple mocha espresso, extra foam, and extra hot.

Darren is not alone. Americans are notorious for their love of java. Sounds pretty normal, right? Besides, what's the big deal about a daily cup of coffee? Not a big deal from Darren's perspective, but a *very big deal* from a financial perspective.

Here's the real jolt. Let's say you buy a cup of coffee before going to work each morning for a year (50 weeks × 5 days = 250 days). After each preference is added in, and a tip, let's say that the cup of coffee costs $4.

If you were to save that money instead, you'd be $1,000 richer by the end of the first year! If you were to invest that $1,000 each year at a 9% rate of return for 45 years, you'd be $574,186 richer! (The assumed rate of return is based on a classic portfolio of 60% in stocks and 40% in bonds, which has returned an average gain of 9% in the market over the past 75 years.) That's a half million dollar mocha!

Perhaps Darren should consider investing his money instead—and make his own mocha, to go. If he did that, then forty-five years later, at the age of sixty-one, he'd probably be a little less jittery on two counts! First he would have avoided an expensive caffeine habit, and second he would be half a million dollars richer nearer to retirement age.

P.S. If you were to invest that $1,000 each year thereafter at 10% for 50 years, you'd be $1,281,291 richer! That's more than a million dollars earned by investing only five more years at a 1% higher rate of return!

Bottom Line: Wise parents use everyday spending examples to teach their children the power of choice and the wisdom of investing early and often.

Mock Stocks and Investment Games

Turn investing into a game and it will turn into an education. One family created their own Fundland Investment Club, using play money at first. They each picked a stock in an industry of their choice and created the "The Smith Family Fun Fund." Before finalizing their hypothetical choices, they discussed the reasons why they chose their "stocks."

Dad picked his because of its stability and because it fit with his environmental values. Mom picked her stock because of the potential for the company to grow and expand. Sis picked her stock based on past performance. And her younger brother picked his stock because he liked the product and the trendy packaging. While his reason for picking the stock was amateurish (naturally, given his young age), with a little more discussion he'll be able to understand that his pick might be a very good one because other kids, just like him, might also like the product and innovative marketing.

For three months this family traded stocks and played the market. Once everyone got the hang of it, they each became shareholders with their own "real" stock portfolios.

Football and the Market

Another dad applied the concepts of fantasy football and rotisserie baseball to make investing fun. Each child was given $300 in play money and invited to research and select four to six stocks under $100. After drafting and picking their favorites, the rule was: tracking but no trading for thirty days.

For several months, Dad helped them track their holdings. He taught them how to use the educational "key chart" printed in their daily newspaper. This came in handy for making sense of what all those columns of numbers meant. To offset the complexity of economic graphs and stock market listings, Dad kept things simple. He taught his kids how to track their stocks on a "need to know" basis, and gradually expanded as his kids' interest expanded.

After three months of playing the game, Dad announced that he would purchase the stocks that had appreciated the most, so his kids could start their very own stock portfolios.

How to Stock Up

You can capture your children's interest in investing in stocks by making a list of their favorite brands—think computers, clothing, electronics, games, foods, movies, and so forth. Help them find the names of the companies that make their favorite products. Then invite them to research those companies.

Set a limit on how much of your money they'll have available to spend, or how much of their money they'll need to save or earn. Parents can reinforce their spending and family values by saying, "Feel free to buy any stock you like as long as it fits our family values."

Tracking a stock you own, real or hypothetical, can be lots of fun, especially if we simplify the process. Make sure that your kids pick stocks that they'll be able to follow easily, either in your local newspaper or online.

EXERCISE 11.1: Tracking Stocks—Signs and Symbols

To keep the analysis simple enough for a child, he or she needs to know only the latest price of a stock and the amount the price has changed since the last session. These changes are listed as the last two entries of each individual stock's listing.

Here's a chart parents can use to get their children started:

My Stock Report

Name of stock: _____

Name of company (abbreviation or symbol): _____

Purchase price: _____

Date of purchase: _____

Tracking from: _____ to _____

Date	Latest Price*	Change in Price**	Bull or Bear? (+ or –)

* The latest price of the stock is based on the last stock market session. It is usually abbreviated as "last" or "close" at the top of the stock market listings.

** This is the amount of the price change (usually indicated as "chg" or "net chg") during the last session. For example, ". 34" means that the stock increased in value by 34¢, and "–. 34" means that the stock decreased in value by 34¢. While 34¢ may not seem like a lot, for someone owns 100 shares this equates to a gain or loss of $34, respectively.

Let's try a simple example. Suppose your child selects a company that specializes in healthy snack foods, called "Go Green, Go Lean." He buys three shares at $32.00 each. In three days (a nanosecond in the investing world), the stock gains 66¢. By completing the last column, your child can see at a glance whether each day in the market was a bull day or a bear day (kids love animal analogies). Your child's stock report might now look like this:

Stock Report Example

Name of stock: Go Green, Go Lean Foods

Name of company: GGFoods

Purchase price: 3 at $32.00 (total: $96.00)

Date of purchase: 6/16

Tracking from: 6/17 to 6/19

Date	Latest Price	Change in Price	Bull or Bear? (+ or –)
6/17	32.91	.91	+ Bull
6/18	33.05	.14	+ Bull
6/19	32.66	–.39	– Bear

For older children, a fourth column can be added to their stock report. It uses a percentage as the measure of change in value and is usually listed in the stock index as "% chg" or "net chg." While typically incremental from day to day, a percentage change is a good indicator of significant gains or losses over longer periods of time, such as one year or five years.

To Buy or Sell?

Of course, tracking a stock every day is not necessary, and may be daunting to a child. If they track their stocks intermittently, that's fine, too. The important thing is that they be given the opportunity to practice their tracking and comparative analysis skills, not to mention the opportunity to practice their math skills! If they lose money in the process of not tracking their stocks, then the learning gained is far more important than the money lost.

Allowing kids to purchase a stock of their choice, for real or for play, and teaching them how to track its progress, will help them get excited about their holdings and keep them involved in the "work" of successful investing. It also helps them learn that investors are called "investors" for a reason—it takes an investment of both money and time.

Bottom Line: Wise parents use mock stock opportunities and investment games to help their children understand how to eventually stock up for real.

Investing in the Next Generation

It becomes more apparent every day that the single, biggest reason to teach your children to invest in their financial future is that government and employer support is chancy, at best. While intentions are good, future delivery is questionable.

If what kids see about everyday money is iffy, then the benefits of the savings they can't see must be in another galaxy.

Someone had better tell the next generation—in advance—they are going to be responsible for their own future financial security, independence, and freedom. It could be painful to watch the results—for us and for them—if we don't teach our children to begin saving early.

What better time to get into the habit of saving than in childhood? Kids have two extra special advantages on their side—a long time horizon to capitalize on compound interest, and someone to take care of the everyday expenses. Now that's a deal too good to turn down!

In order to teach kids the importance of saving, it's helpful to think like a kid. Few kids connect the dots between money and its function in the twofold climate of "e-money" abstraction and affluence.

Did you know, for example, that many kids think that an ATM machine is a printer that actually prints money on demand? Or that the "silver credit card" Dad always carries in his wallet pays for purchases just like cash? Or that the only kind of CD is a compact disc? If what kids see about everyday money is iffy, then the benefits of the savings they can't see must be in another galaxy.

Wise parents teach their kids how to invest so that they won't run out of money before they run out of life.

CHAPTER 12

Sharing

Time, Talent, or Tithe?

This chapter explores ways to teach kids, from toddlers to teens, about sharing their time, talent, or tithe, either as part of the family or as an individual. You'll learn how to help children select and research a charity, and how to raise kids who want to volunteer based on their interests and values. You'll also discover that there are times when sharing is not a good idea.

Care to Share? Jill's Fancy Dance

There was a knock at the door. Sixteen-year-old Jill rushed to answer it. "Oh," she said, clearly disappointed. "Mommm … it's for you!"

When Mom arrived at the door, she saw her neighbor and the familiar donation can in her hand. Mom grabbed her purse and started looking for some money. Not finding anything but loose change, she called to her daughter. "Jill, you just got paid—how about donating some money to the Natural Disaster Relief Fund?"

"What! I need my money for the prom!" was the reply from the couch.

Embarrassed, Mom pulled out her checkbook and wrote a check. She was too angry to speak when she returned to the family room. She was appalled at her daughter's insensitivity and her lack of awareness of the many less fortunate people in the world. Mom realized that Jill didn't have a clue about how "the other half lives," nor did she apparently care.

Any rationalizations that Jill's behavior was "typical teenager" went out the window as Mom realized that her own generosity had made no impression whatsoever on her daughter.

Until that day, Mom thought that her philanthropic contributions to worthy causes over the years would teach Jill to follow in her footsteps. Not so. Instead of modeling Mom's generosity, Jill either ignored it or resented it. A lifetime of receiving without giving anything back taught Jill to learn how to take but not how to share. Mom knew she needed to make some pretty drastic changes, and soon, if she was going to have any success teaching her daughter the rewards of sharing with others.

Pay It *What*?

Jill works at a clothing store several times a week after school. She spends every dime she earns, either when she is out with friends or on being fashionable. Mom understands that she doesn't have any real control over the money Jill earns as a retail clerk. Money Jill earns is her money, unless she spends it in a way that creates a problem for Mom. (For more information about your how to handle the "It's my money!" issue, see "Allowance, Earnings, and Paychecks" on p. 350.)

However, Mom can use Love and Logic's principles of "shared control through choices" by strategically giving Jill lots of thinking and decision-making opportunities. In other words, there is no choice about *whether* Jill will share, but there will be plenty of choices about *how* she shares.

Here's how she broaches the subject of charity with Jill, one day after school:

Mom:	"Jill, have you ever heard of 'pay it forward'?"
Jill:	"Huh? Kinda … not really." (hoping the conversation will end right here)
Mom:	"It's a way to give now to keep the spirit of giving alive later. When someone gives to us and we don't have the means to return the favor at that time, we can 'pay it forward' to someone else later."
Jill:	"Yeah … and so …"
Mom:	"Or, if we are unable to repay in kind, we think of some other way to express the spirit of giving. It's a cycle. We repay generosity by being generous ourselves."
Jill:	(yawns and stretches)
Mom:	(smiles and sits down beside her) "A simple example is when the person ahead of you in the tollbooth pays your toll. They literally have 'paid it forward' so that when you drive up to pay your toll, you have benefited from their grace and generosity. And so generosity gets passed around and around."
Jill:	"Is this about giving my money away or something? Because if it is … I am *not* giving any of my money away!"

What's going to be most effective in this situation—sharing what you want to say, or sharing through choices? Extending this conversation, or ending it?

Short Spurts or Long Squabbles?

Mom wants to say, "All you think about is yourself." But she stifles herself and says, with a smile, "That's fine. There are lots of other ways to share. We can talk about this later." The authors of Love and Logic teach parents to neutralize resistance by picking up the conversation another time. Which just so happens to be after dinner:

Mom:	"Hey Jill, I have been thinking about that 'pay it forward' idea …"
Jill:	"Oh no …"
Mom:	"Would you like to know what some other kids have tried that doesn't involve spending their own money on others?"
Jill:	"Yeah, I suppose … do I have a choice?"
Mom:	"We can always talk about this later."

Jill:	"No … go on."
Mom:	(smiling) "Well … some kids organize a fundraiser to raise money to donate to a worthy cause. How would that work for you?"
Jill:	"I'm too busy. Besides, that sounds like too much effort."
Mom:	"Other kids decide to go to a fundraising event that has already been organized and donate their time to help out. How would that work for you?"
Jill:	"Like how?"
Mom:	"How do you think you could find out?"
Jill:	"On the Internet?"
Mom:	"Probably."
Jill:	"Maybe … later … my time is tight."
Mom:	"Other kids decide to donate some sort of talent or gift they have as a way to give to an organization. How would that work for you?"
Jill:	"I don't know."
Mom:	(smiling) "Well … you are very resourceful, dear, and you have figured things out for yourself before. I'm sure you'll come up with a way to be helpful. We'll talk some more later."

Notice how Mom did not back Jill into a corner by insisting she make a decision. She strategically planted the seeds of her expectations with an introductory conversation, yet presented Jill with lots of choices. The "we'll talk about it later" strategy also gives both parties some much needed "wiggle room." Mom's strategy defuses resistance and increases the chance of Jill taking ownership for her own sharing ideas.

Wares or Fairs?

Their dialogue continues over the next couple of weeks. Mom continues to offer lots of thinking and decision-making opportunities in *short spurts* of conversation, to avoid any power struggles.

For example, Jill is given choices about whether she would like to help feed the hungry, or clothe the needy. And whether she wants to share her time, her talent, or her money. And, based on those choices, whether she wants to pick the Positive Start Shelter's annual drive for used clothing, or the local church's homeless dinner on Fridays.

Once Jill "gets" that Mom is not giving up on this idea, she makes her decision. Having seen her fair share of street people, Jill decides she wants to help people dress warmly and "not in ragged clothes that smell."

With some coaching and supervision from Mom, Jill researches and agrees to help out the Positive Start Shelter. But she reminds Mom, "I am not giving them any of my hard-earned money." She has made it very clear that she still wants to spend every penny on becoming a fashion statement.

Is Mom stuck in her efforts to teach Jill the value of sharing? No problem for Mom. Wise parents remember that many power struggles can be averted as long as kids are given the opportunity to choose. Jill can still choose to share her time, talent, or both, if she feels like she has no change to spare. The Three T's—time, talent, or tithe—offers a "no excuse" policy. (For more information about the exchange of money for time, see "Ways to Waiver" on p. 421, under the section "The Three T's: Time, Talent, or Tithe.")

Mom can use steps 3–5 in Love and Logic's five-step problem-solving guide to see what idea works best for Jill. (For a quick reminder about the steps, see "Accountability 101: How to Guide Kids to Own and Solve Their Problems" on p. 55.)

For example, if Jill chooses to share her talents, she could volunteer to be one of the people who help organize the annual clothing drive. In Jill's case, she could use her on-the-job retail experience by sorting, pricing, and displaying donated clothing. Or she could recruit her friends to collect used clothing with her.

What will Jill decide? Let's see what both success and resistance bring.

Jill Will or Jill the Pill?

What If Sharing Meets Success?

What happened? Well … Jill enlisted the help of her friends to collect used clothing from the neighbors, relatives, and friends at school on behalf of the Positive Start Foundation. She later shared that she felt "overwhelmed by people's support," and that she collected more clothes than she and her friends ever expected.

Mom was pleased by her daughter's experience. She was afraid at first that it wouldn't work. She was afraid that her request to share was going to be met with lots of resistance and Jill's latest mantra: "Oh Mommm."

Mom discovered that if she encouraged Jill in an area she was keenly interested in (clothing) that also involved social time with her friends (collecting the clothing together), it would increase the odds of success. By offering her lots of choices, time to decide, and support throughout the process, Mom watched her daughter embrace the idea that giving has its own reward.

Wise parents remember that many power struggles can be averted as long as kids are given the opportunity to choose.

What If Sharing Meets Resistance?

But what if Jill argued with Mom about this "stupid sharing idea"? Mom was ready. She would use her favorite one-liners to neutralize any emotional moments, like "Nice try" or "I know." Remember, lots of empathy first, then the consequence.

What's a good consequence for Jill if she flat out refuses? Mom can use Love and Logic's delayed consequence if Jill says, "I'm not sharing and you can't make me!" Love and Logic recommends a delayed consequence whenever you don't know what to do. This gives both the parent and the child time to think and calm down in the heat of the moment.

Jill's mom can delay the consequence by saying something like this: "Ohhh … poor decision. That's a problem for me. I'm going to need to think about this. But try not to worry." By delaying the consequence, Mom can keep her dignity intact without lectures, warnings, and threats. And Jill is left wondering what kind of trouble, if any, she has bestowed upon herself. Anticipation becomes it own consequence.

Mom can also use the same ideas that Andrew's mom used in Chapter 5 with two tweenage sons who did not want to do their family contributions. Andrew's mom used empathy, a delayed consequence, and the next available "moment of leverage" to motivate. Let's see … didn't Jill say she has a prom coming up? Or, how about cell phone use?

Love and Logic recommends a delayed consequence whenever you don't know what to do.

Pay It Backward

Half a day later, feeling calm, Mom decides that if Jill is not going to share, then the things Mom shares with Jill are now in jeopardy. With time to think about it and make a plan, Mom can cancel Jill's cell and text messaging services for starters, followed by numerous other cancellations of services that Mom provides, such as use of the car, the computer, and the TV—if necessary. These are all things that Mom "shares" with Jill.

Here's a dialogue about how Mom might deliver the consequential news to her daughter:

Jill: "Mom, my cell phone isn't working! I tried to text Danny today and it wouldn't work!"

Mom: "That's a bummer! … Remember the other day when you told me you weren't going to share or volunteer?"

Jill: "Uh … yeah …"

Mom: "And I said I needed to think about it?"

Jill: "Yeah …"

Mom:	"Well … I've made my decision. I canceled your cell phone contract today until further notice."
Jill:	"You *what*?"
Mom:	"Yes, I decided that I share only with people who are grateful or in need. Since you don't seem to be in either place, I decided to make a change."
Jill:	"You can't do that!"
Mom:	"I know. It's a bummer, and you still have a choice to change your mind. Let me know what you decide."

Prepare to Share

Notice that the same consequences can be used whether the resistance is about sharing at home or sharing in the community. That's because sharing is about contributing.

Kids should not be entitled to receiving if they are not giving. If your kids won't pay it forward, then neither will you. No give, no take. Just be sure to use lots and lots of empathy before delivering the consequence, to prevent the potential for the consequence to backfire. Empathy is the "love" that's an integral part of the "logic."

Bottom Line: Wise parents use the contributions they make to their child's life to prepare the child for learning how to make contributions to the lives of others.

Sharing: The Third S

Spending, saving, and sharing are reserved for people who manage their finances well enough to do all three.

Sharing our money, as first introduced in Chapter 3, on allowance, is the last of the Three S's—spend, save, and share—for obvious reasons. It is, from a monetary point of view, the most optional among the three choices.

People who are in chronic debt never get past overspending. So they rarely experience the security of saving without borrowing, or savor the delights in sharing their abundance with others. Spending, saving, *and* sharing are reserved for people who manage their finances well enough to do all three. When we are fortunate enough to have the knowledge and willingness to apply sound economic principles to our income, of course it's appropriate to share some of it with others.

Sound financial practices are based on prioritizing the "spend, save, share" formula as discussed in previous chapters. Setting priorities is based on your value system and common sense. For kids, it's best to teach them first how to spend money for what they need (just as adults need to do), then how to save for what they want, and then how to share their abundance with others. Each has its educational perks:

- Wise spending practices teach kids the difference between their needs and wants.
- Wise saving practices teach delayed gratification.
- Wise sharing practices support an attitude of gratitude rather than entitlement.

"No! It's Mine!"

It's easier to introduce the concept of sharing as soon as your child understands the concept of ownership. As soon as that happens, "Mine!" becomes their second favorite word, after "No!" Ask any toddler to share his toy with you, and watch him pull it toward himself as his smile turns into a frown, or his eyes fill with tears.

Sharing is not natural, and like many other important things in life it needs to be taught. (For more information about age-appropriate sharing, see "When Sharing Is *Not* a Good Idea" on the next page.)

The earlier you get children engaged in the process of sharing, the more successful the experience, as long as we remember the importance of choices. Don't assume your child will learn by your sterling example when it comes to sharing. Have them *do*, not watch you!

The earlier you get children engaged in the process of sharing, the more successful the experience, as long as we remember the importance of choices.

One single dad shared that he volunteers for the annual "Feed the Hungry" food drive. He slips his toddler into his backpack and off they go with a little red wagon to collect canned goods. He added that before he brought his daughter along, people would say, "I gave at the office." But with his child gurgling as a backdrop, they always managed to find something from their pantry. This became an annual experience. One neighbor took pictures for him each year to chronicle the event, thereby providing additional teaching opportunities as his daughter grew.

Another mom never donated anything without participation from her children. They baked cookies together for the bake sale, sold PTA popcorn after school to their friends, helped to clean up after the Little League Carnival, and joined Mom for her 3K walks for disabled children. By the time her children grew to teenagers, the joy of giving time and effort became a habit.

When Sharing Is Not *a Good Idea*

Most parents agree that it's important to teach the virtues of sharing. Yet many parents would also agree that any strides made in teaching kids how to share tend to go out the window, especially when it comes to sharing personal property with siblings and friends.

Naturally, children should be encouraged to share. We want them to experience the goodwill and pleasure that come with voluntary sharing. The key word here is *voluntary*. But we tend to make the mistake of requiring them to share before they are developmentally or psychologically ready.

Think of a typical eighteen-month-old child. They usually do not want to share anything, and like to say that everything is "my" or "mine." Developmentally, they are simply not ready to share (except as mimicking behavior).

Now, think of typical siblings. The same problem often exists with them (and with their friends, too). While they may be more ready to share developmentally as they get older, they may not be ready to share psychologically.

Forcing kids to share usually results in them clutching their possessions more tightly. Obligatory sharing often undermines the goodwill that might happen more naturally under circumstances of choice.

Mandates rarely come from the heart.

What does this have to do with teaching kids about being charitable? We make it harder to teach our kids the benefits of being charitable in the future if we push the issue of sharing personal property too soon or too often. Charity is about teaching kids to put their toys, time, talent, or tithe where their heart is. When we force them to share personal possessions, we tend to have trouble getting our kids to share other parts and pieces of themselves down the road.

The Readiness Factor

What should we do instead? The solution to this dilemma lies in Love and Logic's principles of shared control and choices.

Let's say Adrian doesn't want to share a toy with his younger sister, Kelsey, who's grabbing the toy because she wants a turn. Ask Adrian if he would be willing to share the item with Kelsey—this is key to sharing control and offering choices—*when he is finished, or when he is ready to share*. Most kids will then cooperate, because they are being asked to share when they are ready. Again, like Jill's story, no choice about whether the child shares, but plenty of control and choice about *when* the child shares.

Wise parents understand that sharing *anything*—beginning with toys and expanding into the bigger gifts of time, talent, or tithe—is best "handed" to them as a choice.

Sharing How-To's

On the surface, giving away money looks easy. But deciding how much and when, for what purpose and to whom, can be a challenge. The story of Jill and her mother illustrates several important factors to consider as you teach your kids how to be charitable.

Sharing raises four basic questions:

- Why share?
- Which cause?
- To whom?
- How much?

Why Share?

Whether we give for self-preservation when we are young or to leave a legacy when we are old, sharing reinforces our abundance.

One of the first questions kids may ask is: "Why should I share?" or "Do I really have to do this?" A great way to answer many of your children's questions is to hand the question back to them (the "dumber" you are, the smarter they become). Parents can ask genuinely: "Why do *you* think it's important to share?"

Your child's answer will give you the perfect place to begin the conversation, because you now have *their* perceptions about sharing. That's the starting point. Based on their answer, you'll know if your child needs to learn that there are people who are less fortunate. Sometimes children act the way they do because they have no perspective about other children who don't have anything at all. How could they know, if they have nothing with which to compare?

"Why share?" is certainly a valid question. Different people have different motivations. Some people like to give globally to make the world a better place, while others give locally to make their community a better place. We may give for political, religious, legal (e.g., tax deductions), social, familial, cultural, and moral reasons, to name a few.

Regardless of the reasons why people share, most of us find that when we give to a cause we believe in, we feel good by doing good.

Whether we give for self-preservation when we are young or to leave a legacy when we are old, sharing reinforces our abundance. We can teach our children that because we are blessed to have enough of what we need—time, energy, talent, or money—we can afford to give some away.

Which Cause?

Charitable causes are everywhere. There are environmental, political, and community causes. There are humane societies, medical research facilities, hospitals and hospices, and senior citizen organizations. All actively courting our generosity.

Part of what makes parents successful in teaching kids about charitable giving deals with—surprise!—choices. For example, Jill wasn't interested in Mom's suggestion to feed the hungry, but she *was* interested in clothing the needy. Wise parents allow their kids to choose a category first, for example the environment, and then choose among organizations dedicated to the environment.

One mom complained that her son's fundraiser at his elementary school held little significance for him (PTA and PTO leaders take note). She found it very difficult to motivate his support for something that seemed meaningless. That's understandable. There's simply too much cause and too little effect. Collecting money for an unknown endangered bird species in Southeast Asia, for example, might be about as motivating as the government asking adults to raise money to increase their income taxes.

A Cause That Connects

Choice is key in coming up with a cause that resonates with your child. Let your child pick a cause he or she is intrinsically interested in, so that the reason to give is obvious. It helps them grasp the concept of what they are doing and why. The younger the child, the more important his or her interest is to a successful and committed sharing experience.

For school-age kids and older, encouraging them to choose their own cause connects the child to his or her current aspirations and dreams. If your child is interested in becoming a firefighter, for example, find a way to match his or her interest to your community's firefighting fundraisers. If your child dreams of becoming an actor, encourage him or her to donate their time, talent, or money to the local theater.

Finding a cause that connects reaps triple benefits. First, your child is providing a service, while shadowing other adults in an area of their interest. Second, he or she is gaining some valuable life experience about how the world works

Let your child pick a cause he or she is intrinsically interested in, so that the reason to give is obvious.

outside the family. Third, they learn something about themselves, their interests, and their capabilities in the process.

Sweet Charity

Notice how this simple guideline to connect the child to the cause creates a beautiful side effect at any age. Whenever your children can shadow adults doing what they think they might like to do someday, you have an investment that pays itself back tenfold.

Did Jill's volunteer experience outside the retail sales environment give her another perspective about clothing and people? Did she gain experience that can be transferred to the workplace? Did she get to meet new people with similar interests? And did she learn that not everyone is as fortunate as she is?

Jill's mom used her daughter's combined passion for friends and fashion to inspire her to learn the value in sharing. A good match between a child and the cause makes it fun, and helps to keep the child enthusiastic about his or her contribution.

Bottom Line: Wise parents help their children discover a charitable cause that matches their interests with their abilities.

To Whom?

Teaching kids to share wisely paves the way for making good decisions about the integrity of charitable requests in the future.

Once you have a cause, the next decision is to select an organization. In deciding to whom to give, the best choice involves both our hearts and our heads.

It's important to teach your children how to choose wisely when choosing charitable organizations. Unfortunately, we are all familiar with scams developed by unsavory organizations posturing as legitimate nonprofits. Teaching kids to share wisely paves the way for making good decisions about the integrity of charitable requests in the future. In this way, your children's charitable contribution skills will be well honed by the time they are senior citizens!

For younger children, start small and supervise pre-selected sharing opportunities that are hands-on experiences. Naturally, the more involved you are, and the more tangible the experience is, the more pleasure a young child will feel by giving.

A Memorable March

During the selection process, explain to your child why you are giving your time or talent to a specific organization. For instance, one mom explained to her son the gratitude she felt because he had been born healthy. She told him about the March of Dimes and the research it funds in the areas of prenatal examination, and detection and correction of birth defects. Each year, as she continued to march for dimes, Mom added to her explanation about why the cause was important to her based on her son's level of understanding.

More importantly, when she marched during her son's infancy, pushing him in the stroller, she had pictures taken to memorialize their time together. As he grew, he walked with her—perhaps not as far, but it was still quality time with Mom. They made memories singing silly songs together. (Notice that this same principle is used for developing the spirit of making family contributions. There is wisdom to combining yourself, the contribution, and fun to create success while making community contributions, too.)

As her son grew, he took over canvassing the neighborhood as Mom followed and watched from curbside while winking to the neighbors! Over time, Mom's interest in the March of Dimes inspired her son as an adult to adopt the organization as his favorite charity.

The key is to involve your children in the evolutionary process of learning; no bystanders allowed. Otherwise, the feeling of giving does not get locked into their experience, and the purpose behind sharing is lost.

The key is to involve your children in the evolutionary process of learning; no bystanders allowed. Otherwise, the feeling of giving does not get locked into their experience, and the purpose behind sharing is lost.

Approaches to Selecting an Organization

There are several approaches you can use to encourage wise selection of charities. Some parents introduce their own favorite charity to their children, as in the example set by the March of Dimes mom. These parents simply pick a nationally known and respected organization that has a chapter in their locale. The "Make a Difference Day" is an example, a national network whereby people team together in their local area to provide community service.

Other parents want their children to learn how to select a charity from the ground up. The approach you use will depend upon the age of your child, your time and money, and your family values.

Dig Before Donating

If you want to teach your children the steps in picking out their own charity, teach them the importance of asking for written information before they donate or contribute. Coach them on how to read the information critically, to determine if the organization's goals seem compatible with their initial desires and values.

Invite them to research the organization's promotional brochures or website for the answers to questions such as:

- What kind of volunteer opportunities exist if I donate my *time*?
- What kind of help is needed if I want to donate my *talents*?
- What percentage of my *money* directly benefits the cause?
- Who should I contact to learn more about how to get involved?

Reputable charitable organizations issue an annual report. Have your children look for the tax-exempt 501(c)(3) status required by the IRS to be a legitimate nonprofit. Explain the purpose of a mission statement and solicit *your child's* interpretation of that mission statement by asking them if they agree completely, or only partly, and why. A "pros and cons" discussion provides kids wonderful opportunities to learn how to make decisions based on their interests and values. (See "The 'T' Chart" exercise on p. 95.)

Guidance Before Giving

As in the adult world, you want to teach your children to select causes and organizations that have fiscal and societal integrity. Educate older children how to understand the organization's achievements, and its fiscal responsibility in terms of how it spends its donations. One philanthropic parent used the correspondence he received from his bequests to foster a discussion with his children.

Invite them to share *what they have learned* about the values inherent in the organization and how the organization provides its service to others. Notice how some of these same steps provide an excellent foundation for teaching kids how to make sound financial investments (versus charitable) for themselves as well.

Finish the process by asking your children questions about their selection. This supports the *act of thinking* through their choice of organization thoroughly. In this way, your children become trustworthy stewards of their—and yes, perhaps your—charitable donations in the future.

Teaching children to make intelligent charitable choices is a life lesson. Even if your child is fortunate enough to inherit a trust fund, and is wealthy enough to become philanthropic early in life, everyone benefits when our children learn how to give to others wisely.

Once the questions about *which* organization have been answered to your satisfaction, it's time to decide how much.

The Three T's: Time, Talent, or Tithe

Most of us think about writing a check when it comes to giving. For many busy adults, this often *is* the easiest thing to do. But for children, it's not very personal, or practical. Plus, some of life's most poignant lessons can be found in the value of giving gifts that do not involve money.

Naturally, kids don't have a lot of money to share. That's perfectly okay, in fact preferable at times. That's because it automatically leaves parents with two more choices to offer their children that are more personally engaging—time or talent instead. As Jill's story illustrates, the Three T's offers a "no excuse" sharing policy.

Time and Talent

Time and talent blend together, especially with kids. It's hard for kids to donate their time without also donating whatever "developing interest or talent" they have at the time.

Choosing how much time and talent to donate involves the same age-appropriate principles and many of the same skills as choosing an organization. Invite your children to research this decision just as actively as they researched choosing a charity. This includes a look at the organization's special events and programs to see where they might fit.

Sharing talent matches a child's "activity of interest" with the charity. Part of the child's search will be to figure out if what they want to give is a match for the needs of the charity. Naturally, for younger children, parents will need to be more actively involved in the decision; older children who are developing their capacity to make their own selections will require less guidance.

The Talent Search

Volunteer opportunities for kids are everywhere. They include stuffing envelopes, animal care, trail repair, selling tickets, answering the phone, cleaning up a section of the highway, or serving as a museum docent or theater usher. Some of the more popular fundraising ideas for charitable organizations that can include kids are: a car wash, a bake sale, a local garage sale, a community auction, or a talent show.

Kids can easily create their own service projects, too. With a little encouragement and supervision, they can offer to pull weeds for the neighbor, recycle bottles, pick up trash strewn about their area, or deliver the mail and newspaper to a house-bound resident.

These and many other volunteer opportunities in our communities can be found in the local newspaper, through online volunteer databases, or at a local volunteer clearinghouse.

The Time Search

Sharing time, of course, is a matter of scheduling. Invite your children to think about the use of their time more thoroughly by asking questions that begin with "When," "What," and "How." This provides wonderful opportunities to learn time management skills, and offers excellent preparation for learning how to juggle the variety of tasks required in adult life:

"When do they need me?"

"What do I need to do to find out?"

"How many hours do I have to donate?"

"How will this fit with my schedule, and with my parents' schedule?"

This is also a great time to introduce a calendar and to show children how to plan, so they can honor the time commitments they make to others.

Tithe

Of course, time and talent are not the only things kids can give to others. They can also make monetary contributions. It's called tithing, and it's another way to share our abundance.

The issue is not the amount of the donation; the issue is that your child is learning how to share what they have with others who have less.

How much money we give naturally depends on one's financial situation. While tithing 10% is most often associated with religious and spiritual causes, donating a percentage of one's income can be applied universally to any kind of cause.

There is no right or wrong amount of money to give. The issue is not the amount of the donation; the issue is that your child is learning how to share what they have with others who have less. Your approach with your children will depend upon their age, their charitable financial know-how, and your family values.

Some people use a "wait and see" approach when making a monetary donation once they have fulfilled their basic needs. Others find that a yearly donation works better for them, and some folks simply collect spare change when they have it to give. However frequent, it's best to keep the size of the donation proportionate to one's income.

Many parents have found success in requiring younger children to structure their charitable giving on a recurring basis, such as at a weekly church collection. Other parents tend to use a less disciplined approach, as long as their children are sharing some part of themselves.

Jill's mom, for example, was wise not to force her teenager to share her money. Mom got a second chance with her stepson, Cody, six years old. She began encouraging Cody to give away his unused toys first. Younger kids can learn all the same virtues of "tithing" by giving away unused toys and possessions in good useable condition. This was followed, as he got older, by the "allowance plus" approach, whereby he dedicated $2 per month to a charity of his choice. (Mom matched Cody's contribution to model the act of giving.)

Cody will learn early that the need to contribute *something* is a fundamental part of a more fulfilling life.

Ways to Waiver

Some parents find it effective to waive the monetary giving requirement if their children are volunteering in ways that involve their time and talent or their toys. For example, if you want your child to make a $5 donation, then the child can donate a toy or possession equal to $5. If your teenager wants to donate their effort, instead of sharing their earnings or allowance, they can donate an amount of time equal to the money they are choosing not to donate.

A Heritage of Helping

For some families, giving is a multigenerational family tradition. I (Kristan) learned about a family for whom helping out has been a tradition for four generations! Fifty years ago, one thoughtful man realized that senior citizens could stay in the comfort of their own homes (without having to move out to nursing or retirement homes) if they could get help with one thing they could not do without—at least one healthy, balanced meal every day. This wise gentleman knew something else seniors needed—companionship.

So he developed a Meals on Wheels program for his local community. He began to model helping others, and since then this value has been passed down from generation to generation within his family. The vision, begun three generations ago by the patriarch of the clan, has inspired family members to cook and serve meals to hundreds of house-bound senior citizens for over five decades.

Sharing was never just an option for any member of this family, it was a duty. Through the process of volunteering, the children were introduced to ideas and people that enriched their lives in return. Who knows how our children will be influenced through the eyes of a volunteer if we can give them similar opportunities?

While we contribute because it feels good to do good, it can boomerang. The same man who brought the Meals on Wheels program to his community became one of its beneficiaries. He had an accident and was bedridden for a short time. Whereas once he was the benefactor, he became the beneficiary, and so have all his children and grandchildren as well as many seniors in between.

> ### A Need, Indeed?
>
> Sharing can be a successful, even a multigenerational family affair, as long as it's collaborative. Family traditions tend to become unpopular over time unless we remember to keep the importance of choice in mind. Kids will tend to embrace cherished family traditions *if* they have a part in shaping and changing them over time.
>
> Trying to guilt our children into volunteering is not a "feel good" experience, for you or the child, nor is it effective. Emphasize what your family can contribute and how each child can help, instead of focusing on what the beneficiary doesn't have. (For example, "You can bring contentment to the family we have adopted by helping me prepare and deliver supper" instead of: "Some kids go to bed hungry.") Parents are on their way to reaching their goal of "many happy charitable returns" if they can create opportunities for their children to walk away with the experience of knowing they really did make a difference.

Making a Family Match

To generate ideas, adapt the same process you used to make your list of family contributions; just change the title to "Our Community Contributions" (review step 1 in the "Family Contributions Balance Sheet" exercise on p. 106).

As ideas are shared, entire families can get involved in what interests them the most. One family adopts another family in need and gives them gifts for the Annual Holiday Toy Drive. Another family asks each child to gift a less fortunate child of similar age by pledging to earn enough money to buy him or her a new toy. Using the appeal of rhyme, this family dubbed their sharing program: "One Good Deed for One In Need."

Here are six tips to making the best match between your family and the organization:

Six Steps to Making the Best Family Match

1. Match schedules.
2. Match family goals.
3. Match skills and abilities.
4. Match values to causes.
5. Match attitude with gratitude.
6. Match words with actions.

Step 1: Match schedules.

Make sure that the hours you volunteer fit everyone's schedule. Better to commit to fewer hours and honor your commitment than to sign up for too many and feel hassled. This way you avoid exhausting yourself, frustrating your family, and shortchanging the organization.

Step 2: Match family goals.

Think about your family's goals when selecting a place to volunteer. Pick an active volunteer job, such as trail or park maintenance, if fitness is a goal. If cooking is something you would all like to learn how to do together, select accordingly. That way, when you go out to make a difference in the life of someone else, you have made a difference in your life, too. It becomes the gift that gives twice.

One family devoted one day every three months to community service. They rotated the responsibility for selecting the organization so that every family member's favored cause was represented. It was a bonding experience all the way around—with the family, with the community, and between benefactor and beneficiary.

Step 3: Match skills and abilities.

Similar to age-appropriate contributions and jobs listed in this book, be sure to match your children's ability with the volunteer opportunities. Will your child be able to do what is asked of him or her? Is it age-appropriate? Does he or she need to be trained?

If your children are making their family contributions at home, then some of the same abilities and skills learned at home can be transferred to their volunteer efforts. If they have been part of a team effort at home, then making contributions to the community as part of a team will also be familiar. For example, if they contribute by cleaning up the kitchen at home, then they can contribute to the crew that cleans up the community's soup kitchen. (For age-appropriate suggestions, see "Charity Begins at Home" on p. 425.)

Step 4: Match values to causes.

What are you interested in as a family? The environment? Animals? Serving the needy? Match your family values to the goals of an organization.

Opportunities abound in any community. You will find them among the old, the young, the infirm, and the disabled—or anyone else who is in need, temporary or otherwise.

A quick search online using your zip code will reveal all kinds of kid-friendly opportunities in your area. For example, raise funds for wildlife conservation, deliver hot meals to house-bound seniors, read stories to the blind, or create cheerful cards for people in nursing homes or hospitals who are sick or injured.

Step 5: Match attitude with gratitude.

Our children are always watching and learning from what we do. If you *feel* grateful, express it .Thank your children for the gifts they give you with a hug, a word of appreciation, perhaps even modeling the written word in a thank you note for a carefully selected or handmade gift. (Handmade gifts are particularly special, because the maker invests their mind and their heart in each creative step.)

Talk to your children about the meaning of giving—for the giver as well as the receiver. "How do you feel?" "How do you think the other person feels?" "What do you think it would be like not to have enough food to eat or to feel lonely?" Help your children connect the dots: giving warms the hearts of both givers and receivers because it shows that you care enough to take action. Play a game of "count your blessings"; or have family members name things they are thankful for, alphabetically from A to Z.

If you've laid the foundation for making family contributions, then the idea of making community contributions is a natural extension.

Step 6: Match words with actions.

Are you familiar with the phrase "charity begins at home"? Children do as we do. If you've laid the foundation for making family contributions, then the idea of making community contributions is a natural extension.

Make sharing generously a core family value throughout the year. It can be a fun exercise to just brainstorm ideas for sharing your blessings with others year-round.

Whether you tithe regularly at your house of worship, send occasional donations to the victims of a natural disaster, get involved in a direct fundraiser for medical research, or support the local soup kitchen daily, your children will learn the importance of helping others through the gift of your example.

* * *

Taking these steps increases the chances of making a match that works for everyone involved. When families perform volunteer activities together, it helps strengthen the bond within the family, and with the community they serve. Serving the community alongside their parents teaches kids compassion and civic responsibility. It also paves the way for future generations to place value on helping a neighbor in need.

Charity Begins at Home: Age-Appropriate Ideas

What if your child's initial enthusiasm about sharing wanes? Jill's mom used a basic principle to motivate her daughter to share, a principle that can be used for children of any age. She offered choices that included her daughter's interests *at the time*. Wise parents keep the spirit of sharing alive by building on their child's ever-changing interests and growing abilities.

Here are a few suggestions by age group:

- *Young children:* Don't do charity alone. Include your kids on your errands to the local Goodwill or Salvation Army outlet. Enlist their help culling and collecting outgrown toys, clothing, and household items, and then donate the items together. Or use nonprofit wish lists to match unused household goods with community needs.
- *School-aged children:* Take kids to nonprofit events. Be a role model by getting the whole family involved in community outreach several times a year. Involvement in PTA and PTO projects can include the entire family, not just Mom or Dad. Make it a family tradition to contribute your collective time and talent to your community by delivering food baskets, adopting a child during the holiday season, or visiting a retirement home. The family that shares together also cares together.
- *Tweens:* Encourage your child to turn his or her complaints and gripes into action. If he or she thinks that there should be a recycling program in the neighborhood, or that the cafeteria food at school stinks, support them in doing "something about it" using the Three T's principle of offering choices.
- *Teens:* Use your own charitable donations as an opportunity to talk with your children about what led you to the decision to share your time, talent, or money with this particular organization. Support your teen in matching their interest to a cause, all under the umbrella of choice. At

a time when teens are beginning to individuate, encourage volunteer opportunities toward the direction of potential future careers. (For more ideas about the importance of encouraging a reluctant teen to share, see "Sharing: An Antidote for the Troubled or Entitled Teen" below.)

Sharing: An Antidote for the Troubled or Entitled Teen

One of the best antidotes for entitled or troubled teens is to create opportunities for them to get "outside of themselves" and volunteer. Sharing can help lost kids find their purpose in life. Wise parents channel their teen's developmental angst to be free and independent into helping those in need be more free and independent. This helps get teens out of their singular world and into the communal world of others.

For troubled teens, it is especially important for a parent or significant adult to accompany the teen while volunteering. This type of "side by side" modeling demonstrates your care and concern for *them as well as others*.

Here are a few ways to get your teen interested. (Notice how they follow Love and Logic's principle of combining their interests with their developmental age—most involve driving a car and can be done either with you or with their friends):

- Be a companion to people with disabilities by going to the theater, concerts, or sporting events.
- Visit a retirement home to read or write letter for the residents.
- Make a meal and deliver it to someone who is ill or house-bound.
- Collect school supplies for needy students from local businesses.
- Buy and deliver gifts to a needy family, not just during the holidays.
- Visit hospitalized children or make "get well" cards and deliver them to people in the community who need cheering up.
- Provide cleanup after a natural disaster
- Join a mission or take community service trip.
- Tutor an older person in how to work their computer or other electronic devices.

Whatever your teen decides, talk about the ways in which their offerings could or have helped others. For example, if your teen is a part of a school choir that visits a retirement home, talk about the cheer that your child's singing may bring to an otherwise dull, lonely, or routine world. Children do not always un-

Wise parents channel their teen's developmental angst to be free and independent into helping those in need be more free and independent.

derstand the positive effect their choice may have on others, because many of them have not had the experience of being hungry, homeless, or unemployed.

Wise parents remember that, when it comes to feeling better about ourselves, there's is no better prescription than a conscription to volunteer.

What Sharing Teaches Our Children

What does sharing teach? There are some very practical reasons why it's important to teach our children to share. Sharing is necessary just to get along in the world. Sharing resources, space, and ourselves in relationship to everything around us is a lifetime lesson.

The whole idea behind teaching our children to share is teaching them the value of, and the value in, community service. Sharing teaches those essential financial values used throughout this book: delayed gratification, needs versus wants, time and money management skills, but especially gratitude versus entitlement. Sharing one's abundance is one of the greatest lessons we can teach a generation of potentially entitled kids.

Selfless acts of service and kindness are the perfect remedy to the selfish attitude of "I want it now." Through sharing, we discover who we are and what we're made of.

There are spiritual reasons to teach sharing as well. Sharing teaches kids that sacrifice is a byproduct of the ideals we hold and cherish. The experience of sharing has a deeper meaning if a part of our self is vested in the process. Children learn lessons in compassion, gratitude, and altruism. Finally, our "good" boomerangs back in the pleasure and goodwill that come from voluntarily giving to others—and that's a pretty good investment for all.

Epilogue

Will the Chickens
Come Home to Roost?

It's always a challenge to see the advance of time before it actually arrives. This chapter is a short and sweet reminder about the importance of *your* financial security, independence, and freedom.

Financial Prevention, Not Tension

An ironic twist of fate is that the final chapter in a book about money is Chapter 13. In financial terms, "Chapter 13" is one of several ways to file for bankruptcy. It's a court-mandated reorganization plan that is financially restrictive. No fun at any age.

Which is better—experiencing "bankruptcy" as a child, or experiencing bankruptcy as an adult? We all know the answer to that question. Let your children experience a kid-sized bankruptcy when they are young, to increase the chances that they won't have to when they are older.

Your children will have many opportunities to make financial boo-boos when the price tags are affordable by following the steps in this book. Love and Logic teaches that the road to fiscal fitness is paved with mistakes and learning from the consequences.

Even if you have adult children who have not left home yet, or have returned, it's never too late to learn. There is still hope. The beauty of Love and Logic is that these principles will still work at creating self-reliance at any age. By applying the principles of the Four C's: Self-Concept, Control, Choices, and Consequences, young or adult children can mature into responsible, resilient, fiscally accountable people.

Life's Fiscal Circle

Our last chapter brings us full circle to the first chapter for another reason. If you recall, we looked at the top three reasons for teaching kids about the importance of money: First, life is hard … without enough money. Second, the school of hard knocks is expensive. And third, an ounce of prevention is worth a pound of cure. But there is a fourth reason—one that is key to your financial future:

Your kids may well be your future financial caretakers.

Consider the following scenario: You are looking forward to the "empty nest" phase, when your kids have finally moved out for good and are raising families of their own. Perhaps you are dreaming about traveling, taking up a hobby, and discovering the joys of being a grandparent as you enter the next phase of your life.

Time flies. You retire and ease into a more relaxed pace of life. You no longer have the pressure and responsibility of working longer hours. Finally, you've reached that time of life when you get to enjoy some of those things that so far you've only dreamed of doing.

Naturally, circumstances change as you age. Perhaps your energy is not quite what it used to be. Your health may become compromised. You find that the tables have gradually turned. It seemed like only yesterday that your children were dependent on you for care and support; now you are becoming more dependent on your children.

Before you know it, they are managing more of your affairs, including your financial affairs. Eventually they will be managing your estate or family trust, and choosing your retirement or nursing home.

Will you be prepared when the time comes? Will your children be prepared?

Underwrite Your Future

Fiscal life has a way of coming around full circle, almost by surprise. Whereas once you were in the financially responsible position to help your children, you hope that, when the times comes, your children will be in the financially responsible position to help you.

> Wouldn't you prefer someone with experience and a good track record
> when the time comes to give up fiscal responsibility?
> Someone who will have knowledge about what to do with your life savings?
> Someone who knows how to manage your remaining money wisely?

In short, will your children be ready when the fulcrum of financial responsibility shifts from you taking care of your children to your children taking care of you?

Millionaire Babies or Bankrupt Brats? is a way to underwrite both your future and your children's future *together*. With the help of this book, the authors of Love and Logic invite you to embrace the opportunities to raise fiscally fit children. Raising kids who are respectful, responsible, and fun to be around is a great step toward making sure your golden years with them are … well, golden.

Open to any page—anywhere in this book—to begin your move toward a more prosperous and abundant future for your children, and yourself, today.

You can do it! Your kids can do it!

List of Charts

List of Exercises

Index

W

Y

About the Author

Jim Fay's background includes thirty-one years as a teacher and administrator, fifteen years as a professional consultant and public speaker, and many years as a parent of three children. He serves both nationally and internationally as a consultant to schools, parent organizations, and the U.S. military. Jim believes his major accomplishment in life is the development (along with Foster W. Cline, M.D.) of a unique philosophy of practical techniques for enhancing communication between children and adults, known as Love and Logic. Jim has taken complex problems and broken them down into simple, easy-to-use concepts and techniques that can be understood and used by anyone. Hundreds of thousands of people have expressed how Love and Logic has enhanced their relationships with their children. Jim is one of America's most sought-after presenters in the area of parenting and school discipline. His practical techniques are revolutionizing the way parents and professionals are looking at how we deal with children; how we help them to become responsible, thinking people; and how we help them enhance their own self-concepts.

About the Author

Kristan Leatherman has pursued a variety of exciting careers, from politics to nonprofit, from broadcasting to small business. Yet it wasn't until she became a teacher that she discovered her truest calling—helping parents with the challenge of raising respectful, responsible, capable kids.

Since that time, Kristan has gone beyond the classroom to make a bigger impact in the lives of more children by working with the adults who are raising them. As her passion evolved, Kristan developed her own educational consulting practice as a facilitator and speaker, family life consultant … and now founder of the Millionaire Babies Project and coauthor of her first book.

The Millionaire Babies Project grew from Kristan's presentations to hundreds of parents and teachers, whose questions invariably lead to lively discussions about how to handle the enduring challenges of raising financially capable and responsible kids. While this may seem a daunting task in today's complex world, Kristan is dedicated to providing simple tools and effective solutions that adults need to raise happy, self-supporting kids. This commitment is reflected in the practical and straightforward style of *Millionaire Babies*.

With a master's degree in counseling and twenty years of experience, Kristan has provided individual consultations and presented seminars about life skills to a variety of schools, colleges, community service organizations, and businesses at local, regional, and national conferences and venues from coast to coast.

Want to learn more about Love and Logic?

Love and Logic is a philosophy of raising and teaching children that allows adults to be happier, empowered, and more skilled in their interactions with children. Love allows children to grow through their mistakes. Logic allows children to live with the consequences of their choices. Love and Logic is a way of working with children that puts parents and teachers back in control, teaches children to be responsible, and prepares young people to live in the real world, with its many choices and consequences. Visit our website at www.loveandlogic.com or contact us at 800-338-4065 for a complete catalog, list of seminars in your area and to sign up for our free weekly e-mail tip!

Want support to make the skills and strategies in *Millionaire Babies* a habit?

Kristan can help you can master the principles found in *Millionaire Babies*. Services include coaching and private consultations for parents, grandparents, and families, and educational workshops for businesses, community service organizations, and schools. Online services include a list of Web-based financial resources, updates, and networking opportunities with other readers.

To learn more about Kristan's Millionaire Babies Coaching Program and the Millionaire Babies Project, or to schedule Kristan for a workshop in your area, contact:

kristanleatherman@sbcglobal.net
530-879-9126